The Seeker's Handbook

The Seeker's Handbook

THE COMPLETE GUIDE TO
SPIRITUAL PATHFINDING

John Lash

Harmony Books
New York

Copyright © 1990 by John Lash

Published by Harmony Books, a division of Crown Publishers, Inc., 201 East 50th
Street, New York, New York 10022. Member of the Crown Publishing Group.
HARMONY and colophon are trademarks of Crown Publishers, Inc.

Designed by Iris Weinstein

Manufactured in the United States of America

Library of Congress Cataloging-in-Publication Data
Lash, John.
The seeker's handbook / by John Lash. — 1st ed.
p. cm.
1. Spiritual life—Handbooks, manuals, etc. I. Title.
BL624.L365   1990
291.4'48—dc20   90-34458   CIP

ISBN 0-517-57797-6
10 9 8 7 6 5 4 3 2 1
First Edition

FOR ISIS-SOPHIA

Nuestra Madre Pagana de Santa Fe

eye of many windings

ACKNOWLEDGMENTS

E|ven though I know as well as anyone that the fear of making mistakes is a great deterrent to learning, it has never deterred me one iota from *teaching*! So first and foremost I want to express my appreciation to all those students who have followed and supported my work down through the years. They, more than anyone else, have assisted me in the process of synthesis and distillation that has, at long last, produced this book. Without them I would have been a voice crying in the wilderness. I hope they will find in *The Seeker's Handbook* a kind of amends for all the difficulties I've posed that have not—or not *yet*—born out in viable truth for their personal lives. Thanks to them especially for absorbing the spiritual shock of a good many wild-eyed Mobies I've off-loaded to gain myself some clearance and balance, and let it be known that lacking their courageous ears I would certainly have turned my best secrets over to the Russians long before now.

Among my other invaluable allies, I must thank Oda Simonsen and Magna Brown for believing in me through many changes of direction; to Sharon Wagner for the initial cue; and to Mela Leavell for all her generosity in many forms. And special thanks to all the kind, courageous investors in MUSA.

Finally, to my beloved companion, Joanna Harcourt-Smith, I feel the kind of gratitude that comes from receiving a long-awaited inheritance, a gift from the child to the man, to which she has been the most intimate ally and loving witness. Finding in her life a teaching of empathy with God, I have also found the ways to heal some of the old theological wounds that afflict those planetary spies who, like Parzival, seek what remains to be done after the Grail has been won and passed on.

CONTENTS

ix

Part III: The Lexicon

PREAMBLE

Into the Labyrinth

L ike you, I am a seeker. My quest began with dreams in early childhood, followed in my teens by some disturbing inner experiences
that were inexplicable in the context of what I or anyone around me knew
at the time. Quite soon, I was led to worldwide travels and other, purely
spontaneous, mystical experiences, followed up by years of esoteric studies and various disciplines of self-work. It is a quest that still continues,
a journey I have come to see as defined by no ultimate goal, but rather
by the shifting horizons—sometimes close, sometimes distant—that appear and dissolve with every step along the way.

My analogy for the seeker's quest is the *labyrinth,* the maze of winding
paths that intersect at unpredictable places. At each crossing of paths there
is room for pause and contemplation, but the figure of the labyrinth is all
movement, all change and exploration. The labyrinth has no single, fixed
center—rather, a kind of magnetic center that shifts as the journey shifts.
Mysteriously and often elusively, each winding path leads toward the
heart of the design, a movable center located wherever the seeker is
exploring at any moment. At each crossing within the maze there is a kind
of mandala, a point to rest the gaze and take bearings. But like the looking
glass in Alice's adventure, each mandala is merely a membrane, and in
going through it, the seeker plunges on again along the winding track of
the labyrinth.

Like so many others, I set out into the labyrinth looking for the eternal
principles, the time-tried formulations of ultimate truth. I did find them,
because they do exist. They are like pictures and hieroglyphs carved at
certain turnings on the walls of the winding passageways. But I discovered that they cannot be taken as goals, as final end points of questioning.
They are helpful markings encountered again and again at different turnings along the way. Because they are age-old and eternally recurrent,

having been inscribed by the many seekers who previously passed this way, they provide a sense of deep-felt confidence, the familiarity of having trodden with others along ancient and well-marked paths.

But in addition to the eternal truths, there are the ongoing, unfinished, still-to-be-worked-out truths. One of my discoveries in the labyrinth is the vital distinction between finding yourself and finding your purpose— which are, respectively, the dominant themes of seeking in the East and the West. By a long process of clarification and sorting, I have been able to identify these and other paradigms as the invariant figures of the labyrinth: what I like to call the principles of right seeking.

"Knock and it shall be opened unto you. Seek and ye shall find."

Yes, but what shall ye find? For me, wandering through the labyrinth only became a clear process of self-unfolding when I realized that seeking is a paradoxical act. It is goal-oriented yet open-ended. Seeking leads to finding, yes, but only in a partial and incomplete way, and beyond that it leads to ever and ever more seeking, better seeking. What is well found opens the way to more seeking, if it does not shut down in righteous conclusion.

When I was nineteen and in India, I worked myself into a state where it seemed impossible for me to go on, even for another moment. I did not see how I could survive, either as the particular human "person" named on my passport or as a pure, impersonal spirit. In a moment of overwhelming anguish, I heard some kind of "higher power" break through and advise me in a tough, familiar tone, "You'll get by on your looks, kid." In spite of myself, I had to laugh—though I had a long way to go before I understood what I was laughing about.

Since I now know that my whole life has been dedicated to the discipline of clear seeking, I can put it in the most easygoing way, inconceivable to me back when I first got that odd, jarring message: Good seeking leads not only to finding, but onward to better and better looking. So the ultimate goal of all seeking is to become more and more good at looking. Whatever we may find through seeking does not end the search, but leads us to become better and better at good looking.

We all get by on our looks, on how good we look.

Today, many of us are alert to the prospect of living in a remarkable time—perhaps so remarkable that it cannot be compared to any other in history. Even though we may strongly suspect that human nature remains the same through the ages, we now seem faced with the possibility of humanity at least seeing itself in a different way than ever before. Surely this is a true prospect, because we are living in a time when human concerns have expanded into the global scale. This is a recent and all-encompassing development, impossible for anyone to ignore. I was a child of the 1940s and grew up in a small town of nine hundred people, yet by the age of five I was overwhelmed by the imminence of global catastrophe. Beyond the small-scale theater of neighborhood conflicts and concerns, I felt the worldwide anxiety of the cold war. Through television, I was exposed to world events and issues before I was able to develop the basic skills needed for dealing with my own personal development. Coming of age in the 1960s, I was shaken by the street cry of "Revolution," the call to an awesome shift of inner and outer realities.

Quite early on, I came to discover that planetization is a leading issue of the New Age, expressed in McLuhan's global village as well as in the ideals of planetary citizenship and world service. It also turns out that my generation, which first experienced the global anxiety of the cold war, now holds the vanguard in the emergence of the world peace movement. All these far-reaching matters have deeply shaped and colored my own personal quest for spiritual awakening.

By a second measure, our time is even more unique: A long development, tracing back to the Renaissance, now results in a situation where the entire legacy of world spirituality is accessible to each and every one of us, if we are inclined to look into it. Every conceivable path of knowledge and discipline, including the doctrines of all the ancient world religions and the long-lost but now retrieved teachings of all the mysteries of the past, plus the wisdom of gurus and guides of the present, both Eastern and Western, is there for the seeker.

The modern spiritual movement is a response to these tremendous prospects, and many people today, in all walks of life and all areas of society, are reacting to the challenges they pose. On my own path, I have trodden certain passageways through the labyrinth more frequently than others, but I have sustained a lifelong interest in all of them. What I hope to offer, after thirty-odd years of seeking, is an overview of the whole design—a kind of floor plan of the labyrinth.

In the central concept and overall design of *The Seeker's Handbook,* I hope to show first and foremost that pathfinding itself can be a discipline. Time and time again I have asked myself this question: What is required for our seeking in all directions—our seeking for God, for ourselves, for a sense of purpose, for the cause of our sufferings, for love, freedom, knowledge, ecstasy, intimacy, meaning, magic, and mystery—to be really worthwhile?

Well, at the outset I believe there must be a commonsense admission that to discover the astonishing potential of our individual lives, we need a discipline, a path to follow. But above and beyond all the spiritual disciplines and alternative paths/methods/techniques we may adopt, there is the fundamental discipline of seeking itself. This point calls for a little thinking, because it implies a crucial shift, and it takes a mental leap to realize that, yes, times have changed, and the situation was not at all like this in the past.

What is at the fingertips of any seeker today—from the shelves of metaphysical bookstores to the pages of a free magazine listing workshops, seminars, and spiritual practitioners—can be overwhelming and bewildering. There was certainly nothing like this in ancient Alexandria, for all its sects, nor in medieval Europe, by any means. Given the enormous array of choices facing the seeker today, spiritual development unfolds now through an entirely new configuration of paths. Never before have there been so many options, and meeting them calls for new approaches, new faculties of discrimination and selection.

As one of the fundamental guidelines to right seeking, I like to propose the principle of four-way balance: Every seeker, in coming to the path that is right for him, seeks (whether he knows it or not!) a balance between deliberate choice and spontaneous discovery on the one hand, and on the other, between gaining from the path and giving to the path. A good part of the discipline of right seeking is asking questions, and a whole sequence of significant questions can be generated from this four-way proposition. It is up to the seeker to work them out. . . .

The Seeker's Handbook is not merely a reference manual, though it will serve as one. Its larger purpose is to make available to other seekers my own skills of direction finding, gained through thirty-five years of exploring the labyrinth. In the prefaces and commentaries distributed throughout the three sections of the *Handbook,* I have set out the principles of clear seeking in the form of paradigms and guidelines. In this way, I hope to provide not only ready access to vital information on all the spiritual paths, new and old, but also the perspective that comes from long-term acquaintance with them.

While the prefaces offer a framework for the modern discipline of pathfinding, the overall design and interweaving of information in the *Handbook* will, I hope, afford the seeker the hard-won advantage of comprehension, above and beyond what the mere information can tell.

The best way I know to find the meaning of life is to seek the life of meaning. This is a very individualistic affair and, in our time, a rather bewildering one. The enormous prospects of our age, offering access to every conceivable path of spiritual development from alchemy to Zen, are attended by enormous risks. For all the wisdom it offers, the labyrinth can be a realm of immense distraction and confusion. Fundamentally there are no delusionary paths, but any path can become delusionary, depending upon how it's approached and traversed. No words are wasted in the Sufi saying, "Counterfeit gold would not exist if there were not real gold somewhere."

The Seeker's Handbook is a gift extracted from the fruits of my own life experience. It is my deepest hope that it will assist other seekers, not merely to become involved in the new trends of spirituality and alternative paths of self-realization, but to attain clear orientation and solid grounding in whatever realms they do choose to explore. Its purpose is to inspire both consistent research and spontaneous discovery. Ultimately, it aims to support and encourage the self-reliant spirit of free seeking.

My own wanderings in the labyrinth have shown me that for all the wisdom of the great teachings, there is no teacher superior to life itself. The most you can ever learn from any path, then, is how to learn from life itself. For me the Great Question is and always has been: How do I come to learn from life itself how to unfold that which is innate and original to me?

It is really a process of learning how to learn, for life itself is, I believe, the infinite treasury of self-knowledge, the ultimate theater of self-initiation.

This seems to be what the quest in the labyrinth is all about—a realization confirmed by the life and work of my own favored exemplars, the world-class mythologists Mircea Eliade and Joseph Campbell.

> Today . . . fortunately, it is everywhere the collective mythology itself that is going to pieces, leaving even the nonindividual *(sauve qui peut!)* to be a light unto himself. It is true that the madhouses are full; psychoanalysts, millionaires. Yet anyone sensible enough to have looked around somewhere outside his fallen church will have seen standing everywhere on the cleared, still clearing, world stage a company of mighty individuals: the great order of those who in the past found, and in the present are still finding, in themselves all the guidance needed. —JOSEPH CAMPBELL,
> *The Masks of God: Creative Mythology*

What I am sure of is that any future forms of religious experience will be quite different from those we are familiar with in Christianity, Judaism or Islam, all of which are fossilized, outmoded, drained of meaning. I am sure that new forms, new expressions, will come. What will they be? I cannot say. The great surprise is always the freedom of the human spirit, its creativity.

—MIRCEA ELIADE,
Ordeal by Labyrinth

For Compassion and Authenticity

GETTING AROUND
THE LABYRINTH

*On the Design and Use
of the Handbook*

W|hile *The Seeker's Handbook* will serve as a reference manual, providing ready access to information on all aspects of the new spirituality (and a fair share of the old!), its larger purpose is to foster comprehension and grounding. To this end, it can be read by meandering through the pages, slowly and searchingly, sometimes following the crossweave that has been carefully inscribed into the contents, sometimes wandering off to make your own tracks.

As a short browse through its pages will show, the *Handbook* covers an enormous territory of themes, principles, systems, practices, movements, scenarios, studies, case histories, methodologies, originating impulses, technicalities, idioms, and leading characters (both human and divine). All of this is pure information, compiled in the most fair and inclusive way I could manage. Any effort to scope out all the current pathways of self-work and inner discovery has to be colored, to some degree, by the personal background of the one who attempts it. This is true for the *Handbook,* which of course results from my personal explorations, though it does not merely impart my personal interpretations. As a teacher of mythology and lifework, I apply the discipline of depersonalization, so that I can offer formal descriptions and objective evaluations to those who need them for their own process of seeking. Assisting others in their lifework, I have learned to give directives appropriate to their quest and unbiased by my own experience, even though derived from it. Hopefully, I have imbued this same spirit of transpersonal clarity into the material in the *Handbook*—though it does retain personal touches here and there.

At best, the *Handbook* is a viewfinder that does not necessarily impose the views of the explorer who designed it.

In every case, I have sought to avoid anything like a propagandistic, persuasive handling of the subject matter. There is already plenty of such persuasive material in print, inviting seekers to identify themselves with one or another spiritual cause or practice or leader, for whoever cares to do so. I hope the *Handbook* does not coax in any particular direction, but is equally helpful to all approaches.

I neither endorse nor oppose any of the practices, principles, or ideologies set forth in the definitions, commentaries, essays, or works cited, nor do I wish to enter into any controversies regarding the origins, development, application, or ultimate results of any of the movements, causes, and teachings indicated. My intention is solely to inform, in the most clear and comprehensive way possible within the given limitations of my own personal knowledge and experience.

In the realm of New Age interests and alternative spirituality, a vast new language has evolved in recent years. This language is highly idiomatic, with a flavor and application all its own. It contains a great many words of ancient origin (most of them Sanskrit) such as *chakra,* as well as newly coined words such as *walk-in.* Much of this special terminology, both age-old and current, is given clear definition in Part III, but the Lexicon serves as something more than a mere dictionary by the way it is interwoven with the other sections of the *Handbook.*

Experience proves that almost every word in the current vocabulary of the new spirituality has a thread of history or myth attached to it, placing it within an immense network of associations. There may be a single thread, or as many as half a dozen, linking a term like *vision quest* to other terms that comprise mosaic sections of an inclusive theme, principle, or scenario. Vision quest, for example, cross-links by one course of association to the large-scale theme of shamanism, the subject of a Ten-Minute Essay. Shamanism in turn interlinks to Native American spirituality, a mosaic that includes in "The Classics and Basics" the breakthrough work *Black Elk Speaks,* containing a dramatic description of a vision quest. By another course of association, vision quest cross-links with *vigil,* a key term in the discipline of the *Arthurian Path,* which in turn opens into the scenarios of the *Grail Mystery* and the *Celtic Revival.*

The richness of the new language of modern, free-form spirituality lies in the vast realms of experience through which it resonates. The *Handbook* is designed for gaining access to all these realms, through a careful but uncomplicated network of the mosaics they encompass. It is set up so that the three main sections—the Classics and Basics, the Essays, and the Lexicon—interweave and complement one another. While each section provides simple and ready access to the material in its category, the overall design integrates the diverse information into a comprehensive whole.

The prefaces for each section and the two longer Essays contain the principles of clear seeking as well as indications on how to use the design features of the *Handbook*. They explain the system of cross-referencing, which is thorough but minimal, meant to foster comprehension but avoid clutter and redundancy. Used casually or worked consistently, the cross-weave can afford the seeker the benefits of long-term familiarity with all the fields to be explored.

The three sections of the *Handbook* are:

1. The Classics and Basics, in four groups: Classics of Eastern Spirituality, Classics of Western Spirituality, Toward the Breakthrough: Key Works from 1900 to the Sixties, and From the Sixties Onward—citing the main works in these areas, author, current edition, the best translations (where appropriate), plus a short review describing the enduring significance of each work.

2. The Essays, including two longer Essays for seeing the whole picture of the New Age and alternative spirituality, and twenty-eight Ten-Minute Essays covering some of the major themes and interests of the modern spiritual movement, the large mosaics of current exploration.

3. The Lexicon, a select list of approximately 1,000 words that make up the operative language of modern spirituality, including both terms in current use and terms of origin, which are background or contextual words. (Although they are as concise and precise as I can make them, these definitions do reflect, more than anything else in the *Handbook,* my own interpretations and opinions. As such, I hope they will at least be stimulating to creative understanding. No definition can be fixed and final, nor should it be.)

May you find the true gold

The Classics and Basics

"One must relate the origin of the medicine, otherwise it cannot work its magic."

—A saying of the Na-Khi, a Tibetan people of southeastern China, reflecting a belief common to many archaic cultures: namely, a medicine or magical gift of spiritual potency only becomes effective for those who receive it when they recall how they acquired it—that is, when its origin is remembered, retold, recited, or ritually reenacted.

USING THE CLASSICS
AND BASICS

S ince the spiritual renaissance of the 1960s, thousands of books dealing with every conceivable area of spiritual growth, religious
renewal, occult exploration, mystical-metaphysical speculation, and self-
actualization have been written or reprinted. As a result of this vast
exposure, the field of independent seeking is wide open today, the range
of options is really enormous, and the literature can be quite overwhelming.

But in any field of knowledge there are primary landmarks for finding
one's way through the vast territory to be explored, and the labyrinth of
spiritual inquiry is no exception. In recent times, the vast array of options
available in the labyrinth has led to its being dubbed, derogatorily, the
spiritual supermarket. Given that there is so much to sift through, the
perennial quest for the meaning of life assumes a form unlike anything
in the past. Where new conditions appear, new approaches are required.

In view of this situation, I have come to see *pathfinding* as a discipline
yet to be adequately outlined, although it is essential to anyone who
ventures into the new spirituality seeking knowledge, practices, or principles to live by. One of the first steps of this new discipline is to learn the
key landmarks, the great spiritual masterworks of the past and present.

Legends of the labyrinth abound in worldwide mythology and folklore.
The baffling construction called the maze, or Troy town, appears to have
been used for some kind of initiation rite, or *ordeal,* as it was formerly
called. Ruins of such mazes are found in Europe from Ireland to Crete,
where the famous labyrinth constructed by Daedalus was used to corral
the dreadful Minotaur. At the cathedral in Chartres, in northern France,
there is an exquisite maze composed of mosaic tile. A brief scene in one
of the videotapes of Joseph Campbell's talks with Bill Moyers shows a
devout young man traversing it on his knees.

In the most famous labyrinth legend in Western myth, the hero Theseus resolves to enter the maze of Daedalus and slay the Minotaur.
Ariadne, the daughter of King Minos, provides him with a huge spool
of thread from her loom. He unwinds the thread as he goes into the
labyrinth and follows it to get back out again. It is interesting to note that
the thread leads him out after he has, by a process of trial and error, found
his way to the central chamber—so the thread merely guarantees that he
will be able to trace back the path he himself has worked out.

Something like this may be said for the great spiritual masterworks of
the past, the sacred books passed down to us from ancient times. They
provide threads to keep us from losing ourselves in the winding tracks
of the labyrinth. They do not compel us to take any particular course
through the maze, but they help us to keep track of where we are going
and have gone. As time-tried tools for pathfinding, they pose the dominant themes and questions that are to be encountered, over and over
again, throughout the long, ever-variant process of self-reliant seeking.
As noted in the Preamble, discovering the eternal principles of human
spirituality endows the seeker with the confidence of treading well-
marked paths. We feel we are in the silent company of those who know
their way around the maze, and we are right. Steeped in their words, we
can gain a strong dose of directive wisdom by sheer osmosis.

In the following selection, I have carefully chosen the Classics, both
Eastern and Western, from among those books that best present original
formulations of the great questions inherent to the spiritual striving of
humanity. These questions appear in endless variations, but they all conform to certain persistent themes, or *paradigms.* This term belongs to the
discipline of comparative mythology, the field pioneered by such modern
masters as Joseph Campbell and Mircea Eliade, although it has lately been
taken up as a popular idiom of New Age thinking (E1.4). A paradigm
is a pervasive structure of meaning that inheres in many different questions and issues: For instance, the paradigm of *guidance,* like all other
paradigms, embodies a structure of meaning, which can be developed
into dozens of issues and questions while the core idea remains constant.
The paradigm of guidance is the root of a few tough quandaries in the
New Age. (See, for instance, E2.3 and E14 on the *Great White Brotherhood,* the supreme organization dedicated to the spiritual guidance of
humanity.)

Another of the primary tasks in the modern discipline of pathfinding
is that of identifying paradigms when one encounters them. This implies

the capacity to comprehend the paradigm, without necessarily identifying with it or reacting to it. For instance, we may hear that someone we know has become the disciple of a certain *master.* Instead of approving or disapproving of this decision, which would be reacting to the paradigm implied in it, we can attempt to comprehend what the individual is doing by looking into the issue of guidance and forming our own questions about it. Paradigms are like bombs with delicate fuse devices—they are massively powerful belief systems that are best handled gingerly. Working to identify paradigms in the masterworks of spiritual wisdom, past and present, keeps the act of seeking clear and open-ended, comprehensive and voluntary. The power of belief is exceeded only by the power to choose what one believes.

In the Bhagavad Gita, the paradigm of guidance assumes a dramatic form in the long dialogue between Krishna and Arjuna; then it reappears again in a very different way in *Parzival,* when the wandering knight encounters the old hermit, Trevrizent, who reveals to him his own life-story; and it shows up in yet another variation, this time as a direct message from author to reader, in Emerson's essay "Self-Reliance." These are just three out of a dozen variations of that single paradigm, which itself is one out of about forty main paradigms covered in the *Handbook.*

Once a paradigm is identified, its variations are endlessly revealing, as the example above readily shows. Tracking paradigms is not merely an intellectual exercise, because when it is done with true absorption—that is, with at least the kind of empathic involvement one experiences by responding to the issues dramatized in a really good movie—paradigms can show us the deep structure of our own belief systems. They illuminate our own options and inclinations, all along the way. For instance, the story of Faust presents a variation on the paradigm of guidance in which power over the human condition is sought by resorting to the guidance of a Satanic being. Yet Faust is miraculously able to turn around this crisis of potential enslavement and the death of his soul, as shown by his experiences in Part Two of the great drama, where he redeems himself in the Underworld—*redemption* being one of the main paradigms of Western spirituality. Once you get the knack of it, tracking paradigms through stories like this can be an enormous aid to personal pathfinding.

Like a picture that's worth a thousand words, every paradigm is worth a thousand choices.

• • •

The Basics, Toward the Breakthrough and From the Sixties Onward, have been chosen for their bearing on pathfinding in the modern spiritual movement, which has unfolded since 1900. They elaborate on the latest variations of many paradigms, such as the question of accessing *ancient wisdom* (in C&B3.9, *The Candle of Vision,* and C&B4.7, *The View Over Atlantis*), or the issue of *conspiracy* (in C&B3.14, *The Journey to the East;* C&B4.2, *The Morning of the Magicians;* and C&B4.12, *The Aquarian Conspiracy*). While the ancient landmarks still serve for good orientation, new approaches to them have been developed by modern pathfinders who have left the Basics as a contemporary spiritual legacy. Now that a whole new cultural, even global, movement is emerging out of their efforts, it is extremely useful to refer back to them now and again. As far as I know, they are still the best resources we have, clear and reliable, outlasting the sensational allure of many current lights. Æ's *The Candle of Vision* (C&B3.9), written in 1935, still excels any contemporary account of awakening the third eye.

Everything presented in this opening section of the *Handbook* is ground-work. Familiarity with these works will support the seeker in venturing into all other fields, since the themes, principles, and practices covered here will be encountered in countless variations, though not always in obvious or well-explained ways, wherever questions of spiritual growth are concerned. All the selections in "The Classics and Basics" have proven to be of enduring value, above and beyond other works of a trendy, ready-access type, which are now legion. While they are not necessarily the easiest books to get to know, they are the most essential to clarification, primarily because these books help us to understand what we're really looking for in the name of spirituality. Given sufficient time and care to be absorbed, they can save us a great deal of confusion and distraction. They are the most rewarding in the long run—and even, in many cases, the most entertaining.

On the other hand, the placebos of pop occultism and quick-fix meta-physics, while often as effective as an advertising jingle, are not likely to produce long-term results. Antoine de Saint-Exupéry wrote: "To live is to be slowly born. . . . Illumination is vision suddenly granted at the end of a long and gradual preparation." In our time, the craving for instant transformation belies an essential failure to see life itself as an ongoing process of transformation, which becomes all the more engaging when we can appreciate how it spreads out in time—how it demonstrates continuity. All the experiential wisdom presented in "The Classics and Basics" contributes to this long-term perspective.

The fifty selections are arranged in four sections:

1. Classics of Eastern Spirituality
2. Classics of Western Spirituality (to 1900)
3. Toward the Breakthrough: Key Works from 1900 to the Sixties
4. From the Sixties Onward

Cross-referencing to "The Classics and Basics" elsewhere in the *Handbook* is indicated by a simple notation: C&B3.1 refers to *Cosmic Consciousness* by Maurice Bucke (see page 28).

In sections 1 and 2, where Classics in non-English languages are cited, recommended translations are indicated by "T:" after the brief review of the work.

In sections 3 and 4, where the more recent Basics are cited, dates of the first editions are given as chronological indices to the progression of these key writings that have inspired and shaped the modern spiritual movement. Most of these books are continuously in print, so there is no need to cite a recommended edition.

Occasionally, terms defined in the Lexicon are used in the brief reviews of the Classics and Basics, but to avoid cluttering, these are not always cross-referenced to the Lexicon by italics. Any term that needs definition can easily be looked up in the Lexicon. Occasionally, reviews include a cross-reference to an Essay, indicated by its number: For instance, E23 refers to the Ten-Minute Essay on shamanism.

Here as elsewhere in the *Handbook,* all the reference material is cross-woven in a deliberate way that invites the seeker to spontaneous exploration, or meandering. The leading themes and clues are spread along all sorts of fascinating trails. Remember, the thread does not guide Theseus into the labyrinth, so he has to meander by his own instincts, sometimes entering a cul-de-sac, sometimes doubling back down a passageway already traversed, but the thread—or in this case, the many threads—help him keep track of where he's going.

In the commentary on *The View Over Atlantis* (C&B4.7), for instance, the reference to *geomancy* leads directly to the Ten-Minute Essay on that subject or, if you are so inclined, to *geomancy* in the Lexicon, with its cross-references to the *canon* and *sacred architecture*. Geomancy > sacred sites > Glastonbury > Grail Mystery, is one of a dozen possible trails of association, for example. Geomancy > Gaia > etheric web > nature mysticism > Romanticism > E22, is another.

Both the Classics and the Basics are convergence points of many and varied associations. Time and time again, the threads lead back to them because they define and redefine the large-scale issues of spiritual seeking. They contain all the vital clues to an ongoing quest that is ever-changing, as different for each of us as are our fingerprints, yet constant and universal in the riddles and paradoxes it proposes.

1. CLASSICS
OF EASTERN
SPIRITUALITY

T here is a wonderful scene in Bill Murray's film of *The Razor's Edge* (C&B3.11) where the protagonist is playing cards with a gruff, hard-drinking English coal miner whom he has befriended in the pits, and their talk suddenly turns to books. They are in the miner's den, which is curiously packed with books, and after a brief exchange the old man is so overcome with surprise and delight that he exclaims, "Wot, ye huven't read the Upanishads!" With an air of great pride and generosity, he pulls out a cherished copy, bound in old, gleaming leather, and hands it over to his young friend. From this priceless moment and this single book, the main character of the story gains the initial sense of direction for his quest to find the meaning of life.

For him, as for so many others, the direction was as it has always been—toward the East.

The Eastern Classics have played an enormous role in the spiritual renaissance since the sixties. Anyone who has found the Upanishads for himself knows firsthand the impact of those teachings, which lead the young seeker in *The Razor's Edge* deep into the heart of the ultimate question: "Who am I?"

All the Eastern Classics point to the way within, the way back to the Source. All of them teach that we have originated, like figures in a dream, from the creative fantasy of a divine Dreamer—the one called Vishnu in Hindu mythology. We awaken to ourselves within the Dream through a peculiarity of our psychic makeup that allows us to be self-reflective creatures. As self-conscious entities we seem to be separate, distinct from all other self-conscious beings. But the Eastern wisdom constantly reminds us that we are not separate in any basic or ultimate way, because the ground-of-being is single and undifferentiated. We are all figments in one and the same consciousness, and Vishnu, who is dreaming us, is never absent or dislocated into some inaccessible otherworld, but right here with us, with-and-in us—if only we can get within ourselves! If we can do that—and the Eastern sources provide us with dozens of time-tried methods for going within—then we will come to the same experience all the great sages and yogis have fathomed. We will realize the ultimate truth of *Vedanta* and the other Oriental systems of transcendental psychology: namely, that the basic self-awareness that enables each one of us to say "I am" is like a lens where the all-knowing awareness of the Divine One is continuously focused, so that the One who is dreaming us can be conscious with-and-in the ones who are being dreamed.

Though the methods vary and the spiritual guidelines of the different Oriental schools can be enormously diverse, the single, common aim of them all is the same: to lead us back to the divine in us. They all assure us that we can discover the profound, ever-playful, all-knowing presence of the Dreamer within our immediate awareness of ourselves, and they all assure us that this discovery, when it comes, is full of ecstasy and light. Whether it be described as *samadhi* in Indian Yoga, direct pointing to the One Mind in Zen, or ecstatic unity with the Beloved in Sufism—the message is the same. This is the doctrine of radical *immanence,* stated in hundreds of variations in the spiritual classics of the East.

Collectively, the Eastern classics make up the so-called perennial philosophy (C&B3.13), often expressed in the simple equations of the Indian teachings:

> *Tat Twam Asi*—"Thou art That"
> *Atma is Brahma*—"The Self is itself the Source"

For every seeker, the ultimate message to be drawn from the Eastern classics is that you yourself are that which you are seeking. They exemplify the way of finding yourself.

Expressing as they do a timeless and universal message, the Eastern classics are monotonously consistent in content. This is not meant as a criticism, for the monotony is, of course, sublime. For years I could not get enough of it, including the hypnotic drone of the music and all the other trappings. The wisdom of the East has a piquant, haunting flavor. It sinks in by a kind of osmosis and the power of its impact is cumulative, so that after a sufficient period of time—the extent of which varies with each person—you become able to rephrase or paraphrase the sublimely monotonous truth out of your own direct apprehension, with utter freshness and surprise, as if you were the first one who ever realized it.

In Zen the paraphrase is developed into an art of ingenious repartee to reveal one's attentiveness to the ultimate nature of things, or *Suchness.* A typical question, or *koan,* goes:

> "Everything returns to the One, but to what does the One return?"
> Answer: It's looking gray enough tonight for more snow in the foothills.

In tracking the paradigms of the Eastern teachings, it is a good practice to remember that there are Western paradigms that stand in a contrasting or counterbalancing relation to them. (The problem of contrasting paradigms is explained in Essays 1 and 2.) For instance, *veiling* is a main paradigm of Eastern wisdom, by contrast to the Western paradigm of the *Fall.*

In the subtle philosophy of the Hindu *Tantras,* what we know as our ordinary state of consciousness is viewed as a case of selective omniscience. Actually we know all there is to be known, all the time, and we know ourselves as existing in perfect union with all things and beings, but innate to this condition of all-embracing wholeness there is a self-limiting process, called *Maya,* by which a part of the whole is selected for involvement in a special and intimate way.

"Boundless and immutable, the ground of God-consciousness veils itself," the Tantras say, so that it can bring forth the endless play of the relative worlds. This paradigm of veiling is the basis of the doctrine of radical immanence, or indwelling. Since the supreme All-Being is self-veiling, there is no true and radical division between Creator and creatures, only an illusion of separation, which may appear to be mischievous or malicious, depending exclusively upon human reactions to it.

It is often claimed that the Eastern teachings stress that the world is illusion, or Maya, but apparition would be a better rendition of this term. The world is not unreal: It is an actual apparition of the Real, which itself is neither audible nor visible nor thinkable. Maya, far from being illusion, is as real as the shrinking of objects at a distance in three-dimensional perspective. You know the spire of the church on the hill is not smaller than your thumb, but its appearing to be is as real as anything else appearing to be in the real world. In Vedanta, in Chinese philosophy, in Sufism, Buddhism, and Zen, this truth is expressed in countless ways, always with an emphasis on how our transient awareness is identical to the changeless, all-supporting One. The self is God, or is at least an aspect of God appearing as a separate reality. And your ordinary mind—when its true nature is perceived in a moment of total clarity and calm, the timeless instant of Enlightenment—is the Buddha-nature.

The Beyond is Within.

The Eastern classics are the inexhaustible wellspring to which seekers through the ages have always returned to renew their commitment to facing the ultimate questions. They are and will always be our primary touchstones to the human mystery.

1. The *I Ching,* "The Book of Changes," a manual for divination based on sixty-four permutations of the eight primary trigrams discovered by the legendary Chinese folk hero Fu Hsi. Its origins are purely mythical, but it was probably put into initial written form around 1150 B.C. and later worked out by Confucius. Its elaborate commentaries are deeply absorbing studies in the issues of choice posed by the vicissitudes of everyday life. In modern hands, the old "yarrow-stalk oracle" of the Chinese sages provides a complete ethical-cosmological system, often sobering, always relevant, full of deep and practical wisdom for facing life's changes. Widely used since the sixties as a tune-up kit for staying in harmony with the universe.

T: Wilhelm/Baynes, in the famous Bollingen edition with foreword by C. G. Jung. The standard edition since its appearance in 1950.

2. *Tao Te Ching,* the classic work of Taoism by Lao Tzu (who lived around 575 B.C.), giving the essence of Chinese mystical wisdom in elegant, poetic shorthand. A revelation of how to live the spontaneous life in exquisite balance between outer necessity and inner mood. After more than 2,500 years, the waters from this deep wellspring of Oriental mysticism are still clear and refreshing. Lao Tzu's style is dark and mysterious, serene and alluring. Everything you always wanted to know about existing in the moment.

T: D. C. Lao (Penguin), with an ample introduction; or try the keen, idiomatic American version of poet-translator Witter Bynner, *The Way of Life* (Perigee Books).

3. *Basic Writings of Chuang Tzu,* the lesser-known but equally wise representative of Taoism in ancient China. Chuang Tzu (who lived

around 350 B.C.) had a lighter touch than his brooding predecessor Lao Tzu. A great champion of spiritual freedom, he celebrated the poet's calling of useless wandering and reveled with clownlike abandon in the many paradoxes of the Way. His sly one-liner "The Tao can be transmitted, but it cannot be received" remains the best and last word on the paradox of nonattainment (E30). Detachment, sly observation of human folly, deep humor, fables, and crazy stories are here, all as entertaining as they are enlightening.

T: Two good versions: *Basic Writings,* Burton Watson (Columbia UP), a wonderful entertainment; and *Chuang Tzu: Textual Notes,* Herbert A. Giles (Allen Unwin), longer and more complete, although the actual extent of the works that can be accurately attributed to Chuang Tzu is not certain.

4. The *Analects,* a sort of Oriental counterpart to the Platonic dialogues. The first expression of pure humanism in world philosophy, a collection of pithy, eloquent sayings and anecdotes from the life of Confucius (K'ung-Fu-Tzu, 551–479 B.C.), whom Voltaire claimed to be "the first man who did *not* receive a divine inspiration"—which Voltaire meant to be much to his credit. How-to insight for practical serenity, taking the recurrent issues of personal choice and social responsibility right down to the marrow.

> "The great learning (adult study, grinding the corn in the head's mortar to fit it for use) takes root in clarifying the way wherein the intelligence increases through the process of looking straight into one's own heart and acting on the results; it is rooted in watching with affection the way people grow. . . ."

T: By far the best version of the Analects is found in Ezra Pound's threefold modern classic *The Great Digest/The Unwobbling Pivot/The Analects* (New Directions), where the poet renders the deep common sense of the old sage into language so clean and strikingly worded that it may become unforgettable, as in the opening lines cited above.

5. The Upanishads, quintessence of the deep wisdom of ancient India, probably written down in the sixth century B.C. but originating from an oral tradition of great antiquity. The first Eastern teachings to be imported to the West (around 1795), consisting of discourses on the soul in relation to death, moral choice, destiny, and the divine. These

discourses state in various forms the perennial message of radical immanence: the identity of the one who seeks God with the God being sought. This is Hindu philosophy exposed to its core, revealing the supreme Eastern paradigm, *liberation,* by contrast to the paradigm of *salvation* (C&B2.7, 2.8), which reigns supreme in the West. The deepest taproots to humankind's primordial revelation of the Self that we have.

T: Juan Mascaro (Penguin), simple, dramatic, clear-toned; or R. E. Hume, *The Thirteen Principal Upanishads* (Oxford UP), an earlier and more literal version, requires long and deep reading, with an extensive preface setting out the basic principles of Indian philosophy, and is more suitable for philosophical study than Mascaro's version.

6. The Bhagavad Gita, an excerpt from the vast Hindu epic poem, the *Mahabharata,* describing a great battle in the time of Krishna, 3100 B.C. Essentially a dialogue between the Lord Krishna (the incarnation of the Supreme Being) and Arjuna (the human seeker), on the nature of the soul, love, suffering, conflict, choice, and memory. Exquisite spiritual poetry, a call to high courage in accepting the changeless reality within the realm of transitory experience. Pocket guide to spiritual impeccability.

T: Juan Mascaro (Penguin), deeply resonant, poetic, compelling. It doesn't get any better.

7. Buddhist Sutras, especially the *Heart Sutra* and the *Diamond Sutra.* Versions of teachings originally received orally in the time of the historical Buddha (sixth century B.C.), these two key works are brief, cogent discourses that direct the mind to self-reflection and insight into the transitory nature of all things. Although the Buddha delivered hundreds of discourses to thousands of followers, tradition reports only three specific instances of Enlightenment among those who heard him. One was a wordless transmission (when the Buddha merely held up a flower), and the other two are described in these short discourses. As evidence of direct transmission they contain the deepest, truest clues for following the Buddha's way of Enlightenment.

T: Lu Ku'an Yu (Charles Luk) in *Ch'an and Zen Teachings,* Vol. 2 (Ryder hardcover), with indispensable commentaries by the Zen master of Cold Mountain, Han Shan, one of the coolest heads who ever lived—superior version, but unfortunately out-of-print. Other translations and commentaries are quite clumsy, but one passable option is *The Diamond Sutra,* ed. R. Iyer (Concord Grove Press), a slim work that also includes the *Heart Sutra* and valuable commentaries on Illusion, Emptiness, and the Eightfold Path.

8. *The Tibetan Book of the Dead,* the famous *Bardo Thodol,* "the book for liberation through hearing on the after-death plane." Actually a manual used for reading to the dead, to assist them in the transitional states *(bardos)* between death and rebirth. Said to have been written around 775 A.D. by Padma Sambhava, the mysterious wildman-sage who initiated the cult of Tibetan Buddhism. Beyond its enormous practical value as a guidebook to the death-experience, it has a lot to say to the living about how we construct our own reality—a piece of wisdom often heard in the New Age, although we are less often told about what happens when it comes time for us to deconstruct it! Paraphrased in C&B4.3.

T: Evans-Wentz (Oxford UP), classic version by one of the first Westerners to be initiated into Tibetan Buddhism; with a mine of esoteric knowledge to be found in the extensive notes of the translator and in the psychological commentary by C. G. Jung; a milestone in East/West studies.

9. *The Zen Teaching of Huang Po,* actually a classic work of Ch'an, the Chinese predecessor of Zen. A sublime teaching on the One Mind, unsurpassed in simplicity and depth, consisting of a record of direct pointing to the Buddha-awareness in the words of the Chinese master Huang Po (tenth century A.D.). Besides Chuang Tzu, one of the clearest expressions of nonattainment on record. A book to be read for a lifetime—and understood in an instant.

T: John Blofeld (Evergreen/Grove), so good no one else has even tried to match it.

10. *The Conference of the Birds,* a long anecdotal poem attributed to Farid ud-Din Attar, a Persian poet of the twelfth century. Enchanting description of a wild menagerie of birds on a pilgrimage to the throne of God, sharing tales and dialogues that express the elusive and wondrous nuances of Sufi mysticism. Full of extravagant whimsy, colorful and amusing, even—or especially—at its deepest. A kind of Sufi version of *The Canterbury Tales,* concerned with the eccentricities of divine nature, God-in-us, as much as Chaucer was with those of human nature.

T: Afkham Darbandi and Dick Davis (Penguin), in rhyming couplets, following the original, divided into short episodes that can be sipped and savored at leisure.

Note: The Eastern classics are drawn from four vast regions of the Orient: China, Tibet, India, and Persia. Numerous other sourcebooks in Oriental religion and philosophy could be cited, but I have left them out due to their obscurity. For instance, from ancient Persia we have inherited the Zend-Avesta in very late versions, which is certainly one of the supreme sacred texts of the Orient to come down to us since the radio came to Florence (E2.2). It does not, however, contain anything of practical relevance to modern seekers. The few available translations are an unreadable mishmash, of interest only to scholars. This is also true of other Eastern classics, such as the Vedas, Zoroastrian prayers, and a good many of the Buddhist Sutras.

2. CLASSICS
OF WESTERN
SPIRITUALITY

F inding yourself is one thing, but if that were all there was to it, then the seeker's quest could be dreadfully self-centered. Considering the Eastern Way alone, we might be led to believe that finding yourself is the sum total, the be-all and end-all, of the human situation, but the Western classics tell a different story. . . .

Take the tale of Parzival, for instance. This is perhaps the central classic of the Western spiritual path. Although there are contrasts, its message is not a contradiction to the perennial philosophy of the East, but an amplification, an actual advance upon the primordial wisdom of the old sages who found God and the All in themselves.

In the story, Parzival is a young knight who knows next to nothing about his own personal history. He enters upon the Grail Quest, without at first knowing what he is seeking or even that he is on a quest at all! Then he becomes involved in a series of encounters that seem accidental, while in fact they provide him with clues to his identity and his unique mission. Unlike the Eastern quest, where the seeker sets out with the deliberate intent of finding God and often has an age-old discipline of seeking (such as Yoga) already prescribed for the task, Parzival's adventure is a slow, awkward, suspenseful process of biographical revelation, fraught with losses and setbacks. The goal of his quest is not defined at the outset, so he only comes to know himself and claim his unique mission as it is progressively revealed to him by life itself, through the dramatic unfolding of his own life story. His spiritual progress is not programmatic, but entirely spontaneous and quite erratic.

This is a strange twist, beautifully and dramatically expressed in the psychological tension of the plot-line in Wolfram von Eschenbach's version. (There are dozens of versions of the Grail Legend, most of them garbled and fragmentary, but Wolfram's narrative is more or less complete and consistent.)

The Eastern paradigm of finding yourself is exemplified in dozens of specific and sophisticated methods: Yoga, Zen sitting, Buddhist ritual and meditation, Sufi dancing. The path-of-union is time-tried and well-plotted, so that the seeker is provided with all kinds of preformulated techniques. Both means and end are clearly given. By contrast, the Western way of individuation and service is a rough-hewn track. With Parzival we are introduced to the paradigm of *self-initiation.* Far from being programmatic, this path is one of trial and error. Moments of spiritual revelation, sudden and spontaneous encounters with the numinous and supernatural, light up the way like flares, but the trip itself is pure serendipity.

To put it by way of another contrast, Parzival discovers that he is someone very special, contrary to the Eastern wisdom that insists we are all one and therefore no one special. In his long quest to become the claimant of the Grail—not by belonging to a spiritual lineage that would guarantee him the rights of succession, but by his independent, if blundering, efforts—he learns that who *he* is matters deeply in the outcome of the quest. He exemplifies the paradigm of salvation: For the wasteland around the Grail Castle is a degenerating world, which even the Grail cannot restore, and the Grail King is suffering from a terrible wound, which causes him continual pain but not death and relief from pain. This grave situation calls for rescue or redemption, and the redeemer must have specific qualifications. Parzival's entire quest consists of a haphazard process of discovery in which he comes to understand how he and he alone is qualified to claim the Grail—and in the growing momentum of this realization, he finally becomes able to ask the right question.

A complete experience of human reality calls for knowing both how you are no one, identical with God, the All, and all other human beings, and how you are someone unique, with a special mission and an original purpose that can only be fulfilled by yourself alone, distinct from all others. Essential to the Western way is the understanding that finding yourself cannot be all there is to it, because there are many things you can discover in the process of finding yourself. It's as if you went up to the attic to find an old pair of glasses, and in the process of searching for them, found all kinds of marvelous things—photos and souvenirs you had completely forgotten, old toys, forgotten letters, ancestral records—which reveal to you the unique design of your own experience and restore you to an awareness of your originality.

Destiny is the old-fashioned term commonly applied to this sense of originality, the awareness that you have something special to do, a unique mission to accomplish. In the East there is no clue to any individual purpose of this kind, but the one unifying purpose of us all is fully and elaborately disclosed. The Western classics complete and advance this common purpose by extending it toward the discovery of an uncommon purpose, thus opening the horizons of human seeking to the new and unknown.

When we read in the Svetasvatara Upanishad, "The Eternal One should be known in the presence of your very own self," or we hear a modern Zen master repeat for the nth time, "Ordinary mind is the Buddha," we know it is the same thing being said—but this is not all there is to be said. From the East we are eternally reminded of the truth that applies for us all, but through the West we discover the truth that applies for ourselves alone. The first is eternally invariable, the second, infinitely variable. Yes, the beyond is within. This is true for us all. But the within is outbound. And the way it unfolds is unique and original with each of us.

Also by way of contrast, the Eastern classics are primarily documents of spiritual and metaphysical truth that came to be set down in literary form, while the Western classics are primarily great works of literature that happen to contain profound discoveries about the human situation. They are not products of a long lineage of spiritual masters who remain forever anonymous, but works of individual genius, outpourings of someone special. They can never be reduced to a universal content, for they remain originally stamped by the characters and personal essences of the ones who produced them.

Due to their high creative potency, these writings call for an effort in cocreative sharing. Beyond the selfless absorption required for the Eastern classics, they demand deep personal identification, a commitment to long-term emotional empathy and intellectual intimacy, so that the dramatic power of the stories can be taken up into the actual unfolding of one's own life story, to illuminate and amplify it in all its details. They involve us in thematic questions, unique to the West as much in the way they are posed as in the way they are resolved: romantic love, cocreation, choice, the nature of free will in relation to the acceptance of divine guidance, power over external nature, individuation, responsibility for creating personal reality, the discovery of biographical uniqueness, cultivation of the inner life, the imperative of beauty. . . .

Incorporating as they do these ever-evolving questions, the Western classics do not merely invite conversion by the persuasion of the eternal argument for Oneness, but they demand commitment to the singular, ever more individualized aspects of that Oneness.

Yes, you are God, as the Eastern classics affirm—but God also evolves, changes. This experimental proposition, based on a dynamic rather than a static conception of God (E1.4), is the essence of the Western quest, the way of individuation.

In the selection of the Western classics certain problems arise which do not apply to the Eastern classics. Since they are all great works of literature, the selection is more difficult to make. There are hundreds of great Western classics illustrating the spiritual plight of humanity—take the complete works of Shakespeare, for instance. It is a question of selecting those which illustrate the basic spiritual themes of the West in the most vivid and accessible way. The *Satyricon* of Petronius, for example, is a masterwork of Western literature with spiritual themes buried in it like rare minerals in crude ore. Dozens of other masterpieces of enduring value could be cited, but the following selections are all distinct in the way that they bring to light the great main themes and questions of the Western way, without the literary form obscuring the inner content. Granted, it still takes personal exertion to get to that inner content and make it one's own, unlike the Eastern classics where the content, the perennial message, is open and obvious—but deep personal identification is the Western way.

Also, with the Western masterworks there is the question of what is truly Western. Most of the classics cited here are European in origin—from *Gilgamesh* and the *Homeric Hymns* up to the Hermetica. But the ultimate realm of the West lies in the Americas (North, Central, and South), and for that vast region the spiritual classics are not easy to identify. As for what might be called Western/American classics, these are conspicuously lacking due to the fact that the spiritual traditions of the New World have been primarily oral—either never written down, or poorly and fragmentarily recorded. Only in the colonial period from about 1600 onward does America begin to have its own literary output, expressive of an emergent spiritual life distinct from the spirituality preserved in the oral folklore and ritual of the native Indian peoples. And then only with the Transcendentalist movement of the mid-nineteenth century does this flower into a spiritual message that is truly American in the modern sense.

Today, with the surge of interest in Native American spirituality (E18), it is useful to define the American classics (such as Emerson's *Essays*) in their own right, distinct from the rapidly growing body of teachings and practices deriving from the native, or *Amerindian,* heritage. As for the folklore and native myths of the Americas, one instance is given here where the oral tradition has been captured with special force and magic in the written word.

1. *The Epic of Gilgamesh,* a Sumerian legend found on clay tablets dating back at least to 1500 B.C. Although it comes out of the fertile womb of the Middle East, this fantastic adventure contains in germinal form many of the key themes of the Western quest: loss of innocence leading to individuation, temptations of power, sexual initiation, the journey to the Underworld, facing and accepting death, the yearning for eternal youth. An exciting adult fairy tale of vast mythic dimensions.

T: N. K. Sandars (Penguin), very readable, nonacademic.

2. *Homeric Hymns,* a group of Greek myths written down around 700 B.C., cameo portraits of the main Greek Gods—Hermes, Athena, Zeus, Hera, Pan—who may be considered to be the directing spiritual impulses behind Western thought and culture. Here is the first full portrayal of Jung's archetypes of the collective unconscious, our oldest spiritual ancestors in the West. The hymns include the complete story of Demeter and Persephone, a formative Underworld myth and the basis of the *Eleusinian Mysteries.*

T: Charles Boer (Spring), an award-winning rendition in vivid, rigorous poetry.

3. *Phaedrus* and *Symposium,* dialogues of Plato from the fourth century B.C. Of all the Platonic dialogues, these two are by far the most accessible and entertaining. Lively conversations exploring the themes of Beauty, Love, and Divine Inspiration, these dialogues are seminal to all later seeking. They initiate the centuries-long quest of the Western spirit to understand and experience the true nature of love, both human and divine. This is philosophy (literally, the "love of wisdom") captured at its flowering, almost as good as being there. The scent of wine is in the air, and you can almost feel the sages breathing garlic in your face.

T: Walter Hamilton (Penguin), accurate and chatty, comes across like conversation that actually took place.

4. *The Golden Ass,* by Apuleius, written around 150 A.D. Funny and racy, a novelistic account of one man's accidental initiation into the mysteries of Isis, at the expense of being changed into an ass. Comic treatment of a profound experience. Good entertainment and a sobering reflection for modern seekers at risk of taking themselves too seriously and developing wild pretensions. Details of the initiation are exact and authentic.

T: Robert Graves (Noonday/FSG), excellent version by a modern master poet.

5. *Parzival,* by Wolfram von Eschenbach, written around 1215. Fine, sinewy, dramatic version of the ultimate Western adventure, the quest for the Holy Grail, illustrating the paradigms of redemption and service. Parzival (or Parsifal, to use the softer French spelling of the name) is the supreme exemplar of what we now call individuation, and his story is full of romance and mystery, populated with characters both salty and supernatural, not to mention a twisty plot with terrific special effects.

T: A. T. Hatto (Penguin), strong modern rendering, with an excellent introduction and afterword, bringing out the figures etched deeply in the grain of the tale.

6. *Tristan and Isolde,* by Gottfried von Strassburg, written around 1210. The greatest love story of the West, which demands to be read with deep empathic absorption to appreciate the psychological depths and nuances it reveals, set out in clear dramatic enactments seven hundred years before psychology was invented. Its tragic ending is not really an ending, for the story goes on, and what it can teach us is as relevant today as it was in medieval times—perhaps more so, considering the stubborn persistence of romantic-sexual dilemmas. Essential background to all modern efforts to fathom the psychology of romantic love, as pursued by Joseph Campbell *(Creative Mythology),* Robert A. Johnson (*He, She,* and *We*), and Denis de Rougemont (C&B3.16), among others.

T: A. T. Hatto (Penguin), clear, strong, psychologically accurate. Gottfried's unfinished version (he disappeared in the middle of writing it, when the Inquisition came to town) with the tacked-on ending by his fellow writer, Thomas of Britain.

7. *The Divine Comedy,* by Dante (1265–1321). Crowning expression of the paradigm of salvation, the culmination of the medieval worldview expressed in poetry of ineffable depth and beauty. Totally cinematic, exquisite in detail, and vast in scope, the masterwork of a Christian

visionary who dreamed a triple spiral of the self-loss, inner ordeal, and final, uplifting redemption of the seeker of love. Shows how we are led by the human to the divine.

T: Many translations in many editions. Best to browse through a few to find one with language suitable to personal taste, or try the modern verse rendering by poet John Ciardi (NAL/Mentor).

8. *Faust,* by Johann Wolfgang von Goethe (1749–1832). The story of a quest for power and immortality in defiance of God, and ultimate redemption by passage into the Underworld, the realm of the Mothers. As significant as Parzival's adventure, this story is the exemplar of the Western struggle to reconcile spiritual power with human weakness. A poetic drama full of rough-and-ready humor, philosophical irony, and startling insight into the hidden worlds of occultism and depth psychology. Read it now, before Spielberg does the movie!

T: Philip Wayne (Penguin), vivid and lively, the most readable and entertaining of the half-dozen good translations. Parts One and Two in two separate volumes.

9. The Hermetica. A collection of metaphysical teachings on God and the soul, attributed to the "Thrice-Greatest Hermes," a master or demi-god of the Egyptian Mysteries. Though not actually Western in content, these discourses are the first truly esoteric writings to be made accessible in the West, thus opening the way for independent spiritual seeking in our culture. The most venerable wisdom of antiquity, hot off the papyrus. Strange, heady stuff that looks relatively harmless, though it served to expose the long-concealed secret of the Mysteries, *apotheosis*—deification of the human. A controversial idea, if there ever was one (E2.2).

T: Walter Scott (Shambhala), in four volumes, though only the first has the essential texts, the rest being elaborate commentaries.

This covers the Western tradition from Plato to the Renaissance, at which time there was a revival of interest in ancient wisdom and occult systems, a kind of metaphysical revival such as we're seeing today.

From the time of the discovery of the New World it was almost three hundred years to the American Revolution. Between 1492 and 1776 some great philosophical works were written, but these are of little interest or practical value to the modern seeker. From the time of the American and French revolutions, however, the massive movement of Romanticism took shape and set in motion many of the main currents that were later to be defined in the modern spiritual movement. On this crucial transition process, see E1 and E2; also, E22 on Romanticism.)

In America the Romantic movement appeared in New England Transcendentalism, which produced two great classics of Western spirituality:

10. *Essays,* written between 1836 and 1864, by Ralph Waldo Emerson (1803–1882). The eloquent expressions of a deep and practical thinker, on the philosophy of individualism, reverence for nature, self-reliance, moral responsibility, destiny, and purpose. These essays treat most of the essential themes of the Western way and provide a touchstone for ever-fresh reflections upon ourselves and the world around us. They should be read and pondered by everyone who is inclined to turn away from our Western way of life because of its apparent superficiality. What Emerson shows is that nothing can be superficial where the powers of genuine self-observation are brought to bear. There is plenty of old-fashioned advice here, with a strong emphasis on learning from life itself how to unfold what is innate. The philosophy of rugged individualism at its taproots.

"The magnetism which all original action exerts is explained when we enquire the reason of self-trust. Who is the Trustee?" (In "Self-Reliance," 1841)

11. *Walden* (1854), by Henry David Thoreau (1817–1862). The journal of a retreat, written long before such retreats were fashionable. Having observed that the "mass of men lead lives of quiet desperation," Thoreau withdrew for two years to a small cabin on Walden Pond near Concord, Massachusetts, to be close to nature and commune with his soul. The result was this famous journal, full of simple and deep reflections, a touchstone to the American mind. Communicates as much through its tone and mood as it does through its content.

Finally, there is one work from the Amerindian heritage that provides access to the vast and deep cosmology of the Native American cultures:

12. *The Popol Vuh,* the creation myth of the ancient Maya, one of the few authentic documents we have from the vast oral tradition of native America. The "Book of the People" is a long, winding tale of magical adventures in the natural world and daring exploits in the Underworld. A massive fairy tale for adults, really strange and really scary.

T: Dennis Tedlock (Simon & Schuster), a superb translation in a storytelling idiom that captures the mysterious dimensions of the oral tradition.

3. TOWARD THE
BREAKTHROUGH

*Key Works from 1900
to the Sixties*

When the sixties dawned, there was already terrific momentum behind what then emerged as the modern spiritual movement. As described in Essay 2, "Traditional Religions and the New Alternative Paths," the historical roots of the current movement are located in the Renaissance, based in events that occurred synchronously with the discovery of the New World. The first distinct shift toward the breakthrough occurred when the Italian scholar Marsilio Ficino translated the Hermetica for his patron, Cosimo de' Medici, in 1463. At that moment a source of ancient wisdom, pointing back to the lost heritage of the Mysteries, became instantly available for independent study and personal application.

Today, enormous amounts of such material are available. The metaphysical bookstores throughout the country—about 2,500 and still counting, according to the 7 December 1987 edition of *Time* (with a cover story on Shirley MacLaine)—are packed with them, and the massive legacy of spiritual teachings of all former ages and cultures is now at our fingertips. The big question now seems to be how well the ancient wisdom of the ages will be absorbed by the Pepsi generation.

For the modern spiritual movement as we see it today, there was a formative period from 1900 to the 1960s. During this time a number of significant works appeared, setting the tone and direction of the movement. These are offerings of spiritual pioneers, writings of primary definition and influence that often contain as much substance as dozens, or even hundreds, of more recent books. In spiritual and metaphysical writings of current authorship, there is an awful lot of rehashing and tramping over well-trodden ground, but what has already been said once and said well is not so easily surpassed.

All the works contributing toward the breakthrough that appeared between 1900 and 1960 speak to us now with remarkable clarity and power. They resonate with the tone of conviction that comes from the pioneers and originators of the movement that now reveals itself in countless trends and digressions. These formative works embody the driving forces of the present-day quest for spiritual awakening, and link us back to the originating agents who gave it definition even before it assumed name and form in the popular mind.

Authenticity matters as much in experiments of occult-spiritual-metaphysical searching as it does anywhere else—in science, business, sports, or the arts. Certainly, this is an understatement, because who can imagine an area of human endeavor where authenticity matters more than it does in spirituality! Yet authenticity in this area is not easy to establish. After all, how can the guidelines be set and who is there to set them? What, if any, are the criteria for authenticity in spiritual teachings and practices? How do we tell the real from the phony, the solid from the specious, in the realms of mysticism, magic, channeling, reincarnation, et cetera? Just because what we call spirituality encompasses the widest spectrum of human possibilities, it stands wide open to the permissive, undiscriminating attitude that anything goes.

And it seems as if almost anything *does* go. In modern spiritual studies and practices, there do not yet exist any reliable criteria for distinguishing what is authentic from what is phony or delusory; although we are, given the hindsight of some twenty or more years in the movement, beginning to allow that fraudulence, brainwashing, and downright exploitation can be perpetrated with outrageous audacity in some areas of what passes for spirituality.

The New Age, if it means nothing else, is a time of exceptional speculation concerning the possibility of certain individuals initiating an enormous experiment in personal and cultural transformation. For centuries going back through history to the earliest roots of human culture, there is evidence of systematic spiritual training—called *initiation*—perpetuated in the Mystery Schools of all high civilizations. In all the traditional cultures, it was initiation into the Mysteries that qualified an individual to assume the status of a self-realized person; and the same remains true in primitive and native cultures today, such as the Australian Aborigines and the American Indians. To initiates fell the responsiblity for directing and inspiring the culture of the populace at large. But today we are facing the edge of a massive transition toward *self*-initiation. For this there are no precedents, no reliable rules or fixed guidelines set down in stone.

In many respects, modern humanity is still quite naive spiritually, quite innocent as well as indiscriminate. The eventual expansion of the New Age movement into a sociocultural revolution depends on its grounding in individual efforts that are authentic and soundly inspired. If we are to go about meeting our individual needs for independent seeking, we will benefit by knowing exactly what those needs are. And there is no better way to identify and evaluate our needs for spiritual growth and self-guidance than by reference to the key works that have given definition to the current era, this New Age of free-form, progressive self-initiation. These works are touchstones to authenticity. A good many of the principles of clear seeking presented throughout the *Handbook,* although they derive from my own experiences, have been clarified and corroborated by the directive wisdom found in these books.

The selections in Toward the Breakthrough are highly varied in theme and content, yet they all share the common feature of being the first of their kind, and not a single one of them has been superseded by anything written to this day.

1. *Cosmic Consciousness* (1899), Maurice Bucke (Dutton). In this pioneering work on the evolution of human consciousness, Bucke proposes a progressive shift in three stages from mere sense awareness to self-consciousness to superconsciousness. His theory is supported by a long, fascinating selection of case histories of mystics, writers, artists, and ordinary folk who have experienced the life-changing moment of spontaneous "c. c." One of the great testaments to the wonders of independent seeking.

2. *The Varieties of Religious Experience* (1902), William James (Penguin). The famous American psychologist interprets conversion, near-death experiences, sainthood, madness, mysticism, and altered states. Covers the gamut of spiritual adventures in a clearheaded way that has yet to be surpassed for its sheer readability. Not a how-to book by any means, but a master study in the psychology of religion that provides a lot of basic orientation to all those strange experiences people are having, nowadays, in the holy aisles of the spiritual supermarket.

3. *Letters to a Young Poet* (1908), Rainer Maria Rilke (Norton, translated by M. D. Herter Norton; or Vintage, translated by Stephen Mitch-

ell). In this slim, eloquent work—short enough to read in a couple of hours but so fantastically compressed in life-wisdom and long-range insight that it calls for years of rereading—the great German lyric poet gives incomparable advice on how to live in vital relation to the world while nurturing the secret resources of the inner life. Indispensable for those who believe that spirituality involves commitment to a creative calling.

4. *The Prophet* (1923), Kahlil Gibran (Knopf). Beautiful, universally stated collection of inspiring aphorisms and deep reflections on all aspects of human experience (love, suffering, childbearing, commerce, wrongdoing) by the Lebanese poet-painter-philosopher whose personal distillation of life-wisdom still blooms like a rare flower along the way of all seekers.

5. *Black Elk Speaks* (1932), John G. Neihardt (Pocket Books). This "Book of Visions" of Black Elk, a medicine man of the Oglala Sioux, is perhaps the most universal expression of the human quest that has come out of the American Indian tradition—as attested by its translation into a dozen foreign languages. It anticipated the present revival of shamanism by a good fifty years, and still stands at a level of spiritual stature above anything else in the field. Black Elk's vision leaves us in awe and humility, open and wondering.

6. *Magic and Mystery in Tibet* (1932), Alexandra David-Neel (Dutton). A thrilling firsthand account of the Frenchwoman who, in 1923, was the first European known to have entered the forbidden city of Lhasa. She describes an unspoiled paradise of magical and mystical wonders encountered among the lamas of the hidden kingdom at the top of the world. Everything that Madame Blavatsky was supposed to have seen and done—though we have no evidence she was ever really there—Madame David-Neel describes in a vivid, highly credible way. Pioneering work that introduced Tibet to the West.

7. *Modern Man in Search of a Soul* (1933), C. G. Jung (Harvest/HBJ). Given as lectures in the early thirties, when Europe was darkening under the black cloud of Nazism, this collection of careful, inquiring essays brings attention to psychotherapy as the modern spiritual alternative to traditional and revealed religion. But beyond Jung's argument for his

own cause, the questions raised and avenues defined are still relevant to the wide spectrum of independent spiritual pathways. Featured in a memorable scene from the movie *The Petrified Forest.*

8. *A Search in Secret India* (1935), Paul Brunton (Paul Brunton Foundation). One of the first stories of a Westerner's spiritual quest in the East, anticipating the wave of India-bound seekers that came to public attention in the sixties. In Brunton's entire body of writing—over thirteen volumes following this one—there is consistent fidelity to the depth of the Indian teachings, but he also goes them one or two better, advancing the Eastern spiritual quest toward new and modern dimensions suitable for the West. Seminal work by a pioneer who stands out as a paragon of sanity.

9. *The Candle of Vision* (1935), Æ, pen name of George Russell (Quest/Theosophical Publishing House). Deep, absorbing autobiography of the Irish mystic and painter, key figure in the *Celtic Revival.* Written with transparent simplicity, full of inner richness, it communicates a sense of intimacy with long-forgotten dreams and lost senses. Contains what is probably the most vivid account ever written of second sight. A testament to the power and mystery of the waking dream.

10. *The Little Prince* (1936), Antoine de Saint-Exupéry (HBJ, a beautiful, large-format edition with the author's illustrations). Naive charm and timeless wisdom combine in this fable by a pioneer of transcontinental flight whose gift of childlike imagination enabled him to produce a parable not by any means for children only. More than fifty years after his first appearance on this planet, *The Little Prince* is still leading us to the discovery of primal magic in the simple things. A reliable touchstone to how honestly and clearly we adults can really see ourselves, free of deviation by our self-importance. Saint-Exupéry's dauntless little adventurer is certainly one of the earliest and most noble representatives of the *inner child* who is so widely and fervently sought nowadays.

11. *The Razor's Edge* (1944), W. Somerset Maugham (Penguin). Classic novel of one man's search for the meaning of life, his courage to reject conventionality and success, his discovery of the Upanishads, and his travels in Tibet. Contains in story form all the ingredients of the modern spiritual quest. Basis of the bold, compelling film by Bill Murray.

12. *The Autobiography of a Yogi* (1945), Paramahansa Yogananda (Self-Realization Fellowship). A warm, intimate, revealing account of the life of an Indian yogi, a prime representative of the age-old lineage of spiritual masters in the Hindu tradition. Includes the famous account of Yogananda's union with God in the moment of *samadhi.* Important work in the dissemination of Eastern teachings in the West, and a best-seller in its time.

13. *The Perennial Philosophy* (1945), Aldous Huxley (Harper & Row). Original, one-of-a-kind anthology covering all the great religious themes and questions of the ages, taken from a wide spectrum of world cultures and woven together by Huxley with a keen, highly readable commentary. Treats every variation of mystical experience and God-seeking, putting them all in perspective.

14. *The Journey to the East* (1956), Hermann Hesse (Noonday/FSG, translated by Hilda Rosner). A book to be read in an afternoon and remembered for a lifetime. Of all of Hesse's works (which contributed immensely to fostering the new spirituality in the West), this fabulist novella from his late period is by far the most magical. Cryptic and elusive, yet strangely direct in communicating the wonder and confusion of the eternal quest. Magical realism at its best, one of that rare breed of story that irresistibly merges into one's own. "It was my destiny to join in a great experience. . . ."

15. *The Murder of Christ* (1952), Wilheim Reich (Noonday/FSG). A brilliant, daring probe into the sickness of modern humanity; challenges the conventional representation of Christ and proposes an alternative way to resolve humanity's main conflict, which Reich sees as a conflict with itself due to setting its will against the life-force. A response to Freud's notion of the death wish, showing how traditional religion in the West has failed, and thus defining the urgent need for some kind of nontraditional spiritual revival in our time.

16. *Love in the Western World* (1956), Denis de Rougemont (Princeton, translated by Montgomery Belgion). An exploration of the meaning of romantic love, delving into the exotic folklore of the Troubadours, Cathars, erotic mysticism, the Sufi connection, and much more. De

Rougemont carries his inquiry all the way through to the cliché of modern romance in relation to illicit passion on the one hand, and conventional marriage on the other. Wise, sophisticated, challenging, this study anticipated the trend of interest in love and intimacy by thirty years, and its mature conclusions (thoroughly European in flavor) may still be ahead of the times.

4. FROM THE
SIXTIES ONWARD

T he new works produced from the 1960s onward all have quite a different character and bearing from those leading toward the Breakthrough. The difference is marked primarily by the great watershed of the sixties, when the New Age first assumed definition as a countercultural event. This development has been followed up in the eighties by a further stage of growth: the initial emergence of New Age interests into the mainstream.

During the developmental period from 1900 to the 1960s, the results of a lot of original, pioneering work appeared in print, but alternative spirituality remained largely a matter of elite interest, more or less unknown to the public at large. Even in the mid-forties, when *Autobiography of a Yogi* appeared and became a best-seller, interest was sparked in Eastern masters, but it was nothing comparable to the widespread exposure they have gotten since 1967, when the Beatles embraced Maharishi Mahesh Yogi as their personal *guru*. Huxley's superb anthology with commentaries, *The Perennial Philosophy,* appeared in the last year of World War II, when the populace at large had other concerns on their minds. It became a must-read for an elite group of questing intellectuals, those rare few who had the time and the inclination to dabble in mysticism.

But already, with the end of the war, other developments were unfolding that would prove to be extremely influential in opening alternative spirituality to wide social exposure. At first, it was soldiers returning from the Asian theater, and later, servicemen stationed in Korea during the conflict there, who served to bring Oriental philosophy and folklore to Western shores. Through firsthand contact with Eastern ways of thought and self-discipline, they became instrumental in a tremendous process of cross-cultural transplantation. Zen and the martial arts were popular among these servicemen, many of whom found their way into the circles of the Beat movement, which flowered through the early and middle fifties. Jack Kerouac's *The Dharma Bums* is one well-known chronicle of this period.

A little-known but crucial event in the dissemination of Eastern teachings in the West occurred in 1965, when the Oriental Exclusions Acts were repealed, opening the way for large-scale immigration from the Far East and India. Since the first appearance of Oriental emissaries to the West at the Conference of World Religions of 1897, swamis, gurus, and *roshis* had remained purely exotic; now they began to arrive in considerable numbers. In the brief span of a few years, America was swamped with all manner of missionaries of Eastern wisdom and ways. Viewed in hindsight, the acceleration has been really staggering: less than a hundred years from Ramakrishna to Rajneesh.

By 1967, when the Beatles brought Maharishi Mahesh Yogi to worldwide media exposure, the image of spiritual masters from the East was becoming well-established. It had in fact already turned into a kind of caricature of itself, as things in the U.S.A. tend to do, curiously and with alarming rapidity, due to a large extent to the distorting overexposure of the media. Also, in the rebellious spirit of the sixties, there was a tendency among adherents of the new movements to be quite exhibitionistic, sometimes flaunting their new ideas and manners. The best-known example is, of course, the devotees of the Hare Krishna movement, founded in 1965 when antiestablishment fever was peaking. Among this group and others, new personal names in Hindi and Sanskrit were adopted to signify the radical change of life-style and identity. Customs of dress, eating, physical austerity, and devotional rituals were also adopted on a wide scale among the counterculture, with plenty of mainstream exposure of the leading cult figures through the national magazines, daily news, and TV talk shows. Whether or not these conversions to Eastern forms of religion— such as Krishna-worship, which is quite traditional in its own right— constitute an authentic instance of finding an alternative path, is a question considered in E2.

Predictably, it was a short step from these rapid and media-hyped developments to clever Hollywood exploitation. I guess you have to be quite an ancient relic, by now, to remember the banal stereotype of a hippie presented in the character of Maynard on "The Confessions of Dobie Gillis." Or Gypsy Boots, who rhapsodized over health food and the Edenic return to nature on "The Steve Allen Show." These were the first faint clues of the New Age seeping into the mainstream. Then, in the early seventies, the pure archetype of a seeker appeared in Kane, played by David Carradine, on the series "Kung Fu." It would be hard to imagine a more perfect and effective characterization of the *warrior,* one of the key themes of the New Age.

By the eighties, the picture had changed enormously from what it was in the sixties. Due in part to the bad press associated with the phenomenon of *cults* (E10), and the nationwide exposure of the Rajneesh scandal in Oregon, it appears that specific instances of "gurumania" are dropping into the background as a much more far-reaching interest in Eastern and alternative spirituality arises within the mainstream. Even if it appears, initially, to be defined by spurious fads (such as *crystals* and *channeling*), this new trend is fed by far deeper currents and may well have long-term effects in the mainstream of American culture.

All the books cited in this section of "The Classics and Basics" reflect the trend toward mainstreaming of the New Age. They are not the products of brilliant forerunners like Paul Brunton or masters of the great overview like Aldous Huxley. For the most part, they are the works of people living today, men and women who are serving as key agents in developing the many facets of the new spirituality on a global scale. These works are testimonials to the enormous social and cultural changes now under way, due to the growing impact of a pragmatic vision of planetary transformation.

As noted in E1, the New Age may be viewed as a late outgrowth, or mutation, of radical socialism going back to heretical sects of the nineteenth century. Its identifiable roots are to be found in the socialist-utopian movements of a century ago, the millenarian cults of the 1840s, which reappeared in the radical counterculture of the 1960s. Now, as humanity approaches the threshold of the twenty-first century, the New Age is shaping into a sociological movement on an international scale—at least in the literate cultures of the West. Planetary *networking* is a common theme in New Age thinking. Although the new spirituality is based upon highly subjective efforts in seeking and moments of personal enlightenment, it comes to expression more and more in external culture, in the media and societal attitudes, taking a long stride beyond the schismatic countercultural activities of the sixties. In short, the New Age appears to have entered a stage of consolidation, with many of its participants devoting their lives to the effort of shaping it into a global program of some kind. Throughout all this, the impulses at work remain fairly consistent, but there is a huge dimensional shift. This trend, fully and vividly described in Marilyn Ferguson's *The Aquarian Conspiracy,* is the wave of the future, potentially strong enough to allow the leading impulses of the New Age to define and shape progressive aspects of social and cultural change.

The sourcebooks cited in From the Sixties Onward are all records of this shift. They reflect what is happening around us in a frame of activity far wider than the esoteric world of those spiritual pioneers who contributed toward the Breakthrough. They indicate how the New Age is developing beyond its superficial features into a new social agenda, a solid and legitimate infraculture, supported by proponents and activists from diverse realms of contemporary life. These are works that have been instrumental in bringing the modern spiritual movement into wide-scale recognition. Some of them have defined new areas of exploration—Tibetan Buddhism, neoshamanism, geomancy. Others are records of private and inner experiences that tell us a lot about why things around us are changing or must be changed. Yet others are significant for the new directions they set, showing how personal efforts in self-transformation and spiritual growth are leading over into discoveries and consequences that can affect hundreds of thousands of others.

In the selection here, I've taken care once again to choose those works that are most universal in their significance, even though in some cases they may belong to a specific genre, such as shamanism or geomancy. The aim is to cite the books most characteristic of the current transition of New Age impulses from countercultural interests into the mainstream effects.

1. *Initiation* (1962), Elizabeth Haich (Harper & Row). Fascinating, often sensational, highly detailed and dramatic account of a woman's memories of her tests and experiences undergoing spiritual training in a former life in Egypt. Probably the most well-written, convincing example of a reincarnational novel to date. Generated a wave of interest in past-life recall and the revival of the Mysteries.

2. *The Morning of the Magicians* (1964), Louis Pauwels and Jacques Bergier (Avon; Stein and Day). An astonishing account of the little-known influences of metaphysical and occult movements behind the scenes of history in the twentieth century. All the rage when it appeared,

although its impressive treasury of outrageous ideas and stranger-than-fiction facts would probably not command as much attention nowadays as what we might see in a TV miniseries. Somewhat sensational, journalistic treatment, but also quite accurate.

3. *The Psychedelic Experience* (1964), Richard Alpert, Timothy Leary, and Ralph Metzner (Citadel/Lyle Stuart). An adaptation in catchy modern idiom of *The Tibetan Book of the Dead* (C&B1.8), written specifically for guidance in going through the *psychedelic experience.* Assuredly of some quaint antiquarian interest (since the sixties almost seem ancient by now), but beyond that, it still holds up today because of its sharp, innovative treatment of typical human hang-ups and blocks that sit like scrappy sphinxes in the way of every seeker.

4. *Understanding Media: The Extensions of Man* (1965), Marshall McLuhan (NAL; McGraw). Dense, dazzling, and difficult, enigmatic and eye-opening, this is the Rosetta stone for deciphering how media works in reflecting and programming our awareness and values, both social and personal. A textbook in the esoteric psychology of modern communication, still as avant-garde as it was when it appeared, although McLuhan has long since gone out of vogue. Considering the role that media technology is now playing in the current efforts to create a planetary culture and expose the masses to New Age options in healing, nutrition, lifestyle, et cetera, McLuhan deserves a careful rereading. Essential for anyone who wants to understand behavioral modeling through media-feedback, though definitely not for the woolly-headed.

5. *Born in Tibet* (1966), Chogyam Trungpa (Shambhala). Rare example of a contemporary account of the life of an incarnate lama, the eleventh Trungpa *Tulku,* who became a rather outrageous figure in American spiritual life. It is significant beyond its specific relevance to Tibetan Buddhism, however, in the way it illustrates a kind of archetypal drama: the uprooting of a native son from his religious tradition and homeland, the exodus from Tibet in 1959 when the Chinese invaded, and the eventual transplantation of a spiritual impulse into a foreign land. Dramatic, well-told inside story of a unique instance of spiritual-cultural transmigration.

6. *The Teachings of Don Juan: A Yaqui Way of Knowledge* (1968), Carlos Castaneda (Pocket/S&S). Although it belongs specifically to the genre of

shamanism, and is in fact a key work sparking shamanism's current revival, Castaneda's first book (originally published as a slim anthropological study by UCLA/Berkeley) transcends the genre it served to define. Perhaps more than any other Western seeker of our time, Castaneda has relocated the boundaries between the actual and the invented, the real and the imaginal, and has related a whole system of experimental psychology for exploring the interaction of the two realms. In the sequence of works following *Don Juan,* right up to *The Power of Silence* (eighth in the series, 1987), he has consistently advanced into areas of the unknown where others have yet to venture or even dare to speculate. Whether he is to be believed or not is quite irrelevant, for if Castaneda has taught us anything, it is that you don't have to believe something to experience it!

7. *The View Over Atlantis* (Original, 1969; revised as *The New View Over Atlantis,* 1983), John Michell (Harper & Row). This breakthrough book on *geomancy,* sacred engineering (Glastonbury, Stonehenge), and the canon of ancient mathematics gave initial definition to the nostalgic longing for ancient wisdom that characterizes so much of New Age thinking. Hinting at the existence of a long-lost world order (symbolized by *Atlantis,* the lost continent), it stimulated a widespread revival in the *Earth Mysteries* and ancient sciences, and reinstated the neo-Platonic concept of an ideal society rooted in sacred traditions. A major influence in the modern effort to find a basis for a workable vision of planetary organization.

8. *Be Here Now* (1971), Ram Dass (Lama Foundation–Harmony). Very widely read description of the devotional path of self-awakening in the Hindu tradition, converted into Western terms as a cookbook for a sacred life. Topical treatment, loose and nonsystematic, providing all kinds of practical and spiritual advice and a Sanskrit glossary at the end.

9. *The Crack in the Cosmic Egg* (1971), Joseph Chilton Pearce (Pocket Books). A stirring account of a man's breakdown and escape from ordinary reality to a new world of inner/outer discoveries, this book affirmed the imperative of breaking away from *consensus-reality* to find one's own version of the truth. Especially stimulating in the way it shows the author's diverse efforts to interpret and explain to himself the breakthrough in mind and feeling he underwent, without at first understanding where it was taking him. Many road maps and way signs for every seeker are

provided by the curious turns Pearce takes on his journey toward another way of seeing life.

10. *Zen and the Art of Motorcycle Maintenance* (1974), Robert M. Pirsig (Bantam). A philosophical novel of one man's adventure in self-discovery, with the emphasis on his efforts to overcome the limits of his rational mind and open to life's unpredictable promises. Warm, winning narrative of a geographical and spiritual journey. National best-seller for several years. For all its charm and accessibility, it is quite heady in places, demanding a lot of concentration to follow the thought-eddies generated in the wake of the errant cyclist.

11. *The Road Less Traveled* (1978), M. Scott Peck (Touchstone/S&S). A major landmark on the broad road of the new spirituality; also a long-time national best-seller. Reflections and directions on the nature of love, problem solving, commitment, evil, grace. All the big issues, well-presented case histories, a lot of good insight on what we're looking for—and how, in some instances, we are looking for it in the wrong ways. Unusually well written, tremendously helpful to self-evaluation. Also, definitive to the strain of Christian humanism within the New Age (para-Christianity).

12. *The Aquarian Conspiracy* (1980), Marilyn Ferguson (Tarcher). A survey of the emergent New Age movement as a whole, tracing some of the historical background (Transcendentalism, the rise of the new physics, brain studies), concentrating on its scientific, technical, and sociological aspects. Here is a sociological overview that will undoubtedly prove influential in bringing to maturity the trends it describes. Oriented to the mainstream, this vision of a planetary network facilitated by a vanguard of evolutionary agents in all fields of human endeavor is strongly pragmatic and optimistic, painting the picture of a vast evolutionary shift that can make the world a better place to live for all people, especially those living in California.

The Essays

Things have roots and branches; affairs have scopes and beginnings. To know what precedes and what follows, is nearly as good as having a head and feet.

The men of old wanting to clarify and diffuse throughout the empire that light which comes from looking straight into the heart and then acting, first set up good government in their own states; wanting good government in their states, they first established order in their own families; wanting order in the home, they first disciplined themselves; desiring self-discipline, they rectified their own hearts, they sought precise verbal definitions of their inarticulate thoughts (the tones given off by the heart); wishing to attain precise verbal definitions, they set to extend their knowledge to the utmost. This completion of knowledge is rooted in sorting things into organic categories.

—TA HSIO,
"The Great Digest"
of Confucius
(Ezra Pound translation)

USING THE ESSAYS

I t was the lovable old wizard Einstein who said that wonder is the true basis of all seeking, common to both the religious and scientific realms. Yes, but sometimes I find myself wondering, "What is wonder?"

The word comes from a rare root, *wundor,* which only appears in Old English and Germanic. Originally, it referred to the effect of something miraculous or supernatural, the impact of a divine power intervening in the world. In mythological language, this is called an encounter with the numinous or sacred. In ordinary use today, wonder seems merely to denote curiosity or distracted pondering. But surely in the sense Einstein meant, it means more than this.

For the child, wonder is obviously the natural state of apprehending the world. Innocence and awe fill the mental and emotional life of all children as they encounter a fluidly changing world, not yet locked into the static categories of interpretation that will soon enough be imposed upon it. For children, as well as for primitive peoples like the Australian Aborigines, wonder is the state of immediate contact with the mysterious forces within the world, powers not to be controlled or fully explained by human beings.

As adults, we still continue to feel wonder, but in an ambiguous way. It is something of a mixed blessing. Normally, if someone says, "I wonder," that person expresses not merely an open-minded interest in something that is not yet understood or defined, but also a sense of confusion, a halting outreach to something uncertain, which perhaps can never fully be known. For the adult, the germ of childlike wonder persists in the depths of consciousness, but it becomes problematic.

Asking the right questions is one of the first principles of clear seeking. What inspires us all through life to keep open and keep looking at the world in new ways is the primordially given germ of childlike wonder, the Edenic longing to know, to taste the fruits of the Tree of Knowledge. The Luciferic promise, "Ye shall become as Gods, knowing good and evil," is a main theme of New Age thinking, and rather a problematic one at that (as noted in E2 on the question of the Theogenic Idea). In any case, no matter how this promise is interpreted, it does expose us to the awesome challenge of exploring human potential to its far limits, if it has any limits. The truth is, we have no final idea, and no reliable way of measuring, the extent of human potential or its hypothetical extrapolation, divine potential. We can only wonder about it.

But wondering, while it definitely involves us in a kind of disorientation, a state of tentative unknowing, still keeps us open to more and more looking. To wonder is to behold in wonder, even if we do not quite know what we are beholding. In his tremendous study *The Act of Creation*, Arthur Koestler notes that the Greek word *theoria* originally described a state of awesome wondering before the revelation of supernatural or divine forces. To theorize, then, is to work into our wonder, to advance by thinking and questioning into the realm of something unknown, which lures and captivates us more deeply the closer we approach. If all theory were just this and no more—that is, careful and systematic asking—then it would never shut down in righteous conclusions or pat solutions.

As children, we are given wonder naturally, but as adults we need a discipline to keep it alive. To get by on our looks, we have to keep the looking open.

In the process of doing so, we often do not initially know what we are looking for or where to look for it. Truly independent, open-ended seeking always starts in the unknown, in a condition of doubt and uncertainty. In fact, it is being uncertain that keeps us open to explore new dimensions of experience. If we ever think we know it all or have all the answers, if we fall into the delusion of possessing final and absolute certainty about anything whatsoever, we automatically shut ourselves off from progressive learning and growth. The child in a state of wonder wants to know everything, longs to search and discover, with no sense of limits to the process. This glorious condition of openness was regarded by many of the Romantics, such as English poet and nature mystic William Wordsworth, as the primary condition of soul-innocence required for the discovery of our innate divinity.

The testament of worldwide spiritual teachings offers us two prime examples, one Eastern, one Western, of seekers who kept their wonder open and came through it to spiritual awakening: Prince Siddhartha and the "holy fool," Parzival.

Siddhartha grew up as a pampered prince, locked away in a palace where he knew nothing of the harsh realities of the world. One day, venturing beyond the palace gates, he saw the alarming sights of poverty and death—and he began to wonder. . . .

Parzival, likewise, passed his early years in seclusion. His mother, Herzelaide ("Heartache"), had suffered the loss of her husband in the exploits of knighthood, and she sought to protect her gentle, awkward son from a similar fate. But when some knights in full armor suddenly appeared in the secluded wood where they lived, Parzival mistook them at first for angels, so dazzling were the reflections from their armor; then he realized they were ordinary men and he set off with them to become a knight himself.

After some years of traveling and jousting, Parzival happened upon a strange castle in a tangled forest in the midst of a wasting land and, without knowing quite what he was seeing, he beheld the spectacle of the Holy Grail, displayed in a glorious candlelight procession in the main hall of the castle. Overwhelmed and bewildered by the magical radiance of the relic, he began to wonder. . . .

Eventually, the holy fool is led to the supreme attainment of the Grail—that is, the spiritual responsibility of serving humanity through his unique and original sense of purpose. This occurs by a process of self-discovery that unfolds, spontaneously and haphazardly, in the context of life itself. Yet all of this is not sheer accident and blind groping. All through his adventures, Parzival is given clues for his pathfinding. He is not guided by anyone, but his interactions with others have the effect of assisting him to become self-guiding. As the pure fool, he is someone in whom the innocent power of childlike wonder still lives and eventually becomes transformed into the highest spiritual gift, the capacity to ask the question.

The question he finally asks, the Grail Question, is: "Humanity, what ails thee—and how can I serve to alleviate thy suffering?"

The adventure of Siddhartha, who eventually becomes Gautama Buddha, runs a different course. Appalled by the suffering and fatality of the human condition, the young prince resolves to undergo each and every discipline of spiritual training until he finds the one that will lead him to full release, the total liberation of Nirvana. He wonders how human suffering can be transcended, and he tries every method available. But in the end he gives up all the methods. His was the supreme test case, because he had to master the methods of meditation and yogic self-control before he could give them up: You can't sacrifice what you haven't experienced!

Up to the last moment, Siddhartha does not see the paradox in his approach to gaining Enlightenment. Then, sitting under the Bodhi tree, he realizes that to transcend human suffering he must also transcend all the methods he mastered in the attempt to transcend it. He achieves full, unexcelled Enlightenment at the moment he realizes there is nothing for him to attain—this is called the principle of nonattainment. So, when asked what he gained through achieving Enlightenment, he is able to answer, "Absolutely nothing."

This answer is, of course, troubling and unsatisfactory—though it does make us wonder. . . . What the Buddha meant was that he came to realize Suchness, the primordial and unalterable presence of the "self-nature," which was there from the start and was not in any way affected by his practices and efforts. As one Zen master put it, our true nature is never lost to us in moments of delusion and distraction, nor is it gained at the long-sought moment of awakening. This is radical Zen teaching.

In returning to direct awareness of the self-nature, the Buddha-nature, Siddhartha also returned to the state of original wonder. His path took a different course from the one Parzival traversed. Siddhartha restored himself to pure wonder, pure and direct beholding of the divine nature of all things, by letting everything that stood in the way of it be cleared away. His was the path of ultimate undoing.

Parzival's quest, on the other hand, culminated in his entering the path of service. This is purely a Western ideal, contrasting to the Eastern goal of total liberation from all human conditions and obligations. As I have noted in Essay 2 and elsewhere, these are contrasting paradigms that, now for the first time, present themselves simultaneously to the modern seeker who faces options for self-realization derived from the entire legacy of worldwide spiritual wisdom. It is the unique challenge of the seeker in our time to reconcile and harmonize these paradigms in a self-evolved life-path of his or her own choosing.

As both examples show, the discipline of pathfinding is paradoxical, consisting as it does of spontaneity and design (Parzival), and of mastering practices and letting them go (Siddhartha). If someone enters into the spiritual practice of the Cabala, we may refer to that person as being on a path. Hopefully, it is a path suitable to the fruitful unfoldment of that individual's innermost potential. But the results to be gained by following a path—Sufi or Southern Baptist—depend to a great degree on keeping wonder open by cultivating the paradoxes of seeking illustrated in the lives of these two great exemplars.

Before you know anything about, say, shamanism, you may often ponder it and express your curiosity: "I wonder about shamanism. . . ." But how often do you find someone who has practiced shamanism for years and who can still wonder about it?

Cultivating paradox is one way to keep the wonder open. Asking progressive questions is another. Applying the four-way proposition, described in the Preamble, is yet another. And, finally, sorting things into organic categories is one of the best ways to keep the seeking mind inquisitive and open-ended. The old Chinese commentary, the *Ta Hsio,* calls this process "the completion of knowledge"—not to mean that knowledge is ever complete in the sense of knowing everything, but in the sense of having an overview of what is to be known, what is to be explored and wondered about. . . .

One disturbing thing I have often observed about people engaged in New Age interests is the tendency to become immersed exclusively in a single path or discipline, or, on the other hand, to pursue a trivial, dilettante interest in a number of different paths. In the first case, there is a closing-down of focus, a lack of appreciation for the larger design of meaning, and in the second, a disordered sense of the larger design without specific mastery of any aspect of it.

These, it looks to me, are the two main pitfalls of spiritual seeking in our time. Sorting things into organic categories and cultivating an awareness of the relative significance of all paths is truly a completion of knowledge that might compensate for these aberrations.

The thirty Essays in *The Seeker's Handbook* are meant for orientation in the process of pathfinding, before any particular path has been chosen. They call up the powers of wonder and foster the act of spontaneous discovery. Good seeking, which leads up to the path that can best enable us to fulfill our innermost potential, right up to the full dimension of our innate divinity, depends on good looking. And good looking is a process of surveillance, looking over the many and varied prospects with a clear, comprehensive view of what they present.

The first two Essays are longer and divided into sections. They build up the main approaches to the fundamental issues of the New Age and alternative seeking. The information presented in them calls for deep

consideration and long-term assessment. Because the issues and developments explained in them can be massive and overwhelming, some sim-
plification is provided by the breakdown of the sections. Throughout the
Handbook, they are cross-referenced by section: For instance, E1.3 refers
to section 3 of Essay 1, "Main Currents and Master Visions," where some
of the leading theorists and dominant themes of the New Age are
described.

The remaining twenty-eight Essays are short enough to be read in ten
minutes or less. In their brevity they allow for rapid scanning over the
whole field of New Age interests, while the cross-references following
them afford access to the kinds of thematic associations that come from
deep acquaintance with the subjects being surveyed. Reading the Essays
systematically, thread by thread, can stimulate the experience of long-term
comprehension at the same time that it keeps the mind open to wonder and
allows it to meander from one subject to another. The threads that connect
the Essays reveal diverse patterns of commonality and contrast within the
overall weave. For instance, Essay 8, "Christianity as an Alternative Path,"
contains six main threads leading to other paths by allusions, parallels, or
contrasts that are not immediately obvious, although they become so after
long familiarity with the matters in question. Thus Essay 8, while revealing
a special pattern of its own, resonates and contrasts with other sections of
the overall weave, so that the seeker's attention is drawn easily into a
natural flow of associations: from the varieties of alternative Christianity to
the question of channeling from the Christ (E7), to the modern revision of
the Solar Mysteries of Anthroposophy (E4), to the struggle of the Romantics to recreate Christianity in their own image (E22), and so on.

The Essays form the backbone of the *Handbook.* They are intended to
present an expansion of the main interests of the new spirituality, but in
a concise form. Through long familiarity, the realms of Eastern and
Western wisdom reveal themselves as an enormous weave of sometimes
concordant, sometimes conflicting principles. The Essays expose the patterns of the weave, and seeing the patterns makes it possible to choose
knowingly among the prospects of self-actualization afforded by each
interest or path. Beyond that, it also allows for a syncretic or multi-
disciplinary approach to numerous paths.

In spiritual matters, everything is organic. Where there is no flexibility,
there is likely to be fixation. Where the perspective is narrow, the path
often comes to a dead end.

"Things have roots and branches," for sure.

ESSAY 1

Defining the New Age

*The decisive moment in human evolution is perpetual.
That is why the revolutionary spiritual movements that
declare all former things are worthless are in the right,
for nothing has yet happened.* —FRANZ KAFKA,
*Wedding Preparations
in the Country*

1. "Paradise in the Making." The archetype of a perfect world.
   Social idealism in the Renaissance and the New World. The roots
   of the New Age in millenarian sects of the nineteenth century.
   Occult symbolism on the dollar bill.
2. "Socialism and Superhuman Plans." Orage and the New Age.
   The Bailey-Blavatsky scenario of Himalayan masters. The progressive vision of planetarization in Dane Rudhyar, coming
   down to the "Aquarian Conspiracy."
3. "Main Currents and Master Visions." Pathfinders and theorists
   of the New Age. Fifteen prominent themes. The outlines of a
   new agenda for humanity.
4. "Now, About That Paradigm-Shift." Thomas Kuhn and the
   structure of revolutions. Dominant paradigms in world-religion
   and the new physics. Human potential and divine potential in
   contrast.

1. PARADISE IN THE MAKING

Most great ideas run a course from archetype to cliché, and the New Age is no exception. Long before it emerged into popular jargon, it was an archetype expressive of a primary and deep-rooted belief structure—what the great mythologist Mircea Eliade called a mytheme (myth-theme). As such, it appeared under various names—the Golden Age, Eden, Utopia, Terrestrial Paradise, City of God, New Jerusalem—but it always expressed the same need for humanity to perfect itself or to recapture a long-lost state of perfection. Saint John the Divine evoked it in his vision of "a New Heaven and a New Earth" in the book of Revelation, and Plato argued for it passionately, using the lost Atlantis as a model for the perfect society. For the most part, the vision remained abstract, an intellectual sand castle or a mystical dream, impossible to achieve on earth yet essential in reminding us that we are far less than we might be.

The mytheme persisted and it gradually mutated, as mythemes tend to do. After all, the vision of a New World and a New Age, even a New Humanity, is a product of the human imagination, and it must grow and change as the human condition itself changes. "Paradise" is a universal theme in worldwide mythology, but down through the centuries there have been many different approaches to achieving it on earth. For a long time, the idea of a utopian society was considered feasible as long as its implementation was directed by superhuman beings, by the Gods or their appointed representatives, who were often viewed as demi-Gods or descendants of the Gods—like the pharaohs of ancient Egypt or the emperor of Japan to this day. The ancient pattern of theocracy, or rulership by divine priest-kings, provided the basis for an ideal society, because the leaders themselves were looked to as the perfect exemplars of the "divine plan" or "mandate of heaven" on earth.

It was only in the European Renaissance that the mytheme took on the outlines of an actual social program that could be implemented by ordinary human beings. At first, this was purely a theoretical proposal. Thomas More's *Utopia* of 1516 described the perfect social order as a humanistic, classless society where all religious creeds were tolerated. Francis Bacon's *New Atlantis* of 1629 imagined England as the perfect state of the future. Both works were political tracts that criticized the bad conditions of the times and posed secular approaches to social change, more or less independent of religious and spiritual principles.

But the utopian idealism of the Renaissance, although it affirmed that a perfect society could be created by its own members, did not go very far into the excruciating difficulties of how it could be created. Proposals and directives along practical lines only began to emerge as the mytheme underwent enormous ferment during the era of the so-called Enlightenment. Abstract and theoretical scenarios for the perfect world on earth gave way to more realistic programs of social progress. In fact, it was during the Enlightenment that the great God "Progress" was invented, the God who eventually led Western society into the Industrial Revolution and who still reigns today in the minds of many in the world.

But already, in its early formative stages, the shift toward scientific and materialistic progress was questioned by some members of society, who felt that basic spiritual values were being excluded. Something like a prefiguring of the present New Age dawned at the time of the Great Awakening in the 1730s. This movement had its initial flare-up in Europe, but it was in the New World of North America that it attained its strongest convulsions. It began with a wave of fundamentalist Christian revivalism—please note—and although it did not last long, it alerted the general populace to the need for radical religious and political reforms. Most significant of all, it persuaded many people that progress toward a perfect society could only be achieved if it was inspired by a spiritual vision of universal renewal.

At that time America was still very much the New World, a designation with large mythical connotations. It was viewed as the land of ultimate refuge and new beginnings—not only by the Pilgrims who founded Plymouth Colony, but later on by a vast migration of heretical sects, odd cults, and utopians of many different stripes. These spiritual outcasts came across the Atlantic in vast numbers from 1650 onward, setting up communities that in some cases have lasted even to this day: the Amish, the Mennonites, the Moravians, the Hutterites. Right up to the time of the Civil War, there were hundreds of such settlements in the New World, most of them in the region of New England. They went by many names— Pietists, Perfectionists, Bible Communists—but they were all seeking the same goal: to create a counterculture, as we call it today, based on the spiritual ideals of self-sufficiency and cooperation.

Many of the recurrent themes to be encountered in the New Age today were common concerns of these heretical communities—for instance, the Second Coming. As early as 1694, one sect in Pennsylvania, calling itself the Society of the Woman in the Wilderness (because they read in Revelation that the true mystical church of the future was described as a woman, the Bride of Christ), declared the imminent appearance of the Lord. So eager were the members to be alert, they set up telescopes on the roofs of their churches and keenly scanned the skies for any sign of his return.

In the remarkable cult of the Shakers, the Second Coming played an even more important role. Originating from schismatic movements in France and England, the Shakers—so called for their behavior of writhing and shaking in rapturous fits when the Spirit came upon them—established themselves in America in 1776 under the leadership of a dynamic Englishwoman named Ann Lee. The Shakers, or United Society of Believers in the Second Appearing of Christ, as they called themselves, believed that Jesus Christ would indeed return—but as a woman. And Ann Lee, so they believed, was the chosen one. This reembodiment in the female was essential to their religious views, which required a restoration of all things to harmony and balance. They held Christ to be the actual Spirit of God who had chosen to live as a man the first time, but must appear as a woman the second time around.

The Shakers were but one among many groups that can all be classed as communitarian. For them the ideal instrument of God's will on earth was the community. They hoped to achieve the perfect society by selfless adherence to strict principles of social-spiritual unanimity. Many of them were passionately convinced that a new era of history was beginning, a new age was dawning. Historically, these groups have come to be called millenarian, because they believed in the end of the current phase of historical time and the beginning of a new age of social-spiritual perfection that would last a whole millennium.

Of the dozens of such groups, while some were pragmatic and secular, others were fanatically religious. Among the Shakers, for instance, celibacy was strictly enforced because sexual union between man and woman was viewed as the sin that had resulted in the Fall—a (or perhaps *the*) dominant paradigm of the West. Brotherly love and communal labor were encouraged, with men and women treated as equals, but there was no sexual mating and so the cult depended on new recruits for its survival.

Other groups, however, were based on radical pragmatism supported by the idealistic philosophy of Free Thought, rather than the principles of old-time religion. These were dedicated to communitarian self-help and libertarian morals. The most famous of these groups was Brook Farm, established in 1841 near Boston. It was inspired by the ideals of Transcendentalism in combination with the radical programs of Charles Fourier, an early French theorist of socialism. Another famous utopian community, Oneida, was founded in 1847 by people who believed that their entire community, rather than a single individual, was destined to serve as the instrument for the reembodiment of Christ. Oneida became scandalously well-known for its espousal of free love in the form of "complex marriage," a serious violation of conventional monogamy. Its leader, John Humphrey Noyes, proposed that all men and women should be able to enjoy each other in the pleasures of "amative love," dependent solely upon the practice of the man retaining semen so that the act did not result in propagation. (This age-old practice, common to Tantric and Taoist sexual rites in India and China, was otherwise completely unknown in the West at that time.) Needless to say, the Perfectionists at Oneida were accused of holding wild orgies, and their spiritual claim to a communal embodiment of Christ was condemned, along with their social-sexual views.

Looking back at the events of those times and reading some of the literature, it is impossible not to get the impression of encountering something very familiar. This is the sixties, no question about it—but it's the 1860s! Both the language and behavior of the radical sectarians brings to mind that famous decade of revolution, the era of the hippies, Provos, and Diggers. One of the first native communitarians, for instance, was Shadrach Ireland, a wild-eyed visionary called "The Man" by his followers, while he himself referred to his unwed significant other, Abigail, as his soul mate. Shadrach perished, it is said, in a rash yogic attempt to demonstrate that he could raise himself from the dead in three days.

While the practice of amative love at Oneida was a radical exception, most of the utopian communities did share the common aim of abolishing the nuclear family. Children from the system of complex marriage were raised by the community as a whole, and whether sex was encouraged or discouraged, all of the groups hoped to achieve harmony between the sexes, so that the evils of jealousy and possession had no place to take root. It all sounds so familiar, quaint, and pathetically futile.

Through the nineteenth century, the wave of sectarian reform advanced simultaneously on two fronts. All the groups were in agreement that pragmatic programs were necessary to change human society, on the one hand, but religious and spiritual principles were necessary to change human nature, on the other. Now here is cause to pause and ponder! Can human nature actually be changed? The belief that it can happened to be a leading proposition in the moral ideology of the Romantic movement, which peaked between 1775 and 1825, though its repercussions went on for decades. English poet and philosopher Samuel Taylor Coleridge dreamed of going to America after the Revolution with a soul mate of his choice and a group of eleven other couples, making up the archetypal set of twelve as the seed-nucleus for "an experiment in human perfection." His dream never materialized, but it was taken up in spirit by thousands of other refugees like those who founded Brook Farm, Oneida, the Ephrata Community, the Amana Society, and dozens more.

Today these utopian experiments are forgotten, and they seem rather trivial by comparison to the large-scale issues of our times—terrorism, world famine, environmental crisis. Yet these communitarian and millenarian sects were the first frail shoots of the modern spiritual movement now unfolding on a global scale. The New Age as it appears today has its immediate roots in the utopian socialist movements of the nineteenth century. Over against the young God Progress, who demands to be worshipped in endless feats of scientific and economic "improvement," the radical sectarians of the eighteenth and nineteenth centuries proposed the wispy alternative of a free society based on organic unity and spiritual dedication. History is different today—and the differences call for some careful assessment, as we shall see—but the essential conflict is the same. The New Age is the progeny of social-spiritual cultism, still trying to assert its cooperative philosophy against the controlling, power-mongering attitude of the Establishment.

Surely the most sensational evidence of the New Age impulse in American history is to be found right under our noses in the symbology of the one-dollar bill. As Joseph Campbell explains in *The Power of Myth,* the Great Seal and other images on the dollar disclose many clues to the idealistic thinking of the Founding Fathers. He interprets the eye in the triangle as a symbol of reason, arguing that ours was the first nation in the world established on total faith in reason as a pure instrument of God's will. He also relates the bald eagle to the Greek God Zeus, and points out other touches of Hebraic and Pythagorean symbolism in the design of the dollar.

By a more esoteric interpretation, expounded by Manley Palmer Hall and other esotericists of this century, the symbolism of the dollar bill was wholly devised by Masonic and Rosicrucian initiates who worked behind the scenes to formulate the American republic. Benjamin Franklin, it is said, was contacted and recruited by the Rosicrucians upon his visit to England in 1757, and by some accounts the Comte de Saint Germain was himself present at the signing of the Declaration of Independence.

There is a strong tradition in the esoteric folklore of the twentieth century that asserts the guiding hand of certain masters and high initiates in the conception and organization of the United States. This may be pure fantasy, but it belongs to the type of conspiratorial thinking that so often appears in the circles of the new spirituality, and as such it is a force to be reckoned with.

As for the dollar, it is certainly a mine of esoteric symbolism. Originally designed by William Barton in 1782, the bill contains on its back face a set of curious symbolic devices clearly identifiable as Masonic or Rosicrucian emblems. The number thirteen is prominent, no doubt in reference to the thirteen original colonies, though it also signifies (esoterically) the emergence of a new seed-nucleus for the future out of the archetypal perfection of the twelve: Twelve plus one equals a new phase, a replication of the twelve at a higher stage of evolution. The eagle who holds thirteen arrows and a branch with thirteen leaves was a phoenix in Barton's original design. This alchemical bird, which is periodically reborn from the ashes, was an emblem of renewal, common in ancient symbolism from China to Greece. Above the bird is a rosette containing thirteen stars in the shape of the Seal of Solomon (or Star of David, as it is more commonly known), and triangles composing the star each form a Pythagorean *tetrakys,* the supreme model in Greek esoterics of the four-plane, ten-point world-system taught in the Mysteries. On the left-hand side of the bill is a pyramid of thirteen levels with a capstone in the form of a radiant eye in a triangle, symbol of the overseeing power of the divine self (or master consciousness) in the ancient Egyptian/Masonic Schools. In the banner below it are the Latin words *Novus Ordo Seclorum:* "The new order of the ages."

So whatever its fluctuating value as legal tender, the American one-dollar bill is a clear-cut emblematic declaration of a New Age.

2. SOCIALISM AND
SUPERHUMAN PLANS

Though inspired by religious and millenarian principles, most of the utopian groups of the nineteenth century were actually experiments in proto-socialism, eventually superseded by the socialist movement, formally established in 1912. This progression can be seen in the use of the term "New Age" itself. It first appears as the title of a journal distributed by the social utopians of Ham Common in England. This was in 1843, at the peak of the millenarian religious revival in America. In that early usage, the term was still rooted in the social-spiritual idealism of the small and scattered sectarian groups, so it remained quite limited in scope. But by the time it first appears in the twentieth century, both its premises and the scope of its applications have changed enormously.

There are three significant appearances of "New Age" in the twentieth century, before it passes over into a common idiom to be used both by those who declare themselves part of the movement and those who know practically nothing about it.

The first time, it shows up as the name of a literary and political journal whose editor was a remarkable man, one of the most fascinating and least-known pioneers of the New Age.

In 1906 a periodical called *The New Age* appeared in London. It was established by a free-lance journalist, A. R. Orage (1873–1934), who received some of his financial backing from a world-famous liberal of the time, George Bernard Shaw. Orage was an energetic man of great personal and intellectual charm, who proved to be an important catalyst in the cultural, political, and literary events of his day. His patron, Shaw, was a prominent member of the Fabian Society, a nonpolitical group dedicated to educating the public in progressive socialism. It was highly influential in the formation of the Labour party in England. Orage directed *The New Age* in part as a platform for the liberal views on social and economic matters espoused by the Society, and in part as an outlet for experimental writing.

An amusing and racy talker, capable of fielding all kinds of intellectual propositions with wit and clarity, Orage not only worked exhaustively for the ideals of cooperative socialism, but he also championed the cause of many new and unrecognized poets and novelists who later came to be known as key figures in the Modernist movement. He supported the vanguard of new writers of the day, such as Ezra Pound and Katherine Mansfield, with whom he maintained close personal relations. Considered a genius in his time, Orage is known to this day for his exceptional wisdom as a talent spotter and literary critic.

In addition to his intense commitment to political and literary matters, Orage also took a deep interest in the occult and spiritual teachings that were being absorbed by the literati of Europe and America at the time. Before the First World War, there was a massive influx of occultism and Eastern religious teachings into Europe. Through the influence of the Symbolist movement, the Theosophical Society, and Spiritualism, a great many strange ideas were being entertained—reincarnation, higher bodies, masters, Yoga, and astrology. Orage read Madame Blavatsky and C. G. Jung diligently, and within his circle of immediate friends, past lives were chatted about in a but-of-course way, no doubt laced with witty historical and literary allusions.

From 1914 onward, Orage became deeply involved in the teachings of the enigmatic Western master G. I. Gurdjieff, who was making a sensation with his dance troupe and his proposals for a regime of radical spiritual training to free people from their sleeplike unconsciousness. In 1922, Orage joined the master for a while at his School for the Harmonious Development of Man at Fontainebleau, outside Paris. Then for seven years he toured the United States and lectured to raise funds for the movement Gurdjieff had founded. Many of his friends and fellow workers were shocked when Orage left *The New Age* at the height of his powers to become a humble and hardworking devotee of the baffling Gurdjieff. Orage himself confessed he could offer no adequate explanation except that he had to go off and "find God."

When Orage named his periodical *The New Age,* he had in mind the social utopians of the Ham Common, whose principles he hoped to continue and expand through British guild socialism, but by the time he left the journal he was living out the impulse of the New Age in quite a different way. His decision to follow Gurdjieff set the standard for a good many seekers who came after him, trying to find God by taking up the ideas and practices of different masters.

In the second specific instance, the use of the term New Age comes a little later—actually in the very year Orage died, 1934. At that time an Englishwoman named Alice A. Bailey began transcribing a series of messages in the form of letters that she was receiving telepathically from someone called The Tibetan.

Bailey, as it turned out, was to become the direct successor to the outrageous Madame Helena Petrovna Blavatsky, who had founded the Theosophical Society with Colonel Henry Steele Olcott in 1875. In her massive, sensational best-sellers on the "Wisdom Religion," *Isis Unveiled* and *The Secret Doctrine,* Blavatsky first introduced the scenario of a hidden order of superevolved men, advanced souls selflessly dedicated to the service and guidance of humanity—the mahatmas, or Himalayan masters. These masters, she claimed, were the "elder brothers of the race," men qualified by their high degree of moral and spiritual evolution to be the sole guardians and transmitters of an enormous body of ancient wisdom, the mother lode from which all known religious and spiritual teachings have been derived. After preserving the "Secret Doctrine" for centuries, they were now ready to come forth and establish direct working contact with humanity, even to the point of reaching the masses, which had never before been done in the long history of their organization, the White Lodge (later to become known as the Great White Brotherhood). Upon contacting her, they told Madame Blavatsky that they had been searching for over a century before choosing her as their main emissary to the modern world. Alice A. Bailey, who encountered her master while walking in the Hollywood Hills, appears to have been the next one chosen to continue their message and extend the groundwork laid by the eccentric Russian seer.

In the course of more than thirty years, Bailey produced a vast amount of channeled material, as we are now in the habit of calling it. She describes in great detail the organization of a secret group, a planetary hierarchy of benevolent masters who are directing human evolution from superhuman heights of vision and compassion. The letters she received from 1934 to 1949 were eventually collected and published in 1957 under the title *The Externalization of the Hierarchy.* In the first letter, the Tibetan master Dhal Khool ("D. K.") refers to the transition from Pisces to Aquarius and the coming of a New Age when all of humanity's problems will be solved, through the collaboration between the masters and those who recognize them and elect to work as their faithful agents in world evolution.

Now, this is a long way, a huge jump, from the modest aims of nineteenth-century communitarians like the Shakers and the Oneidans, and a long way as well beyond the national-scale socialism of Orage, but the same principle is in effect. This immense scenario—the master plan to be implemented through the organization of the Great White Brotherhood in its contemporary form—has been largely ignored today, much as Brook Farm and Oneida have been forgotten. Most people active in New Age circles are quite unfamiliar with the Bailey-Blavatsky scenario, and the planetary hierarchy of guiding masters does not figure prominently in their efforts and designs, though it does resurface occasionally. Yet it was through this expansion of social-religious utopianism into the planetary scale that the New Age outgrew its previous limits and assumed its global dimensions.

The third significant instance of the term New Age shows up in 1975 as a direct, deliberate follow-through of the Bailey-Blavatsky scenario. Blavatsky herself had claimed that in the seventy-fifth year of each century the masters introduce new efforts for the implementation of their plan. In conscious response to this cue, Dane Rudhyar published in 1975 a book entitled *Occult Preparations for a New Age.* Here he gives indications of a new civilization on earth, whose emergence is to be carefully orchestrated by Avatars like the masters of the "Trans-Himalayan Occult Brotherhood" announced by Bailey and Blavatsky. Rudhyar explains how this emergence will occur in the timing of the transition between the Piscean and Aquarian ages, which began with the spread of the Industrial Revolution at the same time as the rise of the communitarian and millenarian groups; and he cites five hundred years as the expectable period for this enormous transition to be completed.

Today Dane Rudhyar is best remembered as the brilliant mind who succeeded in converting the archaic idiom of astrology into a consistent psychological language for modern use, but he was not only that. He was also a Renaissance man of enormous vision. Writer, philosopher, painter, musician, esotericist, Rudhyar was a practical visionary dedicated to the higher education humanity needs in order to become responsible for evolving its true potential, especially its culture-creative abilities. He was primarily concerned with the New Age as a time in which humanity might become fully responsible for its own destiny. In *Birth Patterns for a New Humanity* and *The Planetarization of Consciousness,* he elaborated at length on the New Age themes of paradigm-shift and global transformation, with emphasis on the individual work of self-initiation as essential to large-scale changes. As a whole, his work presents a solid theoretical framework for full-scale global transformation and cocreation.

With Rudhyar, the mytheme of the New Age undergoes yet another mutation, bringing it to its current phase. The vision of local and communitarian renewal is fully extended into the global scale and it becomes conspiratorial rather than merely sectarian. From here it is only another

jump to Marilyn Ferguson's *The Aquarian Conspiracy,* which appeared in
1981.

Throughout this entire development there is a clear three-phase progression: First, the post-Renaissance program of an ideal society created
by ordinary human beings who embrace extraordinary principles, leading
to the utopian socialism of the nineteenth century.

Second, the amplification of this into the grand scheme of superhuman
adepts and spiritual masters who are guiding the transformation of human
society according to a master plan to be implemented on the planetary
scale.

And third, the recentering of the planetary program in local and individual efforts, dependent upon self-initiation and a vast collaborative or
conspiratorial effort in networking—"Think Globally, Act Locally," as
the bumper sticker says—with the question of a master plan of divine or
superhuman guidance left undecided.

3. MAIN CURRENTS AND MASTER VISIONS

Since the early 1980s, the New Age has been emerging into the mainstream of social life in the United States, and all these background developments may now appear remote and irrelevant in the face of the rapid
and tremendous exposure it is receiving. Yet this exposure, produced to
a large extent by the national media, can be deceiving if it conceals the
vital question: What are the main impulses of the New Age and how are
they actually being accomplished?

Most of these impulses derive their current profile from the work of
ardent pathfinders like Orage, and progressive theoreticians like Rudhyar. Other significant thinkers who set the pace for the changes now
unfolding in modern spiritual life are Sri Aurobindo with his vision of a
divine community on earth, culminating in the creation of Auroville in
southern India; Teilhard de Chardin, the French archaeologist and visionary, with his conversion of the dominant Western paradigm from *Fall* to
flow (E2.4), and his concept of planetization as the result of humanity
growing together into a conscient organic entity with the omega-point of
Christ as its cellular nucleus; Buckminster Fuller with his innovative
solutions to architectural and environmental problems, his invention of

the geodesic dome, his theory of synergetics, and his futuristic concept of planetary resource management aboard Spaceship Earth; Oliver Reiser with his proposal of cosmic humanism formulated in an eight-dimensional model of planetary dynamics, including human beings as cells involved in the "embryogenesis" of a gigantic global organism; and Nicholas Roerich, the little-known Russian mystic and Luminist painter, with his Pax Cultura based on the idea that culture is sacred and requires humanity to enter the stage of achieving its divine potential by creating a new culture out of its own initiatives, global in extent and compassionate in its expression of humankind's common spiritual ideals.

The work of these and other visionaries looking toward life on the planetary scale remained largely an esoteric concern until the spiritual renaissance of the 1960s. Then, with the psychedelic revolution, the popularization of Yoga and astrology, and the influx of Eastern masters, the New Age entered its present generation. Today the ground-breaking work of a dozen or so forerunners is being implemented and advanced by thousands of networking agents who define the many fronts of New Age activism. The books cited in C&B4, "From the Sixties Onward," contain some of the leading signals of this global conspiracy. Current developments are rapid and far-reaching, and the tide of change being inspired by the serious proponents of modern spirituality (rather than those who merely indulge in its trendy, superficial aspects) is more and more evident by the decade. From the 1840s to today and onward, the utopian impulse inherent in human nature continues to build into a socioreligious front of immense implications. Although its viable cultural outgrowth is still difficult to assess, the New Age is certainly assuming its own distinct character as what I call an infraculture, rather than a counterculture. Within this phenomenon there are a number of consistent themes and issues that appear again and again in many variations:

ancient wisdom—the restoration of sacred technologies, revival of the Mysteries (as in the later work of Jean Houston, a key figure in the human potential movement), interest in lost civilizations and mythico-religious systems of knowledge (Mayan hieroglyphs, astrology, Chinese geomancy, Native American folklore and ritual), shamanism, and the revival of "archaic techniques of ecstasy" (Eliade);

Gaia—the return to an awareness of the earth as a living being, even a sacred being; including the fascination with sacred sites and the effort to establish a spiritual philosophy for ecological concerns. Closely

linked to the Goddess revival and the rediscovery of the feminine;
indwelling—the shift away from the traditional Western religious orientation of transcendence, which places God outside human nature
and beyond the limits of human consciousness, in favor of seeking the
"God within" or "becoming God" (Theogenic Idea) rather than set-
tling for a mere relationship to God as a supreme but inaccessible
being, like an absent parent; the quest for direct contact with and
instruction by divinity, sometimes posed in terms of "contacting your
higher self";

masters—either those who may be guardians of a divine plan, which
they impart to a conspiratorial elite of followers, or those believed to
have attained a special state of God-consciousness, who can simply
stand as radiant beacons on the way of others seeking Oneness, superconsciousness, union with God;

planetarization—the unification of humanity in all realms of society and
all walks of life according to a central principle of integration and
higher purpose (Christ, the Omega-state, Second Coming), the
"global village" of McLuhan and the "Aquarian Conspiracy" of Marilyn Ferguson, implemented by an avant-garde of visionaries dedicated
to world service, the "seed men" in the new culture-creative agenda
of Dane Rudhyar, the "cocreators of the quantum leap" in the inspirational strategies of Barbara Marx Hubbard;

channeling—the access to information not normally available, which is
believed to come from discarnate human beings or from superhuman
entities and star-guides inhabiting other regions of the universe. Regardless of what one thinks of the information it provides, the phenomenon itself highlights the conflicting paradigms of guidance and intervention (E2.4);

holistics and healing—involving a new worldview that calls for an interdependent and cooperative outlook in everything from medicine to
mysticism, sharing pain and sharing ecstasy. Includes the rallying cries
of "healing the planet" and "healing the inner child," to which millions have responded by pursuing radical changes in their personal
lives and finding different ways to view the world at large. Places
emphasis on our common responsibility for world hunger and the
environmental crisis, proposing all kinds of new approaches to healing
and nutrition; revolutionary methods of exploring the mind/body
connection; full acknowledgment of the power of attitude in shaping
events; and the adoption of reprogramming techniques such as self-

hypnosis, neurolinguistic modeling, and subliminal command of mental and physical habit formation;

East/West studies—interdisciplinary work such as the melding of science and mysticism in the new physics, or the application of Oriental methods of meditation to Western problems of stress and dysfunctionality;

martial arts—what might be called the mystique of the warrior, a way of life that has become immensely popular in film and fictional writing; paralleled by a revival of the Western tradition of the Grail Quest and the Arthurian Stream, with its damsels in distress and knights battling supernatural monsters. This revival encompasses everything from ta'i chi to esoteric pathworking by imaginal stimulation of Kundalini, thence to "the Force" in *Star Wars,* to Dungeons and Dragons beneath the streets of Chicago;

paranormal events and psychic powers—including everything from spoonbending to telepathic contact with extraterrestrial beings, this being the one aspect of the New Age singled out for sensationalist exposure by national media, with the effect of trivializing the deeper issues and distorting the whole picture, since it comprises a mere sliver of the spectrum of serious interests and practices;

reincarnation—access to the deep self and the memory of former lives, hopefully with the result of releasing blocked potential and living more fully and fruitfully in the present, though equally liable to enmesh the seeker in the distraction of make-believe scenarios and romantic hype-dreams that afford escape from the real prospects of living in the here and now;

Earth changes—including the sensational prospects of tectonic plate upheaval, pole-shift, famine, and plague; a fulfillment of the mytheme of the Apocalypse, often explained as a kind of planetary catharsis by which the earth rids itself of cancerous and degenerating growths. In its saner aspect, includes the environmental movement and the new science of ecology, based on the hope of becoming cocreative with Gaia (the living Earth);

service and group effort—often said to be a special feature of the Aquarian worldview, demonstrated in increasing numbers by people who forgo pregiven social roles and the exclusive drive for economic gain in favor of a mission to assist humanity. Usually enacted by taking part in a vast network of collaborating agents (Alice Bailey's "New Group of World Servers"), becoming a "planetary citizen," or joining the "critical

mass" who are attempting to realize a common vision of social change
by contributing what each one has learned and gained on his or her
chosen path of self-realization.

Whew! This staggering array of prospects represents the raw makings of
a totally new agenda for humanity—and this is not all. Finally, we have
to consider what is perhaps the most pervasive and powerful theme in the
New Age agenda:

> *cocreation*—the ultimate secret of the ancient Mysteries and alchemy,
> initially thrown open to independent seeking in the West through the
> translation of the Hermetica (E2.2). Here is the bottom line of human
> potential, which the Romantics seem to have stumbled upon more or
> less by accident. Their grandiose claims asserting the God-like creative
> potential of each and every individual, wild and woolly as they were
> at the time, are now commonplace in the New Age and appear in many
> and various expressions, such as "You create your own reality," and
> "The world is a hologram generated by the mind."

Cocreativity, as usually interpreted, means that we are responsible for
creating the world we inhabit. In the new physics, this is explained
through the hypothesis of the reality-structuring powers of the human
mind, or brain. In ecology, it extends to the responsibility for taking care
of Earth. In New Age metaphysics and medicine, it is widely applied as
the basic principle of self-actualization and self-healing—though the question of how we are actually responsible for the illnesses we contract is a
difficult one. In the widest sense, it shows up in every variation of New
Age philosophy where the element of *attitude* (see the Lexicon) is taken
as decisive, not just in the perceiving but in the actual shaping of the
events of our lives. This is, fundamentally and practically, what the clichés
of "consciousness-raising" and "awareness" are all about.

The theory of cocreation is also implied in the above themes of planetarization (often imagined as a conspiratorial coworking with the masters)
and group effort or world service (in the Live Aid concert of 1985, for
instance). These activities emphasize the outer-directed, organizational
aspects of cocreation, evident in more and more widely promoted and
publicly recognized efforts to produce a global, cooperative society.

At the basis of these outer-directed activities there is a fundamental
understanding that cocreation is an outgrowth of "self-work." This is the

task of evolving the innate potentials of human nature and, perhaps, even going beyond humanhood toward the experience of "human divinity." According to some prominent teachers of cocreation, such as Jean Houston and Barbara Marx Hubbard, *love* is the power that connects the finite personal self with the "God within." It is this inner link—called in the old Yoga psychology of India the *antahkarana,* "inward-arching bridge"— that must be cultivated for an individual to become empowered as a cocreator, capable of carrying out specific tasks in the outer world. This is a great responsibility and a glorious privilege, to say the least.

As above, so below. As without, so within. Since we ourselves are inwardly and innately potential Gods, we must be capable of cocreating the world outside and around us—or at least capable of carrying on the creation of the world, since it seems to have already come a long way without our assistance. This is a task of divine service, presumably possible if we can learn how to make reality after our own image, just as we ourselves were created in the image of our divine Maker.

Easier said than done.

4. NOW, ABOUT THAT PARADIGM-SHIFT

To many, all the above themes and trends may seem barely plausible, an enormous hocus-pocus of wild speculations that leave the vital issues of everyday life lost in magical dust. To a good many others, these prospects are all feasible, and they are merely waiting for serious volunteers to take them up. The agenda is written; it only remains to be implemented.

But are the vast possibilities of social and individual change proposed in the agenda of the New Age really capable of producing vast changes in the way people live, all around the world and in the not-too-distant future? The answer to this question is not a simple yes or no. It depends largely on your viewpoint, and especially on how you see, and support, the great paradigm-shift. For the New Age, this is the ultimate roll of the dice, and the cosmic ivories have yet to hit the table. While they're still rolling, let's consider the odds for a moment.

Early in the 1960s, a historian named Thomas Kuhn published a book entitled *The Structure of Scientific Revolutions,* in which he proposed two startling ideas: first, that the great advances in science come from the sidelines, resulting from the work of eccentrics or outsiders who do not belong to the Establishment; and second, that these advances in scientific knowledge do not occur in a regular way, through consistent research along well-established lines, but rather in sudden, spectacular shifts.

Both of these ideas are rooted in Kuhn's fundamental notion of the *paradigm,* a word from the Greek *paradigma,* meaning "pattern, structure." A paradigm is a framework-of-thinking that determines an entire worldview. For instance, the paradigm of geocentric motion in ancient astronomy: At one time it was believed that all the planets, the Sun, and the stars revolved around Earth, as the Moon actually does. This paradigm was overthrown by the theory of heliocentric motion worked out by Copernicus around 1530. This paradigm was in turn superseded by Einstein's theory of relativistic motion, proposed in the Special Theory of 1905.

Presently, we are still going through a great paradigm-shift in the sciences, the outcome of which will have an enormous effect upon all aspects of our lives. It can be characterized in a number of ways, as shifts from:

> observation to participation;
> atomistics to holistics;
> mechanical to organic;
> mastery over nature to harmony with nature

It is the deepest hope of many people in the New Age to contribute to the successful completion of these shifts.

Although Kuhn was primarily concerned with these and other paradigm-shifts in the realm of science, his ideas were rapidly taken up by progressive thinkers of the 1960s and eventually applied in a general sense to other areas of culture and personal experience. For many people today, exposure to one or more of the leading themes of the New Age (as outlined in the previous section of this essay) has resulted in a sudden and revolutionary paradigm-shift, a total change in their belief systems and their ways of viewing the world. As Kuhn emphasizes, the paradigm-shift is not something that is figured out or worked out; rather, it just tends to happen. Suddenly, life is seen and lived in an entirely different way.

Paradigms are the tectonic plates of our human-made reality structure.

They are massive belief constructions that support our activities, and each one has enormous and far-reaching implications. For instance, take the Darwinian paradigm of evolution, on the one hand, and the biblical paradigm of creation. Between these two lies not merely a difference of ideas, but entire continents! Each of them supports different ways of living embodied by millions of people. Those who live on the Darwinian plate have a different worldview and a different culture from those who live on the biblical plate.

A shift of these tectonic plates, massive as they are, is often revealed by the smallest variation in a person's outlook or behavior. Back in the 1960s, when daddy's darling returned home one day wearing beads and bells, there had been a tectonic jolt, though perhaps no one in the household could detect its origin or put a name to it. For many years, the paradigm-shift to Eastern wisdom might be subtly indicated by the scent of *ajarbhattis,* Indian incense. Today it might show up in the detail of a crystal hung from the rearview mirror in a Saab or BMW.

There is nothing at all trivial about these examples. Anyone who has ever witnessed the great paradigm-shift in a personal instance knows how brown rice, a miniature pyramid, or a subliminal tape can announce the advent of a different world. When the geological tectonic plates shift, huge masses of the population are displaced and their reality is disrupted, even reduced to a shambles. With the paradigm plates, it is a different kind of phenomenon, more akin to a ripple effect, which reveals itself through one person at a time. In a perfectly normal, happy household of two parents and three children, Danny may come home one day with a magic pentagram on his neck chain. He is now fascinated with magic and within a few months he may be reading Aleister Crowley. The tectonic structure of reality has shifted, massively, but only one member of the population has been directly affected.

One of the most convincing aspects of the New Age is the tremendous power of the paradigm-shift in individual cases like this. Here is true "conversion," as described in the pathfinding research of William James (C&B3.2). Although this term is more often confined to the realm of fundamentalism, it is equally applicable to the experiences that bring people into the New Age. And just as fundamentalists hope for a domino effect, through which their belief system will spread by wild contagion to the entire human race, New Agers believe in a geometric amplification of the great paradigm-shift. This is variously described as a "quantum leap," the activation of "critical mass"—both terms borrowed from modern physics—or, more recently, by analogy to the phenomenon of the "hundredth monkey" in ethology.

Which brings us back to the question of odds. By its mere numbers, the New Age is not an impressive movement, though it continues to attract more and more attention from the mainstream due to high media exposure since the beginning of the 1980s. So far, its agenda of extraordinary hopes is being seriously implemented by a small network of people in the English-speaking countries. These are the planetary agents and executives in Marilyn Ferguson's "Aquarian Conspiracy," those who personify and promote the transformative power of the autonomous individual in an (ideally) decentralized society. According to the prevailing view among the new visionaries, this avant-garde of spiritual pioneers, as it grows in resolution and gains more technological resources, will forge out a new course for humanity, and the masses will respond in greater and greater numbers to their direction. Those who have experienced a paradigm-shift of their own are already forming into a core-group who will not only set the direction and pace for the rest of humanity, but will serve as the critical mass for sudden and large-scale changes in social and cultural behavior.

Such is the theory, at least. But the odds of the New Age manifesting in our midst in the next ten or twenty years, as many of its adherents claim, do not depend solely on the catalytic power of its critical mass. There is another factor of crucial importance, which has not been sufficiently considered. This is the issue of conflicting paradigms.

One of the marks of the present age, which makes it different from any preceding time in history and forces upon us the responsibility to develop a *discipline* of pathfinding (as I have noted in the Preamble), is our exposure to many contrasting paradigms at once. In the past, for centuries, whole populations of people remained confined to a single tectonic plate, a single, all-encompassing belief system. Today, one individual may be exposed to dozens of different paradigms. From Kuhn's study of scientific revolutions, we have derived the general idea of a paradigm-shift, which can be widely applied to the personal and planetary changes now in progress. But in the current age we are faced not merely with the option of shifting from one paradigm to another, but with the far more difficult task of reconciling paradigms.

I discuss the problem of how to reconcile conflicting paradigms in Essay 2, but to round off this attempt to define the New Age, let's take the paramount example of two conflicting paradigms that, in sum and essence, reveal the deep schism between the new spirituality and the old. This concerns the way we conceive the relationship between the human and the divine.

In the fountainhead of Western spirituality, the Hermetica, we find the following assertion:

> Willing then that humankind should be at once creatures of nature and capable of immortality, God compacted the human of these two elements, the one divine, the other mortal; and being as it is thus compacted, it accords with God's purpose that the human is not only better than all mortal beings, but also better than the gods, who are made wholly of immortal elements. [My adaptation from the Latin, based on the Scott translation, Shambhala edition.]

Here is yet another expression of the Theogenic Idea, the core principle of the Mysteries. It proposes that within human nature is potential divinity, which is capable of being infinitely evolved, so that the human can ultimately become deified, elevated to the level of a God—or, according to this outrageous passage in the Hermetica, a level even superior to the Gods!

Compare this with a statement for the human potential movement, written at Esalen by George Leonard and Michael Murphy in 1966: "If the divine is present in an individual soul it must be sought and found in man's institutions as well. For people will not readily achieve individual salvation without a saving society."

What Murphy and Leonard are proposing here is a social program for evolving the divine potential of the individual. This is, in essence, the most precise and concise definition of the New Age one could imagine. This proposal lies in direct continuity with the progression we have traced, showing how the mytheme of paradise worked its way down to the heretical sects of the nineteenth century. But now we are considering not merely how a group of people might implement for themselves the actualization of a divine plan on Earth, but how a whole society might be created to acknowledge and support the unfoldment of the divine potential within each of its members.

Terrific idea. But this notion of divine potential is very problematic. In the modern philosophy of self-actualization, it is seen as inseparable from human potential. The ultimate aim of the new spirituality is to develop the one through the other—somehow!—and so achieve human divinity.

Also, the paradigm of *theogeny*—evolving ourselves into Gods—stands in radical contrast to the fundamentalist paradigm of *religion*—which is simply "binding back" to that from which we have originated. It is the difference between evolving to become an equal to God (or the Gods), and merely remaining as we are, limited to the human state, but having a relationship to God. In fundamentalism—and there are both Eastern and Western forms of it—there is no allowance for a divine potential in us, available for infinite development. We are merely creatures in relation to our Creator, and the relationship is all that matters. Needless to say, the New Age paradigm of theogeny is likely to be viewed as sheer heresy and even dangerous, arrogant blasphemy by fundamentalist standards.

But even among dedicated agents of the new spirituality, this question of human/divine potential is unclear and fraught with confusion. As the clichés go, "We are all Gods" or "We are all one with God" and "We create our own reality." This philosophy can readily assume the form of self-serving narcissism, for which the New Age is frequently criticized. It can also lead to all manner of delusions and pretensions. If we are indeed becoming Gods—for I think it's safe to say we're not at the full stage of self-divinization yet—then it might be wise to resort to a turn of phrase I've often used and call ourselves "Gods in diapers."

Until the way we define and achieve our humanity is reconciled with the way we imagine and evolve our divinity, both the premise and the outcome of New Age aspirations are better left in process, subject to perpetual reevaluation and revision. In the meantime, Kafka's astute observation (page 50) probably holds true for the new spirituality, which is as yet greater in the scope of its expectations than its achievements. And the quest to achieve a perfect world on earth, while it must and will go on, can wisely be qualified by the comment of the ancient historian Sallust (around 50 B.C.), who observed of the Greek myths: "None of the events described ever happened, but they are always happening."

ESSAY 2

Traditional Religions and the New Alternative Paths

The new Religion. Yes, there will be a new church founded on moral science, at first cold & naked, a babe in the manger again, a Copernican theory, the algebra & mathematics of Ethical law, the church of men to come without shawms or psaltery or sackbut, but it will have heaven & earth for its beams & rafters, all geology & physiology, botany, chemistry, astronomy for its symbol & illustration, and it will fast enough gather beauty, music, picture, poetry.

—RALPH WALDO EMERSON,
Journal, March, 1848

1. "From Authority to Discovery." What, if anything, makes spiritual seeking different in our time? Impressive statistics and critical mass. Reconciling human potential with divine potential.
2. "How the Radio Came to the Beach." Historical roots of the New Age. The retrieval of the Hermetica, making the Theogenic Idea accessible to independent seeking. Hit tunes of 1471.
3. "The Great Transmission." Initial discoveries of Eastern wisdom and its dissemination in the West. The Occult Revival in Europe and the spiritual renaissance in America.
4. "Teaching an Old God New Tricks." Facing the options and alternatives of modern seeking. Conflicting paradigms and their reconciliation. Beyond alternatives to innovations. A critique of cocreation.

69

1. FROM AUTHORITY TO DISCOVERY

If there is really nothing new under the sun, as King Solomon claimed, then any talk about a new religion, or even alternative paths of spirituality, has to be approached with some sober, cautionary questions. What's so new about the New Age, anyway? What's so important about retrieving and reinstating lost traditions of ancient wisdom? What's so different about the religious seeking of humanity today that it can be set apart from the perennial quest for God stretching back fifty centuries before it? Can there actually be any such thing as change, or—wild idea!—even progress, in humanity's perpetual striving to know itself, to fathom the ultimate nature of reality, to contact and communicate with the divine, and to comprehend the relation between human and divine?

If there is not just a difference between the two, but an actual advantage of the new alternative paths over the old traditions, it has certainly not yet come to the attention of the masses. Looking at the global picture, it is fully obvious that humanity is still satisfied with the age-old belief systems that seem to provide all the answers, making it unnecessary and perhaps even foolish to look elsewhere. Consider for a moment the statistics on the "old-time religions":

Roman Catholics	900 million
Muslims	840 million
Hindus	650 million
Protestants	328 million
Other Christians	395 million
Buddhists	308 million
Jews (Orthodox)	18 million
Sikhs	16 million
Shamanists	13 million
Confucians	6 million
Baha'i	4.6 million
Jains	3.4 million

It looks like these time-tried blockbusters are not doing too poorly after all. It may be a few more years before they are at risk of being overthrown by the new spirituality. The belief systems they embody still hold enormous appeal for the human mind and emotions. Their paradigms are still adequate to the spiritual needs and questions of the vast majority of the human race. So states the testimony of numbers, anyway.

To date, there are no reliable statistics on involvement in the alternative paths of spirituality, nor are there likely to be any for a while. Due to the chaotic and marginal nature of the modern spiritual movement, it is impossible to tell if its numbers have yet risen even to the level of a "dead" religion, like Jainism, or to the level of the most recent addition to the family of world-scale religions, Baha'i, established in 1893. Even though twenty-six million people are reported to have watched the 1986 TV miniseries based on Shirley MacLaine's autobiographical account of New Age conversion, "Out on a Limb," a massive defection from the old-time cults has yet to occur.

But here it is not statistics that matter. As so many enthusiasts of the New Age have explained, the tremendous changes now facing humanity depend upon a spearhead of forward-looking individuals who concentrate in themselves the new potential of the total species. They make up "the benign conspiracy for a new human agenda," as Marilyn Ferguson describes it. They embody the small critical mass necessary to catalyze world-scale change. They are inspired and empowered by the conviction that something incredible is about to happen, or is already happening though not statistically evident, a paradigm-shift of which the full-scale ramifications will be vast (E1.4). Even if they comprise—for the moment—no more than an infinitesimal fraction of the total population of the planet, they are the leading agents of global change, whose power and vision are not in the least diminished by the vast numbers of followers who are not, as yet, following them—and who for the most part do not even know they exist.

The enormous confidence in world change, and perhaps even sudden, spectacular world change, exhibited by so many people of the new spiritual outlook, is often mistaken for gullibility and ridiculed as positively Pollyannaish. The viability of New Age optimism, if it is to depend upon something more than wishful thinking, has to be grounded directly in the personal experience of dramatic conversion, individual paradigm-shift, and metanoia (the act of thinking beyond whatever one has been taught to think). At best, it emerges as a vital force in the minds and lives of those catalytic individuals who have acquired the conviction that there really is a shift taking place from the old ways to something never seen before. But what kind of shift is it, exactly?

First and fundamentally, it is the shift from authority to discovery. It is the phase-over from a way of life dictated by beliefs and principles that have been inherited without question or resistance to a way of life directed by a completely new outlook, a new set of principles gained through the individual feat of free exploration. Granted, all religious experience may be, in the last analysis, structurally and even emotionally the same. It is, after all, based on two factors that are archetypal and perennial: the need to relate to God and, borne out of this relationship, the striving for ways to accept and perhaps even resolve the troubling issues and conflicts posed by the human condition. If philosophy can be defined as systematic inquiry into the meaning of life, religion is the belief system that attempts to validate the meaning of life in relation to a superhuman being, or even within the context of a superhuman scheme.

Yet if the new alternative paths are no different in their motive and striving from traditional religions, they *are* truly different in their imperative of finding the answers for oneself, instead of receiving them hand-me-down. The new paths are forged from efforts in self-discovery and experimentation rather than blind adherence to traditions consisting of prefab answers, with strict limits put on the process of questioning. Discovered rather than inherited, the alternative paths are open roadways of high risk, cutting new tracks that run far afield from the well-trodden ruts mapped out by formula religion.

Above and beyond all else, independent seeking is the primary mark of the new spirituality. But even free seeking in the spirit of Emersonian self-reliance requires some kind of framework, a consistent course to follow, so it is well worth asking what distinguishes the framework for spiritual growth provided by the alternative paths from those of the traditional religions.

Essentially, this is a difference between systems: to be exact, the difference between a system for being guided and a system for becoming self-guiding. Quite an enormous difference, when you come to think of it!

Within the traditional framework of, say, Islam, the individual is guided by the preset parameters of the belief system. These include spiritual and ethical laws and a set of behavioral standards, even a dress code. Each religion consists of a set of ruling paradigms, expressed in dogmas and principles of faith. Obedience to these pregiven standards of thought and behavior is the main requirement for participation in all the traditional paths.

With the alternative paths, principles and standards are not lacking, by any means, but they are adopted as experimental tools for self-guidance. Since they are voluntarily assumed, the act of obedience is set aside in favor of the activity of free-form experimentation. The alternative path merely provides a tentative framework for this experimentation. The typical seeker in the new spirituality is not out to obey, but to learn. To a very great extent—far greater, in fact, than has yet been realized by many people in the modern spiritual movement—the new spirituality is a commitment to self-education, and hopefully to a well-rounded education. It amounts to what we might call a form of higher education, a course of studies and training, freely and voluntarily undertaken by the individual who aspires to become self-actualized.

All this should be clear as a bell—in theory, at least. In practice, it is rather more complex and often quite confusing. The confusion arises because seekers who head off on alternative paths often end up traversing them as if they were no different from the old, pregiven, authoritarian systems.

Now, it is interesting to note that within each of the traditional religions there do exist alternative paths, which are lesser known and demand something more than mere obedience. For instance, the alternative path within Islam is Sufism, an exotic strain of mysticism that was forcibly repressed after Mohammed came to power in 622 A.D. Sufism is obscure and heretical, outside the mainstream of Islamic religious organization. It is viewed askance by Muslim fundamentalists but holds great attraction for Westerners. And there are other similar alternatives within each of the traditional religions.

In Judaism, there is the Cabala, a complex system of moral and metaphysical principles, closely associated with the dubious arts of ceremonial magic; also, the eccentric wisdom of the Jewish mystics and heretical splinter groups such as the Hasidim.

In Christianity, there are Gnostic, esoteric, and even erotic variants of the Christ myth, as well as Christian Science and what may be called para-Christianity. The Quakers, Shakers, the Amish, or Dutch Mennonites, and a good many others of the heretical utopians of the nineteenth century were splinter groups within the Christian fold.

In Buddhism, there are Tibetan Buddhism and Zen, which are neither understood nor cultivated by the 300 million orthodox Buddhists of the world.

Of course, every variant of mainstream religious activity tends to develop into an orthodoxy of its own. Tibetan Buddhism, for instance, is a hierarchical program consisting of rigid principles of succession and astonishingly complex formulas of thought, and Japanese Zen is also rigorously formulaic; yet both these paths remain alternatives within the wider field of conventional Buddhism. Zen principles and practices as known to Western converts would be viewed as crazy stuff, indeed, by a simple Buddhist monk from Burma or Thailand.

To a great extent, it is these alternatives within the traditional Eastern religions that have attracted so many Western seekers since the 1960s. Sufi, Zen, Subud, Taoism, Tibetan Buddhism, erratic and ecstatic devotional sects of Hinduism that are viewed as somewhat wacko by Hindus themselves—these have acquired large and loyal followings in the West. Thinking this over a bit, it gives one pause to wonder what is really meant by "alternative paths." Is there really something in the nature of the path that makes it alternative, or is it merely a matter of how the path is pursued once it has been entered? Here, I find, is a point of serious confusion, which cannot be avoided unless we distinguish carefully between the two meanings of the word *alternative*.

In its primary or obvious meaning, *alternative* simply denotes the optional over against the obligatory. It refers to something assumed in a free and voluntary way, as explained above, rather than taken on by inheritance or under the enforcements of external society and long-standing tradition. In this sense, to switch from Baptist to Buddhist is an alternative for someone whose sociocultural background demands that he become a Baptist. And the reverse is equally true: Switching from Buddhist to Baptist is also a valid alternative for someone culturally obligated to become a Buddhist. Yet we do not normally think of the Southern Baptist persuasion as an alternative path.

The secondary meaning is more subtle and crucial, for it concerns the way a path can be dealt with, above and beyond the mere option it presents. In this sense, any path can be alternative for those seekers who explore it on their own terms, independent of what is expected of them by the orthodox adherents of the path. More exactly, a path becomes alternative when it is turned to the specific purpose and/or needs of the seeker who enters it, rather than being adopted as a pre-fixed agenda. It turns out, however, that seekers who do this are rather rare. There is a great deal of alternative seeking in the new spirituality that amounts to nothing more than a shift of blind obedience from one pregiven framework to another.

One sees this over and over again in cases where independent seeking does not remain independent for long. A young woman from Iowa, for example, may reject Bible Belt dogmas and indoctrination into the inherited principles of Baptism, with all the demands and obligations of outlook and behavior, even the dress code, that come with it. For a few years or perhaps only months, she looks around, doing a little independent seeking. If she lacks a discipline for pathfinding, her seeking will be somewhat haphazard. Then, before you know it, she comes upon a path—say it's Sufism—and this seems to be what she's looking for (as the saying goes). So, she gives up Sunday churchgoing for long rounds of Sufi dancing, and she may become as identified with the principles and practices of her newfound belief system as she would have been with the original one her parents and peers tried to force upon her.

So where's the "alternative" in this?

This is but one of dozens of examples that could be cited, because this is the norm rather than the exception in modern seeking. Similar cases are evident everywhere in the life stories of people who undergo paradigm-shift or sudden conversion into the New Age. What they reveal is (to me, at least) a troubling pattern of becoming involved in alternative paths *as if* they were inherited ones. The young lawyer from Long Island who goes over heavily into the Gurdjieff work after casting off the shackles of the Protestant paradigm may find himself committed to an orthodoxy at least as strict and nonallowing of independence as the one he has so arduously rejected. And so on, through hundreds of variations.

So if independent seeking is the primary criterion for the new spirituality, it does not necessarily remain in effect once the commitment to an alternative path has been made. We must acknowledge that although modern seeking begins with the impulse toward self-discovery and self-guidance, more often than not it does not remain open-ended. Typically, seeking leads to finding, and finding leads to the same kind of identification that occurs with strict adherence to the traditional, pregiven structures and strictures of the old-time religions.

This is a strange affair, but one wonders if it could really be otherwise. If seeking is not meant to lead to finding, then what's the point? After all, it lies in human nature to become identified with what one believes, does it not?

So, what *is* the fundamental difference—if any—between believing in what we are told to believe, and believing in what we choose to believe after discovering it for ourselves?

Here is a question—a terrific question, I would say—that is best left unanswered, because it may be just this question, and others generated from it, that needs to be kept alive and evolving, if we are finally to understand what free seeking along alternative paths really entails. We must "live the question," as the poet Rilke demanded, and by doing so stay open to developing paths that can be kept open.

In the meantime, there is a good working definition of *alternative,* in the second sense, to help us along the way: It denotes any path that provides a provisional framework for the seeker to become self-guiding. And I've discovered that seekers who adopt this definition can and will, *if* the pathfinding is kept open-ended, surpass the given limitations of their chosen paths. In other words, you can take the path of Sufism (or any other) to places no one else ever took it. We do not enter paths merely to conform, but to explore and surpass, to revise and redefine the paths themselves. Those who can show this kind of outgrowth are the true progressive seekers of our time, as they have been in all previous times as well.

2. HOW THE RADIO
CAME TO THE BEACH

So progressive seeking is an open-ended process in which the seeker changes the path he or she enters. And this is not all, because in our time the very act of finding a path to enter can itself be viewed as a crucial feat of spiritual development.

Through the many years it has taken me to find my way around the labyrinth and learn how to assist the pathfinding of others, I have repeatedly come back to one clear and striking observation: The steps leading up to the option of entering a certain path are just as significant as the steps taken upon that path, after one has entered it.

There is a close analogy here between the life of the seeker and the life of the artist. We all know that enormous interest and effort go into researching the biographies of artists to find out how the events of their personal lives contributed to their work. If we are really interested in an artist such as Hermann Hesse or Georgia O'Keeffe, for instance, we are eager to know about the relation between that person's life and his or her work. The same should apply for alternative paths, for it is living that leads to seeking, as life leads to art. What someone has learned, say, from twenty years of work with the Cabala is not more significant than the course of life-events that brought that person to the Cabala in the first place. I call this the principle of Free Approach.

Bearing this point in mind, it is very interesting to look into the life-events that led humanity in the West into the new spirituality. As I stated in the Preamble, our situation today is really exceptional, really different from any time in the past, due to the availability of so many options for the independent seeker to explore. For this, we need a discipline of pathfinding, a way of sorting out and evaluating the options. At the outset of this enormous task, it's only natural to ask where and when the first option arose. How did this new and daring impulse toward self-actualization, this exploratory drive, this heady, high-risk attraction to the sometimes lonely, often uncertain road of self-reliant seeking, actually originate? What got us started on this winding quest within the labyrinth?

Well, as explained in Essay 1, the sociological impetus for what is now called the New Age did not appear overnight in the 1960s. It had its immediate origins in definite group efforts of the preceding century, the communal striving of the utopian socialist sects that fled to the New World to create a paradise on earth through the voluntary efforts of their members. Though these movements died out for the most part, the seed-impulses inspiring them lived on. This explains the historical roots of the modern spiritual movement, but to detect the exact origins of the new paradigm of self-reliant seeking, we have to look back to an extraordinary event that occurred in European intellectual life more than five hundred years ago.

Given the rapid shrinking of the world in our time, it is not hard to imagine a remote Pacific island where native kids, using their ancestral skills to catch dinner in a lagoon, cope with their nonancestral boredom by listening to the latest rock hits blare from a boombox perched on a nearby ledge. For centuries the fishing had been done in silence, attended only by the sighing of the wind and surf, or perhaps accompanied by chants and songs—but there had to be one day, a single, decisive day, when the first radio was brought to the beach.

This analogy is, I think, both facile and inescapable. One of the recurrent (and often tragic) demands of modern life is to accept the startling rapidity and irreversibility of changes like this. They are widely evident all around us in society and nature, all too obvious and numerous to cite.

It takes centuries to produce a rain forest, but only a few years to destroy it. In many cases it takes no more than a single day for things in our lives to become quite different from what they were for centuries in the past.

For the modern spiritual movement now unfolding around us, there was a single day like this, a unique historical moment when the first radio was brought to the beach. It did not look like a radio, of course. It appeared as a bundle of musty manuscripts, later to become known under the collective name of the Hermetica. To this day, it is not known where these arcane writings originated, though they may have been copies of copies of copies of masterworks of ancient wisdom once filed away in stacks of the famous Alexandrian Library, destroyed by fire in 415 A.D. For the most part, they seem to date from the second or third century A.D. In any case, they were collected around 1450 by the Byzantine scholar Georgius Gemistus, known as Plethon. His name is practically unknown to the modern seeker, though he ought to be remembered with gratitude as the man who *sent* the radio to Western shores.

Although he lived and worked in Byzantium (present-day Istanbul), Plethon was in close contact with the Italian court of Cosimo de' Medici, a brilliant Renaissance prince and generous patron of the arts. In fact, it was Plethon who inspired Cosimo to found the Florentine Academy, one of the most active and influential centers for learning in Europe at the time. In the city made famous by Michelangelo and Leonardo, a thriving community of intellectuals and artists gathered at the Academy to discuss philosophy, theology, music, romantic love, and all manner of esoteric issues.

Around 1460, Cosimo de' Medici set his best scholar, Marsilio Ficino, to the task of translating the works of Plato from Greek into Latin, to make them accessible to the intellectual elite of the time. Cosimo was a humanist who supported the personal quest for truth, independent of the Church though not necessarily in conflict with it, and he wanted to see the great ideas of the Greek philosopher freely and openly discussed by the well-bred lords and ladies of his court. Then an emissary sent by Plethon brought a collection of thirteen rare manuscripts to Florence and placed them in Ficino's hands. Since he is only described as "a monk from Macedonia," without a name, the man who actually *brought* the radio to the beach must remain forever anonymous.

After looking the manuscripts over and discussing their content, Ficino and his patron were stunned by what they now possessed. These writings, they realized, were hand-me-down versions of the sacred teachings of

Hermes Trismegistus, or "Thrice-Greatest Hermes." They must have originated in the Mystery Schools of Egypt, among the Priesthood of Thoth, the Egyptian God of medicine, writing, astronomy, and the sacred arts. If this was so, it meant they belonged to an ancient tradition of spiritual wisdom that predated Plato and all the other classical Greek philosophers, as well as Moses and all the accepted biblical authorities. As Ficino put it in his commentary, "In that time in which Moses was born flourished Atlas the Astrologer, brother of Prometheus the physicist and maternal uncle of the elder Mercury whose nephew was Mercurius Trismegistus." Here we see the human powers of mythmaking at work, resulting in an ancient lineage that is all the more credible for being so deeply and passionately imagined.

Hermes—the Greek name for the Egyptian God Thoth, equivalent to the Roman Mercury—was already known to Ficino and his patron through a few references in classical writings, which spoke of him as a God-like hierophant belonging to a lineage of remote antiquity and enormous spiritual stature. But having nothing but second- and third-hand clues to go on, they had been unable to learn anything concrete about the "Hermetic wisdom" he represented. Now, in a single day, they had their hands on the source material itself.

Cosimo was ailing at the time he received the Hermetic manuscripts from Byzantium. Since he was convinced they contained never-before-available teachings derived from the fountainhead of Western spirituality, the Hermetic Mystery Schools of Egypt, he insisted that Ficino set aside his translations of Plato and get to work on the Hermetica. In this single command, he affected the course of spiritual development in the West to a profound degree. He introduced an option to the usual course of classical learning undertaken by all educated people who cared to acquire spiritual maturity, conceived as moral and intellectual culture in those days. The established curriculum of his time was based exclusively and inflexibly on the works of Plato and the Greek masters, on the one hand, and on the age-old authority of the Bible on the other. In choosing the Hermetica over both Plato and Moses, Cosimo opened the way to independent seeking—which only becomes possible when options are made available.

Ficino completed the translation in 1463, less than a year before Cosimo died, and the rare texts of the Hermetica were printed in Latin in 1471, twenty-one years before the discovery of America by Columbus. They were immensely popular in their time, Ficino's translation alone

going through dozens of reprints. To the eager spiritual seekers of the
Renaissance, the Hermetica was a tremendous find. It provided access to
a lost tradition, a hidden body of ancient wisdom consisting of principles
and guidelines for spiritual development stated in a way not to be found
in the volumes of conventional philosophy and religion. Ficino's translation was an act of retrieval with immense ramifications.

Later the Hermetica went through a whole series of translations into
other European languages, but it was not until 1924 that it was finally
rendered into English by Sir Walter Scott.

The Hermetica is the supreme fountainhead of Western spirituality,
the mother lode of all later esoteric and metaphysical systems, but reading it today, more than five hundred years after the radio came to the
beach, is not likely to produce any thrills for the modern seeker. These
rare treatises on ancient cosmology and sacred psychology are forbid-
dingly dense and dull, fraught with dry abstractions and woolly im-
ponderables. One has to read with intense care for any of the path-
breaking ideas to come through, fresh and startling, with the force of
their original revelation.

Given what's available today in your average metaphysical bookstore,
it's no surprise that the Hermetica are practically ignored. Yet reading
these old texts *can* be exciting, given the right expectations and a skill for
good looking. At the very least, they can still offer a heady experience
in tracking paradigms (Preface, C&B). For instance, take just one document, known as *Asclepius III.* A close reading of this text (about forty-five
pages) will absorb you in a breathtaking repertoire of themes: a Supreme
Being ruling the manifest world; the impossibility of the existence of a
Void; the intellectual light flowing in the souls of the Gods; the two kinds
of Gods (thought-detectable and sense-perceptible); the incorporeal nature of the thought-world; the atmosphere as the actual medium where
the Gods work; the universal hierarchy (an unbroken chain from highest
to lowest); the omniscience of God; the astonishing assertion that matter
is actually invisible (though it becomes visible in discrete forms and
shapes); the existence of universal types informing the array of individual
appearances; the presence of change in the cosmos and changelessness in
eternity; the assertion that God is bisexual; the assurance that the procrea-
tive power endowed in all creatures is a joyful and glad effect of God's
love and may even be viewed as a sacrament by which the diverse essences of the sexes are infused into each other; an explanation for the
presence of evil or demonic elements in human nature; a crucial descrip-

tion of the human being as a hybrid of divine and human elements (considered below); human-made Gods (idols) and their potencies; the periodical necessity for a world-purge (flood theme); the periodic regeneration of the world; an assertion that God is identical with good purpose and that all of creation is likewise good; the twofold working of the cosmos (reflecting, in different parts, the dynamics of time and of eternity); the cyclical nature of time (numerically limited) and the fixity of eternity; the identity of the "divine mind" with eternity; the source of all error in human perception (due to the discernment of events at intervals of time, rather than in the unbroken continuity of timelessness); the difference between mind and thought; the divine gift of reason; the invention of and intercourse with animal Gods as practiced by the ancient Egyptians; a brief comparison of destiny, necessity, and order; a few comments on the after-death trials of the soul; rounded off with a plea for piety and the love of God—after which the participants in the dialogue go out for a nice vegetarian dinner *(ad puram et sine animalibus).*

Not too bad for some musty old parchments that were probably still smelling of trail dust and mule sweat when they were placed in Ficino's hands. Unfortunately, it would be possible to read the Hermetica at length, plowing through any number of passages like this, and not really get to the point that makes these writings so crucial to modern, independent seeking. Returning to our main analogy, we might say that the radio played a lot of old tunes, unlikely to get us snapping our fingers today, but it did also broadcast at least two huge hits. These memorable tunes were the *Theogenic Idea* and cocreation.

The first one occurs in *Asclepius III,* in a passage cited above, concerning the contrast between human potential and divine potential. The text states that "God compacted the human of these two elements, the one divine, the other mortal." In short, the human is not merely or exclusively human, but a hybrid of human and divine elements. And the Hermetica goes on to assert the outrageous notion that "being as it is thus compacted, it accords with God's purpose that the human is not only better than all mortal beings, but also better than the Gods, who are made wholly of immortal elements."

Now, this proposal that amalgamated with human nature is potential divinity, or Godseed, as Jean Houston calls it, is the fundamental assumption of the Theogenic Idea. Its implication is clear to anyone who can carry the tune: We are capable of evolving from humans into Gods, even going the Gods one better. Through a second birth (palingenesis), we

can attain transhumanization or deification (theotetis). A pretty sensational idea here. When this idea appeared in the Renaissance, it became
accessible as a goal for independent seeking, whereas previously it had
only been possible within the strict framework of the Mysteries.

As I've already noted (E1.4), this idea of divine potential is extremely
problematic. The ancient masters must have known this, for they kept it
and (even more so) the means of fulfilling it under tight wraps. But since
the translation of the Hermetica, it has become an open game. Going
along with it is the second hit tune of 1471—the flip side, you might
say—which proposes what those who achieve deification are obliged to
do with their time, which is limitless, and talents, which are superhuman:
namely, engage in cocreation.

This theme is stated in various ways throughout the Hermetica, but
especially in one clue in the twelfth book, written in the form of a
dialogue between Hermes and his son, Tat:

> Mind, my son Tat, is of the very substance of God, if indeed
> there is a substance of God; and of what nature that substance
> is, God alone precisely knows. Mind then is not separate from
> the substantiality of God, but it is, so to speak, spread abroad
> from that source, as the light of the sun is spread abroad. In
> men, this mind is productive of God's workings. Hence some
> men are divine, and the humanity of such men is near to deity;
> for the Agathos Daimon said, "Gods are immortal men, and
> men are mortal gods." [My adaptation from the Greek, based
> on the Scott translation, Shambhala edition.]

As unstartling as it may now seem, this is truly a momentous disclosure.
Complementing the proposition that we can evolve into Gods, it asserts
that we are capable of taking up the workings of God. The European
intellectuals who first read the Hermetica were not only inspired by these
two options, but they found in those texts a treasure trove of metaphysical
notions concerning how to achieve them. This came as an electrifying
breakthrough, even though the deification achieved through initiation
was not itself entirely unknown to them. From classical times, almost
anyone in the know was aware that immortalization was attained in the
Mysteries. Back as far as 400 B.C., Aristotle had expressed the gist of the
Theogenic Idea in his *Nicomachean Ethics*: "We must not follow those who
advise us mortals to think of mortal things, but we must, as far as we can,

make ourselves immortal." High advice, here, though he did not go into how to achieve it.

Now, it is one thing to admit the possibility, in exceptional cases, for a human being to be transformed into a living God, a divinity on earth who is capable of carrying out the ongoing work of creation, but quite another to present the initiatory privilege of deification as if it were accessible to free and independent seeking and to expound on how to achieve it. Yet this is exactly what the Hermetica did for those who read and studied it in depth—and it is precisely what a good many New Age teachings, derived from diverse sources and expressed in a multitude of ways, are doing for thousands of people today, long after the hit tunes first released in the Hermetica have been forgotten.

3. THE GREAT TRANSMISSION

When the Hermetica surfaced, the New World had not yet been discovered, and it was still a long time before other developments began to unfold that would lead to another feat of retrieving ancient wisdom. While the Hermetica was circulating among the intellectuals of Europe, the spiritual teachings of the East were completely unknown, and they were to remain so for almost three hundred years. Then, around 1750, an obscure French scholar, A. H. Anquetil-duPerron, arrived in India, where he was to spend about five years. When he returned to Europe, he brought with him another kind of radio: a collection of fifty discourses called the Upanishads, and parts of the Zend-Avesta, the sacred writings of Persia, which he had translated into French. Once again, practically overnight, another option to Western Christianity and classical philosophy became accessible. At first it was available only to scholars, but quite rapidly was discovered by the leading intellectuals, artists, and writers of the time, who in turn made it known to the public at large.

In Europe it was the time of the Enlightenment, the era when Reason was glorified as the rule and solution of all human affairs, and the young God Progress was conceived. During this period, the old European traditions of metaphysics and esoteric wisdom derived from antiquity were being broadly and consistently debunked. Ironically, just as they were being put aside for modern rationalism and Cartesian logic, a fresh infusion of ancient teachings began seeping in from the East.

Around the same time that Anquetil-duPerron was foraging the ancient wisdom of India, Sir William Jones, who founded the Royal Asiatic Society in 1784, proposed a common ancestry of the Greek and Sanskrit languages. Jones was the first person to draw parallels between Hindu and Greek Gods, dropping clues for what was later to develop into comparative mythology. His researches initiated an enormous chain of developments that led through a succession of now-forgotten scholars right up to the enormously popular mythologist Joseph Campbell.

Another major phase in the great transmission of Eastern wisdom to the West occurred in 1822 when Champollion, a young French polymath, translated the Rosetta stone. This was a small slab of basalt found in the Nile delta, inscribed with a text in three different scripts: Greek, Coptic, and Egyptian hieroglyphs. Until then, nothing at all was known of the nature and meaning of the obscure, extremely elegant picture writing of the ancient Egyptians. Working on the assumptions that all three scripts presented translations of one another, Champollion came up with a brilliant though approximate translation of the hieroglyphs. Suddenly, it was as if an immense doorway cracked open, and a dazzling beam of light from ancient times came flooding into the present. The restoration of Egyptian religion and mythology was an immense contribution to the free spiritual life of the West.

In the same year as Champollion's decipherment, the German philologist Wilhelm Grimm established "consonantal shift" according to a set of linguistic laws that enabled scholars to make comparative studies of Oriental and Western religions. For instance, it become possible to correlate the Greek Zeus to the Indo-European *deiwos,* from the root-verb *dei-,* "to shine, radiate," the basis of our English word *deity.* Now Jones's hypothesis of Greek/Sanskrit parallels could be fully confirmed, and extended to dozens of other languages as well. This was another enormous and relatively rapid leap toward what we now call East/West studies, a major facet of the new spirituality.

Meanwhile, another Frenchman, M. E. de Polier, serving in the British military in India, had discovered a set of ancient texts called Vedas and sent them on to Europe, where they passed into the hands of another German scholar, Max Müller. From 1875 until his death in 1900, Müller supervised the translation and editing of *The Sacred Books of the East,* which eventually ran to fifty-one volumes. The entire set can still be found in the more well-stocked metaphysical bookstores, though there is little in these awkward, plodding translations, most of them positively awful, that can serve the needs of contemporary seekers. Nevertheless, the *Sacred*

Books remain with us like a massive wall of ruins, useful to buttress more recent constructions.

At the very same time the Eastern classics were being imported to the West and initially translated, an intrepid young explorer named John Lloyd Stephens was penetrating the steamy jungles of Central America, where he came upon magnificent ruins. Through the 1840s, as the utopian cults were sweeping into North America (E1.1), Stephens unearthed the lost culture of the ancient Maya, which he described in rich detail in his *Incidents of Travel in Central America, Chiapas and Yucatán,* a best-seller of its time. While European scholars were busy unlocking the secrets of the Egyptian hieroglyphics, a whole new set of hieroglyphic symbols came to light, most of which have not been deciphered to this day. With Stephens's discoveries the esoteric lore of Mysteries in the far West became accessible in all its spectacular and enticing complexity, although it is still a long way from being comprehensible.

Throughout the mid-1800s, a dense synchronicity of historical developments crucial to modern spiritual life continued to unfold. In New England Transcendentalism rode the same tide as the utopian movements and flourished as a bright signal of philosophical wisdom, from about 1836 to 1860. Its key figure was Ralph Waldo Emerson (C&B2.10), who promoted the perennial philosophy of radical immanence and made a passionate case for the virtues of independent seeking. Over against the Puritan paradigm of religion, he expressed the Theogenic Idea clearly in a number of places in his essays. His friend Henry David Thoreau was one of the first people on the American continent to possess an English translation of the Upanishads.

Transcendentalism was fiercely antimaterialistic. It is interesting to note the same reaction in Europe during the time that scientific materialism was being codified in such theories as Darwinian evolution and the new field of thermodynamics. Intellectuals and artists of the era responded with an enormous wave of interest in occultism and metaphysics. Much of it was initially stimulated by work in hypnosis and mediumship pioneered by Baron von Reichenbach and Friedrich Anton Mesmer in the late 1700s. Elaborate reports of events in the spiritual world, made by Emanuel Swedenborg, the eccentric Swedish visionary, were tremendously influential in drawing attention to supersensible realms, and later proved to be seminal to the doctrines of the Symbolist movement. Spiritualism, séances, table-knocking, and communication with the beyond were all the rage in Victorian circles.

All these factors converged quite rapidly into the European Occult

Revival, which is generally viewed as being focused on a single figure, a defrocked Catholic priest who called himself Eliphas Levi and posed as a latter-day magus, a mastermind of transcendental magic (the title of his best-known work). Levi drew attention and often fanatical admiration from the social elite of his time, and his influence upon some of the best minds of his generation is still puzzling, since most of his output was turgid and incredible. His fame and influence were exceeded only by an even more outrageous figure, Helena Petrovna Blavatsky, who founded the Theosophical Society in 1875 and introduced humanity at large to the occult Brotherhood of the Himalayan masters (E2.2).

One of the most fascinating ways to investigate the Occult Revival in Europe is to explore the art and literature it inspired, which included some of the greatest works of the premodern era. Around 1875, the Symbolist movement constellated in a set of artistic enclaves in England, France, Germany, Holland, and Belgium. This was the period often referred to as the Decadence, when the leading intellectuals, artists, and writers proposed the superiority of the inner life over the realm of conventional affairs and taste. The Decadence represents the final throes of Romanticism in its radical reaction to bourgeois materialism. Its main thrust was initially defined by the German Romantic poet Novalis, whose theory of magic idealism probably contains the earliest germ of the New Age dictum that you can create your own reality. Infatuated with the mysteriousness of life, positing the reality of dreams and imagination over the secure conventions of mundane existence, Novalis and others of his persuasion cultivated mythomania to a fine art. On the dark side, the experimentations by the main artists and writers of the Decadence led to dangerous quests into the occult, the unconscious, and the underworld of drugs. In America, the leading representative of this trend was Edgar Allan Poe. Today the dangers of naive mythmaking and New Age make-believe must be carefully evaluated next to the record of those exotic and often aberrant seekers.

As Blavatsky was reaching her peak of fame in both Europe and America, the first World Congress of Religions was held in Chicago in 1897. One of the young Zen monks who attended the conference was D. T. Suzuki, later to become the first Zen master widely known in the West, as well as a major contributor to East/West studies. Another participant was Swami Vivekananda, a disciple of the Hindu saint Ramakrishna.

It was not until after the Second World War, however, that this enormous tidal wave of events fully crashed on Western shores. Throughout the era of Modernism (centered around 1910), many artists and writers in Europe and America continued to take a deepening interest in the Eastern traditions, but there was little or no spillover of this to the masses. After World War II this changed drastically and rapidly. A great many veterans who had served in the Asian theater brought back with them an intense interest in Oriental paths, martial arts, and metaphysical systems. When the Beat generation emerged in the early 1950s, it served to introduce all these interests, especially Zen, to the public at large. Alternative paths were initially promoted under the banner of Beat nonconformity and social rebellion. Then in the 1960s the massive influx of Indian gurus began, the Hare Krishnas hit the streets at the same time as LSD did, Yoga was taken up by *Vogue* models—and the rest is (our brief and sensational) history.

From Ramakrishna to Rajneesh, it all took less than a hundred years.

4. TEACHING AN OLD GOD NEW TRICKS

Today, when we are so inundated with New Age programs and alternative paths, it is obvious how the Great Transmission has provided us with an appealing array of new options for spiritual development, while the two main propositions set out in the Hermetica, theogeny and cocreation, still remain to be worked out in clear and practicable terms. We in the West have shown ourselves far more susceptible to Eastern influences than to the challenges of our own indigenous tradition of "progressive occultism," the modern continuation of the Mysteries. One can only wonder, How come?

As noted in the previous essay, it was probably the Romantics of the European movement (centered around 1820) who first proposed that we can change human nature. In fact, the Romantics were obsessed with the Theogenic Idea, which they seem to have stumbled upon by accident, like a bunch of adventuresome kids who barged into a high Druidic rite while playing in the woods. Paraphrases of the Idea show up everywhere in their poetry and theories. For instance, Shelley writes in a letter, "Let us believe in a kind of optimism in which we are our own Gods." And cocreation is equally evident, usually expressed in terms of the Romantic doctrine of the Imagination, viewed as a God-like capacity to create your own reality. In his famous long poem, *The Prelude,* English poet William Wordsworth presents a testimony to Romantic soul-making and declares its dominant concerns:

> Of Genius, Power,
> Creation and Divinity itself
> I have been speaking, for my theme has been
> What pass'd within me . . .
> This is, in truth, heroic argument.

Like all the hard-core Romantics, Wordsworth wanted to have religious experience free of religious organization, dogmas, preset formulas, rules, and regulations. He wanted to discover Genius, unfold the power of imagination, contribute to creation, and contact divinity—all on his own terms, completely apart from any pregiven religious dogmas or organizations. Among his American counterparts in the Transcendentalist movement, Ralph Waldo Emerson was one prominent voice who spoke in the same way of ending religion in all its inherited forms and starting over from personal experience. Emerson and his peers, like the great poet Walt Whitman, had high hopes for the complete displacement of religion by Romantic spirituality, so that a newly inspired culture could arise (as suggested in the passage from Emerson cited at the beginning of this Essay). Whether or not the New Age can and will fulfill their hopes remains to be seen.

But as the statistics show, the vast majority of people living on earth at the end of the twentieth century feel otherwise. They still prefer the framework of a traditional, preestablished religion. They want their relationship to God to be supported and validated by a time-tried framework. They prefer ready-made beliefs to those that can be developed via free exploration. To a great extent they accept the necessity of intermediaries who stand between them and a higher power, however they may conceive it. They look up to religious authorities such as the pope, and whatever they may experience as their own private, subjective relationship to God, they want it to be secured and maintained within a predetermined framework of practices and principles.

In contemporary idiom, it is fashionable to speak of "spirituality" as the aim of modern seeking, by contrast to "religion," which usually connotes the orthodox Western sects, Catholicism and Protestantism. To say that the Romantics wanted to have "religious experience" independent of "religion," then, is to say that they wanted to cultivate the free spiritual life, to work out for themselves the pathways leading to theogeny and cocreation, and to envision and accomplish on their own the ultimate expression of those momentous propositions. Beyond options, they were aiming for innovations.

In their spirit, Mircea Eliade has stated his faith that "new forms, new expressions" of religious/spiritual experience will appear in our time (see Preamble). Since there is nothing "new" (historically) either about Eastern wisdom or the ideas presented in the Hermetica, we are left wondering if the radical innovations so passionately wished by the Romantics are really possible. Keeping this in mind, we can perhaps set up a guideline for modern seeking in these terms: Practical evaluation of both Eastern and Western paths calls for looking into how they can really lend themselves to innovation, to reaching ahead to new dimensions of spiritual experience and religious renewal.

But in the New Age as much as in conventional religion, it appears that tradition is far more appealing than innovation. As already noted in defining the word *alternative,* many people attracted to the new spirituality are merely trading off one pregiven set of beliefs and practices for another. The New Age, so far at least, seems to be about having options, certainly, but it does not commonly pursue them toward radical innovation.

But can there actually be any such thing as innovation in humanity's spiritual life, anyway? Is it really possible to teach an old God new tricks?

A great question, here. It brings us back directly to the issue of conflicting paradigms (E1.4). Let's say, for starters, that *alternative* means not only posing options (according to its primary sense), but also providing for innovations. In other words, alternative paths that are really worthy of the name will be syncretic and pluralistic, uniquely amalgamated from diverse sources, freely adapted to the specific needs of the individual seeker and, ultimately, applied and expressed in some form of highly personal creativity. If this is possible, it requires combining the elements of different paths into new, innovative practices and expressions. It demands encompassing and reconciling diverse paradigms.

We are looking here at paradigm-mix, above and beyond the much-acclaimed phenomenon of paradigm-shift. Take, for instance, the Eastern paradigm of *transmission,* upon which the continuity of spiritual lineage is based, by contrast to the Western paradigm of *self-initiation.* The latter is exemplified in the life story of Parzival, contrasted to the life story of Siddhartha (in the Preface to the Essays). Since the difference between these two paradigms is perfectly clear, it is easy to see how they each generate a different course of action, and how they each answer to a different set of needs. The need to find oneself is fulfilled through the Eastern paradigm, the need to find one's purpose through the Western. The first is a path-of-union, the second a path-of-service.

Clear enough, yes. But it is also pretty obvious that these paradigms can be confused and will not be, perhaps, so easily reconciled into a third and innovative set of options. Make finding yourself your purpose and you may end up living in an ashram with little to do but provide amenities for the master. Try finding your purpose by Eastern methods and you will be exasperated to learn that you have none, that you are no one special with nothing special to do!

But if you wanted to combine these paradigms, taking the best of both and going them one better toward a new expression of spiritual achievement, how would you do it?

Dozens, perhaps even hundreds of similar conundrums can be posed, drawing upon the most common paradigms from East and West. Apart from the contrast between divinity and humanity, which remains the most problematic paradigm-mix of the New Age, there is the fundamental contrast, in a few variants, between

enlightenment	and	*salvation;*
illusion	and	*sin;*
Maya	and	*Fall.*

If we wanted to put it on a bumper sticker, it would say something like, "Shall It Be Fixed or Found?"

As seen in the Theogenic Idea, Western spirituality is dominated by the doctrine of essential transformation: the gradual and progressive development of a pregiven potential or essence, the Godseed in us. Not only are we a hybrid of divine and human elements, but both are prone to be evolved, with the divine eventually absorbing the human so that full "immortalization" is achieved. But we in the human state suffer under the results of the Fall, the dominant paradigm of Christian civilization. We live in a messed-up and deviated world, not at all what the Creator intended it to be. As we evolve toward divinity, we also raise and restore ourselves from this fallen condition. In this scenario, the basic demand of the Western paradigm is to restore and redeem the human condition, to fix the world and achieve *atonement,* making up for what has been ruined or lost.

In the East, on the other hand, it is held that the *Godhead* resides in the human soul or mind and even pervades the whole world-process as an immanent and inviolable presence. It does not have to be developed— indeed, any idea of developing or evolving it is quite absurd. If it evolves at all, it evolves in cyclic repetitions, with no advance or gain. Divinity plays hide-and-seek with itself and, periodically tiring of the game, rolls over and falls into dreamless sleep for a few billion years. But asleep or frolicking in cosmic dream-play, it is full and complete, and all it requires is to be found and reclaimed. Then there is *at-one-ment,* union or reunion with the Source, which is changeless, flawless, and ever-present. To reach this union of ordinary awareness with the eternal ground, we must un- dergo a process of removal, reduction, surrender. But the state of *veiling* imposed upon us is not a *Fall,* not a deviation and a removal, for within it the Godhead is fully and dynamically present. There is nothing to be restored, redeemed, or rescued from sin and corruption, as there is with the Western paradigm. The supreme reality is not to be fixed, but merely found.

So, is the world a game of hide-and-seek with divinity lurking in *play* behind every face and appearance, or is it all toil and trouble, with humanity struggling against enormous odds to work its way out of its fallen state of sin and alienation? Is the essential spiritual question about *illusion* or about *sin?* In other words, is human nature to be wrong on occasion, or are we really capable of being bad (i.e., *evil*)? And is this "karma" we generate (the moral consequences of our choices and ac- tions) something we can merely erase, or do we have to change it?

These are but a few of the twisty questions the seeker faces in the discipline of tracking down paradigms to the point of seeing the exact language dictated by the belief systems that inform them. Tough work, but someone's gotta do it.

How can conflicting paradigms such as these be aligned and merged into a new story, including and surpassing them both? This is not going to be easy, but it could be a great innovation. It could also be the kind of challenge we really need, to come up with new forms of spiritual/ religious experience. And even if some of these contrasting paradigms cannot be reconciled, it is crucial to allow clearly for their differences. In the belief system of Christian fundamentalism, for instance, *revelation* is a paradigm that insists that the manifestation of God to humanity is over and done. It occurred with the prophets and saints who were directly inspired by God to write the Bible, the fixed and unquestionable testament to God's will and word. Over against this, the paradigm of *indwelling* in mysticism allows for a continual and ongoing revelation of God to each one of us. These two paradigms appear to be completely irreconcilable.

A good way to assess the efforts and theories entertained in the new spirituality is to ask what paradigms they contain and look at how they are being handled. In a few cases, some really innovative progress *is* being made, leading to the emergence of new visions to guide and inspire humanity. In the work of Teilhard de Chardin, for instance, the Christian paradigm of the Fall is undergoing a wonderful transformation, due to what Teilhard does with Christ. Instead of envisioning Christ as the vindictive Lord who separates saints from sinners in the awful, adversarial showdown of the Last Judgment, so popular with fundamentalists, Teilhard proposes the "Omega-state," a condition of total organic and societal unification of humankind, for which Christ serves as the magnetic center, drawing the entire race together in loving unification (E1.3).

And ever so brilliantly, he locates this unification in the future, according to the Western view of moral and spiritual growth as a time-bound evolution, directed toward specific ends and aims. He throws off the old paradigm of *hierarchy* for holism, and by describing the Omega-state as "not above, but ahead," he converts its informing dynamic from *Fall* to *flow*. In this new paradigm of flow we are all flow-bound toward the state of the ultrahuman, in which we fulfill our humanity by growing into vitalistic unity with the supreme representative of the human spirit, Christ. Going by Teilhard's vision, we would no longer say, "I'm falling in love with you," a cliché rooted in the Fall paradigm; rather, "I'm flowing with love in you." Now there's a real innovation.

Nevertheless, for Teilhard's brave inclusion of the Theogenic Idea of progressive deification in his Christocentric vision of world-evolution, he was strongly censured by the Catholic church and remains today on the fringes of theological heresy—one of those outsiders who breaks the deathgrip of the old paradigms.

Another instance of conflicting paradigms occurs in the implicit philosophy expressed in the cliché, "You create your own reality." This view is often equated with the master paradigm of *cocreation,* yet it is not quite that.

Both in the new physics and the advanced brain/mind theories often allied with it, we see an attempt to overthrow the paradigm of *evolution,* the hallmark of nineteenth-century materialism. The belief system informing this paradigm states that the universe and all it contains, including human beings, has come about by a billion-years-long process of natural development, in which consciousness plays no effective part. Countering this with elaborate theories extrapolated from relativity and quantum mechanics, proponents of the brain/mind school hope to come up with a scheme to explain how human consciousness largely creates the world it perceives, even to the extent of projecting it apparitionally as a hologram constructed by the brain. Often going back to Oriental philosophy to bolster their arguments, the new physicists are trying to prove that our own minds have vast reality-structuring capacities, some already operative and some yet to be developed, which work as powerfully as the forces of nature to construct the world we inhabit.

In all this we can see an attempt to overthrow evolution for a new paradigm that includes the reality-structuring powers of human consciousness—which might be called self-creation. The New Age cliché, "You create your own reality," while it is not always associated with the sophisticated speculations of brain/mind studies and paraphysics, is a clear-cut affirmation of self-creation, but not of cocreation, as often assumed. In the paradigm of cocreation, the key is in the *co*: It means creating with. As understood in Western alchemy, cocreation is collaboration with Nature and God. It is founded in the ability to imitate Nature first, and then go beyond it, exceeding or improving on what Nature does. It is creating with Nature, and by extension, with God (or the Gods), conceived as the Source of all natural wonders, including the human mind.

The emergent paradigm of self-creation is an all-or-nothing affair. Those developing it attempt to show how the brain or mind alone creates the world; or in New Age optimism, how your attitude alone determines what happens to you. Though these approaches are often taken for expressions of cocreation, they fail to include the *co,* the conjunctive aspect of the process. If, say, the mind does create reality but only in part, what are its operative boundaries, what is created without it, and how does it converge its reality-structuring functions with other functions working externally to it in the world at large? Nowhere in the latest theories are these questions being addressed.

Likewise, in the general attitude of cocreation shared by most people in the new spirituality, the question of *what* we are cocreating with—and how!—is rarely asked. The naive assumption of narcissistic self-creation is so appealing that the difficult questions about the exact dynamics of convergence are usually overlooked. This is perhaps the most serious flaw in the outlook of people who hope to transform the world. It would be a good idea, perhaps, to set some boundaries and separate what can be changed from what has to be accepted as is.

So instead of saying, "You create your own reality," we might convert the language of the paradigm to say, "We cocreate a shared reality."

In the final analysis, it may really be beyond human limits to push options into true innovations, opening up totally new dimensions of religious/spiritual experience, as the Romantics aspired to do in their "heroic argument." But if it really *is* possible to teach an old God new tricks, then it might be wise (as I have long suspected) to play *with (co)* God for a while before making the arrogant leap to playing God. And how do we play with God? Well, I guess we first need to become devoted to learning how God plays, then get into it and eventually introduce a few of our own original turns to the game.

What if cocreation turns out to be, after all, something like child's play on the divine level? Discovering that would certainly shift us in a new and different realm of experience. It would also require a complete reevaluation of what we call religious experience—some modest approaches to this being sketched out in the Afterword.

THE TEN-MINUTE
ESSAYS

E ach of the Ten-Minute Essays concludes with the Crossweave, showing the thematic associations that link the subject matter of the Essay
to the Classics and Basics and to some of the other Essays, as appropriate.
Please note that cross-links to C&B refer to what is to be found in the work
itself, not necessarily in the brief review of the work given in Part I.

ESSAY 3

Alchemy

Alchemy is as fascinating as it is inaccessible. Among all the treasures of ancient wisdom, it is the most difficult to retrieve, yet it holds the promise of immense possibility: discovering the way to work harmoniously with nature.

As its best critics have pointed out, the knowledge developed by modern science is aimed at exploiting and controlling nature. This has brought us some wonderful results—such as hydroelectricity, jet planes, and transistors—and some devastating side effects. Is this the inevitable price to be paid for scientific progress, or is there another way?

By contrast, alchemy was originally conceived and practiced as a holistic science of super-nature, a method that merely imitated and extended the processes already active in nature. "Let thy work be guided solely by nature" is a rule often repeated in the old texts. When the alchemists looked upon nature, they saw gradual and consistent processes of transmutation: plants propagating through the seasons, coal turning into diamond. In a spirit of complete humility, they conceived their own task as collaborative and coevolutionary, a sacred trust to be fulfilled by devout service to the ongoing process of creation. In the work of transmuting base metals, such as lead, into gold, they were simply imitating and accelerating the processes already present in nature, rather than working against them, or attempting to control them.

Although there were certainly a great many impostors and con artists among the alchemists, there is strong evidence that in some cases, at least, metallic transmutation was actually achieved. Also, it is now well verified that many of the medical and pharmaceutical formulas of the alchemists were legitimate. Another curious fact is that a good many of the discoveries that led to modern chemistry were made by alchemists. For instance, Jan Baptiste von Helmont, who is credited with full attainment of the philosophers' stone and metallic transmutation, is on record as the discoverer of carbon dioxide. This is one case among many that seems to indicate that the old masters deliberately turned over what they knew so that it could be incorporated into the laws and definitions of chemistry. This puts a new slant on the long-favored theory that dismisses alchemy as a crackpot pseudoscience that preceded chemistry.

Alchemy was pursued in great secrecy, probably to avoid the accusations of sorcery and black magic, with which it could easily be confused. Most of the surviving alchemical lore comes down to us in the form of private notebooks full of obscure scribblings and bizarre illustrations. Alchemical imagery is fantastic and fascinating: mermaids, homunculi, hermaphrodites, snake and bird creatures representing different states of the work, trees, unicorns, and all manner of odd apparati. This symbolic and emblematic language is practically impossible to decipher unless we are privy to the actual experiences that inspired the alchemists to create it.

While it is easy to locate the time when alchemy fell into decline—by 1650 it was almost entirely phased out—it is impossible to determine when and where it began. The Eastern traditions of alchemy in Chinese, Indian, and Persian cultures are very ancient, corresponding to the earliest religious practices. In Taoist Yoga, it was pursued as a discipline for achieving somatic transformation by converting the natural forces and fluids of human physiology into the "immortal foetus," and ultimately attaining physical immortality. Almost identical practices and aims were found in India, and still underlie the theories of Hindu Yoga to this day. The quest for physical immortality is a primary aspect of archaic, Oriental alchemy.

In the Western traditions of alchemy, both physical immortality and actual gold-making also figure as prominent aims, but the deeper emphasis is on spiritual immortality and creative empowerment. However, unlike the goal of physical immortality in the Far East, spiritual perfection was not for the Western adepts an end in itself. Moral perfection was sought along with life-extension so that the alchemist would be fit and able to dedicate him- or herself to the ongoing work of cocreation, taking an active role in God's divine plan—a task that might take centuries! In their view of nature, which closely resembled the teachings of the ancient Mystery Schools, the alchemists saw God's creation as incomplete and, to complicate matters even more, partially deviated from its intended purpose by counterevolutionary forces. Their "mission impossible" was to correct the aberrations and carry the divine evolutionary process through to the end that God, the Infinite Intelligence, had originally intended for it. For this, they needed all the time they could get, by contrast to their Oriental counterparts, who sought escape (via immortality) into a state of complete timelessness.

Alchemy represents the pure ideal of divine science as divine service. Besides posing a high model for physics, it provides the prototype for modern soul-making. C. G. Jung, the founder of analytic psychology, initiated the modern revival of interest in the Great Work, which he took as the paradigm of individuation. In its imaginative/metaphorical aspects, as a path of self-exploration and psychic-emotional development, alchemy is certainly the ultimate model for essential transformation, while in its practical prospects it is also the supreme paradigm of cocreation.

But the high promise of alchemy is hard to appreciate, and almost impossible to apply, because all the alchemical lore that has come down to us is so complex and obscure. It would require an enormous feat of retrieval and clarification to render it into a form applicable as an alternative science, or even a remedial physics. Although some rare work in metallic and herbal alchemy is being done today, it survives mainly as a metaphorical system for inner work. Tragically, it remains very much a lost science at the very time when its holistic, healing secrets are most needed.

CROSSWEAVE

To the Classics and Basics:

2.8 on the infamous Western alchemist who made a pact with the Devil, only to come out on top in the long run
2.9 on cocreation as soul-making, as presented in the language of the Hermetic tradition
3.1 on the cosmic consciousness of alchemist Jakob Boehme
4.2 on a modern alchemical legend, Fulcanelli

To Other Essays:

2.2 on the disclosure of cocreation and the Theogenic Idea in the Hermetica

2.4 on essential transformation and problematic aspects of cocreation, crucial to a modern re-creation of alchemical science

4 on occult teachings concerning the intervention of counterevolutionary forces

13 on the Gnostic belief that error and incompletion are included in God's creation, a view shared by the alchemists, which profoundly shaped their vision of their work

15 on magic compared to modern science on the one hand (control-system) and alchemy on the other (collaborative effort)

16 on cocreation as the supreme aim of the Mysteries

21 on serial reincarnation of Western masters who are dedicated to divine service in the Great Work

26 on the physiological and hormonal "nectars" in sexual alchemy

ESSAY 4

Anthroposophy

I n adopting the term "Anthroposophy" Rudolf Steiner was intent upon countering the bias of Theosophy, the movement in which he participated for thirteen years. In replacing the "wisdom about God" with the "wisdom about the human being," Steiner initiated an immense endeavor and lived up to it with impressive, almost superhuman efforts. In presenting his version of progressive occultism to the modern world, he established three fronts.

First, he presented evolutionary teachings, including clairvoyant readings from the Akashic Record on the spiritual history of humankind. His contribution in this field was enormous and it still stands out from all other attempts to re-create the lost history of humankind, because he took such painstaking care to correlate the information he presented with the evidence of history and science. His reincarnational studies, worked out on his deathbed, are unsurpassed for their depth and sophistication. Steiner often applied the term "spiritual science" to his work, arguing that matters of the occult could be investigated by a consistent scientific method. He even attempted to create such a method by developing a system of epistemology derived from his studies of Goethean science. He claimed his readings of the Akashic Record were as valid as any other kind of scientific finding, free of questionable psychism and naive mythmaking, because they were based on an exact method of extending normal cognition into supersensible realms. Deeply dedicated to the modern ideal of independent seeking, Steiner never demanded that others either take him on pure faith or remain lost in speculation, though the methods of verification he proposed are often so tedious as to discourage the spirit of free inquiry.

Second, Steiner pioneered the modern psychology of esoteric development, the path of self-initiation and its practical applications to everyday life. In this vein, Steiner presented what he claimed to be secret teachings in the tradition of the Rosicrucians, the Western agents of the Mysteries. He took personal responsibility for the first public disclosure of their techniques, which had always been passed down orally and in strict secrecy. In his manual of esoteric training, *Knowledge of Higher Worlds and Its Attainment,* he broke the long-standing rule of restriction to oral transmission—a daring deed that may have brought upon him the enmity of certain occult societies who did not see it fit to release this information to the public at large.

Third, he developed the "daughters," or offspring, of modern occultism in the form of indications given to artists, doctors, ministers, dancers, farmers, scientists, architects, and teachers. These were Steiner's practical directives for culture-initiation and cocreation. On this front, he initiated a number of new schools of medicine, painting, architecture, agriculture (biodynamic farming), dance and curative therapy (eurythmy), and education (Waldorf Schools), which still survive to this day.

For Steiner's purposes, the communication of modern occultism required the use of the spoken word, so he transmitted his message for the most part orally, in over seven thousand lectures, many of them arranged in courses or cycles. Working tirelessly, he was also able to write about thirty books and to consult privately with thousands of people.

All of Steiner's work is deeply Christocentric. His lecture-cycles on the Gospels are unsurpassed for their beauty and depth. A key reason for his split from the Theosophical Society was his objection to the Luciferian or Gnostic bias of Madame Blavatsky and her followers, and the deemphasis or even derogation of Christ as the supreme historical Avatar. By contrast, Steiner emphasized the tradition of Christocentric Rosicrucian teachings, stating that the resurrection of Christ was a physical event that implanted the seed-forces for the future regeneration of the entire Earth. His interpretation of the Second Coming, which he considered to be the single most important occult event of the twentieth century, places emphasis on humanity's responsibility to cocreate the event by deepening its awareness of vitalistic ("etheric") communion with the Earth.

In Steiner's vast and complex scenario of planetary evolution, the "Christ Impulse" is seen as mediating between the deviating influences of other extrahuman beings who have become enmeshed in our evolution. He developed a whole system of esoteric psychology to describe the workings of these beings, the Ahrimanic and Luciferic forces, because he believed that only by detecting their influences can humanity stay on its true course and integrate the central, regenerating force of Christ in the correct way. This is both the most controversial and the most difficult aspect of his message. Sadly, Steiner's painstakingly developed criteria for distinguishing what is authentic and progressive in spiritual work from what is delusory or retrogressive have been largely ignored by the majority of leading thinkers in the modern spiritual movement. Yet these criteria define the esoteric character of his work and are without question his most valuable contribution to modern spirituality.

More than any other Western master of our time, Steiner succeeded in laying the foundation for an extensive reinstatement of the Mysteries in a practical and contemporary form. In the twentieth century, there is no other work comparable to his, either in depth or extent, yet it comes down to us today all the more difficult to receive because of its cumbersome bounty.

CROSSWEAVE

To the Classics and Basics:

2.8 where the deviant temptations of the Luciferic and Ahrimanic forces are blended in the figure of Mephistopheles. (Steiner considered the legend of Faust to be a great parable of modern humanity's spiritual plight. The complete play in two parts is presented annually at the world headquarters of the Anthroposophical Society in Dornach, near Basel, Switzerland.)
3.9 on an example of spontaneous mystical access to the Akashic Record, contrasting to Steiner's rather arduous program for cognitive training to perceive the supersensible worlds
3.14 on the "League," perhaps a fictional representation of the type of Western Brotherhood to which Steiner belonged
4.2 on Steiner's position as the number-one enemy of the Nazi occultists
4.11 on an attempt to develop a Christocentric system of modern spiritual values, parallel to the strong moral emphasis in Steiner's esoteric philosophy

To Other Essays:

1.3 on the theme of the Second Coming as an aspect of planetarization, widely developed by Steiner in his teachings on the Christ Impulse
2.1 on the challenge to become self-guiding, emphasized by Steiner in his bold deed of disclosing secret oral teachings

2.4 on the question of preferring Eastern ways over the Western path of "progressive occultism," and the necessity of having practical directives for cocreation

3 on the belief in deviant forces (Luciferic and Ahrimanic) inherent to alchemy

8 on Esoteric Christianity, as presented in its modern revival by Steiner and others

13 on the Gnostic view of deviant forces in our evolution

14 on Rosicrucianism, which Steiner represented as the supreme historical instrument of the Great White Brotherhood, and on the work of the *Manus,* which he attempted to redefine as a free deed of service undertaken by the self-initiating modern seeker

19 on the true nature of occultism, presented by Steiner in contemporary form, hoping for it to be admitted as a legitimate science

28 on Theosophy, which provided Steiner with an audience for his initial teachings but from which he eventually defected due to deep ideological differences

ESSAY 5

Astrology

A strology is probably the oldest example on record of the holistic paradigm, the model of organic structure in which all parts are interdependent with one another. According to a main argument in the New Age worldview, humanity in former times felt and responded to the earth and its cosmic environment in a more living way than we do now. For ancient humanity, in some ways wiser and more sensitive than we are, the whole world was animated, vital, pulsing with the rhythms and moods of a single organism.

Moreover, ancient wisdom continually reminds us that the Gods imbued creation with mathematical norms, elegant formulas revealed in the design features of nature and calculable in the golden section and the Fibonnaci series. Thus, the complete holistic paradigm comprises both organic aliveness and total mathematical (not mechanical) order. Astrology is based in this ancient intuition of an all-living design, harmonically integrated from plants to planets, and synchronized by recurrent cycles and rhythms.

But the applicability of this design concept to human nature is a problematic leap that has never been fully or satisfactorily established, down to our day.

Astrology has an immensely long history. It is evident in the earliest stages of mathematics and astronomical science. Although it was originally practiced as a royal art, applied exclusively to predict and interpret events in the lives of the great theocratic rulers, it went popular in the Hellenistic era (around 200 B.C.) and has been so ever since. The astrology columns in newspapers have been thriving for a hundred years, and now appear in everything from airline magazines to New Age journals.

The fact that astrology appears prominently in trivial forms does not preclude it from being a serious matter, but there has been a great deal of difficulty in establishing it as a legitimate science. The most well-known (and well-meant) attempts to do so come from the French researcher Michel Gauquelin. By exhaustive statistical research, he established that certain planetary patterns do indeed coincide with certain vocations. If this is taken as solid proof that astrology is scientific, it still leaves open the question of how to apply it. Should we, for instance, study the charts of newborn children and preprogram their education based on the inclinations shown by the planets and aspects? Other proofs for the working of an electromagnetic field that configures the human nervous system into definite patterns of behavior have also been developed. But even the best proofs seem pointless due to an unavoidable catch-22: Those who are willing to believe in astrology don't need the proofs, and those who might be convinced by scientific verification aren't inclined to believe in it in the first place!

But the question of its scientific validity has little to do with the modern practice of astrology, anyway. This is led by the humanistic school, originated by Dane Rudhyar in his breakthough work, *The Astrology of Personality.* Rudhyar managed to establish astrology not as a scientific system that needs to be reconciled with physics, but as a symbolic language useful in psychological diagnosis and counseling. Treating it as a master paradigm, comparable to the *I Ching* on the one hand and Jungian psychology on the other, he brought astrology over from nineteenth-century fortune-telling into modern form. He shifted its aim from making predictions to creative exploration of life-directions. Unfortunately, the language of the humanistic school is not widely observed by practitioners who continue to speak as if the planets cause our behavior and our actions can be foretold. This situation will persist as long as astrology is seen as a genre (specious or legitimate) of physics, rather than a genuine (though rather odd) branch of semantics.

The main problem with astrology, it seems, lies in the proposition of twelve consistent personality types. While we may admit the existence of certain recurrent design patterns in nature, it is not so easy to allow them where *human* nature is concerned. Though often expressed in the most banal of clichés, astrological typology is enormously appealing because it confers immediate order and meaning upon the chaotic complexity of human experience. Besides, we love to hear about ourselves, and others love to be given the power to tell us. While astrology continues to be in some respects no better than hyped-up fortune-telling, its genuine side appears in its serious application to one-on-one counseling and self-help.

For instance, Emma Jung, wife of the pioneer psychologist, worked diligently on charts for all of Jung's clients, providing him with astrological indications that he then assimilated to his own method of depth psychology.

Technically, astrology consists of a fourfold framework: *houses,* which describe life-situations and contexts of growth; *signs,* which describe attitudes and behavioral norms; planets, which describe motives; and *aspects,* which describe psychological complexes or life-issues.

There are dozens of different schools of astrology, whose members tend to be exasperatingly clannish. The literature, which is chaotic and overwhelming, varies from the inane to the sublime. Astrology is not easy to learn, though it is unfortunately quite easy to fake. Serious students usually give themselves two or three years of solid apprentice work before hanging out the star-spangled shingle.

Looking back to its root-metaphor, it is worth asking if the principle of universal concordance in astrology is a two-way street. If so, then human beings ought to be able to influence the planets as much as be influenced by them. Paracelsus, a great adept and astrologer of the Renaissance, certainly thought so when he declared that "the human is greater than the planets." Yet this crucial paradigm-shift has yet to be incorporated into modern astrology, which, though concerned with human psychology, leaves the planet Earth completely out of the picture.

Although often viewed as the most prominent aspect of the metaphysical revival since the 1960s, astrology remains both the most conventional and the least credible of New Age belief systems.

CROSSWEAVE

To the Classics and Basics:

1.1 on the master model of organic design inherited from the East, which Rudhyar and others have closely correlated to the astrological paradigm
2.7 on Dante's view of cosmic/hierarchical design, typical of the medieval model-making that still pervades astrological thinking today
2.9 on numerous references to the mathematical regularity of cosmic order (for example, in *Asclepius III,* cited in E2.2)
3.7 on the revival of astrology as an attempt to solve modern humanity's need

for a key to the "inner life;" also, on "a theory of types" perhaps applicable to astrological typology

3.12 on the ancient system of vast time-cycles, or *yugas,* basis of Hindu astrology

4.7 on the close relation between geomancy and astrology

To Other Essays:

3 on alchemy as the supreme paradigm of cocreation, for which astrology could, perhaps, provide the timetable—though it has yet to be cultivated to this end

12 on the astrological and mathematical correspondences applied in geomancy

15 on the use of astrological formulas in magic

27 on the Tarot as a tool for frivolous fortune-telling or serious self-examination, complementary to astrology

ESSAY 6

Celtic Revival

T he concern for retrieving and reinstating ancient wisdom, so characteristic of the new spirituality, assumes a remarkable form in the Celtic Revival. In this special case, it involves nothing less than the resurrection of an entire culture. The Celts were fantastic storytellers, adventurers, and bons vivants who never wrote anything down, so they had no scriptural body of ancient wisdom to leave behind them, as the Hindus and Chinese did. What they did leave is more difficult to define, though its outgrowth was and still is enormous.

The Revival of the present day can be traced to an event in the European literary scene about a hundred years ago. The Irish Literary Renaissance (often called the Celtic Twilight) was an offshoot of late Romanticism that incorporated many elements of spirituality and occultism. It arose in the middle of the nineteenth century with Irish poets and folklorists who began to seek out their lost cultural roots. They went back to the land and the people, the peasants and fishermen, and gathered the old stories, fragments of myths, the gay and tragic songs. Out of this rich treasure trove they attempted to recreate Irish culture and revive the Celtic folk-spirit.

The generation following the first revivalists included eminent figures such as the Irish poet William Butler Yeats and his friend the mystical painter-poet Æ (G. W. Russell). Led by a dynamic aristocrat named Lady Gregory, the second-wave revivalists created works of modern art and literature, including a national theater, infused with the elements they had salvaged from the perishing culture of their native roots. The movement they initiated had an enormous influence both in Europe and America, serving as the test case and prototype for others who sought to tap into the deep vitality stored in regional folklore and aboriginal culture. It provided a model still applied to this day, worldwide, wherever creative people attempt to produce literature and art from inspirations rooted in their native soil.

Today, the Celtic Revival continues to grow on several fronts. In the late 1960s, it expanded into a popular movement, more widely recognized in Europe than America. The Celts were a nomadic people whose clan-based colonies extended at the time of Christ from the westlands of Ireland and Wales far into the Middle East. Geographically, the current Revival is centered in northwest France among the Breton-speaking people of Brittany; and globally it is evident in a popular resurgence of Celtic music (akin to American folk music in the 1960s), and a massive interest in the stone circles and megalithic structures believed to have been designed and constructed by the ancient Druids, the priest class of the Celtic nation-tribes. Though these geomantic studies have been confined largely to Europe, an extension into America has been unfolding through the work of a maverick Harvard archaeologist, Barry Fell, who claims to have found Celtic structures in New England and as far west as Oklahoma. As more evidence emerges that the ancient seafaring Celts were able to cross the Atlantic on a routine basis, it may open the way for a Celtic resurgence on American soil.

Apart from their regional and historical aspects, there is something universally appealing in the Celtic mood and worldview. Celtic matters seem to hold a tremendous appeal for the adventuresome in spirit. The Arthurian Path, a subgenre within the Revival, is the authentic Western counterpart to the martial arts of the East. Chivalry, though it is unlikely to be revived in a literal way, provides an attractive model for discipline of the passions and an idealistic orientation to the feminine. The exploits and romances of the Arthurian knighthood are more than the stuff of fairy tales. Encounters with supernatural forces, similar to those described by Castaneda and other present-day revivalists of shamanism, are widely and dramatically described in Celtic myth and legend. These ordeals and magical battles are now being reinterpreted as initiatory experiences: For instance, the knight's vigil in the graveyard can be directly compared to certain Tantric rites of empowerment. One revivalist, Gareth Knight, has produced an entire system of spiritual training by blending Celtic lore and legend with Cabalistic pathworking, Yoga techniques for mastering Kundalini, and creative visualization.

Among the many popular indications of the revival is the widespread fascination (largely among teenagers) with Dungeons and Dragons and all manner of demonic and elemental critters, seen in dozens of films such as *Beastmaster*. Tolkien's little hobbits, who inhabit his "Middle Earth," are a revivification of the mischievous fairy folk of Irish/Celtic lore. *The Mists of Avalon* was a New Age best-seller, and runes are all the rage. These are Celtic matters.

In many respects, the Celtic culture of the past offers an ideal model for the planetary culture of the future. It was decentralized and highly mobile, like the emergent network of present-day planetary agents. The Celts were a vital, restless, passionate people, fiercely independent, skilled in warfare, loving of adventures (especially romantic ones), and enthralled with story-telling. The tale of Tristan and Isolde, model of the Western conflict between love and passion, comes down to us from them, as does the legend of the Holy Grail. Even the importance given to Mary Magdalen in the Gnostic gospels is supported by Celtic legend, which tells of her exile in southern France, a region now becoming widely known for its sacred sites. In Celtic myth there is perhaps the germ of an emergent planetary folklore, as seen in the immense popularity of the Camelot saga and the fascination with Avalon (a Western Shambhala?) and the Otherworld.

Perhaps more than anything else, it is the magical potency of Celtic lore that attracts people today. For modern seekers, the Revival may provide a new and exciting approach to rediscovering the magic of life, threatened near to extinction by media dominance and "special effects" of our technology.

CROSSWEAVE

To the Classics and Basics:

2.5 on the Celtic legend of Parzival, exemplar of the Western Quest and historical agent in introducing the paradigm of self-initiation
2.6 on the tragic but instructive tale of the most famous lovers in the world (or at least tied for the top with Romeo and Juliet!)
3.9 on a firsthand account of natural clairvoyance, by one of the leading figures in the Irish Literary Renaissance
3.10 on a playful French/Celtic variation of a trip to the Otherworld
3.16 on the conflict between love and passion, as seen in the romance of two Celtic lovers, with a full commentary on its modern ramifications

To Other Essays:

2.3 on the Occult Revival in Europe, in which Yeats was a key figure
7 on *A Vision,* one of the most famous and well-composed instances of channeling, received through the wife of W. B. Yeats
8 on the Grail Mystery, central to esoteric Christianity
12 on the ruins of the Celtic westlands, including such sites as Stonehenge and
Newgrange; and on the growing fascination with runes as well as ruins
14 on speculations that the Arthurian knights (and their cousins, the Knights
Templar) served as an arm of the Great White Brotherhood
16 on the Solar Mysteries of the Celtic Druids
21 on the matter-of-fact view of reincarnation held by the Celts
22 on the vogue for ruins established by the Romantics
23 on Slavic and Native American traditions of shamanism, describing battles
with supernatural forces similar to those found in Celtic and Arthurian lore
29 on aboriginal witchcraft and commerce with the supernatural host of the
earth, common in Celtic lore

ESSAY 7

Channeling

W hile astrology signaled the metaphysical renaissance of the 1960s, in the 1980s it was channeling that brought the attention of the mainstream to the New Age. This is an interesting shift. Does it mean we have become more interested in receiving messages from beyond than in knowing about ourselves?

In any case, channeling is as old as the hills. All through the cultures of the ancient world, channels were active. In those far-gone times they were called oracles. In Greece the most famous was the medium or "pythoness" of Delphi, a grotto where beautiful ruins can still be seen. Like many of the other great oracles, she prognosticated on serious decisions concerning the state, and dispensed personal counsel to sincere seekers, whom she advised to "Know thyself." Short and sweet, and a lot more practical than the fantastic spoon-feedings being dispensed by channels in our day.

Michelangelo decorated the ceiling of the Sistine Chapel with five sibyls (another old term for channels), setting them alongside the biblical prophets, who may be viewed as channels in their own right. People who fall into trances and prophesy are clichés in ancient literature and culture. Old crones and midwives in the European tradition of Wicca were able to channel spirits as a matter of course. Slavic shamans and Native American medicine men were channels. Sufis are channels for God who aspire to become as oceanic as God is.

A dramatic revival of channeling occurred with the rise of Spiritualism late in the nineteenth century, when it was called table-rapping or spirit-mediumship. This was a matter of worldwide attention, as much as anything could be in those times. Then after the First World War, it picked up even greater interest, due to the need for so many people to contact their "lost boys," the young men who had died in unprecedented numbers in the first truly global conflict. In England, especially, séances and spiritualistic channelings were all the rage, and prominent, clearheaded people like the famous astronomer Sir Oliver Lodge came forth in public with startling evidence of life after death and communication from "the beyond." Sir William Crookes, a well-known physicist, was another prominent figure of the time who compromised his reputation by displaying a serious interest in mediumistic phenomena. He was influential in the founding of the Society for Psychical Research in 1882. Table-rapping and Ouija board readings were widespread in Victorian times, and England remains to this day the strongest bastion of Spiritualism. This is a worldwide phenomenon, always associated with mediums and trance-speaking.

In America channels were legion, but by far the most famous were the Fox sisters of Hydesville, New York. Although they attracted enormous press, they never concerned themselves with anything very deep or serious. In its most recent revival, channeling has taken on a more grandiose aspect. Einstein and Gandhi speak from the beyond, and spirit-guides from other galaxies bring tidings of massive Earth changes and wit and wisdom from the Pleiades or Alpha Centauri. Channels are very fond of espousing the Theogenic Idea that "You are all Gods," which they state in endless and not very original variations. They are equally prone to sensational scoops on evolutionary enigmas and planetary conspiracies, carefully sticking to matters that cannot be verified.

Channeling comes in several forms. In the heyday of Spiritualism, table-knocking and extrusion of ectoplasmic phantoms under deep trance were fashionable. Madame Blavatsky and Alice A. Bailey wrote directly from telepathic dictation. The wife of Irish poet W. B. Yeats produced a remarkable system of esoteric psychology by voice-channeling, which Yeats recorded in fifty notebooks and condensed into *A Vision.* Around the same time, one of Aleister Crowley's wives received *The Book of the Law.* Other well-known literary channels brought forth *Oahspe, The Urantia Book, The Aquarian Gospel,* and *The Course in Miracles,* to name but a few. With the advent of audiovisual technology, channeling appears to be reaching another high point, with volumes of channeled material in print and high-profile mediums, seen on tour and on tape, coming in and out of fashion like shoe styles.

Channeling, like spiritual masters, is a New Age issue that raises some very challenging questions, though these are rarely entertained by the people who become spellbound by the channels. For those attracted to channels and willing to accept the advice and information they dispense as authoritative, there is of course no need to validate the phenomenon. Their popular appeal—however skin-deep it may prove to be—is probably due to the way they offer a fast and easy answer to the perennial human need for guidance and supernatural intervention, especially in our troubling times. For better or worse, channels are the spiritual authority figures of the New Age.

Even if channeling proves to be no more than a passing fad, it ought not to come and go without telling us something about ourselves. Is its enormous appeal an indication that we feel powerless, unable to gain access to vital information we believe we need, whether it be intimate knowledge of ourselves or fantastic disclosures about social problems in long-lost Lemuria? Is channeling, as its most radical critics believe, merely a symptom of schizophrenia? And if so, why is schizophrenia showing up in this form at this time in our culture? And finally, is channeling something we can do without, or is the message being transmitted through it an indispensable one that cannot be accessed in other ways?

Whether channeling or satellite TV will be the world's favorite form of entertainment in the year 2000 remains to be seen.

CROSSWEAVE

To the Classics and Basics:

1.6 on the possibility of viewing the Lord Krishna as an avataric channel for the God Vishnu

1.8 on a reverse instance of channeling: Instead of sitting around to listen to the dead speaking from the beyond, we read to them!

2.2 on the possibility of viewing an ancient poet like Homer as a channel for the Muse

2.3 on Plato's comments on mania (in the *Phaedrus*), describing four kinds of divine madness, which may be related to psychic possession and channeling

2.12 on the oral tradition of sacred transmission, common to all ancient cultures, which suggests a long continuity of channelers who preserve the story of creation and other mythic material essential to the guidance of the people

3.1 on the phenomenon of cosmic consciousness, in which full self-consciousness is retained (usually), by contrast to the deep trance experienced in channeling, when personal identity is obliterated

3.2 on channeling as a variety of religious experience, including the "conversions" exhibited by those who join cults centered on channels

3.5 on an epic instance of a Native American "spirit vision," showing a shamanic variant of channeling

4.4 on electronic media as the ultimate form of feedback in which humanity channels itself!

To Other Essays:

1.2 on the implementation of hierarchical guidance from the masters through telepathic means

2.1 on being guided versus being self-guiding

4 on the influence of deviant extrahuman beings (of two kinds), whose possible role in channeling is rarely considered

8 on the question of telepathic contact with Christ, a huge issue in the New Age and a special concern in Esoteric Christianity

9 on channeling (energies and entities) through crystals

10 on cults, such as those that often form around popular channels or their productions

14 on channeling the masters

28 on Madame Blavatsky's visit to the Fox sisters

ESSAY 8

Christianity (Alternative)

V iewed as an alternative path, Christianity comprises a half dozen little-known and fascinating variants.

1. *Christian mystics,* from the early pioneers, such as Saint John the Divine, to the soaring hearts of the Middle Ages like Hildegard of Bingen and Richard of Saint Victor, through the Renaissance ecstatics like Saint Teresa, down to those in our time, such as the writer Thomas Merton and the poet William Everson (Brother Antoninus)—a motley and marvelous crew.

2. *Eastern Orthodox Christianity,* including Russian mystics like Saint Seraphim. In the theology of the Eastern church, Christianity achieves a passionate depth practically unknown in the West. The existential theology of its greatest modern thinker, Nicholas Berdyaev, is unsurpassed in its brilliant treatment of suffering, freedom, and evil. Vladimir Soloviev, Symbolist poet Andrei Biely, Vyasaslav Ivanov, and Lev Shestov are a few of the leading agents of Russian spirituality.

3. *Gnosticism,* consisting of a vast cosmology and a set of gospels all its own. The underdog of world religions.

4. *para-Christianity,* a name that can be applied to a variety of modern paths, starting with New Thought, Christian Science, and Science of Mind (as represented by Mary Baker Eddy, Marcus Quimby, Emmet Fox, and others) and coming down to *The Course in Miracles.* These teachings are the main source of most contemporary views on cocreation, which they treat as a matter of mental discipline ("positive thinking" or attitude control). This strain also includes the inspirational psychology of M. Scott

Peck, immensely popular in New Age circles, and some prominent apostles of recovery. Para-Christians, like paralegals and paramedics, practice all the moral and ethical principles observed by conventional Christians, but they do so while keeping for the most part outside or alongside *(para)* the dogma-bound, churchgoing crowd.

5. *esoteric Christianity,* supposedly founded by Saint Paul in collaboration with Dionysius the Areopagite (New Testament, Acts 17:34). This is an underground stream fed in part by Gnostic currents and apparently incorporating some systematic teachings of the Solar Mysteries, as seen in the grand scheme of the "Nine Hierarchies" described in the work of the Pseudo-Dionysius. Most serious Christians, even the far-thinking and self-searching ones, seem to be completely oblivious to this rich and enduring stream. Its covert existence through the Middle Ages and the Renaissance is a fascinating tale of subversion through which Christianity became assimilated to Platonic and neo-Platonic thinking. Its cross-fertilization with alchemy was crucial to the deep continuity of Western spirituality, as C. G. Jung wisely noted. This strain includes the Grail as a numinous relic and symbol of the Western path of redemption. From the nineteenth century on, it has been somewhat revived in the works and visions of Swedenborg, William Blake, Novalis, and the English and German Romantics who sought to co-opt the Christ myth to their own purposes. It also appears in the esoteric systems of Rudolf Steiner, Max Heindel, Valentin Tomberg, Corinne Heline, and other teachers of Christocentric cosmology.

6. *Christian spiritualism,* last but not least, a strange and often muddled fusion of old-time Christian faith with psychic phenomena, contacts from the beyond, UFOs, conspiracy theories, and what have you. In America, it comprises the hundreds of small congregations that keep themselves away from public exposure, but it has also come to wider notice through a number of alleged cases of "channeling the Christ." In South America, it shows up as a phantasmagoric melange of Christian imagery and ideology with candomblé, Macumba, tribal folklore, and Brazilian glamour. This is southern hemispheric fundamentalism at its weirdest.

It is interesting to observe that as a wave of religious revival and TV evangelism sweeps across America, involvement in these variations of

Christianity is also on the rise. Considering that Christian fundamentalism concerns itself with many of the same themes and issues that are being explored in the new spirituality, the current revival of conventional, dogma-bound religious faith may turn out to be more than a pendulum swing that lasts a decade or two. It could persist as long as the new spirituality itself is in gestation—that is to say, by some estimates, for centuries.

In any case, although it draws little or no attention from the national media (interested only in fundamentalist mania or wacko cultism), alternative Christianity is a force to be reckoned with. It answers to the failure of traditional Judeo-Christian values and rejects its end-of-the-world scenario, or historical Armageddon, in favor of direct revelation and global communion (Second Coming). Its resurgence has been precisely timed by the dawning of the nuclear age and the simultaneous discovery of the Nag Hammadi gospels in 1945. For a significant few, the dogmatic righteousness and doomsaying of the old-time Christianity are now unacceptable, yet it is still the Oriental paths that dominate alternative seeking in the West.

And no wonder, since evolving a new Christianity from any or all of the strains described here raises some questions—concerning the divinity of human nature, the origin and purpose of evil, the foundation of freedom, the achievement of self-change and self-direction—that are not so easily resolved. As the mytheme of the Second Coming is a paramount concern of the new spirituality, the question of achieving telepathic contact with Christ, or with each other *through* Christ, is a crucial one for modern seeking. How to *imagine* Christ in different ways from those we are taught by conventional Christianity is the common challenge of all these alternative strains.

CROSSWEAVE

To the Classics and Basics:

2.5 on esoteric Christianity in the Grail Legend
3.1 on spontaneous mystical experiences, sometimes interpreted as contact with Christ

3.7 on the causes of the spiritual disillusionment in the modern world, opening the way for interest in alternative paths

3.12 on the modern Christian mystic, Therese Neumann, who experienced the stigmata

4.11 on the psychology and ethics of para-Christianity

To Other Essays:

1.3 on the mytheme of the Second Coming

2.4 on Teilhard de Chardin's attempt to convert the dominant paradigm of Christianity from Fall to flow, with Christ envisioned as the flowpoint of our evolution toward the ultrahuman

4 on Steiner's Christocentric occultism, an attempt to reinstate the Solar Mysteries, and his radical interpretation of the Second Coming

13 on what is perhaps the most potent, promising strain of alternative Christianity, suppressed for almost two thousand years

16 on the supreme importance of Christ in the ancient Solar Mysteries

17 on the Christian mystics

20 on the para-Christian aspects of recovery

22 on the Romantics' attempt to re-create the myth and ideology of Christianity to their own liking, freed of all doctrinal and organizational structures

ESSAY 9

Crystals

I f we go by what the media tell us about alternative seeking, there is much ado about crystals. With channeling, they are the most faddish interest in the New Age.

The current interest in crystals may be due to the need for technology for spiritual development, in keeping with the modern demand for instant results. The crystal, it is said, is a tool for accessing psychic powers and invisible forces, a handy device for focusing personal desire and acquiring rare forms of knowledge. It might even be called the computer chip of today's spirituality, the miraculous object that gives instant access to lost secrets and hidden realms.

The use of crystals for charms and divination is, of course, very ancient. In these practices, the crystal merely serves as a lens for looking into other worlds, into the past or future, or into the interior, subconscious dimensions of the gazer's own mind. Popular modern applications of the crystal are many and varied: for healing; lucid dreaming; communication with invisible spirits or extraterrestrial intelligences; casting spells and achieving desires; and strengthening of inner forces, such as desire, memory, and mental acuity.

Studies and practices with crystals seem to fall into two categories. On the one hand, there is a more or less scientific approach to crystals, or at least an attempt to make research and experimentation with them into a legitimate science. This approach is often allied with radionics, using instruments and detectors to measure the "energy fields" of crystals. A whole new science of healing has sprung up with the crystal technology being developed along these lines. It is often closely allied to the ancient wisdom of aboriginal cultures, which used crystals extensively in their folk religion and ritual.

On the other hand, crystals are employed for personal use in self-empowerment, attracting one's desires, repelling negative or resistant forces, and contacting other realms for guidance. In this context, they are often associated with fabulous scenarios, such as channeling from the Pleiades. Mythmaking along these lines usually picks up the ominous theme of the last days of Atlantis, the legendary continent said to have been destroyed in a war waged with crystals.

Radionics, as it appears today, is a direct extension of the pioneering work done early in the nineteenth century by Friedrich Anton Mesmer and Baron von Reichenbach, exploring what was then called "animal magnetism" and the "od force." Out of this work emerged the pseudo-science of hypnotism, which played an enormous role in the spirit-mediumship of the late nineteenth century. At the very time when Spiritualism was peaking, Scottish physicist James Clerk Maxwell was working out some equations that were to provide the jumping-off point for Einstein's computations in relativity theory. These were called field equations. Around the same time, English inventor Michael Faraday proposed the theory of electromagnetic induction. Though these advances in science remained quite distinct from Spiritualism at the time, they came in the twentieth century to be amalgamated with it; so now we speak quite casually of energy fields and electromagnetic induction with reference to the human body or even the mind.

More recently, the Russian parapsychologists have been delving extensively into the behavior of "bioplasma," which reminds us of the "ectoplasm" of Spiritualism. Practitioners of crystal technology argue that the human bioplasmic field is sensitive to crystals—easy enough to say, but the puzzle remains, How and where can there be an interface between the inorganic radiation fields of crystals and the vast spectrum of biological/biochemical/organic radiations that comprise life as we know it, actively and consciously?

The explanation generally given is that crystals emit "energy"* of certain kinds. To some extent, this is sense-detectable: Some crystals will warm noticeably when held in one's hand. But those who work with crystals claim they possess vast fields of emanation, beyond what is sense-detectable. Just as a huge magnet is surrounded by a field, or as the very air we breathe is permeated with all kinds of radio and TV waves, so crystals are described as transmitters and receivers of certain "energies," of many types and wavelengths. Presumably, the entire realm of crystals is part of an active field of emanations consisting of many bands. As a magnet throws off a magnetic field, crystals throw off fields that are

*A word I don't like to use. See Lexicon for my antidefinition.

responsive to psychic-emotional processes (or "vibrations"), as well as to thought formations (telepathic radiations). They are said to absorb, intensify, and transmit such radiations. The thinking that supports this theory seems to draw upon the archaic concept of "magic" as a control-system in which crystals serve as tuning devices.

Crystals are said to be extraordinarily precise in their properties: Quartz does things tourmaline will not do. In their use for healing, they are applied as specifically as prescription medicines. While some neophytes may adopt them as little more than good-luck charms, crystals are taken very seriously by those who use them for healing, shamanic practices, meditation, biofeedback, divination, channeling, and awesome feats of self-improvement. The old gypsy woman who reads the crystal ball has been replaced by high-tech wizards who apply their skills to everything from curing cancer to discount brokering.

Crystals and rare gemstones have, of course, been coveted and worshiped down through the ages. Certainly the sheer beauty and astonishing configurations of crystals account to some degree for their appeal. It is very difficult to assess their real significance, however, due to serious interest frequently being compromised by all manner of fabulous claims made about them. Perhaps the ultimate test of crystal technology will come in their practical application, not only in personal healing and creative visualization but, say, in heating. If crystals could serve as generators to produce light and "energicity" (a possible replacement for electricity), then we surely would find ourselves living in a New Age.

CROSSWEAVE

To Other Essays:

3 on metallic transmutation in alchemy, an age-old concept surprisingly absent from crystal theory
7 on channeling energies and entities and the connection of crystals with Spiritualism
12 on divination with crystals as an aspect of geomancy
15 on the theory of magical influence, often invoked to explain the powers of crystals; and the use of crystals in amulets and charms
23 on the frequent use of crystals in neoshamanic practices
29 on crystals in traditional witchcraft

ESSAY 10

Cults

T he statistics on cults in America are not impressive: about six hundred groups, with memberships of ten thousand at best in a few, one
thousand or less for most. This is taking the word *cult* in its broadest
definition: including everything from groups long ago accepted into the
Establishment, like the sect of Christian Science, to the merest slivers
comprising fifty or even a dozen members. In the past two decades, some
of these have claimed enormous numbers of converts. Transcendental
meditation and Scientology, for example, have cited statistics in excess of
a million. Certainly, this many people may have been touched by those
cults, at one time or another, but the core-groups remain very restricted
in numbers, and there is rapid turnover.

Somewhat more impressive is the number of sects and splinter groups
within conventional Christianity—about eight hundred at any given
time—comprising a total membership running into the hundreds of
thousands!

As usual, the media has given us an overblown picture, yet the principle behind cults is not to be dismissed as trivial. The Manson family and
Jonestown are two signals so deeply imprinted in the American psyche
that they are unlikely to fade for a long time to come. Scientology, known
for its fascist approach to recruitment, its mercenary attitude, and its
enormous legal budget, has contributed widely to giving cults a bad
name. To meet the challenge, numerous watchdog groups and a couple
of deprogramming units are now in operation, even beginning to deal in
some cases with Christian fundamentalism, which may be viewed as a cult.

Since Manson, Jonestown, Rajneesh, Scientology, and the Moonies,
the word *cult* has become inseparable from threats of brainwashing,
soul-soaking, and spiritual dry cleaning. At worst, it evokes visions of
orgies, human sacrifice, and black-hooded figures eating babies. It is

unfortunate if the lurid sheen of the word serves to prevent intelligent people from discerning how it points to something extremely common in our *cul*ture: namely, behavior modification. As Aldous Huxley and others have warned, this is something to be reckoned with in the present age. It is pervasive in the media and advertising, in forms considered to be entirely acceptable. The emphasis on status and appearance in advertising is intended to create cultic experiences centered on totem products. Beer commercials, for instance, exude a tremendous cultic appeal, as do fashion fads. Levi's 501 jeans are extravagantly pitched as cult gear. On the other hand, the widespread use of prescription drugs can be seen as a feat of technocratic management in which a handful of pharmacologists and medical experts preside over vast cults whose members are united by frequent ritual ingestion of the eucharist (Valium, Lithium).

The CIA has been described as a "cult of intelligence." Any group managing special resources or information (NASA or NBC or the KKK) tends to assume the features of a cult. These comparisons are not as farfetched as they may seem, for all that makes a cult like the Manson family different from the examples given here is its savage profession of antisocial attitudes and aims. Cults are everywhere in our culture, but they become notorious and dangerous (in public opinion) when their aims are threatening to the existing social order or traditional values. Every cult, whether it be the CIA or Scientology, stakes its identity on the possession of special power, techniques, or information. Often there is a charismatic leader attributed with supernatural connections or divine inspiration. Cults that seek to overthrow the current order of things necessarily have to keep their programs secret and set themselves apart. Most of the cults that come to national attention through the media exhibit a messianic character, often derived from Eastern religion.

Techniques of behavior modification remain as yet a special study for experts, but one of the beneficial side effects of the infamous cults of Charles Manson and Jim Jones may be a slow awakening of public interest in all aspects of mental and behavioral programming. The psychology of cult involvement is a new frontier, opening rapidly. One obvious point is how cults can serve as countercultural refuges for the disillusioned and dispossessed. Membership provides a new identity and group support for those who cannot establish a support system within conventional society. The cult can confer special meaning on the painful experiences of rebellion and alienation. It gives much-needed personal validation—perhaps even the sense of serving a divine cause, beyond the appreciation and sanction of normal people—at the same time as it takes away the autonomy and judgment of the member. Cultism at its lowest common denominator is the polar opposite of independent seeking.

There is much public education to be done before cults can be viewed with compassion and objectivity. Lacking this, it is perhaps helpful to view cults as a dangerous and tragic perversion of the community impulse. So much of New Age vision predicts or calls for massive transformations in society that can only come about, realistically, through the activation of cultlike cells, evolutionary vanguard groups, like the utopian sects of the nineteenth century. Cultism in its notorious forms is a perversion of group effort, one of the key themes of New Age ideology. It is a form of cancer appearing in the cellular life of the emergent social/planetary organism.

CROSSWEAVE

To the Classics and Basics:

To Other Essays:

8 on repressed and forgotten splinter cults within Christianity
13 on the main countercult to conventional Christianity
15 on the grave problem of Satanic cults in America
16 on the Mystery Schools as cults or culture-generating centers of spiritual training
19 on the common root of the words *cult, culture,* and *occultism*
24 on the Eastern masters who often attract large cult followings in the West
29 on the problem of applying the cult label to harmless practices that defy or offend conventional habits of belief

ESSAY 11

Eroticism/Goddess Revival

One basic claim of the new spirituality is that humanity in former times lived in much closer communion with nature than we do today. Our ancestors, right back to the caves, felt the earth and sky as living entities, sources of bountiful food and vitality, animated through and through with spiritual forces to be worshiped, celebrated, and feared. Was this empathic closeness to nature accompanied by an entirely different experience of sexuality? The definition of "erotic" depends on how we answer this question.

Originally, Eros was a Sun God in the Orphic Mysteries, the projection of the Solar Logos as pure vitality, infusing the Earth with its "solar-phallic" ray. The ritualistic union of "Father Sun" and "Mother Earth" was commemorated vividly in the huge constructions of the passage-graves (so named by archaeologists), consisting of a vaginal channel and uterine chamber to receive the fertilizing ray of the Sun. This is eroticism at the highest level of religious experience.

Among ancient peoples, erotic experience was probably "polymorphous" (to borrow Freud's term): a sensation of vital excitation, not confined to the sexual organs. The shuddering delight of contact with a sacred or numinous power was something essential to all religions in past times, when the divine was felt within nature as a supernatural presence. For a Greek to have an erotic sensation was probably as common as it is now for someone to be "turned on" by a pop song on the radio.

According to a long-standing tradition in the East, erotic sensation (including the sexual but not confined to it) is equatable with the bliss of union with the divine. In Tantric teachings, both kinds of bliss, sexual and spiritual, are said to be *samarasa,* "same-tasting." This belief recurs in a watered-down way in Plato's *Symposium,* where Socrates, normally the paragon of modesty and self-deprecation, is made to declare boldly that he is a master of eroticism, due to his tutelage by the sibyl Diotima. With Plato, erotic bliss is derived from the pure contemplation of Beauty—thus providing the lead for a kind of supernatural esthetics in the West, culminating in the Decadence of the 1890s. A high esthetic flowering of eroticism appeared in twelfth-century France in the Albigensian culture where the Troubadours sprang up. Since their time there has been no major cultural efflorescence of the impulse.

A Greek bas-relief showing a prostrate man with a winged woman positioned over him in the Tantric posture known as *maithuna* may have been connected with the Mysteries of Eros and Aphrodite celebrated at Corinth. In any case, there is a long history behind this image, referring back to the universal mytheme of theogamy, or intercourse between humans and Gods. The belief in sexual intercourse as a sacred rite goes well back into Paleolithic times. The oldest evidence on hand points to the worship of woman as an embodiment of the Great Goddess, or Divine Mother. As such, she is fully earthbound and yet invested with celestial powers (wings). Before the discovery of patrimony, her capacity to bear children was viewed as a divine mystery, not dependent upon sexual union with the man. This left the act free to be experienced in other ways, especially as a rite for receiving *mana,* spiritual power. The veneration of the *lingam* (phallus) and *yoni* (vulva) is without question the oldest religious practice of humankind. This is difficult to appreciate today because it refers back to a time when the generative powers were viewed as divine gifts, even vehicles for the manifestation of superhuman forces, rather than mere devices for personal gratification (either through sexual pleasure or egotistical self-extension in one's progeny).

Sacred prostitution probably arose as a formalization of the caveman's natural awe for the Goddess, incarnate as woman. It flourished for thousands of years in the East and Asia Minor, as well as in other cultures from Polynesia to Scandinavia. Erotic imagery still thrives in Hindu and Tibetan Buddhism, especially in the *yab-yum.* The erotic statuary of India is unsurpassed for its outrageous celebration of sexual rapture. The long Hindu poem, the *Gita Govinda,* describes in the most exquisite and explicit language the mad love-play between Krishna (human embodiment of the world-dreamer Vishnu) and Radha, his mortal consort and a married woman into the bargain.

It is a long way from ancient sacred sexuality to the *Kama Sutra* and even a longer way still down to Masters and Johnson and the "sexual revolution" of the 1960s. However, the evident failure of that revolt serves well to point up the argument that eroticism cannot be revived without grounding it in the sacred. Although Christianity and other fundamentalist belief systems like Islam try to keep them separate, sexuality and spirituality are Siamese twins who cannot survive unless they are attached, even if it be by an adversarial bonding. Mircea Eliade (in his book *Yoga: Immortality and Freedom*) is one of the rare few who have written in a brilliant, tasteful way of ancient sexual mysteries. Today, eroticism survives in a trivial form in the popular revival of Tantra and the Tao of Sex.

Drawing upon the feeble but ever-recurrent tremors of eroticism is the current attempt to reinstate the Goddess, to renew our understanding of the feminine. The Goddess Revival that has shaped up in the 1980s appears to be a spiritual aftergrowth of the feminist movement, far exceeding its original dimensions. This involves a great deal of new research into matriarchies, as well as feats of mythmaking to countermand the paradigm of the Fall and lift the blame placed on Eve as the cause of all our sorrows. In the Gnostic gospels, as well, the feminine is restored to a high role in the revelation of divinity on Earth, for Mary Magdalen is described as the closest personal ally to the God-man, Christ. In the most radical view, she is even viewed as the one who makes it possible for God as man to complete the mission of becoming God as fully human.

In spite of its sensationalistic aspects, eroticism may be viewed as a vital, though poorly developed, element of the new spirituality. It is a deep volcanic core capable of upheaving the main tectonic paradigms upon which morality and civilization, as we now define them, precariously depend.

CROSSWEAVE

To the Classics and Basics:

1.2 on Lao Tzu's famous evocation of the feminine, of the "Spirit of the Valley"
2.1 on sexual initiation as an archetypal stage of the hero's quest
2.2 on the Goddess Aphrodite, described right down to her intimate smells
2.4 on eroticism in the Mystery Cults of the Middle East
2.6 on the "love potion" mistakenly taken by Tristan and Isolde—symbolic of the tragic, uncontrollable power of erotic passion as viewed in the West

3.2 on the sublimation of eroticism into "theopathic" ecstasy (especially in Saint Teresa)

3.15 on the modern denial of Eros (identified with Christ as the personification of pure and perfect vitality) and its subversion into fascism

3.16 on the Western dilemma of passion versus love and the cults of Eros in twelfth-century France

To Other Essays:

1.1 on the application of Tantric/Taoist views of sexuality in the utopian cults of nineteenth-century America

1.3 on the themes of *ancient wisdom* and *Gaia,* both of which imply the superiority of spiritual empathy with the earth enjoyed by humanity in former times

2.2 on the description of human generative powers as God-given instruments for pleasure and spiritual interfusion between man and woman, found in the Hermetica

13 on the figure of the Fallen Sophia in Gnosticism

15 on sexual ritual in magic

16 on the Solar Mysteries as the basis of ancient solar-phallic religion

17 on the resemblance of sexual pleasure to mystical ecstasy

18 on the preservation of spiritual communion with nature among Native Americans

22 on the concept of the "noble savage" in Romanticism

23 on the possible origins of shamanism in ecstatic worship of the Goddess

25 on the erotic/hedonic elements of Sufism, where ecstatic union with the divine is described by analogy to drunkenness and sexual union

26 on the most sensational aspects of erotic spirituality

29 on the revival of Goddess-based religion in neopaganism and witch cults

ESSAY 12

Geomancy

W hile it often appears to be one of the most fashionable or even faddish aspects of the New Age, geomancy has a profound foundation. As indicated in John Michell's classic, *The View Over Atlantis,* it involves the attempt to recapture a lost vision of planetary organization, to plot out the original physiology of the Earth.

To revere the Earth as a living being is perhaps the basic demand made by the new spirituality upon modern habits of materialism. As the argument is often stated, the Earth *was* regarded as a living being in times past. This attitude was typical of the old nature religions of paganism, common to all cultures from the Chinese to the American Indian. It is widely believed that this attitude prevailed until the time of the Industrial Revolution, when the exploitation of natural resources on the global scale began. Geomancy, which concerns itself in the widest sense with recapturing a vision of the living earth, is an attempt to reinstate the feeling of reverence and communion between humanity and its global habitat, the wise and nurturing realm of Mother Earth, who is the supreme embodiment of the Great Goddess.

Sacred sites, megalithic structures aligned to the four seasons and the stellar and planetary movements, ley-lines linking power-points in long, straight arcs across the landscape, geometrical and numerical designs incorporated into ancient temples, dowsing, geodesics, Earth-chakras, runes, labyrinths, the golden section, the Gaia hypothesis, the vibrating mesh of the planetary etheric web, Nazca lines, the Glastonbury Zodiac, giant figures inscribed in the landscape, the Great Serpent Mound of Ohio, medicine wheels of the Rockies, pyramids, stone circles, dolmens and underground chambers used for initiation, dragon-currents running over valleys and mountain ranges, electromagnetic fields and telluric emanations of the planet, plottings of astronomical and mathematical

correspondences—such are the ingredients of the fascinating lore of geomancy. A good many of these require reinstating the lost lore of ancient
wisdom; others are purely modern extrapolations of what our ancestors
knew. The great attraction and promise of geomancy may lie in its potential for evolving into a new planetary science, a kind of Earth-based
physics in which our vital interplay with the natural dynamics of our
planetary habitat is reestablished and actively, conscientiously preserved.
Geomancy points to the ultimate art and science of ecological conserva-
tion. To its practitioners, it is the supreme example of unified field theory.

In practice, geomantic work involves a small cadre of dedicated students who form a sort of cult. There is a great deal of inside information
and special lingo, rapidly unfolding into a whole new genre of planetary
folklore. Because of its global nature, this group of geomantic activists
tends to be scattered across the planet, but it remains closely integrated
by newsletters (such as the legendary *Ley-Hunter*), small organizations,
and personal networking.

While the new science is being developed by this core-group, there is
a burgeoning of popular interest in the more accessible aspects of geomancy. PBS programs on the inexplicable wonders of ancient ruins are
becoming more common. These are bound to hold the attention of even
the most skeptical viewers, for the sheer miracle of ancient engineering
required to move and precision-fit the massive stones of the Giza Pyramid
or the Peruvian temple fortress of Suycamanco is enough to cause anyone
to pause and wonder, and there are hundreds of examples of such feats.
Due to the tremendous appeal of such enigmas, world tours of sacred
sites are now becoming highly popular, and not just to those in New Age
circles. The appeal of geomancy in this regard is quite universal, and it
may indeed contribute immensely to fostering a new sense of planetary
awareness in modern society.

Along with the reinstatement of reverence for the Earth as a living
being, geomancy involves the question of emergent psychic powers and
otherworld or extraterrestrial scenarios. For instance, wherever sacred
sites are located there is always the possibility of entering into contact
with the ancient spirits, the elemental powers of the landscape or the
pagan Gods and Goddesses associated in folklore with those sites, as
found in countless tales of the Celtic Otherworld. This requires the
opening up of psychic centers, the sensitization of the human etheric
body—like a tuning fork—to the environing currents of the planetary
etheric body in which it is embedded. Those who meditate under dolmens or in the King's Chamber of the Great Pyramid, for instance, report

having psychic impressions or out-of-body experiences or visions of pictures in the Akashic Record concerning what formerly happened there.

On the other hand, a strong extraterrestrial factor is often evident in geomantic explorations. The Nazca lines, for instance, are continually cited as proof that ancient astronauts have visited the Earth and inscribed it with figures and designs that may have served them for a landing strip. Zechariah Sitchin builds his entire scenario upon this premise, for which he finds evidence in Babylonian inscriptions. Even more convincing are the alignments of sacred structures such as the Mayan temples and Newgrange in Ireland. These prove beyond any argument that the ancients possessed a sophisticated and exact knowledge of vast time-cycles involving the solstices and the equinoxes, lunar standstills, planetary periods, star ascensions, and much more. One inference drawn from all this startling and somewhat overwhelming data is that the ancient initiates, such as the Druidic masters of the Solar Mysteries, must have been in contact with extraterrestrial civilizations—and so many students of geomancy are concerned with how to resume this contact in our time.

CROSSWEAVE

To the Classics and Basics:

4.7 on the great overview and theoretical framework that established the genre

To Other Essays:

1.3 on the themes of *Gaia* and *planetarization,* widely elaborated through the theories and practices of geomancy
2.3 on the discovery of Egyptian religion, opening the way for extensive research on the Great Pyramid and other ancient feats of sacred engineering
5 on the astrological system of the *houses,* originally derived from geomantic figures inscribed on the ground
6 on the fascination with ruins in the Celtic Revival
16 on the evidence of the Solar Mysteries in the worldwide distribution of sacred structures aligned to the solstices and equinoxes
18 on the medicine wheels and sacred sites of the West
22 on nature mysticism and the love of ancient ruins in Romanticism
29 on the renewal of natural religion and the feeling for Earth as a living being, a common conviction among the advocates of Wicca

ESSAY 13

Gnosticism

G nosticism, as it appears today, is a huge shambles, the ruin of a once vast and magnificent structure. Historically, it is defined as an elitist religion of unknown origins, suppressed in the fourth century when the Catholic church came to power. For a long time, accounts of Gnostic beliefs came exclusively from its fierce opponents, the early Christian fathers, who only cited its theories for the purpose of refuting them. This is like having the prosecutor's dossier on a case tried almost two thousand years ago, and trying to reconstruct from it the viewpoint of the defendant!

By the best guess, Gnosticism may be the remnant of a vast system of theological and cosmological teachings that go back thousands of years. Until 1945, the prosecutor's dossier was the main source of information about it, but with the discovery of the Nag Hammadi gospels and other apocryphal scriptures buried for as long as sixteen centuries, much new material has come to light. Still, Gnosticism as we have it today consists of a mere handful of fragments, like a heap of glass slivers from the ruins of a massive stained-glass window. Much of what remains is bizarre and baffling in one way or another. In spite of the fragmentary condition of the evidence, the strangeness of the Gnostic worldview comes across with startling force.

In what once must have been a complete scenario of world evolution, the Gnostic texts describe not only the creation of the universe and the human race, but also the deviating or counterevolutionary influences that caused the divine plan to work out in a different way from what was originally intended. "The world came about through a mistake," as *The Gospel of Philip* says. It must be understood, however, that the world meant here is exclusively the sensory/material world, not creation as a whole. The Gnostics believed that higher beings called the Aeons, who are creative emanations of the Godhead, produced most of the invisible and immaterial universe. But then an alien entity, called the Demi-urge, intervened in the creation process at the level of the material realm that human beings inhabit. This is like saying that a group of architects and engineers did the initial work on a building, including the foundation, the supportive framework, and the vast system of electrical and plumbing installations, but when it came to the furnishing and interior decoration—that is, everything that would actually be seen and used by the people due to inhabit the building—another company took over and fitted it out in ways that were not compatible with the original intent of its creators. This is a complex idea, with mind-boggling implications. Typical of Gnostic thinking, it introduces all kinds of strange and troubling considerations.

In further elaboration of this strange scenario, the Gnostics described how one of the creative Aeons—Sophia, or Wisdom—was so passionately attracted to the fallen realm of the Demi-urge that she herself fell into it, thus becoming the Fallen Sophia. In the lower world she undergoes a series of spiritual agonies described at length in the Gnostic texts, only to be rescued in the end by Christ, the Savior-God who descends from the higher Aeons and assumes human form. In the Gnostic view, Christ is not the only savior, for the serpent in the Garden is taken as a *benefactor* who introduces to humanity the Theogenic Idea, "Ye shall be as Gods," working through his chosen instrument, the primordial woman, Eve.

Both Gnosticism and Christianity are soteric (or soteriological) religions, centered on the figure of a savior (soter) or redeemer who came to rescue the world from its fallen state, in keeping with the paradigm of salvation. While it does exhibit some anti-Christian elements, no doubt due to its adversarial relation to the early Church, Gnosticism is fundamentally Christocentric. It is even held by some of its radical advocates to be the true and original from of Christianity. It maintains, however, that God is to be found exclusively within the human self. It sets knowledge over against belief, and raises intuitive learning above blind obedience. It is deeply concerned with the extrahuman deviations of human intent and the apparitional nature of the material world.

Although Christ figures as the supreme Avatar who links the fallen realm of humanity with its long-lost source, the Gnostics maintained that his appearance as the man Jesus was not strictly physical but apparitional. To them Christ was an actual God, a superhuman being who performed a kind of magic show by appearing temporarily in the guise of a human being. But the magic was effective because it introduced into the fallen realm of the senses the power to see through the illusionary magic of the Demi-urge. However, this power is only accessible to those rare few initiated into Gnosticism. In some Gnostic texts, Christ is depicted as laughing scornfully at the folly of those who do not comprehend the supernatural trickery he is performing.

Gnosticism was condemned by the Christian fathers for this elitist outlook, as well as for its claim that Christ's appearance on Earth was a magical event, its practice of pagan sexual rites, and its high regard for Mary Magdalen, whom the Gnostics viewed as the closest confidant to Christ, and the embodiment of the Fallen Sophia. Most objectionable of all was the Gnostic assertion that those who were truly close to Christ kept his teachings to themselves or only shared them discreetly with a few other intimates. Obviously, this completely undercut the imperative of the Church to go forth and convert the world.

Gnosis means direct knowledge of the divine, without the need of mediation, but the ancient texts that have surfaced since 1945 provide no indications of how it might be achieved. Thus, Gnosticism poses great difficulty for modern seekers by its lack of any practical methods for developing direct contact and communication with God within. Nevertheless, a kind of Gnostic revival is unfolding as these long-lost scriptures get wider exposure. Many people who encounter this material are attracted by its alternative view of Christianity, as well as by the opportunity it affords to see the feminine in a new light. For all its troublesome obscurities, Gnosticism continues to stir up deep responses in many people.

CROSSWEAVE

To the Classics and Basics:

2.8 on Mephistopheles, the tempter of Faust, as an agent of deviant or counterevolutionary forces

2.9 on the traces of Gnosticism in Hermetic philosophy

2.10 on Emersonian self-reliance as a Gnostic principle of independent seeking

3.4 on Gibran's type of sentimental Gnosticism

3.6 on Gnostic and Manichean aspects in the worldview of the Cathars

Note: Though Aldous Huxley dealt extensively with Gnostic ideas in his novels, he seems to have totally ignored Gnostic source materials in compiling *The Perennial Philosophy* (C&B3.13). This is a serious omission, though understandable due to the scarcity of the materials at the time.

To Other Essays:

1.2 on Blavatsky's Himalayan masters as a kind of Gnostic elite corp

1.4 on Gnosticism in the Hermetica, especially in the Theogenic Idea (the inherence of a divine potential in us)

2.1 on the need to become self-guiding, a criterion for spiritual authenticity among Gnostics; also, on the issue of obedience versus "higher education," or spiritual development, as a learning process

2.2 on Gnostic elements in the Hermetica

2.4 on the paradigm of salvation, central to the soteric philosophy of Gnosticism

3 on Gnostic elements in alchemy, especially the work of deviant powers and the incompletion of lower creation

4 on Gnostic elements in Anthroposophy

8 on Gnosticism as the main historical alternative to Christianity, for centuries only acknowledged in its role as the underdog and scapegoat of conventional faith

11 on sexual-erotic practices often found among some Gnostic sects who viewed sexual intercourse as a sacrament

28 on the Gnostical bias of Theosophy

ESSAY 14

Great White Brotherhood

T here are few clues telling how and where the scenario of the Great White Brotherhood originated. In its modern version, it goes back directly to Madame Blavatsky; but this explains only the origin of the current scenario, not of the GWB itself. A tricky point, this. Unfortunately, those who perpetuate the scenario tend to invent its history, making it difficult to see what actual history it may have.

Scholars and historians have by now solidly established the existence of the Mystery Schools of ancient times, though it is impossible to locate or date their origins—thus leaving plenty of room for invention. Although there is little or no historical grounding in New Age circles, it accords well with personal mythmaking to incorporate the lore of the Mysteries as evidence of spiritual attainments in previous lives, even going back to Atlantis and Lemuria.

But it is one thing to accept the Mysteries, and quite another to propose a worldwide organization for them. As one account goes, there was a "Mother Lodge" of purely superhuman or "Luciferic" beings who guided humanity from its earliest stage of evolution. This gradually developed into an elite corps of half-human, half-divine leaders who presided over the various racial groups. Even historical records show that the original form of civilization was *theocracy*: rulership by Avatars or demi-Gods, such as the Egyptian pharaohs and the Chinese emperors. Viewed with an eye to the GWB, these may be seen as sacred lineages descended from the Mother Lodge.

The ultimate model of theocratic culture was Atlantean civilization, described by Plato as under the rulership of ten priest-kings. By other accounts, there were ten primary oracles, or centers of spiritual training, on Atlantis. After the Flood, migrations went out from these to all parts of the world, and the post-Atlantean Mystery Schools were established, encompassing everything from Chinese astronomy to Egyptian therapeutics to the North American Medicine Lodges. (In comparative mythology, this is called dissemination theory.) To this day, the most convincing evidence for the worldwide uniformity of the GWB is to be seen in megalithic structures such as Stonehenge, the Great Pyramid, and the Mayan/Aztec temples of Central America, which exhibit astounding similarities of geometric design and alignment.

In the occult revival of the Renaissance, there was a great deal of gossip and even political controversy about the existence of secret brotherhoods. These seem to have appeared as latter-day specializations of the Mysteries. Right up to the dawn of the twentieth century, they were believed to be influential behind the scenes of historical and cultural events. Speculations along these lines provide endless entertainment for those who are attracted to conspiracy theories.

Somewhat less programmatic, but equally conspiratorial, is the loose scheme of covert organization suggested by the legend of the Secret Chiefs behind the Golden Dawn. A paragon of sanity in this scene was the Western master Dion Fortune, who, coming from a Christian Science background and undergoing a long nervous breakdown due to what she believed to be psychic attack, countered the Golden Dawn by setting up her own secret society, the Fraternity of the Inner Light, in 1924. She wrote novels, developed a clear science of occult pathology, and used sexual magic. Her efforts to revive the Temple Mysteries were clean and noble compared to the murky power-games of most Golden Dawn participants.

Madame Blavatsky claimed to have penetrated Tibet around 1850, about a hundred years before the expulsion of the Tibetans from their homeland. This raises the "Tibetan Question": Is there some obscure relation, which has never been made fully clear, between the Himalayan masters of the Theosophical scenario and the Tibetan lamas? Although the masters who worked through Blavatsky and Bailey were in fact Hindus, the master Morya goes by the name of "The Tibetan." Yet the existing body of Tibetan Buddhism clearly does not present itself as representative of the GWB.

Other threads of association to the GWB are found in the varied and fantastic accounts of the Masonic and Freemasonic orders, some of whom claim descent from the Mother Lodge or its Egyptian outposts as late as 2000 B.C. Needless to say, wherever the GWB is cited as the power behind a present-day group, it is invested with a long and fabulous history going back to Atlantis, or even Lemuria, thus asserting an enormous claim to spiritual authority. Groups as various as the Arthurian Knights and the Kahuna priesthood of Hawaii have been described as arms of the GWB.

Rosicrucianism also claims to be an external, historical organ of the GWB. Traditionally, the Western masters who come by this brand name are attributed with the ability to direct their own incarnations in chosen periods of historical time when they are most needed. Picking up directly on their previous efforts, they are able to operate as secret intelligence agents dedicated to maintaining responsible historical and cultural continuity, exactly in the manner of the ancient initiates of the Mysteries or the *Manus* of Brahmanical tradition. Usually, they remain obscure, behind the scenes, though occasionally they appear as well-known historical figures: Benjamin Franklin, for instance, is said to have been one of several Rosicrucian agents among the Founding Fathers. His epitaph, in which he compares himself to a book that will reappear in a new edition, suggests a bold conviction concerning reincarnation.

Since the 1960s, a number of spiritual teachers have openly claimed to represent the GWB. Most notable are Elizabeth Clair Prophet, who founded the Church Universal and Triumphant in 1958, and Omraan Mikhael Aivanhov, a Bulgarian working in France since 1938. Prophet's church is busy maintaining its worldwide missions, and for years the headquarters of Bailey's Arcane School was the United Nations—fitting enough, since her detailed description of the GWB resembles nothing so much as a vast bureaucracy developed along ancient hierarchical lines.

CROSSWEAVE

To the Classics and Basics:

1.1 on one example of spiritual and ethical teaching imparted to humanity by a superhuman or semihuman being, the Chinese *Manu* Fu Hsi

1.3 on Chuang Tzu's frequent reference to Luciferic beings, or "dragonmen," who appeared in ancient times and provided the models of morality and culture to humanity in its fledgling state

2.5 on chivalry and the organization of the Arthurian Kings as a kind of sacred lineage encharged with the transmission of the Grail; also, on the possibility of viewing the Round Table as a facet of the GWB

2.7 on viewing Dante as a Western master who previously incarnated in ancient Greece as a priest of the Orphic Mysteries and returns in the Middle Ages as a lyric poet who reverses the old myth of descent: Instead of Eurydice drawing us into the Underworld, Beatrice leads humanity into the Upperworld
2.8 on occult symbolism in Goethe's long dramatic poem, confirming allegations that he was initiated into a Rosicrucian brotherhood
2.9 on Asclepius and Hermes Trismegistus as exemplary theocratic demigods acting as officiants of the GWB
2.12 on the Quiché Maya as an ancient surviving thread of one sacred lineage originating with the GWB
3.6 on the nature of the lamaistic hierarchy and the Tibetan Question
3.14 on "the League," a fictional representation of a Western arm of the GWB
4.1 on a classical account of the GWB in ancient Egypt
4.2 on secret societies behind world events in the twentieth century, with much reference to Gurdjieff, claimed by his main disciple, J. G. Bennett, to have contacted a Persian/Sufi strain of the GWB
4.6 on the initial disclosure (developed more extensively in later books) of the ancient lineage of Toltec sorcerers, which may be viewed as yet another arm of the GWB
4.7 on the evidence of megalithic structures pointing to the worldwide uniformity of occult astronomical and geometric knowledge (the sacred canon of proportions)

To Other Essays:

1.1 on the mytheme of paradise on earth, the perfect civilization ruled and guided by the Gods, taking Atlantis as its model
1.2 on the Bailey-Blavatsky scenario of the planetary hierarchy, the most recent attempt to reinstate the GWB
1.3 on planetarization as a progressive attempt to shift the GWB model from a hierarchical to a cooperative scheme
2.1 on the problematic paradigm of *guidance,* which always comes up when the GWB is considered
4 on Rudolf Steiner as a possible representative of the Rosicrucians, charged with the difficult task of breaking their long rule of strict oral transmission
10 on the dangers and attractions of cults, viewing the GWB as the great granddaddy of them all
12 on the worldwide existence of megalithic structures often taken as evidence of the global organization of the GWB
16 on the history and character of the Mysteries, viewed as separate regional arms of the all-encompassing GWB

19 on the role of the *Manu,* or culture-initiate, the exemplary officiant of the GWB

21 on serial reincarnation as a technique used by the Western masters believed to be operating in the GWB

24 on the popular conception of spiritual masters, more often than not completely aside from the GWB

27 on the universal system of symbols and images used by the GWB, similar to the occult language called Senzar by Madame Blavatsky, and possibly represented in the Tarot

28 on the soapbox where it all began

ESSAY 15

Magic

T he English scholar Sir James Frazer, author of *The Golden Bough,* once proposed that magic was a primitive system of cause-and-effect, an archaic pseudoscience. Frazer was right, though he did not sufficiently understand the dynamics. *Magic* comes from a root meaning "large." It refers to the worldview of former times, now utterly lost, in which all beings and things were felt to be contained in a womblike totality, often called the Macrocosm; magic was a control-system that drew upon the powers of the Macrocosm. It was, as Frazer thought, a primitive application of cause-and-effect, but an indirect one, quite different from what is applied in science today.

Take, for instance, the cliché of a magician who wants to cast a love spell to attain the favors of a woman. In this situation there are three factors: magician, spell, and woman. Now, the magician does not merely work the spell and direct it upon the woman. Rather, the magician draws upon a system within which he knows himself, the spell, and the woman to be included. The assumption that underlies all forms of magic is that the Macrocosm, the great world of primary causes, defined by the external seasons and the planetary orbits, works upon all things, rather like a huge mill wheel or dynamo. The method of magic, then, was to create a projection of personal will or desire (in the form of a verbal formula, rite, amulet, et cetera) and turn it over to be worked upon by the Macrocosm, which in turn produced the desired effect upon the third component—in this case, the woman. This is not cause-effect as science understands it, but a preconceived effect (devised by the magician) released into the Macrocosm (the dynamic field of all causes) and then returned as an achieved effect (enchanting the woman) in the Microcosm, the lesser world of mundane and human affairs. "As above, so below."

So Frazer was right, though he did not see the complete picture.

Magical causality, far more complex than scientific causality, was rooted in the holistic paradigm of dynamic order, the all-inclusive Macrocosm, according to a way of thinking that has been entirely lost in the analytic/ atomistic method of modern physics. Frazer's notion of "sympathetic magic," referring to the affinity between the magical rite and the object to be affected, is in fact applied by a threefold *interval* (see the Lexicon) from the device (spell, amulet, or whatever) through the Macrocosm to the person or event to be affected. This explains why ceremonial magic always had to involve a detailed reproduction, through rite and symbol, of the precise components of the Macrocosm: planetary signs and sigils; great care for the timing ("planetary hours"); the use of the cardinal points; crystals and gems; astrological, metallic, and herbological corre- spondences; et cetera. All this was necessary to project, or "seal," the microcosmic will of the magician into the "great world," and all the work of producing the magical result was then done by the great world, di- rectly, and only indirectly by the magician.

But no matter how carefully it may be reconstructed, the dynamic of magical causality is no longer convincing, because our current way of thinking has departed so far from its premises. We are apt to snicker at the abracadabra of ceremonial magic, unable to appreciate how seriously it has been brought down through the ages. Its two most current flare-ups, first in the Renaissance and then in the European Occult Revival from 1850 onward, were vastly influential among artistic and literary circles of the times. Most of what remains today, however, is the spurious popular brand of magic typically advertised in the back pages of tacky tabloids, promising the fulfillment of all your dreams and the achievement of any goal through "adeptus rituals for vigor, vitality, ecstasy, and dominance." The last word is a dead giveaway, because magic, even in its trivial modern forms, still appeals as a control-system. It is billed as the surefire method of "getting your way" in the world. It is directed toward concrete results—usually sexual satisfaction, wealth, and power over personal af- fairs.

The desideratum of wielding power assumes its most extreme form in black magic, or actual Satanism. Of its three degrees (see the Lexicon), the first involves a philosophy of selfish, separatistic dominance, a total perversion of the principle of dynamic inclusion. That practices to this end do indeed exist is becoming more and more widely recognized in America, largely through alarming news concerning the disappearance of children (about 220,000 a year) and reports of ritual abuse, perversions of sexual and excremental functions, and human sacrifice. Even the association of heavy-metal music with Satanic activities is a disturbing signal, not to be ignored, because the personality disorders that may be suffered by adolescents due to the extreme anxieties of our time can readily be directed into psychotic paths. The example of the Manson clan remains a sobering lesson in this regard, but with Manson, as with other examples of self-proclaimed Satanists, it is impossible to distinguish the deliberate and programmatic perpetration of magical atrocities—if such there be— from acts of criminal insanity.

For all its darker shades, there is a clean, legitimate tradition of magical practice as a method of psychological self-exploration and inner work. This grew out of the European Occult Revival, originating with Eliphas Levi and coming down through Aleister Crowley to Israel Regardie, the most intelligent modern exponent of magical theory and its allied psychic technologies. Crowley himself was a sensationalist and a hobbyist of black magic, rather than a dangerous psychotic specimen like Manson. He introduced the spelling "Magick" to distinguish the ancient art from the trivial entertainment of card tricks and pulling rabbits out of hats. Much of the Crowleyesque approach refers back to Egyptian ceremonial magic and hierophantic science, which he cleverly synthesized with practices of Tantric visualization and the liberal use of drugs.

In America, magic under the label of Satanism (second degree) has become known primarily through Anton Sandor Le Vey, who founded a school in California in 1966. He advocates self-assertion and hedonistic indulgence of all the passions and animal desires, leaving open the question of whether or not magic is to be applied as a control-system for dominating others.

CROSSWEAVE

To the Classics and Basics:

1.1 on a classic example of the philosophy of dynamic inclusion, in which the two poles of the "great world" are represented by Heaven and Earth (primary trigrams) and from this polarity a complete system of ethical laws is worked out, reflecting the belief that human affairs conform to a harmonious, supervening order, or Macrocosm. (In short, the *I Ching* rests on the same paradigm as magic.)

2.9 on the archaic principles of Macrocosmic/Microcosmic correspondence, tremendously influential among the intellectuals of the Renaissance who revived magic in association with Platonic philosophy

2.12 on ritual and shamanistic forms of magic, described as actions of the Gods working in the Macrocosm to produce events on earth, such as the creation of humanity

3.6 on ritual evocation and exorcism among the Tibetans, one of the best examples of the survival of magical technique into modern times

4.1 on Egyptian initiation and hierophantic science, one of the classical sources of magical technique

4.2 on the survival of magic in degenerate and psychotic forms; also on Satanism, believed to have been practiced by the Nazis

4.6 on the esoteric psychology of magic in Native American shamanism, especially as applied to altered states

4.9 on various attempts to reconstruct in modern terms a magical view of the world (that is, a dynamic interaction between subject and world that is inexplicable to the consensus-reality)

To Other Essays:

1.3 on the theme of the *paranormal* as it reveals a chaotic recognition of magic by modern thinking

2.4 on cocreation as a possible advance upon the archaic concept of magic, since it proposes creating with the Macrocosm rather than merely through it

3 on alchemy as a cocreational system, by contrast to a strict control-system

5 on the supreme holistic paradigm of all-inclusive order, often used as a code-system in formulating magical rites

6 on the magical attraction of the Otherworld

9 on the use of crystals in psychic technology, closely akin to magical theory

11 on the ancient or primitive sense of being included in a totally animated world, basic to magical theory; also, on sexual intercourse as a magico-religious rite

19 on the occult sciences, long equated with magic before both magic and occultism became discredited due to the rise of empirical science

26 on sexual magic, specifically

29 on the practice of invoking the forces of nature in Wicca, a reevaluation of archaic theory

ESSAY 16

Mysteries/Mystery Schools

B y far the greatest feat of retrieving and reinstating ancient wisdom lies in reclaiming the Mysteries. So far this has been a task largely assumed by scholars, for which there is little or no appreciation in New Age circles, due to the lack of historical perspective among modern seekers. Nevertheless, like a vast invisible ruin, the framework of the Mysteries pervades many aspects of the new spirituality.

Historically, the picture is quite clear. The Mysteries, or Mystery Schools, were ancient colleges of spiritual training. Everywhere in the high cultures of the past, from China to Mexico to Polynesia, there is evidence of profound spiritual wisdom. Of course, this should be no surprise to anyone, for humanity has always been deeply religious. What is more difficult to appreciate, however, is how this wisdom was in many respects superior to what we have today—not only due to its direct access to the divine, its practical grasp of the universal intelligence working in nature, its system of magical arts and sacred psychology, and the extent of its paranormal and mystical phenomena, but most of all due to its highly sophisticated and systematic character.

The Mysteries were programs of spiritual training, as well-organized as any college course today. The curriculum was rigorous: a long program (from twelve to twenty-one years) of preparatory discipline culminating in a series of trials, called ordeals or orgies. Since physical and mental education alone was not enough to produce a superhuman type, the Mysteries used fear and traumatic shock to effect a deliberate mutation, eventually resulting in the birth of a high genius gifted with an extraordinary constitution and paranormal skills. This elaborate program of "shock therapy" involved scaring the initiate nearly to death in order to set the higher bodies up for reimprinting. (However, nothing of the kind could or should be attempted today, since a totally different set of psychological conditions were involved.)

One of the most famous sites of initiation was the Great Pyramid of Giza, crudely assumed to be a tomb by modern archaeologists. According to descriptions given by Rudolf Steiner, Manley Palmer Hall, and Peter Tompkins, initiation in the Egyptian Solar Mysteries concluded with a three-day trance-sleep in the stone sarcophagus of the King's Chamber. In a state similar to suspended animation, the initiate endured a near-death experience, with the ego and astral bodies being lifted away so that the etheric body could be entirely reimprinted or reprogrammed, and the initiate emerged as one reborn with God-like attributes.

Secrecy regarding the Mysteries was strictly enforced by the death penalty right up to the time of phase-out, after the Advent of Christ. Nevertheless, it was widely known even among the common people that initiation into the Mysteries resulted in immortalization; that is, the elevation of the human being to the status of a God, with the potential of physical immortality, or at least life-extension. What was not known, however, was that this *result* of initiation was not its final *aim;* or perhaps it was deliberately misrepresented as the aim. The acquisition of proto-immortality and paranormal powers merely qualified the initiate to go on and accomplish the true goal—the *telos,* initiates being called *telestes,* "those who seek the goal"—which was cocreation. Thus, the Theogenic Idea consisted of these two parts: deification and the work of cocreation, with the first merely viewed as the prerequisite for the second. Both ideas were held to be too dangerous to be made accessible to the world at large.

The initiates who came through training in the Mystery Schools were qualified by their superevolved status to serve as guides and teachers in the societies of their times. They were elevated to the level of the *Manu,* a title for someone empowered to guide and direct human culture through successive stages of historical development.

The Mysteries were designated according to archetypal categories named for the planets. By one account, there was a group of planetary oracles on Atlantis that later evolved into the Mediterranean and Mystery cults of Asia Minor; for instance, the Mercury Oracle grew into the Dionysian Mysteries, remains of which can be seen in the secret caves of Malta, used for underground initiations. Primarily, however, the Mysteries were either Solar or Lunar. The Isiac (of Isis) Mysteries of the Goddess Hathor in Egypt were of the Lunar class, concerned with sexual physiology and selective breeding to preserve the special gene pool for avataric embodiment of the pharaonic line.

Variations were many and complex, for the Mysteries were highly specialized and enormously diverse in character, each school tailored to the culture and race or even the climate where it functioned. There were Hibernian, Eleusinian, Samothracian, Dionysian, Druidic, and Mithraic mysteries, to name but a few. The Chinese priest-astronomers who advised the emperor belonged to a Mystery School, as did the tribal chieftains of Medicine Lodges in North America; hence the myth of the Great White Brotherhood, implying a worldwide organization of the Mysteries.

Beyond their regional diversity, the Mysteries did indeed exhibit an amazing uniformity, evident in the megalithic ruins of sacred engineering from the Andes to the Nile. Here is worldwide evidence of the Solar Mysteries, centered on the myth of a God who comes to Earth through the Sun, and attested by a canon of mathematical and astronomical formulas astoundingly consistent from Polynesia to Persia, Ireland to Egypt. The great passage-graves of Europe and the Temple of Luxor in Egypt attest to the preeminence of the Solar Mysteries, or solar-phallic religion, showing its purest form in the Egyptian and Druidic mysteries. The very program of initiation was often based on a solar model. In the naive tale of the Twelve Labors of Hercules, there survives a remnant of the twelve-phase soul-ordeal undergone by the "Sun initiate," corresponding to the twelve constellations on the path of the Sun. By imitating the passage of the Sun, the initiate became identified with the Solar Logos and empowered to preserve and transmit the primary secret of the Solar Mysteries: the cosmic transference, or anointing, in which a God—Greek Christos, Egyptian Horus, Druidic Mabon—comes from a higher dimension through the Sun to be united with the Earth. This Christocentric myth predated historical Christianity by several thousands of years.

Attempts to reinstate the Mysteries in modern form have been proposed by everyone from Rudolf Steiner to Rajneesh, and the beat goes on. Perhaps the best way of evaluating these efforts is found in the words of Christ: "By their fruits shall you know them. . . ."

CROSSWEAVE

To the Classics and Basics:

2.3 on Socrates's conversational account of his initiation into the Mysteries of Eros by the sibyl Manitea (in the *Symposium*)
2.5 on the Mystery of the Holy Grail as treated in the folklore of the Celtic romances
2.6 on the "Mystery of Love," a difficult one often fraught with ordeals of its own, and still in progress. This designation is not inappropriate, since Gottfried of Strasbourg asserts that the love of Tristan and Isolde is a sacrament so deep and great that it equals or may even surpass the sacrament of the Christian Mass—a proposal that resulted in Gottfried's sudden and permanent disappearance when the Inquisition came to town.
2.7 on the Mystery teaching of the Celestial Hierarchies, rendered into poetic form
2.9 on the breakthrough in which the Mysteries of ancient Egypt were first made accessible to independent seeking
2.12 on a story version of the Underworld Mysteries of ancient Mexico
3.5 on a firsthand retelling of the vision quest involved in initiation among the Mystery Schools (Medicine Lodges) of the American Indians
3.14 on a fabulist account of modern participation in a Mystery School, which Hesse calls the League
4.1 on a firsthand account of the Egyptian Mysteries
4.2 on the exploitation and perversion of fragments of the ancient Mysteries by power-mongering secret societies of our time
4.6 on the revival of the Toltec Mysteries of ancient Mexico via the Yaqui sorcerer Don Juan
4.7 on Mystery teachings embodied in the lore of sacred sites and megalithic ruins, especially the Mysteries of the Grail at Glastonbury and Stonehenge

To Other Essays:

1.3 on the theme of reinstating ancient wisdom, or even updating it, as in the modern attempts at Mystery Schools such as Esalen and Lindisfarne
1.4 on the Theogenic Idea as the primary heresy of the new spirituality: "Gods in diapers"
2.2 on the Theogenic Idea and cocreation, introduced through the Hermetica as an option for independent seeking, rather than an initiatory privilege available only to the elect (hit tunes of 1471)

2.4 on the need for practical directives for cocreation

3 on the supreme paradigm of cocreation

4 on the practical directives given by Rudolf Steiner for modern application of Mystery teachings

11 on the Mysteries of Eros and the sexual symbolism of the passage-graves

12 on megalithic ruins as evidence of the uniformity of the Mysteries (especially Solar)

14 on the worldwide organization of the Mysteries, then and now

21 on reincarnation and immortality relative to the superhuman status attained by the initiates in the Mysteries

23 on shamanic practices in the Mysteries of Native America, including the Maya/Aztec complex

27 on the possible existence of a universal code or secret language held in common by the Mystery Schools in different parts of the world

28 on Madame Blavatsky's revival of the Mysteries in a universal system of "wisdom religion"

ESSAY 17

Mysticism

A lthough mystics have appeared often enough within the confines of the traditional religions—Saint Teresa in Catholicism, for instance— the personal and independent nature of their experience remains uppermost. Mysticism is the quest for firsthand intimacy with God, the Divine, the Source, the Ground. Often defiant and heretical, it accepts no substitutes, and refuses all intermediaries. If free-form mysticism were to flourish on a popular scale, organized, authoritarian religion could no longer continue to exist in its current forms.

By universal testimony, mysticism is an experience of tremendous emotional power. It is definitely a way of knowing through feeling rather than intellect, though it sometimes comes to be translated into intellectual concepts—in the profound theological propositions of Meister Eckhart, for instance. To indicate its non- or superintellectual character, mystical experience has often been described as a path of "unknowing"; whence the title of the classic work *The Cloud of Unknowing.* By the testimony of mystics through the ages, direct contact with God entails the melting of all boundaries and the complete loss of one's sense of individual identity.

Sure, but perhaps it's not all that simple. The two norms of *transcendent* and *immanent* are essential for a clear definition of mysticism. If God is transcendent, then God is not to be sought in the world as we know it but only by passing beyond it, usually in a moment of ecstatic transport. One goes completely out of oneself and beyond all accustomed mental and emotional boundaries to find God in this direction, the path of transcendence.

By contrast, other mystics have claimed that reaching the "God within" is what it's all about. If God is immanent rather than transcendent, then mystical contact entails going as deeply within one's own self as possible. This accords with the Gnostic view of God as an intrapsychic presence, in-here rather than out-there.

In both cases, the God one encounters is equally unfathomable, an immensity that swallows up the conscious mind like "the dewdrop [that] slips into the shining sea" (*The Light of Asia,* Sir Edwin Arnold); but apparently different sensations are entailed. On the path of immanence, in a moment of what Eliade called "enstatic" awareness (staying within), the mystic discovers that God is identical with the innermost "I": God and the self are one. This can be contrasted—intellectually, at least—to the transcendent experience in which God is found not in the "deep self" but in the complete and utter loss-of-self, even in the no-self. One experience involves sounding the innermost self to its depths, while the other involves dissolving the self to annihilation in ecstatic union. Though this distinction is clear enough, personal accounts of mystics of both types are often impossible to tell apart.

The word *mystes* was originally introduced into Western usage by Dionysius the Areopagite, who borrowed it from the lore of the Mysteries. While the experience of God in the Mysteries was the result of a long process of training and intense inner transformation, mystical experience is more often spontaneous, or even haphazard. It can come over anyone and it comes, like ice cream in America, in at least thirty-one flavors.

Two consistent features of mystical experience are the sense of oneness and the sensation of rapture. In some mystical transports, there is total absence of sensory content, specific images, or words. This is equivalent to what the Indian yogis call *samadhi* without seed: superconsciousness without anything to be conscious of, or "consciousness without object," as the Buddhists say. Zen *satori* is also like this: knowing everything by knowing nothing.

But in other cases mystical illumination can be fully animated, saturated with detail, as with Emanuel Swedenborg and William Blake, to name two. This is what the Indian yogis called *samadhi* with seed: knowing nothing by knowing all and everything. Apparently, totality-awareness is sometimes given in a state without content, other times in a complex configuration, with the quality of rapturous absorption (love) being common to both. More often than not, the rapture is accompanied by an out-of-body experience. This extraphysical aspect has been emphasized strongly by some mystics, such as Plotinus, who confessed to a deep sense of embarrassment at having a body at all. By contrast, there is the radical immanence of Tantric mysticism, in which the Godhead is felt to be present directly as a supernatural current streaming through the physical senses and flooding the sense organs—very much an in-body experience.

Mystics appear in all cultures and religious traditions throughout the world. The Christian mystics who have been officially accepted as saints by the Catholic church remain special cases of individuals who have sought and found direct God-contact in an altered state—something that good, decent, ordinary churchgoing folk are not encouraged to do. Since the Renaissance, many independent and secular mystics have appeared. Sufi mystics and Hasidic Jews form a distinct subgroup within the large denominations of Islam and Judaism.

With the rise of Romanticism around 1800, something called nature mysticism became a much-discussed issue. Best exemplified in the writings of the English poet William Wordsworth, it involves returning to a sense of primal innocence and communion with nature, even finding the presence of God in natural forces like the wind and light. Later inherited by the New Age, this view afforded a spiritual foundation for the environmental outlook, initially surfacing as the "back-to-nature" movement of the 1960s.

A formal technique of mysticism does not exist, but the closest thing to it is probably the devotional practices of Bhakti Yoga among the Hindus and Sufis, and some contemplative practices in Christian orders. All these only serve to prepare the individual to receive the moment of mystic illumination, which can only be invited, never demanded or coerced. Mystic transport is always looked upon as a gift of grace.

A mystic is someone whose heart has been at one and the same time broken and healed by an intimate encounter with God.

CROSSWEAVE

To the Classics and Basics:

1.3 on the famous instance of the Chinese mystic who could not say if he was a butterfly dreaming he was a man, or a man dreaming he was a butterfly
1.10 on the many mystic ways of God as understood in the wit and wisdom of the Sufis
2.3 on the four kinds of divine madness or mystical rapture described by Plato
2.5 on the mystical revelation of the Holy Grail, vividly described with many "special effects"
2.6 on the mysticism of Romantic love, in which sexual passion takes the place of rapturous absorption in God

2.7 on Dante's mystical vision of the Rose of Heaven

2.10 on the personal moods and reflections of a Transcendentalist, often tinged with mystical sensibility

3.1 on numerous case studies of mystical and quasi-mystical experiences, especially those involving *samadhi* with seed

3.2 on a careful, cogent analysis of mystical transport

3.5 on the mystical transport of a Native American shaman

3.12 on a classic case of *samadhi* without seed

4.3 on chemical mysticism

4.8 on the Hindu Bhakti path, which often leads to mystical experiences

To Other Essays:

1.1 on the perennial longing to return to a paradisiacal world and recapture Edenic innocence by communing directly with God

8 on mysticism as an alternative form of Christianity

11 on the mystical sensation of nature-empathy, believed to have been common to humanity in former times, and still common among "primitive" or aboriginal peoples today; also, on the resemblance of sexual pleasure to mystical rapture

13 on the quest for God within

16 on the programmatic cultivation of divine potential, resulting in deification of the initiate, contrasted to the haphazard nature of most mystical experiences

22 on nature mysticism among the Romantics

24 on mystical contact and even identification with God, which seems to be the main qualification of Eastern masters—raising the question of how the divine can appear in person in our midst

25 on the play element in Sufism, which has been defined as a "mystico-ludic" path

26 on radical immanence and infrasensory mystic rapture

30 on Zen experiences of sudden enlightenment as examples of *samadhi* without seed

ESSAY 18

Native American Spirituality

T o appreciate Native American spirituality requires, first of all, an understanding of its setting. This calls for looking into what is meant by "oral culture."

A good example is the religious tradition of Hinduism, Indian spirituality and philosophy from the East. The Vedas are among the most ancient surviving texts of Indian religion. They come down to us from remote times, and even though they appear at a very early time (around 600 B.C., by most estimates) in written form, they faithfully preserve the legacy of an oral tradition that may predate the writings by a few thousand years. Just as it is still difficult for us, modern as we may be, to comprehend how volumes of information can be stored in a pinhead-sized computer chip, it is equally (or perhaps more) difficult to appreciate how an oral transmission of such longevity could actually persist and remain consistent.

By analogy, Native American spirituality is, today, where Oriental/ Indian spirituality was in 600 B.C. It is a lost culture we are just now beginning to retrieve. For the most part, it is an oral tradition that has not yet come to be written down. Of the countless American Indian tribes and nations, many had no written form of language, and most of those that did held it to be sacred and never to be disclosed to the white man. Now there is a revival of sorts taking place in Native America, akin to the fast-growing interest in shamanism. Tribal teachings and folklore are being restored and imparted on several fronts, and the figure of the American Indian is emerging from its cigar-store cliché into an important profile in the new spirituality. This is happening as tribal methods and attitudes are being converted into more globally accessible teachings, as in the case of the Hopi prophecies, which are now seen to apply for the whole planet, rather than for an obscure and isolated tribe living on mesas in the southwestern U.S. American Indian spiritual leaders often figure prominently in the world peace movement.

Geographically, both the Americas are included here, spanning from Alaska to Tierra del Fuego. This is a vast terrain, largely uncharted—the New World of modern spirituality. It encompasses a huge variety of tribes, each with its unique ethnological features and its own special lineage of aboriginal teachings. Since the late 1970s, revivalists are appearing within each Indian nation—Cherokee, Hopi, Apache, Sioux. Even though so much of their culture was obliterated by the genocide in the nineteenth century (and, in some cases, the twentieth), some Native Americans are keenly aware of the powerful resources they carry within themselves. The enormous process of healing and retrieval now being undertaken involves to some extent drawing upon ancient roots, but even more so it seems to call for a courageous act of reinventing everything from scratch. The younger representatives, especially those who work through poetry and painting, are giving definition to their long-suppressed culture through personal creativity that often expresses the mood and mystique of Native America in ways true to their roots, yet without direct reliance on the mystic and ritual aspects of their spiritual lineage.

In this vast mosaic of tribes and cultures, there are some common concerns and themes. From the time of the pre-Romantic social philosopher Rousseau, the native inhabitants of America were idealized as the "noble savages" who lived in a state of primal innocence, before the deceits and contradictions of the human-made "social contract." Today the theme persists, and Native Americans, such as the Hopi, are often cited as the best example of a people who live in close communion with nature, who revere and serve the earth as Goddess, observing the wondrous cycles of nature with ritual dances and initiations. All the local cultures of the Americas are deeply animistic, and most of them recognize a monotheistic deity, a single great spirit without, who is often not so well-known as his lesser counterparts, such as the Trickster, Coyote. The curious term "medicine" is a transliteration of the generic root *mana,* referring to spiritual power, supernatural force. In the mythology and sacred psychology of Native America, this concept is still closely allied with the perception of natural and vital phenomena—for instance, the wind in the skies and the breath in human nostrils, brought together in the ritual communion of the pipe (according to one tribal legacy, a gift from White Buffalo Woman, a Manu and benefactor of the tribes). Respect for the great spirit animating all things is an ideal in the holistic philosophy of the New Age, exemplified by the ancient peoples of Native America. Medicine men of the past are becoming planetary shamans of the future, leading non-native seekers on their own vision quest for a sense of purpose and dedication to the earth as a whole.

Empowerment through ritual and the alliance of "animal powers" is a main theme in Native America, though a somewhat problematic one that holds the danger of falling into power games and even power politics. Traditionally, the various tribes were known for squabbling, and today power struggles between medicine men (or women) are fast becoming a part of planetary folklore. Fantastic stories of shape-shifting, telepathy, and manipulation of power-objects (including crystals) are common in this realm, though the sensationalism often serves to conceal the deeper issue of exploitation, to which these ancient but fragile cultures are prone. As the lure and lore of Native America become more popular, trivial and ripped-off versions of the old wisdom are inevitable, and it remains a lesson of discrimination for incoming seekers to choose between the true medicine and the snake oil.

On a deeper level, the destructive use of spiritual power and knowledge is a theme buried deep in the strata of Native American culture. Especially in the Maya/Aztec complex of Central America, we encounter the vestiges of ancient sorcery and the terror-ridden mytheme of the Dying Sun, a kind of counter-Logos to the Solar Mysteries. Just as the Aztecs sacrificed their people in huge numbers to feed the Dying Sun so that the world would not end and their people could survive, we in the West have established the policy of nuclear deterrence in which we save the world from destruction by amassing enough firepower to destroy it a thousand times over! The responsibility to clear or redeem this psychotic complex comes along with the spiritual inheritance of Native America.

Claiming a lineage straight back to Paleolithic times, with a sophisticated body of knowledge regarding the relation between humankind and nature, including elaborate calendar systems, herbology, and priestcraft, Native American spirituality is a treasure trove just now becoming accessible. It remains to be seen if the "big medicine" it preserves offers the right prescription for the grave spiritual ills afflicting the land of its birthright.

CROSSWEAVE

To the Classics and Basics:

2.12 on a rare and extraordinary retrieval of oral culture, the creation-story of the Quiché Maya retold in simple, vivid language that fully preserves its supernatural magic

3.5 on the extraordinary vision of a medicine man who witnessed the destruction of the Indian nations

4.6 on the revival of aboriginal sorcery in Central America, an important step in the emergence of neoshamanism

4.9 on altered states of the kind experienced through the ritual use of psychotropic substances, a practice common to almost all the Indian tribes of the Americas

To Other Essays:

1.1 on the nineteenth-century influx of utopian sects into the New World, ironically illustrating the quest for Paradise by groups of people who were apparently oblivious to the unspoiled way of life of the aboriginal people they were displacing

1.3 on the themes of Gaia and ancient wisdom, for which the Native American cultures are often taken as exemplary models

2.3 on the discovery of Mayan and Aztec ruins in Central America, synchronous with the Occult Revival in Europe

6 on the lost oral lore of the Celts, also now undergoing a retrieval; may perhaps be viewed as the—or at least *one*—current European equivalent to reviving "native culture"

9 on crystals as power-tools

11 on reverence for the earth as a Goddess, typical of all animistic cultures of the past

12 on sacred sites, such as medicine wheels, closely associated with the revival of Native American culture

14 on the long-standing lineages of the Medicine Lodges, possibly viewed as arms of the Great White Brotherhood in the ancient Americas

16 on the Solar Mysteries of Scandinavia, the Mediterranean, and Asia Minor, contrasted to the Mysteries of the Dying Sun among the Maya and Aztecs

22 on the idolization of primitive or aboriginal cultures in Romanticism
23 on the shamanic revival, closely associated with the current interest in Native American spirituality
29 on the comparative aspects of Wicca and aboriginal spirituality in the Americas

ESSAY 19

Occultism

W̲ hen the word *occult* came into use in English about four hundred years ago, it simply meant something that defied rational explanation, like a bizarre accident. Within a short time, however, it took on the connotation of something ancient and mysterious, perhaps involving lost wisdom superior to common knowledge. Then, coming down to recent times, it has taken on the dark tones of something sinister, suggestive of black magic and dangerous cults.

Now, it would be a strange pass if so much counterfeit money were circulated that people came to doubt the existence of real money. Yet this is precisely the problem with *occultism,* the most misused and misunderstood word in the vocabulary of the New Age. Fundamentally and exactly, it refers to the practice (ism) of *cult*ivating hidden forces. In the distant past, right up to the time of the European Enlightenment, the opinion of these hidden forces held by the general public and by the students and "faculty" of the Mystery Schools was quite different from ours today. The modern attitude toward the un- or underdeveloped potentials of the human mind and body is acutely skeptical: Either it denies flat out that these potentials exist, or it views them as the speculative fodder of weirdos and mystics, not to be taken seriously.

Nothing could be farther from the truth, even though occultism today is in so critical a state of disorder that practically none of its traditional elements appear in credible forms. Its reputation is deeply muddied, but essentially it is something quite simple, solid, and utterly practical. To teach speed-reading, for example, is legitimate occultism; so are feats of bodybuilding, or the exercises for controlling involuntary functions demonstrated by Indian yogis. An athlete who can run the mile in less than four minutes or swim the English Channel is achieving something extraordinary through the discipline of *cult*ivating inner potentials that remain totally undeveloped or even unadmitted in the average person. This process of exceeding the ordinary, or norm, by the development of hidden potentials that are present (though latent) in the average person is occultism, pure and simple.

By another approach, occultism may be defined as any practice leading to the development of that which eludes the obvious. For instance, we know that memories are constantly being recorded in the very moment of immediate experience, but even the experts know next to nothing about how this occurs. Occult teachings, both bogus and legitimate, claim to explain the obscure dynamics of such processes as memory, dream-construction, and subconscious association. They are concerned with everything that makes us act, feel, and perceive, through mechanisms we do not normally fathom: You can move your arm to lift a glass and drink without knowing anything about how you actually do it. According to the occult theory widely applied in the ancient Mysteries, if we can be taught to experience these nonobvious mechanisms directly and consciously, then we will also come by special knowledge of how to manipulate and extend our latent capacities in rare and unusual ways.

Practical occultism, in the original and legitimate sense, was the pure science of unfolding human potential, even to the extent where it passes over into divine potential. And progressive occultism was the method of directing culture and masterminding history, carried on by the initiates and adepts of former times, as the story goes. . . . According to esoteric thought, the fruits and attainments of one cultural era are passed on to the next not by accident or casual association: From ancient times this large-scale continuity was the mission of the Manu, the supreme lawgiver and culture-initiate, the guide and director of the inner potentials of the social dynamic in each era, whose symbol was the ark.

Probably the last clear-cut historical evidence of this activity of deliberate culture-transmission is to be found in the Gothic cathedrals of France. According to the planetary folklore emergent with the new spirituality, these magnificent structures bear witness to the vast collaborative effort of a society inspired and directed by masters of high accomplishment, perhaps the last reliable representatives of the Great White Brotherhood. Since the Enlightenment, the secret societies have apparently disintegrated and occultism has fallen into disrepute. With the decline of the Mysteries this special elite corps of evolutionary agents disappeared— some say to work telepathically while remaining behind the scenes in the remote vastness of the Andes or Himalayas—but in the New Age there is speculation of replacing them with a global network of coworkers whose common efforts (group-work) are described in various terms by the leading visionaries of the day.

Since the 1960s there has been a steep rise in pop occultism, including all kinds of ways to increase your psychic or sexual powers overnight, or reprogram your bad habits. More recently, subliminal self-alteration using audio and video tapes is becoming quite popular. Although these quick-fix methods try for an air of high-tech sophistication, for the general public occultism has become degraded into something identified with trashy ads in the tabloids, if not with serial murders and the fantastic beliefs of the Nazis.

There may be no way to eradicate these connotations, wipe out the shades of fraudulence and evildoing, and restore occultism to its right and respectful status. What may be called classical occultism was a vast body of theory and practice applied for centuries to fostering the spiritual growth of a few select members of the human race, and it depended totally upon the framework of the cultural Mystery Schools, where it was preserved. With the loss of this framework, occultism has either died or degenerated into a grotesque caricature of its former glory. The place it might assume in the modern world seems to have been taken over by paraphysics, on the one hand, and the high-tech behavioral sciences, such as neurolinguistic programming, on the other.

CROSSWEAVE

To the Classics and Basics:

2.1 on Gilgamesh, the pure archetype of a culture-hero who undergoes an initiation ordeal for the sake of advancing his culture
2.5 on Parzival, the special example of someone who wins the role of culture-initiate by dint of his own blundering efforts, rather than through bloodline inheritance, thus illustrating the paradigm of self-initiation
2.8 on Faust as an example of the corruption of occultism into personal power-tripping, especially the initial scene when Faust is visited by the Spirit of the Earth, against whom he turns in his selfish quest for gratification
3.6 on the ritual and magical occultism of Tibet, often bordering on the black arts

4.1 on an example of classical occult training in the Mystery Schools of ancient Egypt

To Other Essays:

1.2 on the attempted reinstatement, on the planetary scale, of occult organization of human society, either through the masters (Blavatsky) or free-lance agents (Rudhyar)

1.4 on the problematic distinction between human potential and divine potential

2.1 on the difficult issue of being guided (as humanity was, according to the occult program of the initiates of the past) by contrast to becoming self-guiding (as illustrated in the story of Parzival)

2.2 on the Theogenic Idea and cocreation as fundamental principles of occultism

4 on the issue of practical directives for sociocultural growth, as addressed in the lifework of Rudolf Steiner

5 on the far chance of using astrology to develop an agenda or timetable for directing cultural and historical changes

10 on the degeneration of occultism into dangerous weirdo groups

14 on the supreme example of an organization supposed to exist for the purposes of occult training of a select few and spiritual guidance of humankind as a whole

15 on the theory and techniques of magic as identical, in the original and legitimate sense, with occultism

16 on the curriculum of occult training in the Mysteries

21 on the importance of reincarnation as the method used by Western masters to insure their ongoing influence in preserving the continuity of cultural and historical growth

22 on the demand of the Romantics to claim and explore the innermost potential of the individual, thus initiating an experimental path of self-actualization, which previously had been exclusively (and secretly) cultivated in the schools of occultism

26 on so-called "sexual occultism"

ESSAY 20

Recovery

O ne of the consistent concerns of the New Age is group effort based on spiritual principles. Within the vast spectrum of such efforts, recovery stands as a unique and bountiful movement, a realm of many mansions and diverse streams.

At present there are estimated to be about 120 recovery programs in the United States, some of which have worldwide extensions. All are based upon the same set of fundamental principles set down in the twelve-step model that originated with AA, Alcoholics Anonymous, founded in 1939. Since the late 1970s, recovery has burgeoned in America into a movement of nationwide dimensions, largely through popular absorption of teachings on addiction and dysfunctional families. There are now such groups as CA (Cocaine Anonymous), OA (Overeaters Anonymous), and ISA (Incest Survivors Anonymous), to name but a few.

All the programs begin with the first step: admitting one's powerlessness over something—whether it be a substance (like alcohol or sugar) or an emotional fix, a psychological addiction of any kind (to sex, eating, spending money, obsessing over relationships). No one really enters recovery until he finds the humility of admitting that his life is "unmanageable," no matter how it may appear. From this follows the second step: affirming that a power greater than oneself can restore one to sanity. This is not a religious dogma, and those in recovery take great care to view it as a spiritual program rather than a religious cult, even though the assertion of a higher power (as each one chooses to conceive it) does appear to meet the need for a religious grounding among many people who have become terribly disillusioned about God, especially in America.*

*On the distinction between spirituality and religion, see the Afterword.

All who participate in recovery share a common sense of not having fully lived out the true potential of their lives, or even of not having lived their *own* lives at all. It is widely accepted that most addictive/dysfunctional behavior grows out of family-of-origin situations. This diagnosis implies the Adult Child Syndrome, a core element in many of the programs. It seems, ironically, that we must receive (learn) self-love from others before we can give it to ourselves. The adult whose self-love was inadequately nurtured and supported as a child faces a serious lack of self-worth throughout later life. (Thematically, the Adult Child Syndrome tallies closely with the mytheme of the Divine Child in world mythology, taking the latter as the symbol or representative of the precious, original self of each one of us.)

Seeking to overcome this handicap, people in recovery become deeply committed to clearing the past and establishing a new foundation for living fully in the present. They undertake what might be called therapeutic cognition of karma: seeing into the life-lessons that were encoded, as it were, in family-of-origin situations, parent/child roles, and emotional conflicts of early years. Their goal is to outgrow these patterns, so that their innate potentials are no longer hampered by them. The essence of recovery is karmic and emotional healing, fostered through the sharing of life stories at meetings and entering treatment for intensive work in clearing anger, grieving, and dismantling guilt complexes. Although people in recovery often go into individual therapy, recovery itself is adequate therapy for the great majority of participants, with the support group serving as a kind of superpersonal instrument of healing.

Within the diversity of the programs, certain common elements are evident: the pervasive emphasis on addiction and codependency (sick love), the necessity of overcoming shame, facing the dangers of abuse and self-abuse, setting personal boundaries, mastering the mechanisms of delusion and denial, letting go of compulsive forms of control, and learning surrender to life itself as the greatest teacher. The actual methodology involved is very loose and freely adaptable to all personal variations of need and pacing. People attend meetings simply to share their experiences and troubles, with no analysis or advice given. Enormous respect is shown for personal independence, and the unconditional acceptance that each member has his or her own autonomous process for recovering endows solidarity to the group that extends that acceptance. Members share a deep sense of belonging to a group-spirit with a power and identity all its own, yet the framework is so loose, informal, and nonauthoritarian that there is minimal danger of brainwashing and the usual cult problems. Recovery is not a cult and remains, for the most part, remarkably immune to the dangers of becoming one. It is a group-support system for transformative experiences of communion, catharsis, and self-change.

In its strong emphasis on shame, recovery reveals itself to be a belief system based on the paradigm of the Fall and its corollary, redemption. In a brilliant turn of phrase, one of the leading apostles of the movement has said that the sin of Adam and Eve was not that they did something wrong, but that they felt shame at what they had done. Shame itself, and not something done to make us feel ashamed, is the "original sin," according to this view. In taking shame/sin as what prevents us from becoming all that we can be, recovery proves to be closely allied to the human potential movement, or may even be viewed as a kind of ground-swell of the same impulse that inspired that movement. People in recovery are very clear in working upon basic human capacities such as honesty and self-confidence, in keeping with the emphasis on human potential rather than divine potential. The ultimate aim of the recovering person is to become fully human.

By a radical reorientation to their life histories, those in the "New Time" enter a lifelong path of self-renewal, even self-regeneration—one of the primary ideals of religious striving down through the ages. Though recovery in its principles and methods steers clear of religious structures, as already noted, it does serve the innermost human needs that religions claim to meet. The atmosphere of group sessions is not unlike the feeling of old-time camp meetings with the members witnessing and confessing in testimony to the power of their conversion. Also, the emphasis on forgiveness and making amends in recovery links it closely to similar directives found in the teachings of New Thought and para-Christianity.

CROSSWEAVE

To the Classics and Basics:

1.4 on the oldest surviving body of ethical and moral teachings that are purely secular, exclusively concerned with the cultivation of human potential

2.7 on a poetic illustration of the Fall, with special emphasis on the judgment syndrome of Christianity (Dante describes a sinner suffering in the nine circles of Hell or, not much better off, sweating it out in Purgatory), by contrast to the insistence on a nonpunitive higher power in recovery

2.10 on self-reliance, learning from life itself and other points of down-to-earth wisdom relevant to the discipline of recovery

2.11 on the psychology and ethics of para-Christianity, often adopted as a philosophical framework for recovery

3.2 on the psychology of conversion

3.10 on the quest of the Adult Child

To Other Essays:

1.1 on the sociological impulses toward recovery and regeneration exemplified in the utopian movements of the nineteenth century

1.4 on the problematic distinction between human potential and divine potential

2.4 on the paradigm of the Fall and the contrast between finding reality and fixing it

5 on astrology as a tool for discovering the meaningful design of one's life, an aim shared by those in recovery

8 on para-Christianity

10 on the dangers and attractions of cults, from which recovery appears to be largely immune

16 on catharsis and regeneration in the Mysteries, following a programmatic system of initiation in total contrast to the self-initiatory work of recovery (which, however, does involve parallel experiences of catharsis and regeneration)

22 on the Romantic challenge to change human nature—something that appears to be attempted in recovery, especially in the specific task of mastering codependency

ESSAY 21

Reincarnation

H ere's a tough one, for although reincarnation is not an idea to be easily dismissed, it is also seemingly impossible to verify. Recent public interest in the subject was originally sparked in 1956 with the appearance of a case study, *The Search for Bridey Murphy,* by Morey Bernstein, which became a best-seller and was reprinted in two dozen translations. After some sensational controversy, it was exposed as a fraud, but since then, hundreds of far more convincing studies have appeared, and past-life regression has become a standard practice in many New Age life-therapies.

Yet reincarnation remains as much a riddle as ever—both its mechanism and its purpose being totally obscure.

In the past, reincarnation has been widely accepted as a fact of life more often than not, though it has been viewed in quite different ways by different cultures. The Celts, Hindus, Chinese, Greeks, and American Indians all held diverse opinions on the matter. Among the Celts it was common for the great bards, like Taliesin, to recite their previous incarnations (some human, others not) in "riddling poems" full of beautiful and perplexing allusions, and for the Celtic warriors it was common to pledge repayment of a debt in the next life, in the event of death in an upcoming battle; but this matter-of-course attitude was the exception rather than the norm. Among the Greeks, Chinese, and many other ancient peoples, there persisted the far more common belief in a shadowy afterlife with no certain prospect of reembodiment in human form.

The unclear link between immortality and reincarnation also figures in many ancient views. Most high cultures of the past were theocratic, with the populace at large regarding the pharaoh, emperor, or shah as a God who temporarily assumes human form. Upon death, the Avatar returns to a state of immortality but may enter the world again by a successive reembodiment in the same genetic lineage: Amenhotep I, II, III, et cetera. This concept of restricted immortality with the option to reappear in human form was preserved in many parts of the world for millennia. The same privilege was granted to kings and heroes, but never to ordinary folk. Probably originating in Paleolithic times, as our ancestors observed the cycles of death and reproduction in the animal kingdom, this concept of rebirth appears to be the oldest pervasive belief about reincarnation in evidence. One of the main reasons Christianity had such a shattering impact on the classical world is that its promise of a perfect afterlife for everyone who entered the faith removed this ancient concept from the realm of theocratic privilege and turned it over to the ordinary person.

But immortality—the state of continuing existence in a superworld after death, as Christianity promises—has to be distinguished from recurrent embodiment, the literal meaning of reincarnation. These might be contrasted as final immortality, removed from this world, and ongoing immortality, the capacity to return repeatedly to this world, to keep reliving. Views on the value and purpose of the latter differ enormously. In orthodox Buddhism and Hinduism, rebirth into this world is viewed as an affliction due to a state of deep confusion. Liberation, the dominant paradigm of Eastern spirituality, supports the act of getting off the wheel (of rebirth). But in Hinduism, rebirth is sometimes viewed as a matter of duty, while in Buddhism the Bodhisattva's vow asserts a commitment to continue in the cycles of reincarnation until all sentient beings gain the opportunity to be liberated. In some schools of Buddhism, the term "rebirth" is used in a purely psychological sense to describe a continuous process of blind identification with the not-self, which binds us to suffering and condemns us to repeat the error habitually until we are released through Enlightenment.

In the Western Mysteries it was taught that reincarnation was indeed a cycle of necessity—but one that could be turned, through initiation, into a ritual of responsibility. In the Orphic Mysteries, the interval between Earth-lives was clearly presented in the scenario of the journey through the planetary spheres, illustrating how the immortal soul undertakes a long quest into other worlds after death, with the aim of eventually returning to Earth with new gifts to offer. From this teaching Plato extracted his doctrine of the "anamnesis": the theory that all we know is rooted innately in the memory of what we knew before birth when we lived in the realm of the divine ideas, archetypes, or planetary spheres.

In the present day there is practically no concern for this question of preexistence, or if there is, it is not consistently and systematically pursued in any well-known disciplines of the new spirituality. Rebirthing and past-life regressions aim to explore material from past lives, not from the life-intervals. Also, current interest has shifted to post-existence, with a lot of attention going to after-death and near-death experiences. But for the initiates in the Mysteries, the interval was crucial. They sought immortalization of the soul-consciousness so that they could consciously undertake this journey and return to Earth at a self-appointed time. Through their commitment to cocreation and culture-initiation, they were morally bound to practice serial reincarnation in successive periods of history. Blavatsky claimed something like this for the mahatmas, whose successive historical appearances were described by Alice A. Bailey in some detail. Rudolf Steiner also disclosed the reincarnational biographies of some leading initiates of the West. Needless to say, fantastic claims have been made and the matter has now passed over wholly into the realm of planetary folklore and free-form mythmaking.

The unique curious instance of the reincarnating lama, or tulku, in Tibetan Buddhism seems to preserve the old system of theocratic privilege intact. Just how lamas manage to direct the timing and location of rebirth has not (to my knowledge, anyway) ever been disclosed by the Tibetan masters.

Reincarnation is serious business, deeply enmeshed with ideologies of redemption and liberation, ideas about karma and destiny. Is it a punitive system of cyclic sentences, a reward-system sanctioned by superhuman powers, or an educational program that affords the opportunity to individuate, to grow and learn, and ultimately contribute to the continuity of human evolution? What are we seeking, *relive* or *relief*? And do we relive, again and again, to serve the earth and humankind out of love, or are we driven by blind necessity or sheer delusion?

Although none of the existing answers to these questions may be true or verifiable, it seems to be extremely difficult for human nature to endure living, even if only once, without recourse to such answers.

CROSSWEAVE

To the Classics and Basics:

1.3 on Chuang Tzu's playful outlook on reincarnation as apparitional fun

1.6 on Lord Krishna's long discourse on rebirth

1.7 on the four delusional aspects of human awareness, by which we are falsely led to believe we exist when in fact we don't (in the *Diamond Sutra*)

1.8 on the elaborate process of death by stages, followed by the even more elaborate process of rebirth through the six *bardos*—a major document on the mechanisms of rebirth

2.1 on a typical quest for the final immortality of the culture hero, or Avatar, in Western tradition

2.7 on a vision of the afterlife, leading to blissful absorption into the bosom of God (the ideal of Christianity)

2.8 on Satanic immortality, its fringe benefits and contraindications

2.9 on the immortality of the soul achieved by those who undergo initiation, repeatedly described in lofty terms, though the desirability and conditions of rebirth are left unexplained

2.10 on Emerson's personal convictions about having lived before and living again, shared by many Romantics

3.6 on the fabulous feats of the Tibetan tulkus

3.9 on a vivid account of spontaneous past-life memories

4.1 on the reincarnational biography of a priestess in the Egyptian Mysteries

4.5 on the biography of a modern-day tulku

To Other Essays:

1.2 on the Himalayan masters, sometimes described as assuming different historical personalities, other times as maintaining themselves for hundreds of years in the same body

1.3 on reincarnation as a main theme of the New Age

1.4 on reincarnation viewed, perhaps, as a periodic change of diapers

2.4 on the contrasting ideologies of "relive" and "relief"

3 on the quest for physical immortality among the Chinese alchemists, contrasted to the commitment to relive among Western alchemists

5 on the elaborate system of astrology, applied by some to investigate patterns of rebirth and answer questions regarding karma and destiny

ESSAY 22

Romanticism

I n many ways, Romanticism was the forerunner of the modern spiritual movement. In Europe it peaked at the very time the first utopian socialist communities appeared, yet Romanticism itself was largely a venture of solitary eccentrics who left no coherent program for achieving the immense changes they proposed.

In the widest sense, a Romantic is someone concerned with the divinity of the human as it may be realized and developed in complete independence from external religious authority and organization.* Corollary to this proposition is the belief that human nature can be changed. Of course, this is not a new idea, but it was always a highly guarded one. It is none other than the Theogenic Idea of the Mysteries, which the Romantics seem to have stumbled upon by accident, intuition, or inspired guesswork. By the ancient viewpoint, the potentiality of an immortal soul was granted to everyone, but the privilege of evolving it to its fullest scope was reserved for a few select specimens of the human race who were willing and able to undergo the long and rigorous training program of the Mystery Schools.

With the printing of the Hermetica, this prerogative became available as a free option of self-initiation, open to all independent seekers, though it remained largely (for three centuries, at least) the special esoteric pursuit of a small community of intellectuals. Then the Romantics appeared and proclaimed it in native tongues from the rooftops. They announced the advent of popular spirituality, the religion beyond all

---

*This is, by the way, my personal definition, worked out with much difficulty after a great deal of probing and pondering. I must confess a deep identification with the problem of Romanticism, so this attempt to define the indefinable ought to be, if not authoritative, at least authentic.

pregiven forms of religion, the path of what German theologian Friedrich Schleiermacher called *Selbstbildung,* "self-formation." Because it attempted to take over the perennial themes and issues of traditional religion and adapt them to its own program of passionate self-exploration, Romanticism was pithily described by one critic as "spilt religion." Yes, it was that for sure, but it was also spilt Mysteries, even spilt Gnosticism.

So the Romantics, somehow, spontaneously discovered the ancient principles upon which the Mysteries were founded, and attempted to put these into practice, yet without the age-old guidelines for moral-emotional preparation, or the discipline that was formerly required for initiation. They took upon themselves, by the sheer force of inner inspiration and creative intuition, the work of God-birthing and the sacred responsibility for cocreation. In a completely independent and secular way, liberated from all previous forms of religious and metaphysical discipline, they attempted to achieve a kind of superhumanism, which culminated tragically in the Nietzschean "Superman," a concept taken up by the Nazis and adapted to horrific ends.

Freed from the age-old rules and restraints that defined spirituality and the relation between human and divine, the Romantic venture turned out to be tremendously fruitful for the art and literature of the world, but also tremendously dangerous, leading a good many of its key agents into despair, degeneration, drugs, and suicide. Its final phase, called the Decadence, was a time of magnificent literary and artistic flowering in which a great many of the leading figures were deeply involved with esoteric wisdom and alternative paths.

Today, Romanticism is largely a matter of oblivion to the world at large. The term shows up in high school and college classes on certain poets and painters, but the true spiritual dimension of Romanticism is rarely fathomed, even by the best scholars on the subject; nor is Romanticism generally appreciated in the New Age, which derives so much from it. The Romantics were the first independent voices to speak openly and in purely Western terms of "becoming God," rather than merely maintaining a relationship to God as one of the Creator's creatures (medieval paradigm), or as a noble personality serving God as an instrument of moral and intellectual virtue (Renaissance paradigm). The poet Shelley wrote, "Let us believe in the kind of optimism in which we become our own gods." Like all the other leading Romantics, he believed that the strongest evidence of a God-like potential in human nature lies in the power of the imagination. This is the key faculty to be developed, the basic tool of genius inherent in each and every one of us.

But although the Romantics set fantastic challenges to develop human potential toward divine potential, they left no clear program for achieving them. Coleridge, who coined the term "self-realization," was an opium addict and chronic escapist who dreamed of fabulous schemes but never completed anything. Many Romantics were to suffer similar fates, going into oblivion through drugs or merely through the preference for what they could imagine over what actually existed. Romanticism itself was a chaotic movement polarized and eventually devastated by all kinds of inner contradictions. The Romantics lacked the necessary patience, consistency, and discipline to realize the grandiose prospects they envisioned. They were also monumental hypocrites, often living lives in grave contradiction to their views. Worst of all, they seem to have glorified their personal sufferings, instead of developing the kind of universal compassion for suffering that is promulgated in all traditional religions; and by acting out their passions in morbid and extravagant ways, they left us with the stereotype of the Romantic artist as a self-destructive egomaniac.

Though Romanticism lies in ruins, its heritage remains very much with us. A great deal of popular culture—women's fiction and the genre of the thriller, adventure movies, and TV dramas, "Lifestyles of the Rich and Famous"—is nothing but trivialized Romanticism. On a deeper level, the foundation of the modern environmental movement lies in the nature mysticism of the Romantics (via the Transcendentalists), just as modern psychology is founded in their passionate explorations of the inner life. They pioneered mythmaking and individuation, and their glorification of the "noble savage" set the mood for today's advocacy of aboriginal cultures.

Contrary to conventional usage of the word, *romantic* in the context of Romanticism has nothing to do with love; or if it does, then the meaning is troublingly unclear, because the theory and practice of love were the weakest aspects of the Romantic vision. With few exceptions (such as the French novelist Stendhal, and the late English Romantic D. H. Lawrence), the psychology of romantic love was not understood by its (alleged) exemplars, which is perhaps one of the strongest factors contributing to the downfall of Romanticism.

CROSSWEAVE

To the Classics and Basics:

2.3 on one of the great classical influences in Romanticism, Plato's *Symposium,* which was translated into Italian by Ficino in 1483, after he had completed his work on the Hermetica, and immediately became an item of fashionable parlor talk among the European nobility who aspired to understand the nature of love in its twofold relation to the human and the divine

2.5 on the numerous sexual and romantic adventures of the Arthurian knights, popular with many Romantics who looked back to the Middle Ages as a time of personal heroicism

2.6 on the primary Western conflict of love versus passion, a troubling issue for the Romantics

2.9 on cocreation and the Theogenic Idea, ancient teachings discovered spontaneously by the Romantics, who seemed, however, unable to handle them safely

2.10 on the reflections of the main representative of Transcendentalism, the American branch of Romanticism

2.11 on nature mysticism and the spiritual retreat

3.1 on spontaneous cosmic consciousness among such well-known Romantics as John Keats, William Blake, Honoré de Balzac, and Walt Whitman

3.3 on the life-wisdom of the German lyric poet Rilke, a late Romantic who managed in some ways to fulfill (or even redeem) the lost causes of Romanticism

3.9 on the personal revelations of a Romantic poet and painter who figured strongly in the Irish Literary Renaissance

3.11 on the Romantic quest for the meaning of life

3.15 on the rise of fascism and the inversion of the Romantic philosophy of vitalism

3.16 on the psychology of modern love as a problem inherited from the Romantic movement

To Other Essays:

1.1 on the Romantic longing to reenter Paradise

1.4 on the problematic distinction between human potential and divine potential, never successfully clarified by the Romantics

2.1 on the Romantics' insistence on believing what you discover for yourself, rather than what you are told

2.3 on the Occult Revival in Europe, which unfolded in the aftershock of Romanticism and culminated in the Decadence

2.4 on the necessity of reevaluating the whole issue of religious experience, a challenge set but not solved by the Romantics

6 on the Irish Literary Renaissance, which involved a number of leading Romantics of the day, including Irish poet and mystic W. B. Yeats

12 on the fascination for ruins, which came into vogue around 1800 through the Romantics

13 on the Gnostic imperative of independent seeking, often expressed in the credo of Romanticism

14 on the question of Western masters and secret societies, which may have been influential in "leaking" occult teachings to the Romantics: For example, it is known that Goethe's personal physician was a Rosicrucian, and even as late as the Decadence many writers and painters, such as Paul Gauguin and Henri Matisse, are known to have been directly influenced by self-styled initiates and esotericists of the day

16 on the rigorous program for spiritual training in the Mysteries, totally ignored by the Romantics, who apparently hoped to achieve the results of initiation without going through the work

24 on the distinction between a God-realized person and a person who is actually a God

25 on the concept of human personality as an expression of the divine, perhaps the solution to Romantic "superhumanism"

26 on the hedonistic pitfalls of sexual mysticism, which seem to have been highly attractive to some of the Romantics

28 on the mother lode of modern spirituality, known to have exerted a tremendous influence upon late Romanticism and its outgrowth in Modernism: Both Wassily Kandinsky and Piet Mondrian were deeply involved with Theosophical teachings, for example

ESSAY 23

Shamanism

W hen its present-day practitioners eagerly claim that shamanism is the world's oldest religion, they probably are not exaggerating. Religion is a means of binding back to something—and shamanism may well be what it purports to bind us back to.

In America, starting in the early 1970s, the shamanic revival became a very hot item on the New Age agenda. Speaking in 1974, Mircea Eliade described it as "the most archaic and most widely distributed occult tradition" in the world, and a source of tremendous fascination for modern youth seeking alternative paths. His masterwork, *Shamanism: Archaic Techniques of Ecstasy,* is still the basic text on the subject, though dozens of volumes on pop shamanism have now appeared.

Shamanism is an outstanding example of the revalorization of ancient wisdom and aboriginal cultures. Unlike a good many other revivalist trends in the New Age, however, it sets itself firmly upon historical, archaeological, and folkloric precedents. The magnificent cave paintings of southern France, dating from as early as 35,000 B.C., are often cited as evidence of shamanic art and ritual. With shamanism, the mythmaking, meditations, and rituals undertaken by its modern practitioners have a deep and solid foundation in an enormous spiritual legacy. Evidence of shamanic beliefs and practices shows up all around the world, from Australia to Alaska, Polynesia to Scandinavia. All of it points back to a time when vitality, as manifested in human life and the animal kingdoms, was felt to be imbued with supernatural power—known as *mana, orenda, wakonda,* and dozens of other names. Long before spiritual power became a concept—an abstraction tagged as *Atma* by the Hindus, *Pneuma* by the Greeks—it was felt and seen and encountered as a force at large in the world. For thousands of years before religion as we know it was created, humanity lived in a state of intimate participation with nature and the surrounding cosmos. In the infancy of humanity, shamanism arose as the natural expression of our primeval awe, innocence, and vulnerability in the face of supernatural powers. It was and still is a vitalistic religion of appeasement and empowerment.

Throughout the world, the main features of archaic shamanism are amazingly uniform and consistent. Culturally, it is viewed as a mystical vocation entered by an elect group of individuals (both men and women) who are mysteriously chosen by the spiritual powers. Invariably, the one who becomes a shaman is initiated into the calling by the ordeal of sickness—a sudden or mysterious illness, a fit or attack of mental instability, often accompanied by hallucinations, and sometimes verging on a near-death experience. In less severe instances, the calling comes through unusual and powerful dreams. In any case, the paranormal abilities of the shaman-to-be are awakened and a different person emerges—a figure of spiritual authority and magical power.

In its archaic forms, and in many aboriginal cultures where it persists to this day, shamanic initiation produces a tribal hero, deeply feared and respected. He or she is a healer who effects magical cures, a soul-guide who uses "magical flight" to enter the Underworld or ascend to the Pole Star, a sorcerer who communes with the animal spirits in their native language, and a fierce adversary who may engage in psychic battles and take psychotropic drugs to access dangerous occult realms. Pervasive to all these pursuits is the shaman's capacity to enter ecstatic states by the superexcitation of the life-forces—hence the derivation of the word (see the Lexicon). On the one side, the figure of the shaman merges into the spiritual warrior, a popular role in the new spirituality; on the other side, it closely resembles the mad yogis and wild women of Tantrism, who battle with psychic phantoms and pass all-night vigils in graveyards, dancing on the exposed corpses.

In any case, shamanism is—now as it ever was—a sensational calling, full of bizarre attractions and not immune to spiritual glamour.

In its modern renaissance, shamanism has been reclaimed and redeveloped, initially, by anthropologists and legitimate scholars who saw it as a way to satisfy humanity's need for rediscovering the sacred. According to the prevalent view, shamanism is the ancient methodology of direct contact with the sacred or numinous. It affords personal access to the divine or supernatural powers at large in the world, as well as those concealed within the human mind and emotions. Great pains are taken to distinguish it from voodoo, devil-worship, and sorcery in all its negative connotations—though this would seem to be an impossible task, really, because all the silly and sinister aberrations of shamanism are as rooted in its fundamental premises as are the legitimate forms. Above and beyond all else, shamanism is a path of *empowerment,* impossible to divorce from the inevitable pitfalls of power-tripping. In fact, the ongoing and often vicious episodes of psychic and magical warfare waged by Native American medicine men and some of their modern followers are by now a favorite item of planetary folklore.

In its current revival, some aspects of ancient technique and ritual are being literally restored. A modern practitioner will generally adopt the shamanic drum, mask, and costume, and may accumulate magical talismans like feathers, bones, and crystals, all to be used in solemn rituals for passing over into an altered state. Some contemporary practices make extensive use of astral travel and lucid dreaming to reach the "other side" and perhaps effect changes in this world through acts performed over there. Modern shamans are extremely diligent in studying the ancient and aboriginal lore, which they often adapt to modern situations with amazing ingenuity and sophistication.

Mythologically, shamanism centers on the paradoxical image of the wounded healer. This archetype, because it seems to reflect the spiritual tragedy of modern humanity in a deeply poignant way, may well be the root of shamanism's enormous appeal.

CROSSWEAVE

To the Classics and Basics:

2.1 on a classical version of the hero's quest, involving a shamanic descent into the Underworld
2.12 on fabulous tales and adventures among supernatural beings, passed down in the oral tradition of the Quiché Maya by a long-standing lineage of shamans (jaguar-priesthood)
3.5 on a dramatic first-person account of initiatory illness and the shamanic revelations it produced
3.6 on many wonders and weirdnesses encountered among Tibetan shamans
4.6 on the revival of the old lineage of Toltec shamanism in central Mexico
4.9 on the resemblance between shamanic experiences and the psychological disruption of the seeker who attempts to go beyond the consensus-reality

To Other Essays:

9 on the use of crystals for healing and lucid dreaming, enormously popular in neoshamanic practices

11 on the sense of living communion with the earth and direct access to supernatural powers

12 on medicine wheels and other megalithic ruins, often associated with shamanic practices

15 on magic as a way of drawing upon the workings of the super-earthly realms (macrocosmos), contrasted to shamanism in which direct access is sought to the supernatural powers *within* the natural world

18 on aboriginal and revivalist aspects of shamanism in Native America

25 on techniques of ecstasy in Sufism, contrasted to those found in shamanism

26 on Tantrism, which may be viewed as a specialized form of shamanism directed to the exploration of the supernatural potentialities inherent to human sexuality

29 on nature worship in Wicca, distinct from the ritual supernaturalism typical of shamanism

ESSAY 24

Spiritual Masters

P erhaps there is no idea in the entire range of New Age interests that
has had so powerful an impact on Western thinking as that of spiritual masters. The willingness to believe in such masters and the eagerness
to revere them can be viewed as a response to Nietzsche's gloomy an-
nouncement that "God is dead." This news, delivered at the end of the
last century at the very moment the first migration of Indian masters was
hitting Western shores, has been overthrown today by the testimony of
many people who believe there are those among us who have actually
"realized God," or who embody divinity on Earth—the widest and loosest definition of a spiritual master.

The prototype of a master is the Avatar, a divine being who appears
widely in worldwide mythology, and specifically in the Hindu myth of
the Ten Avatars of Vishnu. The Avatar is a world-savior, a definitely
superhuman being who descends into embodiment on Earth to perform
a deed of service or salvation. In the mythology of the Mayan Indians,
for instance, Hunab Ku is the divinity, the actual God, who assumes
embodiment in the high priest Kinebahan, who founds the lineage of the
Ah Kin, the Solar Priesthood. Similar examples abound all through world
myth, though the distinction between the actual God and the human
Avatar of the God is not always so clear.

With the Avatar, there is certainly a God in the works, a superhuman
entity who assumes human form. But with spiritual masters as they have
become known in the West in the last hundred years, the distinction is
often blurred. Yet a "God-realized" person is not to be confused with
a God: It is a human being who has achieved an exceptional relationship
to God, to the Divine Being—someone above and beyond the usual run
of people.

Traditionally, spiritual masters always come out of a specific lineage.

This goes back to times before history, to the scenario of the ancient priesthoods and holy sages. Most of the Eastern mythologies describe human beings of high spiritual attainment, like the Rishis of ancient India, or the Imams of Arabia. Then, coming down into the time of historical records, there is evidence of many spiritual lineages that claim these mythical figures as their founding fathers. Thus the lineage of the Rishis, at first purely mythical, carries through into the time of the first historical sages and from there right down into the modern sages who appear in the West—though the continuity is purely hypothetical and cannot in any case be fully proven.

Maharishi Mahesh Yogi, the founder of Transcendental Meditation, for instance, claimed to represent a line of descent going back directly to the Indian sage Shankaracharya, who lived either in the ninth or the second century A.D.(scholars disagree), and from him all the way back to the legendary prehistorical Rishis. By this he implied a direct, oral, person-to-person continuity for the lineage—a high claim of authenticity. The same thing is frequently cited in the traditions of Zen: direct oral transmission from one master to another, down the centuries. Another well-known lineage is the special case of the *tulkus,* the reincarnating lamas of Tibetan Buddhism.

While the idea of a timeless spiritual lineage is impressive to many Westerners, it does not figure largely in the most recent crop of masters to attract wide followings: Muktananda, Sai Baba, Sri Chinmoy, Rajneesh. In their cases, popular appeal depends upon the master being viewed as a special God-realized person, regardless of how one got to be that way. In rare cases, a master may be a Westerner whose attainment is believed to equal that of the Eastern prototypes: Da Free John (previously Baba Free John, born Franklin Jones).

Far less known, and difficult to assess, is the question of purely Western masters, initiates who direct their own rebirths and appear in successive historical periods, sometimes as famous figures but more often as obscure agents working behind the scenes. In this curious area, claims of who-was-who are often incredible, historical conundrums and conspiracies loom large, and the problem of how to track serial reincarnations remains unsolved.

The issue of spiritual masters is—or ought to be—deeply problematic for the Western mind, because in the case of the Eastern masters it involves the tremendous question of how we imagine divinity on Earth, God in human form. How does God make an "in-person" appearance in our midst? This remains a great challenge for the modern seeker, though all too often the naive and uncritical acceptance of masters by Westerners has left us, for the most part, quite blind to the exciting possibilities of the question.

CROSSWEAVE

To the Classics and Basics:

1.6 on the appearance of "God in person" as Krishna
1.9 on verbatim sayings of a Ch'an master of the tenth century
2.7 on the appearance of a master as an anima-figure, Dante's Beatrice
2.8 on the dangers of taking the Devil himself as a master
3.8 on a firsthand account of searching for the masters
3.12 on the spiritual lineage of one of the most loved modern masters, Yogananda
4.1 on a dramatic account of a classical master-pupil relationship in the Egyptian Mysteries
4.8 on devotional attachment to a master

To Other Essays:

1.2 on humanity's introduction to the Himalayan masters by Madame Blavatsky
2.1 on the distinction between being guided and becoming self-guiding, a tough question associated with the masters, who sometimes claim to answer it
2.3 on the course of events that brought the Eastern masters to Western shores
10 on the dangers of blind submission to masters
14 on the conspiratorial theory of the masters
16 on the original role of the masters as lawgivers and culture-initiates who emerged from the Mysteries
22 on the Romantic imperative that we must become our own masters, even our own Gods
28 on the Theosophical Society as an external organ of the masters
30 on the peculiar character of the master in Zen

ESSAY 25

Sufi/Sufism

[A]lthough its elusive and magical character makes Sufism—or Sufi, as it is known among its adherents—almost impossible to define, it helps to see it as an expression of the Eastern paradigm of *play.* Essentially, Sufi is a path-of-union, a way of ecstasy. Like its Indian cousin, Tantra, it is oriented toward achieving a state of total and blissful absorption in God. Along the way there is a lot of fooling around and flirting with God, which gives substance to the rumor that the better part of Sufi may be in the foreplay.

It is somewhat inaccurate to call Sufism a sect within Islam, although there do exist definite sects or Sufi orders in the Middle East and by extension in America. But more than a sect or a movement, Sufi is a mystique that invites the seeker to participate in an invisible, pervasive community of spirits. Although there is a great deal of disagreement among authorities as to whether Sufism existed before the time of Mohammed, almost all insiders attribute to it a fabulous longevity. To view it merely as a mystical splinter group located uneasily within the troubled bosom of Islam is certainly too limiting, for Sufism shows all the signs of an ancient native mysticism that has evolved into a sophisticated mystique. It is a technique of ecstasy, comparable to shamanism on the one hand and Hindu Tantra on the other, but with the emphasis on surrender rather than empowerment.

Sufi may be described—though never ultimately defined—according to two primary aspects: the ritual side and the magical side. Ritually, Sufi consists of long and arduous practices of meditation and chanting, which lead eventually into ecstatic states. Some of these, such as the *zikr,* involve a rigorous suppression of the separatistic ego, while others use trance and dance to ease the practitioner beyond the normal boundaries of self-awareness. Since the seeker is taught to view God as "the Beloved" and surrender totally to the divine embrace, unitive rapture in Sufi is often fraught with erotic overtones.

In short, the Sufi actually attempts to become the lover of God. Many of the classical Sufis were closely associated with the Troubadours in France and Spain, producing a cloudy mix-up of mystical and sensual love. There is a hedonistic strain in Sufi, reflecting the belief that one who experiences God as lover will be free to celebrate that love through indulgence in all sensual things. In this view, sex and wine assume a eucharistic value, and there is evidence of this sybaritic variant of Sufi being taken to wild extremes. But for the most part the extravagant language celebrating alcoholic and sexual intoxication in Sufi poetry is purely symbolic, referring to states of emotional and spiritual ecstasy rather than literal indulgence. For instance, the well-known poetry of Omar Khayyám rhapsodizes over "a loaf of bread, a jug of wine and thou." Here the eucharistic substances of the Christian mass (bread and wine) represent the body and soul of the Sufi, and the "thou" is God, the divine.

There is an elaborate and subtle philosophical message in Sufi, which represents in many respects the high flowering of Islamic religious thought. At its historical climax in the thirteenth century, Sufi was dominated by mystics like Ibn Arabi, a master who explored the complex and arduous process of reaching direct, ecstatic union with God by sharing the suffering of God. This is called theopathy, or compassion for God. Sufi here shows its heretical side, because it asserts the exact opposite of the conventional emphasis on God's compassion for humanity and it even asserts that God created the human race so that there would be someone to empathize with it! In this respect, Sufi remains essentially opposed to traditional Christian teachings, which demand that we show reverence and appreciation for God's interest in our suffering.

Thus, Sufi not only affirms the paradigm of *play* over *suffering,* but it turns the paradigm of suffering on its head.

On the magical side, Sufi is a quest for the ultimate dream-experience: experiencing life itself as a dream. In this sense it is very close to Hindu Tantric mysticism and Bhakti Yoga practices centered on the myth of Vishnu, the world-dreamer. In Sufi, however, there appears to be no supreme entity who dreams the world—there is only the conspiracy of all dreamers. One of the great attractions of Sufism is its nonrational, ambiguous, and elusive mood. This is symbolized in the recurrent image of the fabulous Garden of Roses, a mystical retreat found by those who enter into the dream-state while awake. Passing into the "twilight zone" where the divine freely interpenetrates the sense-world is always described as the experience of being caught up in a gentle waft of exquisite perfume. The Garden is a Sufi version of the Otherworld, far away and yet somehow present in this world, like the land of faeries and eternal youth, Tir-na-Nog, described in Celtic mythology.

The image of the winged heart and the fantastic spinning of the whirling dervishes both express the dynamic aspect of the rapturous awareness every devoted Sufi is seeking, but total loss of one's identity in God does not, paradoxically enough, seem to be the ultimate goal. There used to be a lot of argument as to whether or not the human soul can retain its personal qualities after death, or upon being dissolved into God, as "the dew drop slips into the shining sea" (Edwin Arnold, *The Light of Asia,* a long poem on the life of the Buddha). At the height of the Middle Ages the Western mystic Thomas Aquinas disputed this with the Arabian philosopher Averroës, who denied that "personal immortality" is possible, since all elements of personal existence are reabsorbed into the Godhead upon death. This issue is crucial in Sufi teachings (such as those of Hazrat Inayat Khan), which affirm that personality is an enduring quality of the divine presence. This is the deepest and most beautiful aspect of the Sufi outlook, and may provide the solution to the problematic psychology of personal love and the theme of superhumanism, which so tormented the Romantics.

To date, several Sufi lineages have established themselves in America and there are numerous free-lance masters. The magical aspect of Sufi lends itself to wonderful jokes and anecdotes, such as the stories of Nasruddin, as well as to global conspiracies such as those of Idries Shah, who claimed that everyone from Shakespeare to Einstein was a Sufi in disguise. At its far end, Sufi develops into a kind of spiritual clowning, for the Trickster (whether divine or human) is the ultimate adept of play.

CROSSWEAVE

To the Classics and Basics:

1.10 on the Sufi version of *The Canterbury Tales*
3.4 on poetic philosophy by a Lebanese dreamer widely reputed to be a Sufi
3.9 on an alternative view of access to the dreamworld

To Other Essays:

2.1 on Sufi as the alternative path within Islam

2.4 on the paradigm of play, contrasted with the paradigm of the Fall, which dominates conventional religion in the West

22 on the Romantic imperative of the superhuman, which elevates the human ego to a God-like status without allowing for the inherence of divine qualities in the personality, as Sufi does

23 on archaic techniques of ecstasy directed toward empowerment rather than surrender

26 on techniques of sexual mysticism leading to states similar to those experienced in Sufi

30 on the enigma of the personal self (divine or delusional) as viewed in Zen

ESSAY 26

Tantra

I f eroticism is a worldwide garden of earthly delights, its profusion evident from Polynesia to Provence to Peking, then Tantra is the rarest strain in the garden, the finest flower of Eros—and perhaps the last, dying on the vine.

The word *Tantra,* when originally introduced to the West in 1799, meant something strange and sinister. It was applied to exotic scriptures found among the vast amount of Indian lore that was then being absorbed by European scholars. At first sight, the teachings contained in the Tantras drew comparison to black magic and medieval rites of exorcism by then well documented in Europe. Even going by the testimony of the Hindu commentaries, these scriptures were to be viewed as morally question- able, and quite dangerous. To top it all off, it soon came to light that the Tantras advocated sexual intercourse as a rite of union, a sacramental act allowing the divine to manifest itself in human form.

Now, there is probably no more sensational claim in the world than to say that God, the divinity who is both ultimate self and original source of all creation, can be reached on the wave of sensuous rapture generated in the act of sexual intercourse. Sexuality and spirituality have always been carefully separated—not only in the Christian morality of the West, but in all fundamentalist belief systems, including Buddhism and Islam— but in Tantra they are completely fused.

Philosophically, Tantra is a worldview based on the paradigm of the Fall, which, however, takes the conditions of that event as the supreme opportunities to reach spiritual awakening. "As one falls to the ground, so one lifts oneself by the aid of the ground," says a famous scripture. To use sexuality and the physical senses in the service of spiritual awakening is the aim of every Tantrika, not unlike the eucharistic conversion of the sense-world found among the Sufis. In accordance with the play paradigm, Tantra takes the world as the dream of Vishnu and holds to a doctrine of radical immanence, asserting that the Godhead is present to us directly in pure sensation. Sure, but when was the last time anyone felt pure sensation?

Since its popular phase, when the psychedelic generation of the 1960s discovered free love and the *Kama Sutra* almost in the same week, Tantra has automatically come to mean ritual sex. But Sexual Yoga, as it is sometimes called, is a minor part of Tantra as a whole. The full body of teachings encompasses two main schools, Hindu and Buddhist Tantra, the latter including the Tibetan varieties. Most well-stocked metaphysical bookstores display dozens of translations of rare and difficult Buddhist and Tibetan texts, many of which claim to present Tantra, but in the Buddhistic/Lamaistic canon, the word applies almost exclusively to mental disciplines into which sex does not enter. A great many of these works never mention sexuality at all, and although the icon of the *yab-yum* (sacred intercourse) is ubiquitous, it is always interpreted as a symbolic image indicating the union of metaphysical principles (Buddha and consort, compassion and means, Shiva and Shakti, Spirit and Matter, et cetera).

Hindu Tantra, on the other hand, faithfully preserves the deep currents originating from the ancient wellspring of Oriental eroticism, as does its Chinese counterpart, the Tao of Sex. It consists of three aspects: the metaphysical and cosmological teachings; the Bhakti aspect or devotional mysticism centered on the passion between Krishna and Radha; and the explicit sexual disciplines that give Tantra its notorious reputation and come down to us, completely vulgarized, in the Hindu marriage manual, the *Kama Sutra.* Among the leading agents of the Occult Revival in Europe from the middle of the nineteenth century onward, the third aspect became something of a personal obsession (with Aleister Crowley, for instance), resulting in a hybrid form of "sexual occultism," which still thrives in a few strange cults. It shows up today among daredevils of the new spirituality who openly advocate the use of sex as a sacramental tool for inner work and radical self-transformation. Likewise, some revivalists of Wicca are said to use "sexual magick" extensively in their ceremonial rites of empowerment.

The true metaphysical teachings of Hindu Tantra are hard to access, but enormous efforts toward presenting them openly to the West were made by the great revivalist Sir John Woodruffe, whose masterwork, *The Serpent Power,* is still the primary text on Kundalini Yoga. The meditative ritual of raising Kundalini up through the seven intracorporeal centers *(chakras)* was the ultimate technique of ecstatic union followed by yogis down through the centuries. Often practiced by solitary meditation in mountain caves, it was also performed as a sexual rite, usually with the man being instructed and initiated by a woman. Thus we find the exotic tradition of "temple prostitution," widespread in the Far East and into the West as far as Asia Minor and even Greece, where there was a cult of Aphrodite and Eros at Corinth. In all probability, the sensational custom of "woman-worship" comes down from matriarchal times when woman was viewed not only as the source of life, but as the "sacred whore" whose sexuality was the gateway to spiritual awakening. It was developed into a subtle mystical art by the Sufis, who used woman as a sort of lens to catch a glimpse of divinity, and it seems to have been taken up in a purely spontaneous way by the Troubadours, those notorious woman-worshipers who often disguised themselves as womanizers (or vice versa?).

In the ultimate rite of Tantric intercourse, the man and the woman imagine each other as God and Goddess, reinforcing the visualization with rituals of touching, anointing with perfumes, holding postures, and more. By riding the ebb and flow of their rapturous sensations without giving themselves up to physical orgasm, they reach a state of superexcitation that is at the same time an absolute calm, the still point in a whirlpool of oceanic bliss. This practice is said to be rejuvenating in the extreme. It may even involve subtle processes of physiological alchemy in which hormones and sexual secretions undergo a deep transmutation. Special rites using the sexual secretions for sacraments were known to have been celebrated by some of the Gnostics.

This and other fantastic claims often come along with Tantra, which—if they were true and made known to the world at large—certainly might draw a lot of converts, if not inspire a new Inquisition.

CROSSWEAVE

To the Classics and Basics:

2.1 on a famous instance of initiation by a prostitute
2.2 on the Goddess Aphrodite, the main deity in the Mediterranean cults of eroticism

2.3 on the Mysteries of Eros (in the *Symposium*), an old Western variant of Tantra

2.4 on Tantra-like practices in the Mysteries of Isis

2.6 on irresistible erotic attraction (the "love-potion"), considered essential to Tantric practice, though it must be ritualistically controlled

2.9 on various allusions to sexual intercourse as a sacramental rite (passage cited in E2.2)

3.6 on Tantric skills of exorcism and supernatural trickery among the Tibetans

3.12 on Kundalini Yoga as it is practiced by yogis who do not take recourse to sexual union with a woman

3.15 on the sexual experience of Christ (the greatest taboo in the world?), discussed by a modern psychologist and pioneer of sexology who was heavily persecuted for his views

3.16 on Tantra-like theory and practice among Sufi mystics and Troubadours of the twelfth century

To Other Essays:

1.1 on Tantra-like practices among the utopian socialists of the nineteenth century

1.4 on Gods in diapers, sometimes known to consort with Goddesses in black-mesh stockings

2.4 on Teilhard de Chardin's conversion of the paradigm of the Fall, possibly comparable to the aim of Tantric sexual intercourse: the primordial pair, Adam and Eve, representing the perfect essence of man and woman before the Fall, unite and enter the flow that restores them to long-lost unity with the Godhead

3 on alchemy, in which the image of sexual union (called the *coniunctio*) appears as often as the yab-yum does in Tantric art

11 on the worldwide phenomenon of eroticism

13 on the crucial figure of the Fallen Sophia, embodied in Mary Magdalen, a woman reputed to have been a prostitute, but viewed by some Gnostics as the most intimate spiritual ally and carnal consort of Jesus Christ—an example of what might be called erotic Christianity

16 on solar-phallic religion, probably the most deeply guarded aspect of the ancient Mysteries

17 on the often-observed similarity between sexual and mystical rapture

25 on hedonic mysticism among the Sufis

29 on the sexual emphasis in witchcraft, both ancient and modern

ESSAY 27

Tarot

I n all that can be said by way of explaining occultism, esoterics, hermetics, theosophy, metaphysical science, and the ancient wisdom in its countless variations, there is one simple premise that is often overlooked: namely, the idea that life is a school. This view has been promulgated in various ways down through the centuries, though most often a bit indirectly, using the image of a specific tool of schooling, the book. This was an important symbol among the Rosicrucians, whose writings refer constantly to the "Book of Life."

Surely this idea is not strange or hard to grasp. We commonly speak of "reading" people and situations—yes, but how far, or how deep, does this go? Gestalt psychology is a recent science in which life-situations are viewed as pictures that tell us stories about ourselves, or reveal the stories we are telling ourselves (our inner myths). Long before literacy was common and the written word was available in any form, there may have been a primeval science of gestalt psychology based on the condition of human faculties in an earlier, more childlike stage, when picture-thinking, as Rudolf Steiner called it, was the norm. Today, the Jungian work and other disciplines that use imagery and visualization are aimed at getting us to think and feel in pictures.

If there really is a pictorial script for accessing the deep inner language of the "universal mind" or "collective unconscious," then the Tarot may be the best translating device ever invented. The Tarot deck—sometimes called the Book of Thoth, after the legendary Egyptian hierophant, Thoth, known as Hermes to the Greeks—consists of a complete code-system for probing and interpreting the meaning of life, especially in its deeper grain, where recurrent patterns and archetypal images are active. If astrology remains the most long-standing and popular method of finding order and meaning in life, Tarot runs a close second. In fact, in most

Tarot systems, the two are closely associated, with the twenty-two Major Trumps often correlated to the ten planets and twelve signs.

Nothing definite is known about the origin of the Tarot, and its practitioners, quite typically, tend to invent fabulous histories for it. By one account, the imagery of the Major Trumps originated in the Egyptian Mysteries as a set of huge frescoes illustrating spiritual principles and tests, said to have been painted on the walls of an initiation hall located deep in the body of the Sphinx at Giza. Other histories give the cards an Arabian origin. Historians agree that the first known reference to the cards was made in 1480 by an Italian writer who referred to them as having been brought from North Africa. Upward of a hundred decks are available today, most of them of quite recent invention. The best known are the Marseilles, the Crowley, and the Rider-Waite decks.

Though there are many variations of structure and imagery in the modern decks, the prototype of the Tarot is consistent with numerical principles of ancient standing. The full deck of seventy-eight cards is divided into twenty-two Major and fifty-six Minor Trumps, with the latter broken down into four suits of Wands, Swords, Cups, and Pentacles, corresponding to the Spades, Diamonds, Hearts, and Clubs of modern playing cards. This exemplifies the classical model of the four Elements found in all ancient metaphysical systems and now reinstated in the "quaternary" of Jungian psychology. Each suit runs through a progression from one to ten, culminating in the four Court cards—King, Queen, Knight, Page, and variations (for instance, Crowley inserts a Princess). The Minor Trumps refer to social and personal matters as they run their course from initial impulses (Ace) to completion in the world (Ten), with the Court cards usually read as specific types of people involved, or projections of the personality of the querant.

The Major Trumps, on the other hand, represent crucial stages of experience, lessons of self-realization or life-changes of a long-term significance. The symbolism of these cards is highly complex and syncretic, combining imagery from many areas of world culture and mythology. In and of themselves, the Major Trumps are always viewed as a comprehensive model of experience, a complete and self-contained allegory of life. By one popular interpretation, the Fool is designated both as Trump 0 and 22, set apart from the other twenty-one. It represents the human spirit in a state of total innocence and spontaneity, naive and unsuspecting, ignorant of its own true nature before it enters the school of life (zero), and then emerging wise to the ways to the world and fully aware of its own innermost powers at the end (twenty-two). The twenty-one intervening stages are interpreted as a linear course of tests and realizations, or as a more complex arrangement such as a three-leveled model of seven recurrent lessons, through which the Fool progresses. Further elaborations of the main set are developed by drawing upon more and more correlations, including everything from the sacred Hebrew alphabet to the twenty-two amino acids in human physiology. The master scheme of the Major Trumps is totally convertible with other archetypal models such as the Cabalistic Tree of Life, used extensively in ceremonial magic; the signs and planets in astrology; geomantic figures, and even the *I Ching*. Each of the Major Trumps is so rich and complex in imagery that it presents an almost inexhaustible storehouse of meanings.

Due to its extraordinary consistency and depth, the Tarot is truly a sophisticated tool for reading the patterns of life and detecting the options, opportunities, and challenges that it poses all along the way. Unfortunately, the Tarot often suffers from trivialization, being used for silly feats of fortune-telling, rather than for elucidating life's ongoing lessons of growth and change.

CROSSWEAVE

To the Classics and Basics:

1.1 on the Oriental master scheme, or Book of Life, correlated to the Tarot by Aleister Crowley

2.2 on the imagery of Greek mythology, some of which is incorporated into the Tarot (Eros as the cupid in Trump Six, the Lovers, for instance)

2.9 on the extensive teachings attributed to Thoth-Hermes, legendary inventor of the Tarot

3.7 on the stages of life and the theory of types, two modern psychological concepts that relate intimately to the theoretical basis of the Tarot

3.9 on spontaneous clairvoyant recall, revealing images in the Akashic Record, which has often been posed as the ultimate source of the Tarot archetypes

3.10 on a popular version of the Fool as the Divine Child, an archetypal figure in world mythology

4.1 on the doctrines and principles of initiation in the Egyptian Mysteries, often related to the main archetypes of the Tarot

4.4 on the modern dominance of stereotypes and media images, contrasted to the archetypal images provided for self-instruction in the Tarot

To Other Essays:

1.1 on the usual progression from archetype to cliché

2.2 on the disclosure of the Hermetica, writings attributed to Thoth, at almost the same time the Tarot cards are said to have surfaced in Italy—a notable instance of historical synchronicity

5 on the master scheme of astrology, highly regarded and closely studied by C. G. Jung, though the Tarot might have given him even a deeper view into the collective unconscious had he cared to investiate it

11 on the Great Goddess, who appears in many guises in the Tarot

13 on the Gnostic scenario of the Fall, which has been interpreted as the basis of the Fool's journey through the Major Trumps; in fact, the Fool is often shown on the verge of stepping off a precipice

14 on the worldwide secret organization that may have used the Tarot for its universal code-system—something like a symbolic/alphabetic version of IBM

15 on pathworking in ceremonial magic, often practiced by using the Major Trumps in correlation to the pathways on the Cabalistic Tree of Life

16 on theogenesis and cocreation, the main principles of the Mysteries, represented in the Tarot by the Magician (1) and the World (21)

ESSAY 28

Theosophy

L̲ike an abandoned mine, Theosophy is rarely visited by modern seekers in quest of spiritual treasures. Yet as the Lexicon amply shows, Theosophy supplied a good many of the terms in use today, as well as basic themes and principles no longer directly considered, though they inform current interests on all levels. It staked the claim for ancient wisdom and reinstated the paradigm of guidance as one of the most crucial and problematic issues of the New Age.

Madame Blavatsky herself remains a fascinating and enigmatic figure. If nothing else, she was certainly one of the greatest channels of the ages, though it remains a matter of personal opinion whether some or all of her phenomena were bogus. Massive and largely unreadable, her major works include *Isis Unveiled* and *The Secret Doctrine,* plus a dozen volumes of letters, notes, and essays. Much of this material is said to have been received telepathically from the mahatmas, especially "Morya," her personal master. The two main works contain allusions to and quotations from thousands of hard-to-find sourcebooks in ancient religion and philosophy, seemingly too vast for Madame B., who was no scholar, to have collected by herself. The books were sensational best-sellers in their time, largely due to the daring challenge she threw in the teeth of the scientific materialism then prevailing. Everyone in the New Age today who argues the case for ancient wisdom against the follies of modern knowledge is standing on her soapbox.

Blavatsky and Colonel Henry Steele Olcott founded the Theosophical Society in New York in 1875. In his memoirs, *Old Diary Leaves,* Olcott describes the cavalier moment when he lit her hand-rolled cigarette at their first meeting in upstate New York, where they were on hand to witness an extraordinary display of spirit-knockings and table-turning by the Fox sisters, typical of the high vogue of Spiritualism. Later they established the world headquarters of the Society where it still remains, at Adyar, just outside Madras on the southwest coast of India. A tablet in the main hall states the three objectives of the Society: to form the nucleus of a "Universal Brotherhood of Humanity," to encourage spiritual studies, and to investigate the occult or unexplained powers latent in nature and humankind. Other plates bear the emblems and images of the world's religions—Judaism, Christianity, Buddhism, Jainism, Hinduism, Sikhism, Taoism, Zoroastrianism, Confucianism, Shinto, Islam, and Baha'i—as well as the square and compasses of Freemasonry, cited as the oldest occult brotherhood. The motto of the Society appears next to the Seal of Solomon, surrounded by a serpent swallowing its tail: "There is no religion higher than truth."

It is known that Madame B., adventuresome spirit that she was, traveled widely, but her alleged visits to Tibet are semilegendary, the stuff of planetary folklore. Even if she did not actually manage to penetrate that remote land, she did apparently delve into deep territory previously inaccessible to anyone in the West. The main body of Theosophical teachings seems to have been derived from the secret traditions of the Brahmins, the elite priest caste of India. It is notable that Blavatsky's mahatmas, though they reside in the remote fastnesses of Tibet, are of Hindu (or Aryan) stock. Given that to this day Brahminical teachings are closely reserved, Madame B. seems to have mined deeply at rare diggings. Theosophical teachings on cyclic evolution, encompassing Yugas, Kalpas, Rounds, and Globes, are tremendously elaborate, matched only by the prodigious time-reckoning feats of the ancient Maya and Aztecs in America. Nevertheless, the general idea of a master plan for guiding humanity through successive cycles of cultural and spiritual evolution originates here—in its modern form, at least. Like so much of Theosophy, this is largely theoretical and schematic, with little or no indications of how it might be applied in practical directives. This demand was taken up in earnest by Rudolf Steiner, who broke from Theosophy after a dozen years and went on to found his own movement, far more solidly oriented toward practical contemporary applications of ancient wisdom.

In its loosest sense, the term "gnosticism" applies to Theosophy, but in a peculiar counter-Christian variant. Madame Blavatsky and her collaborators (Annie Besant, Leadbeater, and Sinnett) all worked from a cosmic scenario that included the workings of deviant forces in the world drama. Almost as if to antagonize Christians, Madame B. insisted that the Demi-urge of the Gnostics, the lesser God who produced the material-sensorial world, was identical with Jehovah of the Jews. *Lucifer-Gnosis* was the title of the most important Theosophical journal, further emphasizing the heretic bias of Eastern intuitive seeking against the mass appeal of Christian ideology.

At the dawn of the twentieth century, Theosophy had a membership of over one hundred thousand worldwide. Its influence and appeal declined somewhat after the Krishnamurti affair (see the Lexicon). If it is largely ignored by modern seekers, it nevertheless deserves recognition for establishing the modern spiritual movement as a global event. It leaves us with the troubling legacy of the master plan, elaborated by Alice A. Bailey into the scenario of the planetary hierarchy. Today, this is occasionally reinvoked by high-profile channels and advocates of conspiracy theories, but even for those who never heard of the Himalayan masters, the program remains a question to be resolved. Viewing the transition into the Aquarian Age from the Piscean Age as a paradigm-shift from authority to discovery, what are we to make of a scenario that presents the guiding elite of the masters as the ultimate model of spiritual authority? Due to its profound historical and mythographic precedents, it is quite impossible to eradicate or avoid this scenario—though it may perhaps come to be understood as an aspect of personal mythmaking, free-form and optional, rather than as a solid dogma to be accepted or refused.

CROSSWEAVE

To the Classics and Basics:

1.5 on Brahminical teachings concerning the personal quest for liberation, which were always widely accessible to the masses, by contrast to the secret body of cosmological and occult wisdom tapped by Madame Blavatsky
1.7 on the basic teachings of Buddhism, deeply respected by Blavatsky and Olcott, who both converted to this religion upon taking up residence at Adyar
2.9 on Gnostic and Hermetic teachings in the Western stream, somewhat akin to the radical gnosticism of Theosophy
3.6 on the dramatic account of the first westerner (a woman) to penetrate Tibet, as Blavatsky claimed to have done
3.8 on an alternative version of the quest for guidance from the Eastern

masters (particularly Sri Ramana Maharshi, a free-lance mahatma not associated with the Himalayan masters)

3.11 on a novelistic version of penetration into the remote spiritual homeland of the masters

3.12 on a biographical account of the lineage of Hindu yogi-saints, contrasting somewhat to the masters described by Blavatsky

4.5 on yet another view of Tibet, perhaps relevant to the "Tibetan Question"

4.8 on a purely devotional approach to Hindu spirituality

To Other Essays:

1.2 on the role of Blavatsky's vision and Bailey's revision in defining the global dimensions of the modern spiritual movement

2.1 on the issue of being guided versus becoming self-guiding

2.3 on the role of Theosophy in the European Occult Revival a hundred years ago

3 on the inclusion of deviant impulses in world evolution, as understood by the alchemists

4 on Rudolf Steiner's alternative to Theosophy

7 on channeling and mediums in general

13 on the Gnostic view of deviant impulses in evolution, fully and widely attested in Theosophy

14 on the ultimate projection of the Himalayan masters and the Tibetan Question

19 on the true nature of occultism, corresponding to the third main objective of Theosophy

21 on the working of Western masters by contrast to the mahatmas

24 on the belief in spiritual masters in general

ESSAY 29

Witchcraft/Wicca

T he modern revival of witchcraft is a curious affair. In some respects, it seems to have come about as an afterthought of the European Occult Revival, yet it differs in that it draws its advocates from the lower classes, rather than from the intellectual elite who populated the Revival. It began in England in the early 1950s with the efforts of Gerald Gardner, who presented it as "neopaganism," and spread to America during the metaphysical renaissance of the 1960s. Today it is probably the least understood and most maligned path in the new spirituality.

Not that the word *new* can be applied in any sense to witchcraft, or Wicca, as it is known to its practitioners. If shamanism claims to be the world's oldest religion, then Wicca is its closest rival. Basically, its framework rests on the age-old religion of nature worship, which has to be carefully distinguished from the supernaturalist outlook of shamanism. In Wicca, the forces of nature (including human sexuality) are worshiped and revered just as they are, whereas in shamanism, though it derived originally from the archaic worship of the animal powers, nature is surpassed through the exploitation of extraordinary forces within the human psyche.

Both the theory and practice of witchcraft have long been subjects of intense scrutiny by anthropologists and historians of religions. In fact, a key influence in the current revival was Margaret Murray's book *The Witch-Cult in Western Europe,* which appeared in 1921 and surprisingly catalyzed a large popular interest. Murray proposed that witchcraft was the last surviving evidence of a widespread pre-Christian fertility cult. During the Middle Ages, it was targeted by the Church and horrifically persecuted in witch-hunts and burnings, but before that time it was an accepted part of European folk culture. In short, the Church invented witchcraft, ascribing satanic rites and orgies to its practitioners, as a way

of warring against those who remained outside the Christian fold, cling-
ing to old ways and pagan Gods.

To this day, it is practically impossible to understand witchcraft fairly,
without thoughts of withered crones bent over steaming caldrons, evil
spells, and all-night orgies. The word has become a monumental cliché
that effectively serves to hide the simple and harmless nature of Wicca.
Murray called this archaic folk-religion Dianism, after the Roman Goddess of nature, Diana. She is one of the principle deities of Wicca, the
other being the Horned God (or Goat God) who goes under various
names, such as the Greek Pan or the Celtic Cernunnos. The male horned
God and the female Moon Goddess are viewed in Wicca as the primordial parents of us all, comparable to Shiva and Shakti in Eastern Tantrism.
They are not, however, transcendent deities who remain remote and
alien to ordinary affairs. They are present in the workings of nature and
can be sought and supplicated by ritual and meditation. They embody the
eternal self-regeneration of nature, as well as the boundless vitality of the
sexual urge. To worship them and work with them is the goal of Wicca.

To view human sexuality as the instrument and expression of divine
forces was the norm in former times. There is plentiful evidence of this
in the religious eroticism of Tantra as well as in the solar-phallic aspect
of the Mystery teachings. Christianity changed all this and cleverly inverted Pan into the Devil, or Satan, so that thousands of years of human
experience became anathema. Modern advocates of Wicca argue that by
making sins out of natural human impulses (note, for instance, the animal-
istic and aggressive behavior of children, and their complete innocence
regarding bodily functions), the Church put itself in a position to monop-
olize the means of salvation and atonement that are required whenever
these sins are (inevitably and repeatedly!) perpetrated.

Wicca in its purest form is totally undeserving of its evil reputation,
though it is rarely encountered in its purest form. By returning to communion with nature and repudiating Christian morality (along with all its
hypocrisy and judgment), witches and warlocks in the modern revival
seek to live a simple life as caretakers of the earth. The coven (traditionally of thirteen members) is something like a spiritual support group for
nurturing personal growth and sharing knowledge in the use of crystals,
herbs, spells, lunar cycles and seasonal rites, chants and invocations.
Female Wiccans who object to the tainted term "witch" simply call themselves "wise women." Equating Wicca with the lost religion of the Great
Goddess, they aspire to revive the old ways of natural healing and pagan

sensitivity, while male Wiccans occupy themselves with the method and mystique of the spiritual warrior who attempts to fathom the workings of nature in order to become its faithful ally and servant. Wiccans, for the most part, are quite content to be left alone with their odd beliefs. They are not inclined to convert others to their views, nor do they take an adversarial stance toward conventional religions. If all this sounds awfully innocent and well-behaved, it really is—though those in the "craft" are always the first to admit that everything in Wicca depends upon motive.

Here the real difficulty begins, for even if it were possible to allow the genuine and harmless character of Wicca and forget its egregious reputation, the fact remains that many of the people who are attracted to it are not the kind of individuals who are likely to improve its image. In its various American strains, Wicca is inseparable from shameless power-mongering, trafficking in drugs and spells for personal gratification, dabbling with Tantric occultism or ceremonial sex magic and, in general, indulging in narcissistic game-playing at the expense of true spiritual growth. If not held to the purest standards, its theory and practice are so fraught with the dangers of egotism and self-indulgence that they lead easily into the worst aberrations of intent—silly, sinister, or psychotic, and often a combination of the three.

Unfortunately, no matter how deep its original roots or how well-developed its contemporary reformulations may be, Wicca remains a questionable path. Its modern advocates are a long way from restoring the Goddess, and if their claim to revere and serve the forces of nature is true, then they will have to demonstrate in clear and acceptable ways just how they are cocreating with Her, before there is any chance of their ancient craft achieving a wider and more legitimate standing.

CROSSWEAVE

To the Classics and Basics:

2.3 on Greek cameos of Pan and Artemis (Diana), the primary deities of Wicca

2.4 on a hilarious account of initiation into the cult of the Great Goddess

2.8 on a fantastic description of the witches' Sabbath

4.6 on the revival of witchcraft (or sorcery) in modern Mexico

4.7 on the sacred sites of the British Isles, ancient centers of paganism

To Other Essays:

3 on alchemy, also designated by the Christian church as a form of Satanism
6 on Celtic culture, one of the purest repositories of pagan folk-religion in the West
7 on channeling, a mediumistic skill typically attributed to witches
8 on Christian Spiritualism, a metaphysical hybrid that actually incorporates many aspects of Wiccan folklore and beliefs, especially in its Brazilian and Caribbean forms
10 on Satanism, often wrongfully equated with witchcraft
11 on sacred sexuality, Gaia, and the Goddess Revival, fundamental concerns of modern Wicca
12 on sacred sites and communion with the earth
15 on the theoretical basis of magic, common to many Wiccan practices
16 on the solar-phallic aspect of the Sun Mysteries
18 on medicine men and women, Wiccan representatives in the culture and folklore of Native America
23 on the similarities and differences between shamanism and witchcraft
26 on sexual magic

ESSAY 30

Zen

A lthough the Japanese Zen master D. T. Suzuki, who was the greatest native interpreter of Zen, attended the 1897 World Congress of Religions as a young monk, Zen did not become well-known in the West until its adoption by the Beat generation after World War II. In no time it became a cliché, used as a joke to ridicule the odd, nonconformist life-style of the Beats. Bearded bohemians sporting berets who lounged around in smoky coffee houses, reading poetry, were believed to be practicing Zen in some obscure fashion. The jibe is understandable, since Zen has a lot to do with doing nothing.

Zen may be defined as the path of pure spontaneity, though this is misleading as long as we think of spontaneity as something we need to attain. Zen teaches that we both do and don't need to attain it; and herein lies its odd, irrational bent, the source of so much puzzlement and rich paradox. In the Buddhist philosophy that underlies Zen, the state of total, childlike spontaneity in which the human mind attends to what is immediately present to it, without judgment or distraction, is identified with the Void, the source and end of all things, indeed the very ground of being, though more often described in terms of nothingness. To put it concisely, the mind as pure attention is the "Buddha Nature," though in its activity of conceptual thinking the mind distracts itself from its own clear, still essence. The aim of Zen is to restore our participation in the world to the act of pure attending.

Initially, Buddhism did not involve an elaborate framework of analytical and metaphysical formulas, as Mahayana does today. Perhaps its original, stripped-down character is preserved in Zen, where the way to Enlightenment is, paradoxically, no way at all. At best, it can be described as the method of removal, undoing, getting out of one's own way. Zen practice consists mainly of sitting, walking, and doing chores. These simple acts are performed with no particular intent, no goal-orientation, yet they serve as an active meditation in which the practitioner seeks to let go of whatever thoughts and emotional distractions interfere with being fully present to the moment. Everything that obscures pure and total attending may be called "illusion," but this is not so easy to eliminate. Impossible, in fact. As one of the great Ch'an masters, Huang Po, put it, both the arising and the removal of illusion are illusory. He also warned that by seeking Enlightenment we automatically lose it, because using the mind to fathom the mind is pure futility.

Putting this baffling idea into practice is the essence of Zen discipline, which requires full "deconstruction" of the kind of thinking that normally consumes our waking moments. Ordinarily, no matter what we may be thinking about, we think "this must mean that, this leads to that," et cetera. But Zen practice weans us away from this type of mentation, toward direct, preconceptual awareness. Hence the frequent surprises in Zen discourse: "What is the Buddha Nature?" a monk asks, and the master replies, "The cypress tree in the courtyard." This is not meant to identify the Buddha Nature in a conceptual way with the cypress tree, but to redirect the questioner to clear, immediate mindfulness of the presence of the tree. Rather than conceptual logic, a kind of analogy (or ana-logic) pertains here: As monk is present to tree, and tree is present to mind, so mind is present to Void. Because it defies the conceptual formula of this-means-that, this state of "nondualistic" attention is often called No-mind.

Historically, Zen originated in India with Prince Siddhartha, who became Buddha, the Enlightened One; then, through a long line of patriarchs who preserved oral transmission, it was transferred first to China and then to Japan, where it became most rigorously defined. Tibetan Buddhism, in its emphasis on the apparitional nature of all things (Maya) is a distant cousin to Japanese Zen. (See, for instance, the twelve similes of Naropa in the Lexicon.)

The term "Gateless Gate" expresses the central paradox of Zen, technically formulated in the doctrine of *nonattainment.* Originally, it was the historical Buddha himself who claimed to have gained absolutely nothing from Enlightenment—a way of saying that it merely revealed what was already self-evident. But even if Enlightenment is something that happens to you, rather than something you acquire or cause, and even if it only reveals what was already present in the first place, still you must make yourself available for it to befall you. Zen practice consists basically of setting oneself up to be caught by surprise. This requires, however, the difficult task of slipping clear of the illusory notion of self. In Zen, self is viewed as a concept without any actual experience corresponding to the concept, like "antimatter." This radical teaching of *anatta,* "no self," lends a stark, impersonal tone to the Zen experience. Liberation from the fixations of personal identity can open the heart to "compassion for all sentient beings," true, but at worst it can deviate into zombielike depersonalization, a pitfall of Zen.

In Zen all technique is purely tangential, for there is no way to become enlightened—only styles of availability. All ideas and methods for achieving Enlightenment come under the old analogy: the finger pointing to the moon, not the moon itself. Look at the finger and you miss the moon. Likewise, lock into the techniques for being present in the moment, and you miss the moment. Nevertheless, a great deal of Zen as it is practiced today consists of rituals performed with almost militaristic rigidity. Perhaps the true spirit of Zen is better exemplified in the art forms that spring from it: the tea ceremony, archery, flower arrangement, and some of the martial arts. Ultimately, Zen can be viewed as an esthetic stance more than a spiritual technique. The effect of being in total presence is vivid, fluid participation in Suchness, the incomparable beauty of things in the passing moment, the water shaking the moon.

CROSSWEAVE

To the Classics and Basics:

1.2 on Taoism, the Chinese mystical path that shares with Zen the emphasis on "going with the flow," living in spontaneity
1.3 on deep serenity and comic paradox in Chuang Tzu, a pre-Zen master of the identity of contraries
1.7 on the two Buddhist sutras that exemplify the direct transmission of mind to mind supposedly preserved in the lineage of Zen masters up to this day
1.9 on consummate teachings from a Ch'an master who once had the audacity to slap the emperor of China in the face as a gesture of "sudden awakening"!
2.5 for the story of Parzival and his spontaneous "revelation of destiny," perhaps the Western complement to the Zen experience of *satori,* though highly personal in content

3.1 for numerous accounts of spontaneous awakening

3.12 for a classic account of sudden awakening or *samadhi* in the Hindu tradition

4.3 on surrendering to the moment and letting go of all conditioned responses in the psychedelic experience

4.9 on the arduous process of mental and emotional "deconstruction," similar to what is undergone in Zen training

4.10 on one man's experience of Zen in the context of life itself

To Other Essays:

17 on the lack of formal technique in mysticism, a characteristic it shares with Zen

21 on the problematic notion of the permanent self (entelechy, individuality), which reappears in successive incarnations—a concept usually denied in Zen, though it is included with great finesse in Suzuki's interpretations

24 on the many varieties of spiritual masters, among which Zen masters appear like the Walrus and the Carpenter at a fundamentalist rally

The
Lexicon

Well-being I won
and wisdom too,
    I grew and I joyed in my growth;
from a word to a word
I was led to a word,
    from a deed to another deed.

HAMAVAL
(Icelandic Epic)
"Song of Woden As He Hung
on the World Tree"

Using the Lexicon

T erminology is crucial for a clear approach to any field, whether it be real estate or reincarnation. This is especially so for metaphysics and spirituality, where words can often be either nebulous or many-angled—if not both.

In the Lexicon, as much care has been taken in the selection of the terms defined as in the definitions themselves. Although now rapidly coming into popular use, a great many of the words in the new idiom of modern spirituality have not yet found their way into standard dictionaries, while a lot of obscure terms are still included there as a matter of habit. For instance, *Webster's New World Dictionary,* Second College Edition, 1980, lists *Shamash,* the name of an obscure Assyro-Babylonian Sun God, but not *Shambhala,* a word of key importance in the purview of New Age thinking. *The Random House Dictionary of the English Language,* 1987 edition, does not list *Shambhala, enneagram,* or hundreds of other words common to the language of the new spirituality. *The Barnhart Dictionary of New English Since 1963,* published in 1973, lists *retread* but not *retreat, cock-up* and *codon* but not *cocreation.*

Within its special guidelines, the Lexicon does include some words that can be found in the standard dictionary, but only when it gives them a special slant according to their current usage among modern seekers. A word like *transmission,* for example, may be found defined in several ways in any dictionary (including "the part of an automobile that transmits motive force from the engine to the wheels"), but in modern spiritual work it occurs as a distinct idiom, which an ordinary dictionary fails to render.

While including hundreds of terms and expressions that have not yet found their way into the dictionary and conventional reference books, the Lexicon does have its own built-in limits. I have taken great care to select as many operative terms as possible without overloading the Lexicon with special terminology from particular fields: herbology and nutrition, UFOlogy, martial arts, dreamwork, radionics, alchemy, Sufism, Theosophy, Kabala, shamanism, parapsychology, mythology, and so on, into dozens of categories. At present there are literally hundreds of specific fields of spiritual exploration, each with its own array of technical terms, idioms, and slang expressions, but the selection here is limited exclusively to those terms useful for the initial approach to any field. Otherwise, it would be necessary to extend the list of words into the thousands.

Geomancy, for example, is a realm that has generated hundreds of special terms. The best way to master these is by hands-on experience in that realm, but for approaching it, just a few terms are essential: *sacred sites, ley-lines, Gaia, dolmen, dowsing, canon, Glastonbury.*

Another feature of the Lexicon, which takes it beyond the bounds of a conventional dictionary, is the inclusion of special words that set the context of our modern spiritual vocabulary, even though they are seldom directly used. These are terms of origin, like *black arts* and *interval,* not so frequently encountered as terms in use, like *chakra* and *near-death experience,* though they are just as important if we really care to know what we're talking about. These terms of origin derive from various sources such as ancient traditions, seminal books, movements, and teachers, which were formative to the spiritual milieu of our time, though they may have since been forgotten. While terms in use stand in the foreground of current spiritual interests, terms of origin define the background of what's happening now, and when taken into consideration they lend depth and distinction to the language we apply to present-day practices and pursuits.

Due to the specific historical sources from which the modern spiritual movement has evolved, a great many of both kinds of terms trace back to Hindu/Buddhist teachings and practices, though most of them have by now passed over into general use, independent of their origins. For example, *karma* and *chakra* are words used, more often than not, without allusion to the Hindu/Buddhist framework where they originated. In the many cases of words derived from the Oriental mother lode of ancient religious teachings first introduced into the West around 1800, the Sanskrit root-verbs are often explained, not for an academic effect, but to take the meanings back to their origins and thus, hopefully, to insure them against decay into sloppy clichés. Sometimes a word is taken back to its Indo-European root, abbreviated IE, to illustrate deep-level correlations of meaning. The discovery of such linguistic parallels (explained in the Lexicon definition of *Indo-European*) was a major breakthrough toward a global framework for modern seeking.

I have excluded numerous borderline terms that apply to spiritual/ metaphysical seeking yet fall outside the boundaries of the Lexicon because a satisfactory definition can be looked up in any dictionary: words such as *agnostic* (in theology) and *hysteria* (in psychology).

All words are defined of course by other words—but how they are defined makes all the difference. In writing the Lexicon, I have had a lot of pleasure in distilling the definitions to be pitch-perfect rather than letter-perfect. By this I mean that I cannot and do not presume to give fixed and final definitions in any case, but I do hope to offer interpretations that resonate with an accurate pitch of meaning. I have taken great care in the phrasing of the definitions, so that the right pitch of meaning comes through the words, clear and true, like the aftersound you hear in the silence that follows the pealing of bells.

In many cases, of course, precise technical accuracy is required: both *holograph* and the *Shroud of Turin* need to be defined as exactly what they are. With other words this is not conceivable: *Otherworld, sentient beings, involution, divinity, spirituality, human potential,* to give but a few. These I have defined by careful paraphrase worked out through a long process of distillation and synthesis. Then again, words like *monad, Paraclete,* and *infinity* fall unavoidably into the realm of creative interpretation (to say the least). Here I have drawn upon my lifelong discipline in comparative mythology to come up with interpretations that, even if they are of my own invention, are solidly grounded in an understanding of the persistent mythemes and complex historico-religious propositions such troublesome terms imply.

Once in a while there is a neologism of my own making that I include because it has proven useful in my teaching work: *para-Christianity, new time, servation.* There are also some words, such as *life-path, authenticity,* and *self-reliance,* that have been specifically applied to elucidate the principles and guidelines of clear seeking that I've developed. A few definitions bring to light aspects of the new spirituality that seem to have been completely overlooked: *Decadence,* for instance. New Agers don't generally know about this, but they ought to—at least to gain some perspective on the dangers of mythmaking (E2.3).

• • •

In keeping with the overall purpose of the *Handbook*—to offer both pure, ready-to-access information and the findings of a long-term personal quest—the Lexicon is designed both for instant reference and extended perusal. Meandering is the most natural way to get around the labyrinth. This is not aimless wandering but an actual technique of selective association, a method of following threads. The example of Theseus is parallel to Woden's initiation: "from a word to a word I was led to a word, from a deed to another deed." In this process, everyone follows his own inclinations, but the recurrence of certain tracks is inevitable. With discretion and restraint, I have facilitated meandering in the Lexicon by the mosaic of cross-referencing that links word to word, theme to theme, building now and again into those large-scale scenarios the veteran seeker comes to know by heart: *Fu Hsi,* an isolated bit of Chinese folklore, links an Eastern classic, the *I Ching,* to a term of origin, *Manu,* which in turn links to *servation,* a theme in worldwide mythology that involves the conflicting paradigms of *guidance* and *intervention.*

And so it goes. Seekers, greeting each other in the labyrinth, have been heard to say, "Have a nice meander."

All through the Lexicon, cross-linking is ample yet carefully and purposefully selective. To a large extent the cross-linking of word to word and section to section will be self-evident, leading by leaps and bounds of fluid association, but the systematic setup of the *Handbook* offers distinctive plot-lines where it is not so evident.

Cross-referencing within the Lexicon and from it to other sections of the *Handbook* has been carefully indicated, with a minimum of clutter and complication, as follows:

1. Whenever a cross-reference is necessary to complete a definition, the cross-linked term is given in small caps. Example: DOGON, "a tribe in Mali, West Africa," which has little meaning in the new spirituality if it is not cross-linked directly to the SIRIUS MYSTERY. Since the definition is incomplete, a cross-link is provided to another defined word, which completes it.

2. Wherever a cross-reference supplies the clue to a significant thread of association that, when picked up and pursued by meandering, will amplify the definition given into a mosaic, the cross-linked term is also given in small caps. Example: MOTHER WISDOM, with cross-links to VIRGIN, GAIA, SHAKTI, and SOPHIA. Here the cross-linking develops into a mosaic that is essential for full appreciation of the initial definition.

In addition to these tracks I have inscribed into the Lexicon, I have left plenty of opportunity for optional meandering. In the case of *oversoul,* for instance, Transcendentalism, self, genius, Atman, and Aryan are all cross-link words but are not indicated by small caps, so meandering from them is purely optional. A single word in the definition, SUPERMAN, is given in small caps to mark out a specific track leading to *Romanticism,* definition and E22, opening into a full-scale scenario in which the definition of *oversoul* forms a mosaic section.

3. When a word defined is treated in an Essay, the number of the Essay appears in parentheses after it: shamanism (E23), indicating that shamanism is treated in number 23 of the Ten-Minute Essays. Occasionally, when a definition refers to either of the two opening Essays, the reference is indicated by section. Example: 1.1, referring to Essay 1, section 1, Paradise in the Making.

4. Occasionally, when a definition can be amplified by cross-linking to "The Classics and Basics," this is indicated by C&B, followed by the exact reference: C&B2.5 refers to Section 2, Classics of Western Spirituality, entry 5, *Parzival.*

5. In some cases when a definition includes two or more distinct usages of the same word, these are indicated by (1), (2), et cetera. Example: *alignment,* which has a different meaning in bodywork than it does in geomancy.

6. Quite often, when the definition falls into a specific field of interest or recurrent context, this is indicated by "In." Examples: In Sufi, In Geomancy, In Theosophy. Here the context serves as an obvious optional cross-link, not capped to avoid cluttering.

Thus the Lexicon works like a loom, interweaving the other sections of the *Handbook.* At first glance providing clear, concise definitions, it serves in the long run to assist the seeker in building up a confident overview of the whole network of correlating principles and themes applicable in the wide and various genres of modern spirituality.

Since it is not confined to mere definition, the Lexicon invites discovery at every turn. More often than not, the working definition of a word depends upon special connotations, as with the argot used in stone carving or sailing or police work. To know the word calls for knowing not merely what it means, but how it's used. Like a new dialect of English, loaded with loan-words from Sanskrit and Arabic sources, the language of modern seeking is full of odd and mutable significance. Beyond a mere vocabulary, it is a living idiom whose nuances and complexities the Lexicon tries to convey.

A

ABBA (AB-ba) A name for God in ARAMAIC, used by Christ in speaking of "God, the Father" (New Testament, Mark 14:36).

ABORIGINE (Ab-eh-RIDGE-en-nee) Latin, "those who were here from *(ab–)* the beginning *(origin)*." (1) The native people of Australia, also called Bushmen, heirs to a long tradition of shamanism, known for their extraordinary feats of storytelling, and their access to a supernatural dimension called the DREAMTIME. (2) **aborigine.** More loosely, any tribal or indigenous people, such as the Kalahari Bushmen of South Africa, the Alaskan Eskimos, or the Native American Indians of both hemispheres, often viewed as possessing an oral tradition of ancient wisdom reflecting the primary religious values of direct sympathy with nature and love for the earth as a living being.

ABSOLUTE The ultimate reality and source of all manifestation in the universe, undetermined by anything previous to it in time or space; Origin, Source, Beingness, Ground, God as the "First Cause," et cetera. An old-fashioned term rarely used anymore, and perhaps more appropriately replaced by abstract.

ABSTRACT From Latin *ab-*, "from, away" + *trahere*, "to draw." As a noun, that from which all things are drawn or emanate, a reality that is not accessible to conceptual thinking, though it can (just barely) be sketched in a conceptual framework. A good overall term for many ideas and schemes proposed in New Age thinking, such as the planetary hierarchy of Bailey. An abstraction may be conceptually plausible, but the question is, How does it play? In the later work of Castaneda, *abstract* is used to refer to the baffling, unpredictable dynamics of the Spirit, which is known by its direct manifestations in the world, but cannot be preconceived or second-guessed. Unless it can be contacted directly—in some way—God remains an abstraction hinged on a long-range inference that the things drawn out around us must have been drawn out *from* something.

ABSURD That which is removed or away *(ab-)* from the root, or *surd,* a Latin word often used in old metaphysical teachings to mean God as the root of all being: Thus, what is absurd is removed from God, out of touch with the Source. Where one arrives after losing faith in the abstract. See also GODOT.

ACTIVE IMAGINATION In the Jungian work, a technique of conscious reverie, like a simulated form of dreaming, which uses inner VISUALIZATION to trace how the flow of mental and emotional states develops, often following it to the point where it reveals an autonomous meaning or plot, independent of conscious intent, which provides material for self-revelation or essential insights about one's behavior and attitudes. Compare with GUIDED IMAGERY.

ACUPRESSURE The use of massage and the application of pressure to points on the body for healing and directing the flow of vital forces. *Shiatsu* or *Jin Shin Do* in Japanese.

ACUPUNCTURE In Chinese medicine, an ancient method in which needles are inserted into the skin along MERIDIANS at precise locations designated as trigger-points for different bodily functions (digestion, liver metabolism, immune reactions), for the purpose of stimulating and balancing these functions, or simply to improve vitality and ensure the overall healthiness of the system; also used occasionally to replace anesthesia in surgery. Important technique in holistic medicine.

ADDICTION Any blind, repetitive behavior that controls the one who enacts it while it promotes the illusion of being in control; or, the condition of physical and/or psychological dependence on anything that distracts one's attention from the process of developing one's innermost potential. In recovery, one of the primary things to recover from. Esoterically, one of the main symptoms of the human condition during KALI YUGA.

ADEPT Someone who has attained a working knowledge of the laws of the world and the relation between the visible and invisible aspects of nature; especially, someone who can perform feats that defy the known physical laws, such as mind reading, transmutation of substances, appearing in two places at once, or even self-resurrection. Variation on the theme of the OCCULTIST or INITIATE, but especially with the implication of full command over the laws of physical nature. Famous examples: in history, Apollonius of Tyana (around 100 A.D.); in the planetary folklore of the New Age, the Comte de Saint Germain.

ADULT CHILD In recovery, an adult who failed to receive adequate nurturing and support in crucial areas of growth, due to having been raised by parents who were alcoholic or otherwise DYSFUNCTIONAL; therefore, someone hampered in adult life by issues that were not resolved in childhood, especially issues of relationship. An adult child is inadequately equipped to meet or even recognize his or her own needs, and is unable to face life in a happy and effective way—though he or she may be successful at coping and pretense, purely in the cause of survival. Identified by common symptoms such as poor self-esteem, fear of abandonment, the need to take care of others at the expense of self, and attraction to chaotic, insecure relationships—problems that they seek to remedy by REPARENTING and involvement in a TWELVE-STEP PROGRAM. Compare with INNER CHILD.

ADVENT   In theology and mythology, the coming of Christ to Earth, conventionally viewed as the specific instance of the human incarnation of God in our midst: the first coming. Viewed esoterically as a special instance of the descent of an AVATAR, treated as the central event of human evolution in the SOLAR MYSTERIES.

ADVENTIST   Conventionally, someone who believes in the SECOND COMING of Christ.

AFFIRMATION   Any simple statement of an intention for self-improvement, attitude adjustment, or positive management of one's affairs: "I am learning to overcome my fears." Used to apply the power of positive thinking. See also NEW THOUGHT.

AFTERLIFE   Continuing existence after death, described in some ancient religions and in the Mysteries as a kind of pilgrimage taken by the soul through the region of the PLANETARY SPHERES for the purpose of learning things that cannot be discovered on Earth—and perhaps bringing the wisdom so acquired back to Earth for service and self-betterment in another lifetime. See also LIFE AFTER DEATH.

AFTERWORLD   In world religion and mythology, the realm inhabited by the dead, where they exist after physical life has ended; often described as a place of ordeal or judgment, followed by a blissful vacation in the company of the Gods, as in the Egyptian scenario of the Amenti—the blissful fields of Osiris—or the happy hunting ground of the American Indians. To be distinguished from UNDERWORLD and OTHERWORLD.

AGHARTHA/AGARTTHA/AGHARTI   (Ah-GAR-thah) Mythical world-center, navel of planetary intelligence, often described as situated in the interior of the Earth (Hollow Earth) where it serves as the hub for a vast maze of subterranean passageways. Connected by Blavatsky and others with legends of the masters and the Great White Brotherhood. Interesting variation on the labyrinth theme.

AGNI YOGA   (AG-nee YO-gah) A body of practices and teachings developed by Nicholas and Helena Roerich, named after the Vedic God of Fire, Agni, interpreted by them as the "fire of self-sacrifice" to be developed by inner practice and applied to creative living and the extension of ordinary consciousness to far-off worlds. See also Nicholas ROERICH.

AHRIMAN   (AIR-uh-mun) In Persian myth, the supreme adversary of the Good Creator, Ohrmazd. Perhaps the earliest prototype of Satan, the embodiment of antievolutionary power, darkness, and destruction. In some esoteric teachings, the superhuman agent who cooperates in the bias of human intention toward DENIAL, especially self-denial, and who reinforces and exploits its results. Also, the agent of divisive self-will who seeks to accomplish everything by controlling through power rather than by responsible choice to collaborate through love in the all-encompassing harmony of the world. Adj., Ahrimanic. Contrast to LUCIFERIC.

AIKIDO (Eye-KEY-doe) Japanese, "the way of harmonizing *ki* (life-force)." In the martial arts, a technique of self-defense and inner centering that uses stylistic passes and circular movements to cause the aggressive strength of the opponent to work against itself. Developed by Ueshiba Morihei (1883–1969), thus one of the more recent lineages of martial arts.

AIN-SOPH (Ayn-soff) Hebraic, "supreme wisdom," the Godhead as pure light-filled creative intelligence, source of all manifestation. Basic principle in the Cabala.

AIRTIME The time occupied by a person channeling, which leaves him absent from self-awareness and unable to attend to normal affairs.

AKASHA (Ah-KAH-shah) Sanskrit, from the root *kash-*, "to shine, radiate." In the physics and psychology of Yoga and Hindu metaphysics, the fifth element or the fifth state in the progression from solid to liquid to gaseous to thermal. Usually described as an all-pervasive radiant field not detectable to the ordinary senses or mechanical instruments, and supposed to work like a photographic plate that registers the impressions of all events and actions and even thoughts. Compare with the problematic notion of the ETHER.

AKASHIC RECORD OR CHRONICLE (Ah-KAH-shik) Something like a cosmic videotape library, a vast record of impressions recorded in the Akasha, containing the annals of all human deeds, thoughts, and events in history, and accessible for instant replay depending on the possession of special faculties (namely, clairvoyance) by the one who consults it. For instance, events in past lives and things that happened on Atlantis can be learned by reading the Akashic Record. As to what qualifies anyone to read the Akashic Record, this is anybody's guess—but we may assume that the literacy must be acquired somehow, just as it must be for ordinary reading. In an old dispute, Rudolf Steiner claimed that the Atlantean history reported by Scott-Elliot was incorrect, because it was not drawn directly from the Akashic Record, but from distorted reflections on the astral plane—sort of like reading the *New York Times* underwater. Lacking direct access to the Record, some of us have resorted to transcripts.

ALBIGENSIANS (Al-be-GENT-shuns) A community of heretics who lived in southern France in the twelfth and thirteenth centuries (in the region of Albi), until they were destroyed in a bloody crusade commanded by the Catholic church. Their society was extremely liberal, allowing for complete equality of men and women, and total freedom from the repressive morality of the medieval church, though they had a voluntary morality dedicated to high standards of purity. For about one hundred years, their culture provided the fertile environment for the lyrical arts of the TROUBADOURS. Recently, there has been a revival of interest in the Albigensians through fascinating case histories of past-life memories brought to light by people who claim to have lived in their era. See also CATHARS, MONSÉGUR, REINCARNATION.

ALCHEMICAL WEDDING (OR ALCHEMICAL MARRIAGE) (1) The perfect union of spirit and matter, divine and human, ideally reflected in the loving collaboration of woman and man; may be accomplished either within each man and woman individually, or between man and woman or, ideally, *both* within themselves and between each other (four-way wedding). Conscious harmonization of the masculine and feminine traits in the human soul, achieved in the ANDROGYNE. (2) Esoterically, the perfect reunion of human and nature, the restoration of the human form to its divine perfection so that it coevolves harmoniously with the entire natural world and serves to raise nature itself to a higher stage of evolution: the goal of alchemical COEVOLUTION.

ALCHEMY (E3) A word of very obscure origin, probably from Old Arabic *chem,* "earth, matter," said to be an ancient name for Egypt. The practice of accelerating the natural workings of nature to produce supernatural results; thus, the supreme manipulation of matter. The art of transmuting base metals into gold and immortalizing the human body, or, on the moral level, transmutating the human soul into a being of spiritual perfections, able to express divine or potentially God-like attributes. The supreme paradigm of COCREATION.

ALEXANDER TECHNIQUE In bodywork, a method developed by F. M. Alexander in the late nineteenth century to correct body movements and postures by increasing attention to the style and quality of the actions one habitually performs.

ALIGNMENT (1) Loosely, coordination of bodily, mental, emotional, and spiritual functions. Specifically, lineup of the forces streaming through the CHAKRAS. (2) In archeo-astronomy, the layout of standing stones or the axes of ancient structures to correspond to the rising and setting of certain stars or to the sun and moon at key points in the year (solstices and equinoxes).

ALLAH (AH-lah) Arabic, "great one." In Islam, the most common name for the Supreme Being. Described by the great modern scholar and mystic Henri Corbin as the "Angel Most Near to God," rather than God itself, who cannot be named: a being filled with nostalgic sadness, aspiring to know that which originates it (that is, the nameless God beyond it).

ALPHA CENTAURI One member of a double star located in the Southern Constellation of the Horseman (Centaur), latitude forty-three south, equivalent to twenty-nine degrees Scorpio on the Ecliptic. The two closest stars visible to the naked eye at a distance of 4.3 LIGHT-YEARS from Earth.

ALPHA STATE The condition of alert relaxation due to the predominance of alpha waves in the brain: estimated to be 8–10 cycles per second, or twenty millionths of a volt. See also BRAIN WAVES.

ALTERED STATE Any condition of the body, mind, emotions, or perceptions (or any combination of the four) that involves an awareness beyond what is considered normal; especially, any state of consciousness achieved through unusual practices or the use of mind-altering substances such as psychedelics. See also CONSENSUS-REALITY.

AMERICA (1) Continent "discovered" by Columbus in 1492 and named after Amerigo Vespucci, an Italian navigator. (2) Geographic location of the Westland or Otherworld, conceived by many of the ancient peoples of Europe, such as the Celts and Greeks, as a remote paradise of after-death rewards, though often described as plagued by monstrous beings and violent underground forces: thus, a place of extreme spiritual ordeals and rewards, hidden treasures such as EL DORADO. (3) The land of new beginnings, celebrated by William Blake and other Romantics as the locale for the future perfection of the human race, though the process must be attended by severe trials. (4) In New Age folklore, the ideal society, created under the direction of Masonic initiates (E1.1). (5) Also known as Amurka, realm of blind consumerism and down-and-dirty politics.

AMERINDIAN An awkward term sometimes applied to the Native American Indian, as distinguished from the Oriental Indian, or Hindu. Since so much in present-day spiritual teachings comes from the ancient Indian sources of the East, it is often helpful to set the Amerindian apart and give it a distinct meaning. Loosely, it applies to all the native cultures in the three Americas: North, Central, and South. See also NATIVE AMERICAN SPIRITUALITY.

A.M.O.R.C. Ancient and Mystical Order Rosae Crucis. A modern variant of Rosicrucianism, founded in 1915 by H. Spencer Lewis, who claimed a lineage going back to the Egyptian pharaoh Akhenaton. Offers teachings on the higher self and spiritual evolution. Claims to be a worldwide fraternity, with headquarters in San Jose, California.

ANALOGY The logic or system of thinking by comparisons, drawing parallels: The Solar System is like the human body, the planets like organs, et cetera. The most widely applied method of explaining the universe in ancient esoteric/metaphysical teachings, related to the doctrine of correspondences: a planet corresponds to an organ, which corresponds to a metal, which corresponds to a plant, which corresponds to a letter, et cetera. Essential feature in all systems of ANCIENT WISDOM.

ANALYTICAL PSYCHOLOGY Name given in 1911 by C. G. Jung to his work, to distinguish it from that of Freud and others: the science of mapping out the inner workings of the psyche, or soul. See also JUNGIAN WORK.

ANANDA (Ah-NAHN-dah) Sanskrit, "bliss, ecstasy." A concept basic to those Eastern teachings that state that bliss is the nature of the Godhead, the primary and innate quality of all existence, the ground sensation felt when one attains total identification with the self, God, Supreme Reality, et cetera. In

Bhakti and Eroticism, the experience of pure joy attained by selfless devotion to the guru or God or by pursuing sexual ecstasy as a spiritual discipline. Also, the essence of spontaneous being or life itself, the quality of pure vitality that arises once all resistance to it is removed, as imaged in the playful dancing and flirtation of KRISHNA.

ANCIENT ASTRONAUTS Frequent theme in New Age speculations, proposing that the Gods of former times were actually beings of more advanced civilizations elsewhere in the universe, who visited Earth in flying saucers. Popularized by Erick von Däniken, a Swiss innkeeper turned occultist, in *Chariots of the Gods* and other books published in the 1970s. Supposed to be confirmed by such unexplained matters as the great sarcophagus of PALENQUE and the NAZCA LINES. See also EXTRATERRESTRIALS.

ANCIENT WISDOM Loosely, the body of scientific-psychological-artistic-religious knowledge believed to have been possessed by certain high cultures of the past, and now lost or forgotten though it may be rediscovered and redeveloped. Since the era of the Enlightenment (1650), it is no longer fashionable to propose that our ancient ancestors knew more than we do about anything, but most New Age belief systems involve to some degree the revival of ancient wisdom: astrology, geomancy, Yoga, et cetera (E1.3). The "wisdom religion" of Madame Blavatsky is likely the prototype of all present-day variants.

ANDES MASTERS A community of benevolent guides and teachers supposed to live in the high Andes and direct the course of human affairs by supernatural powers. Variation on the theme of the HIMALAYAN MASTERS, probably introduced by the American occultist Brown Landone, who claimed a migration of masters from Tibet to South America after World War I.

ANDROGYNE (AN-dro-jine) From Greek *andros-*, "man" + *gyne*, "woman": thus, an entity combining all aspects of male and female into a harmonious unity. In alchemy, the image of human perfection and wholeness. By some ancient traditions, the original and perfect form of the human being—cited in the humorous account of Aristophanes (*The Symposium,* C&B2.3). Adj., androgynous (An-DROJ-in-us). A fashionable look among some celebrities.

ANDROMEDA GALAXY An external spiral galaxy in the Constellation of Andromeda, the "Fallen Woman." At a distance of 2.3 million light-years, the most distant object visible to the naked eye. Locked onto a mutual gravitational axis with our own ORION GALAXY, its mythological and astrophysical counterpart.

ANGEL From Greek *angeloi,* "messenger, emissary." In many religious traditions, a supernatural being, usually envisioned as winged, who serves as a messenger of the Supreme Being and speaks directly to humans; or sometimes acts as a guardian, as in the guardian angel of Christian tradition. In Hinduism, this guardian is called Agnisvatta, "one who is sweetened by fire (Agni)," and imagined as taking for nutriment the flame located in the human heart, which consumes all suffering and converts it into wisdom.

ANIMA/ANIMUS   In the Jungian work, complementary components in the bisexual makeup of human beings. Both terms are Latin and mean "living, animated." The anima is the feminine aspect of the man's psyche, the woman within the man; conversely, the animus is the masculine aspect of the woman's psyche, the man within the woman. Each is the missing half of the other, which may be integrated or projected outward onto someone of the opposite sex. See also PROJECTION.

ANIMAL GUIDES/INNER ANIMALS   In popular techniques of spiritual work related to Native American spirituality, entities of a magical or imaginary nature, produced by concentration or encountered in dreams, supposed to help and heal, provide knowledge, grant powers. Traditionally, the embodiment of a psychic force, like the black cat who accompanies the witch in European folklore; or the rabbit in *Alice in Wonderland.* Loosely equivalent to the NAGUALS of ancient shamanism.

ANKH   (Aahnk) In Egyptian religion and mythology, the symbol of eternal life yoked by incarnation to the human form, represented by a cross with the upper arm looped like an inverted teardrop.

ANTHROPOSOPHY   (E4). (An-throw-POSS-oh-fee) From Greek *anthropos,* "human" + *sophia,* "wisdom"; hence, "the wisdom of humanity or being human." A modern school of spiritual teachings and practical directives given by Rudolf Steiner. Contrast to THEOSOPHY.

ANTICHRIST   A problematic entity in world history and Western theology, supposed to be the antithesis of unifying spirit, Christ, but predicted to appear in the guise of a loving and benevolent savior. Hence, the false Christ, the trumped-up Messiah. "Sometimes Satan he come as a man of peace," Bob Dylan, *Infidels,* 1984. This is almost an exact paraphrase of the warning given by Christ in Matthew 24:5—"For many shall come in my name, saying, I am Christ; and shall deceive many." See also SECOND COMING.

APOCALYPSE   (Ah-POCK-uh-lips) From Greek *apokalyptein,* "to disclose, reveal." In religious writings, any text that purports to reveal a secret or esoteric message. Specifically, the Revelation of Saint John the Divine, the last book of the Bible, which gives a detailed account of the things to be revealed at the end of the world. Loosely, any end-of-the-world scenario, including the fantasy of extraterrestrial intervention. One of the main themes of the New Age. See also HARMONIC CONVERGENCE.

APOCRYPHA   (Ah-POCK-riff-fah) From Greek *kryptein,* "to hide," as in a crypt. Generic name for religious scriptures considered to be of heretical value, or doubtful authorship. Most famous are the GNOSTIC GOSPELS, which contain incidents and views capable of radically upsetting the established notions of Christianity. There exist both Old and New Testament Apocrypha, excluded by the Church fathers from the official (or "canonical") edition of the Bible, though very important in Gnosticism.

APOTHEOSIS   (Ap-uh-THEE-o-sis) From the Greek verb *apotheoun,* "to deify." The supreme aim of the Mysteries, the raising of a human being to the level of a god, DEIFICATION. Dismissed as mere glorification by those who do not consider it possible, or desirable, to pursue the idea of mutating the human species toward a higher existence. See THEOGENIC IDEA.

APPARITION (1) Loose term for the appearance of spooks and ghosts, usually in visual form, often interpreted as due to the activity of the dead. A phenomenon subjected to extensive experimental research during the heyday of Spiritualism at the end of the nineteenth century, resulting in a number of startling photographs. (2) In a more limited sense, the miraculous appearance of the MADONNA in the form of visual images, usually to children or people of simple, unsophisticated character. Famous instances occurred at Guadalupe, Mexico (1531); Lourdes, France (1858); Fátima, Portugal (1917); Garabandal, Spain (1961–65); Zeitun, Egypt (1968–71); and since 1981 in Medjugorje (Med-joo-GORE-e-uh), Yugoslavia. Initially these Marian visions appear to a single person or a small group (six children at Medjugorje), then they become visible to many more as news of the vision spreads. Often accompanied by spontaneous healings or inexplicable phenomena, such as the sun dancing in the sky. The event at Medjugorje appears to be ongoing, so that the place has become a site of pilgrimage for millions of people from all over the world.

AQUARIAN AGE A term that became popular in the sixties—for example, in a major hit song from the musical *Hair* (1968). Technically, the period of time encompassing about two thousand years when the spring equinox transits through the CONSTELLATION of the Waterbearer, erroneously called Aquarius. In current usage, almost synonymous with the *New Age,* believed to be a time of massive spiritual awakening for humanity. See also NEW AGE, PISCEAN AGE, PRECESSION OF THE EQUINOXES, and E1.2.

AQUARIAN GOSPEL An account of the lost years of Jesus, describing extensive travels in the East where he was known by the name of ISSA. Written under telepathic direction by Emmanuel Levi in 1907.

ARAMAIC (Air-uh-MAY-ik) An ancient Semitic language spoken in biblical times, especially in the area of Palestine where Christ lived. Compare with SACRED LANGUAGES.

ARCANA (Ar-KAHN-ah) Specifically, an old name for the cards of the TAROT, traditionally divided into the Major Arcana of twenty-two cards, and the Minor Arcana of fifty-six cards. Loosely, any knowledge or practice considered to be rare or obscure.

ARCANE (Ar-KANE) Noun and adjective, that which comes from a sacred or superhuman source, or from the secret treasury of inner knowledge and power accessible only to those who discover it within themselves. From Latin *arcere,* "to shut away, enclose" > IE root *areq-,* "protect, enclose." The treasure or secret is protected by its inwardness or latency, so the idea of secret knowledge does not imply withholding or deception, as is often thought. Rather, it implies accessing and activating that which exists within us in a nonapparent or potential way—though the method of doing so may indeed be held under close protection by those who possess it. In pragmatic terms, the INNATE.

ARCANE SCHOOL A modern school for spiritual development founded by Alice A. BAILEY, one of the later exponents of Theosophy and the scenario of the Himalayan masters (E1.2).

ARCANUM (Ar-KAHN-um) In medieval science and folklore, any remedy or cure, but especially a secret one. Also, the treasury of all higher knowledge, containing the keys to all things in creation. Ramon Lull, alchemist, 1235–1315: "The Virgin is the Arcanum of the Art."

ARCHANGEL In esoteric Christianity, a supernatural being responsible for overseeing the evolution of a specific FOLK-SOUL. Also, in special instances, the executive agent of planetary intelligence, such as Oriphiel, archangel of Saturn, who operates in a position of executive management regarding everything that goes on in the realm of Saturn. According to the Christian occultist Trithemius of Spondeim (1462–1516), the seven archangels of the planets also serve as timekeepers, each overseeing a 350-year period of historical evolution and imbuing it with a certain character, directing it toward certain aims. See also MICHAEL, ZEITGEIST.

ARCHEO-ASTRONOMY The scientific study of ancient monuments, such as temples, for the purpose of understanding their construction in terms of geometrical and mathematical principles (canon), and their alignments to certain stars and astronomical points of orientation. An outgrowth of geomancy, this science has come into legitimacy since the early seventies. Its popular reflection is seen in the current rage for visiting SACRED SITES.

ARCHETYPE Greek, "primary imprint." A term introduced in 1919 by C. G. Jung, who originally called it the primordial image. A kind of supernatural computer chip, or active fossil imprint in the psyche, which operates as a repository of emotional forces and information. Supposed to exist in the COLLECTIVE UNCONSCIOUS, from which it shapes and directs human action and attitudes independent of the individual conscious mind. Adj., archetypal. Designated by Joseph Campbell as "mythic image."

ARCOSANTI New Age cooperative community founded in Arizona by the futuristic architect Paolo Soleri.

A.R.E. Association for Research and Enlightenment, founded in 1931 by Edgar CAYCE, located in Virginia Beach, Virginia. A major center for New Age studies in psychology and healing.

ARICA (Ah-REEK-ah) Spiritual movement founded by Oscar Ichazo in Arica, Chile. A synthesis of several disciplines, including Tibetan Buddhism, Yoga, and Zen, into a highly systematic program of exercises and meditations, aimed at achieving the cooperative wholeness of body, mind, and emotions.

ARK Symbol and vehicle of the MANU, the superhuman agent responsible for carrying over the seeds of one cycle of evolution into the next cycle: for instance, Noah in the Old Testament, who gathers the genetic prototypes of all living creatures (animals in pairs) into the vessel he has built according to specific proportions. Among the funerary articles in the tomb of the boy king Tutankha-men was found an alabaster ark with a gazelle prow, fitted out with a canopied storehold containing small urns in which the vital organs of the pharaoh were preserved. As an AVATAR or incarnation of divinity, the pharaoh was held to be the source of all culture and civilization on Earth, and his organs were treated as receptacles for cosmic-creative forces. For these archetypal impulses to be preserved through time, they needed to be safeguarded and transported in a vessel: the ark. Babylonian cylinder seals from 4000 B.C. show the ark with a ram's-head prow. The earliest known symbol for the continuity of human culture; basis of the image of the Goatfish in the constellations.

ARMAGEDDON (Ar-ma-GED-un) Hebrew, "mountain *(har)* over-looking the plain of *Megiddo,* scene of great battles." In the Bible, the place where the last stand of humanity occurs, with the evil being cast out and the good raised up into heaven at the moment of the LAST JUDGMENT. In fundamentalism, the actual geographic locale of the Apocalypse.

AROMATHERAPY In holistic medicine, the use of scents or essential oils for curing illness or producing mood alterations.

ARTHURIAN PATH In the Celtic Revival, the spiritual and moral discipline of the medieval knights, associated with the legends of King Arthur in England and France, a thriving mystique from 600 to 1300 A.D. The idealistic model of CHIVALRY is celebrated in the vast body of literature called Arthurian Romance, which describes these knights, their quests and adventures, their la-dies, and their supernatural foes and attainments, including the legend of the HOLY GRAIL. Technically, a modern form of shamanism using visualizations and power-rituals to develop inner faculties, especially through the transformation of KUNDALINI and inner vitality, in a manner somewhat comparable to the martial arts of the Orient.

ARYAN (AR-ee-un) Sanskrit *arya,* "noble," akin to the Greek *aristos,* "best, superior." Originally, a tribal name for the people who established Indian civilization from 5500 B.C. onward, when India itself was called *Aryavarta,* "Land of the Nobles." Later adopted by nineteenth-century spiritual groups (especially Theosophy) to indicate a spiritual aristocracy, directed by the Indian masters. Also used by the Nazis to denote the master race or Caucasians of non-Jewish descent. Apart from this unfortunate association, it probably refers to those who are noble and elevated above others because they act in the service of God, taking on responsibility in the human realm for what God ordains from the superhuman realm.

ASANA (AH-sa-nah) Sanskrit, from the root *as-,* "to sit." The general name for postures assumed in Yoga, especially Hatha Yoga. Usually designated by descriptive names such as plow, fish, wheel.

ASCENDANT See RISING SIGN.

ASCENDED MASTERS Superevolved human beings who are no longer bound to physical embodiment but remain in contact with humanity to teach and guide. In New Age folklore, these disembodied entities are believed to remain in contact with humanity through CHANNELING. Key agents in the "I AM" MOVEMENT.

ASCETIC (Ah-SET-ic) N. & adj., one who practices denial of the body or senses for the sake of spiritual development. Based on the esoteric theory that systematic suppression of natural functions (such as breathing or the sexual urge) will result in the emergence of supernatural functions: i.e., denial breeds excess. Tested in the occult application of the INTERVAL. In traditional Christian doctrine, one who attains a better-than-thou condition by suppressing certain urges just because they are "sinful," with no implication that superpowers are acquired.

ASHRAM (AHSH-rahm) Sanskrit, from *a-*, "away" + *shrama*, "exhaustion": hence, a retreat from exhaustion. A place of retirement from the world, usually for the purpose of inner self-collection. Often the headquarters of a sect or master.

ASPECTS In astrology, angular relationships between the planets: Mars positioned at ninety degrees from the Sun is in square aspect. Interpreted as revealing different kinds of psychological complexes and behavioral problems, for example, Mars-trine-Jupiter (120 degrees): false confidence leading to inappropriate self-assertion; Venus-opposite-Saturn (180 degrees): difficulty in communicating what one really wants.

ASSEMBLAGE POINT Special term in Castaneda for the mechanism of fixation that causes human awareness to remain rigidly limited to a narrow band of reality, amid the wide spectrum of all possible bands to be accessed. Something like the center of gravity in the AURIC EGG. Moving the assemblage point gives access to altered states.

ASTRAL BODY One of the so-called higher bodies of human makeup, supposed to surround the physical body in the form of a colored oval (AURA) as well as permeate it inwardly; usually described as the vehicle of the passions and personal tastes, or emotional body. See also FOUR-BODY THEORY.

ASTRAL LIGHT One of the most important concepts in the nineteenth-century revival of occultism, now almost completely forgotten. Described by Eliphas Levi and others as the conducting field in the transmission of psychic impressions, silent thoughts, or suggestions, as well as emotional attractions and repulsions; the medium for animal magnetism at its lower end, and subtle manipulations of mental force at its higher. Seems to have been largely ignored in current teachings on magic, perhaps because its functions have now been entirely superseded by electronic media.

ASTRAL PLANE Where we go when we dream, when we experience in a chaotic and inconsistent way those regions of the fourth dimension that are not ordinarily accessible to us within the given limits of the mind and senses. Where we go in the process of astral travel (rather than what we go there in).

ASTRAL PROJECTION   The technique of separating the astral body from the physical at will, to travel to distant places or investigate events. See also OUT-OF-BODY EXPERIENCE.

ASTRALITY   Slang for emotional charge, or the residue of feeling dispersed into the atmosphere by human acts and attitudes.

ASTROLOGY   (E5) The science or language *(logos)* of the stars *(astra)*, applied to the analysis of human character and the prediction of events.

ATLANTEAN MIGRATIONS   In the planetary folklore of Anthroposophy, vast movements out of the mythical lost continent, supposed to have occurred for hundreds of years down to the time of the last glaciation in Europe (circa 9000 B.C.), spreading to all regions of North, Central, and South America, and Europe, Africa, and Asia. Led by the great spiritual teachers of Atlantean civilization, the MANU and other guides, the migratory streams are said to have established the sacred centers of culture in many locales, where they eventually evolved into the vast network of the post-Atlantean MYSTERIES.

ATLANTIS   A lost continent in the Atlantic Ocean, supposed to have been the motherland of all human culture previous to what we now know from historical records. Mentioned by Plato in several places; supposed to have sunk in a series of awesome cataclysms ending around 9500 B.C., the time of the last major Ice Age in Europe. See also LEMURIA.

ATMA / ATMAN   (AHT-mah) Sanskrit, "breath, spirit." The individual soul as a spark or breath of God. See also SPIRIT, BRAHMA.

ATONEMENT / AT-ONE-MENT   A play on words, referring to the two principle paradigms of Eastern and Western religion. From the Middle English *atonen,* "reconcile." Taken in the West to mean the act of making up for something wrong or done wrong, as "atoning for sins." Hence, the paradigm of salvation or redemption, which implies restoration to wholeness from a fallen or injured state. Taken in the East to mean at-one-ment, making what appears to be divided into a whole. Hence, the paradigm of Enlightenment or liberation (i.e., from the false sense of division). In this case, there is no Fall, but only the illusion of separation or a veil concealing the original perfection, which does not need to be fixed, but merely found (as explained in E2.4).

ATTACHMENT   In Buddhism and Indian philosophy, often cited as the primary obstacle to the realization of Atman or the self-nature, universal and independent of all inner and outer identifications. The dynamic of alienation, usually viewed as a major obstacle to spiritual growth and self-realization because of the way it causes us to distort and control our experiences, thus rendering us incapable of seeing or receiving what they really have to give us; although Western attempts at nonattachment often end up, ironically, contributing to our habits of alienation in other ways. Overcoming it is a primary and recurrent theme in Eastern spirituality as well as in Western schools of ascetic mysticism, which encourage giving up all worldly goods and indulgences.

ATTAINMENT   See NONATTAINMENT.

ATTITUDE   The outlook or act-of-attention through which we are engaged in continuous COCREATION with the reality given to us, in a state of partial completion, from without. Probably given its initial formulation in modern language by William James (C&B3.2) around 1900: "The greatest discovery of our generation is that human beings by changing the inner attitudes of their minds can change the outer aspects of their lives." The factor of primary responsibility for how "good looking" we are. See Preamble.

ATTITUDINAL HEALING   The method of treating and curing diseases, both physical and psychological, by changing how one views them and feels about them. Developed by Jerry Jampolsky and others.

AUM   (Home without the H) In ancient Hindu religion, the sacred syllable or MANTRA used for achieving attunement with God, the All, the Source, et cetera. Represents the beginning (a), continuation (u), and end (m) of creation. Also spelled OM in shortened form.

AURA   A field of subtle light and mobile forces surrounding the human body, visible to the clairvoyant as a colored oval. Usually applies to the field of the astral body, extending to about a foot in all directions beyond the reach of the extended limbs. See also FOUR-BODY THEORY.

AURA BALANCING   The technique of manipulating the forces in the aura (by concentration, visualization, use of crystals) to clarify and harmonize the mind and emotions.

AURIC EGG   Old term in Theosophy for the causal body, described as enclosing and permeating all the other bodies. Called the luminous egg in Castaneda. Plotinus (around 300 A.D.): "The body is in the soul." See FOUR-BODY THEORY.

AUROBINDO, SRI   (Shri Or-oh-BIN-doe) Indian philosopher, poet, and social reformer (1872–1950), an early theorist of the New Age concept of uniting with the higher self by coevolution of consciousness and body. Originator of Integral Yoga, author of many books on spiritual development, and inspiration for Auroville, a New Age utopian community established at Pondicherry on the southeastern coast of India in 1968.

AUTHENTICITY   The primary criterion for the validity of spiritual knowledge: that it comes from a source or author that is original and reliable (see C&B3, Preface). Requires no badges or labels. From Greek *authentes*, "one who acts on one's own"; from *auto-*, "self" + *hentes* > IE base *sen-* "to achieve, practice": thus, "self-achieving." See also DELUSION.

AUTOGENIC TRAINING   A method, similar to BIOFEEDBACK, developed from the work of Oskar Vogt and Johannes Schultz at the beginning of the century, using repetitions of simple phrases ("My breathing is deep and easy") to produce tension-release and physiological changes.

AUTOMATIC WRITING   Old-fashioned name for writing under the direction of a psychic entity, without conscious effort or muscular control.

AVALON   From the Old Welsh *Avallenau,* literally "apple-land"; also, a name for the Celtic Goddess of the orchards. A fabulous kingdom or paradisiacal Otherworld, often described as the blissful abode of the dead and the sanctuary of the departed Gods. Sometimes equated geographically with GLASTONBURY in England. Important concept in the Celtic Revival, perhaps the Western equivalent to SHAMBHALA.

AVATAR   Sanskrit, "one who descends, dives down." Originally, in Hindu myth, the physical embodiment of a deity who assumes human or animal form to perform some action for the salvation of the world. The most famous example is found in the Ten Avatars of Vishnu, in which Christ is sometimes included as the ninth, with the tenth, or Kalki Avatar, still to come. In more recent usage in the West, the term has come to be extended, rather loosely, to any SPIRITUAL MASTER who is believed to enjoy a privileged relation to God.

AVESTA   The body of sacred writings of the ancient religion of Zoroastrianism, written in Avestan, a sacred language and the sister tongue to Sanskrit.

AWARENESS   Specifically, self-awareness: that is, the practice of giving attention to finding oneself in the context of one's vital and evolving connection with life and others; the state of being mindful of how things are done, rather than merely what is done; the art of listening to life itself and learning what it reveals. Attunement to the larger, all-encompassing reality of the earth, to humanity as a whole, and to God; appreciation of the Oneness of life or operative planetary unity, and giving expression to this in one's day-to-day ATTITUDE as well as in long-term efforts to fulfill a personal vision in service to the whole. See also INNATE, SPIRITUALITY.

AWE   From the IE base *agh-,* "to be overwhelmed." The primary sensation that arises from direct contact with a divine or superhuman force or entity. Considered by leading mythologists and theologians to be the primary religious feeling of humankind, although the modern age seems to be a time characterized by its complete loss or suppression. The New Age appeal to rekindle a sense of the SACRED is a response to this situation. Perhaps the primary force in suppressing it—its antidote, as it were—is SHAME. See the Afterword for my views on restoring awe through vital contact with the Divine.

AYURVEDA/AYURVEDIC MEDICINE   (Eye-ur-VAY-dah) Sanskrit, "life" *(ayu-)* + "knowing" *(veda).* A system of medicine practiced in India for 5,000 years, using for diagnosis a complex system of factors involving diet, temperament, habits, herbs, color, and gem affinities.

AZTEC (INDIANS AND CULTURE)   A lost civilization of Central America, deeply puzzling as to both its origins and its elimination—which occurred when the Aztecs took the Spanish marauder Cortés to be the Avatar of QUETZALCOATL, the God whose eventual return was predicted by the Toltecs, whom the Aztecs had conquered and absorbed. A major culture in the history of Native America, associated with mystical and religious practices (including human sacrifice) yet to be understood.

AZTEC CALENDAR An elaborate system recorded in obscure hieroglyphs on a huge stone disk excavated from a public square in Mexico City on 17 December 1760. Evidence of an ancient system of time-reckoning used by the Aztecs in computing a succession of five great world-cycles, of which ours is the last, the "Fifth Sun," supposed to end in a catastrophic earthquake. Contrast to MAYAN CALENDAR. See also HARMONIC CONVERGENCE.

AZURAS (Ah-ZOOR-uz) In some esoteric teachings (especially Anthroposophy), superhuman beings who focalize in themselves the ultimate human potential for self-destruction; the agents of SPIRITUAL DEATH, supposed to invade Earth at some undetermined point in the future. Equivalent to the Titans in Greek myth, the Lords of Xibalba (Underworld) in the sacred Maya book of the POPOL VUH (C&B2.12). Many myths tell of botched attempts by the Gods to create the human form, which result in monstrous creatures. Although these are wisely aborted, they apparently cannot be totally eliminated and will at some time in the far-distant future return to confront the human race with its own worst potentials. Frequently featured in *Heavy Metal* comics.

B

BACH FLOWER REMEDIES Distillations made from flowers and given in liquid form, for curing diseases and preserving mental and emotional health. Developed by the English physician Edward Bach (died 1936) from findings made by gathering dew from wildflowers in Wales. Prime example of holistic medicine, drawing directly upon the forces of nature.

BACON/SHAKESPEARE CONTROVERSY A dispute over the theory that the English statesman and philosopher Sir Francis Bacon (1561–1626) and the great English playwright William Shakespeare (1564–1616) were in fact the same person, according to which Bacon is credited with writing Shakespeare's plays. Believed to be supported by the evidence of strange cryptograms and aspects of the bard's works, which themselves are taken to present in a dramatic form certain teachings of the ROSICRUCIANS. Endorsed and explained in full by Manley Palmer Hall, among others.

BAHA'I (Bah-HIGH) A modern religion, founded in 1863 by the Iranian prophet Bahaullah (Mirza Hoseyn Ali Nuri), stressing radical monotheism, the unity of all religions, rejection of organized priesthood and rituals, and careful preservation of all the scriptures from all races containing the words of the chosen ones of God.

BAILEY, ALICE A. English-born exponent of Theosophy (1880–1949), successor to Madame Blavatsky in transmitting teachings received from the so-called Himalayan masters, who elaborated a vast system of esoteric psychology and evolutionary physics (E1.2) and founded the ARCANE SCHOOL (originally located at the United Nations).

BALAM (BAH-lum) Mayan, "jaguar," or "jaguar-priest." In Mayan religion and mythology, literally, the predatory animal of the jungle viewed as a sacred beast or NAHUAL; as well as the title of the supreme master of occult knowledge and magical powers. In comparative mythology, equivalent to the panther of Dionysus as well as the Egyptian guard dog of the necropolis (city of the dead), Anubis. Esoterically, the embodiment of dark powers normally contained within the human metabolism, where they work in the breakdown and conversion of food, but which can be extracted and applied to acts of magical aggression.

B A R A K A (Bah-RAHK-ah) Arabic, "blessing." Spiritual power, gift of divine endorsement or inspiration. Often said to be passed on as a "cloak" or "mantle" from a dying master to his successor, as described in the TRANSMIS-SION from Elijah to Elisha (Old Testament, 2 Kings 2:13). The expression is also used by the Persian mystic poet Rumi.

B A R D Poet-singer-harpist. In the old Gaelic and Celtic cultures, the artist responsible for preserving the folklore and mythology of the people, who usually underwent a long course of training to master a vast body of complex musical forms and an equally vast repertoire of stories, passed down by oral transmission. Like their Arabian counterparts, the "drunken poets" such as Rumi, the bards were mystics and seers, gifted with second sight and access to the OTHERWORLD. Known especially for the "riddling poem," in which they referred, often in baffling and hilarious ways, to memories of previous incarnations. Also known in Celtic legend for the supernatural effects of their art, which could change the weather and produce miraculous cures. It is said that the true test of an accomplished bard was the ability to produce a poem that could kill rats. See also TROUBADOURS and C&B3.16.

B A R D O Tibetan, "limbo, interval." Specifically, the period of time tran-spiring between death and rebirth. The transition through this period is a se-quence of six distinct phases as described extensively in the *Bardo Thodol,* "the book of liberation through hearing *(thodol)* on the intermediate plane between death and rebirth *(bardo)"* (C&B1.8). Likewise, the journey undergone by Dante in *The Divine Comedy* (C&B2.7) can also be seen as a progression through a sequence of bardo-states. Loosely, any interval or limbo-state, especially one attended by ordeal or confusion.

B E A T G E N E R A T I O N From a shortening of the word BEATITUDE. American slang introduced by Jack Kerouac in the early 1950s to describe the postwar generation who rejected the conventional values of American life and, in many cases, sought self-awareness through involvement in alternative paths of spirituality, such as Zen. Known for raucous/maudlin poetry accompanied by jazz and for experimenting with drugs to obtain mystical visions or simulate the sacramental rites of ancient cults (E2.4).

B E A T I T U D E S From Latin *beatus,* "happy, blessed." Sayings of Jesus Christ delivered in the "Sermon on the Mount" (Matthew 5:3–12), in the form of brief pronouncements beginning with the words "Blessed are . . ." (*Makarios* in Greek). Treated by some modern esoteric teachers as formulas for spiritual development: for instance, they may be correlated to the nine aspects of the ENNEAGRAM. Adj., beatific, ecstatic, absorbed in the vision of God or saintlike joy in the communion with the miracle of life itself.

BEATNIK   American slang, first used at the time of the Russian satellite Sputnik by *San Francisco Chronicle* columnist Herb Caen, who added the Russian suffix *-nik* to the term "Beat" in derogatory reference to the members of the Beat generation. A bohemian or unconventional person, often interested in esoteric matters. Predecessor of the hippies of the sixties, a significant agent in the counterculture that has produced the modern spiritual movement.

BELIEF   Any interpretation or framework for viewing reality that is held beyond questioning, either because it stems from direct experience and thus does not need to be questioned, or because it is given in dogmatic form by an accepted authority and thus is not supposed to be questioned. Curiously, the word comes from the Old English *geliefan,* from the IE base *leubh-,* related to the Latin *libido*: "what is desired, or loved." This seems to imply that we believe what we desire (or love) to believe. On the substitution of one belief structure for another, contrasted to the much more difficult process of synthesizing belief structures, see E2.1. Contrasted with FAITH in the Afterword.

BERMUDA TRIANGLE   Mysterious area of the Caribbean where a great many boats and airplanes are alleged to have disappeared without a trace, connected with wild speculation about underwater temples and UFOs. Example of an unexplained phenomenon that exerts sensational interest and contributes to the trivialization of the occult. See other examples under EARTH MYSTERIES.

BETA WAVES   See BRAIN WAVES.

BHAGAVAD GITA   (Bug-uh-vuhd GEE-tah) Sanskrit, "Song of the Lord." Sacred book of Hinduism, the first Sanskrit text to be translated into English, highly influential in the transmission of Eastern spirituality to the West. C&B1.6.

BHAKTI   (BAHK-tee) Sanskrit, from the root *bhaj-,* "to revere, to honor by devotion." In Yoga, devotional love, especially for a master or a chosen deity; the way of achieving union with the divine through blissful surrender. One of the six Yogas.

BHIKKU/BHIKSU   (BIK-hoo, BIK-soo) Sanskrit, "beggar." Common terms for the wandering mendicants who followed the Buddha around, believing that to be the best way to Enlightenment. Implies someone who has renounced the ordinary rewards of life and is totally dedicated to achieving Enlightenment, though he may be a long way from it. Comparable to the SANYASSIN in Hinduism.

BIBLE   From Greek *biblos,* "book." The primary sacred text of Western Christianity, divided into the Old and New Testaments, the former being a history of the ancient Hebrews, and the latter giving various accounts of the acts and sayings of Jesus Christ and his followers. See also APOCRYPHA, GNOSTIC GOSPELS.

BIGFOOT   See SASQUATCH.

BILOCATION   The capacity to be in two places at once, a skill frequently attributed to shamans and wizards. Its dynamics are complex and ambiguous, but it might be achieved through projection of the astral body or through lucid dreaming; or it may involve the difficult task of manipulating the DOUBLE. Described in numerous accounts, some hilarious, some horrible, by Carlos Castaneda.

BIODYNAMICS/BIODYNAMIC FARMING A method of agriculture proposed by Rudolf Steiner at the beginning of the century; uses special methods of cultivating the innate regenerative properties of the earth. Early prototype of organic farming.

BIOENERGETICS A method developed by Alexander Lowen in the early 1950s, based on exercises for communicating with the body and increasing vitality, with a strong emphasis on increasing sexual sensitivity and the capacity to feel pleasure. A spin-off of Lowen's involvement in REICHIAN WORK.

BIOFEEDBACK The process of monitoring bodily signals, such as pulse, temperature, and brain waves, in order to bring them under mental command and, by extension, use them to induce desired mental and emotional states. Widely used by Western practitioners to achieve mental and physical states of control comparable to the feats of Eastern yogis. Described by Barbara Brown, one of its main exponents, as "voluntary control over reflex-functions."

BIOKINESTHESIOLOGY The science of bodily energetics, noted for its technique of muscle testing: The practitioner asks the subject to hold out an arm and flex it, then poses a series of questions, pulling on the arm each time. The degree of resistance or release is interpreted as a direct answer by the body to the questions.

BIOPLASMA Vital force or quasi-electromagnetism of the human body. Term coined by Russian researchers in parapsychology, who call the ASTRAL BODY of occultism the biological plasma body, though it is unclear if bioplasma is the operative force in etheric fields as well. See also PLASMA.

BIOREGIONALISM In ecology and holistic nature studies, the approach to nature through caretaking of the Earth on a local scale by cultivating both practical and poetic sensitivity to natural resources in the area one inhabits.

BIORHYTHMS A system of plotting physical, emotional, and mental fluctuations according to three cycles of twenty-three, twenty-eight, and thirty-three days, respectively; developed early in the twentieth century by Hermann Swoboda and Wilhelm Fleiss and more recently popularized by others.

BLACK ARTS Old medieval term for all kinds of activities held to be questionable by the Christian church: alchemy, astrology, divination, et cetera. The use of this term became imperative when the Church set itself to eliminate all vestiges of pre-Christian worship, such as the reverence of nature-spirits and solar-phallic ritual. Most of these practices were harmless and in no way black; that is, Satanic. Though actual Satanic magic does exist, authentic cases of it are as rare as fleas on a flagpole (E15). The black arts at one time also included printing—considered to be the Devil's craft when it was first introduced! See also BLACK MAGIC, EVIL, LEFT-HANDED PATH.

BLACK HOLE Hypothetical locale in SPACETIME, usually associated with a dying star, where gravitational suction causes all light to collapse inward, resulting in a total conversion of matter to new potential at the atomic level. Originally implied by Einstein's Theory of General Relativity, 1916; later theoretically developed by George Gamow and Robert Oppenheimer (independently) in 1939. Often cited in playful speculations about mysterious points in the universe where normal laws are suspended and it becomes possible to disappear or to emerge in a different dimension: in short, a dodgy scientific hypothesis positing the OTHERWORLD. Key concept in some of the wilder speculations of paraphysics.

BLACK MAGIC The ultimate power trip; the pursuit of complete independence from the rest of the universe, including all practices and forms of thinking that lead to destructive, controlling, isolationary, and manipulative behavior; the quest for control and autonomy at the cost of all harmonious participation in the given order of the universe. See also SATANISM.

BLAVATSKY, HELENA PETROVNA Usually called Madame Blavatsky (Blah-VAHT-skee) (1831–1891). Eccentric Russian adventuress and famous medium, key revivalist of ANCIENT WISDOM, cofounder of Theosophy, long-sought emissary of the masters (E1.2), writer, channel extraordinaire, and formidable honky-tonk piano player. Noted for her spectacular feats of telepathy and magical materialization, performed (as described in the suppressed fourth volume of *The Secret Doctrine*) by the concentration of occult forces in her pinkies, which, when excited by a superfluity of subtle power, were said to resemble Polish sausages in heat.

BLOWGUNNER In Mayan and Central American mythology, image of the SOLAR LOGOS as the God who grants life and takes it away; pictured in the hieroglyph of the *Ahau,* divine breath, cosmic word, SPIRIT. His magical adventures are described in C&B2.12.

BODHI (BOH-dee) Sanskrit, from the root *budh-,* "to awaken, become enlightened." Enlightenment, illumination, the awakening to the ultimate nature of reality of mind or God, the state of perfect clarity and detachment in which everything is seen as a reflection in the mirror of one's own mind—the attainment of which makes one into a BUDDHA. In the life of the historical Buddha, his Enlightenment is said to have occurred as he sat beneath a tree, usually called the Bodhi tree. In Zen, the state of total, spontaneous presence of mind in which the SELF-NATURE is realized.

BODHIDHARMA (BOH-dee-DAHR-mah) Name of the twenty-eighth patriarch in the LINEAGE of Indian Buddhism, who carried the message of the Buddha from India to China around 527 A.D., thus initiating the practice of Ch'an in China, which eventually developed into Zen in Japan.

BODHISATTVA (Boh-dee-SAHT-vah) Sanskrit, "one who embodies the essence *(sattva)* of enlightenment *(bodhi)*." A human being of superevolved potential, able to enter and remain in the state of complete detachment, total serenity, and anonymity, removed from all human concerns and differences, merged with the All, the Source, in the state of Nirvana—*but who refrains from doing so,* so that he or she may continue to be involved with human affairs and contribute toward the liberation of all sentient beings. This commitment to refrain from total withdrawal into the superhuman detachment of NIRVANA is called the Bodhisattva vow. Colloquially, a superevolved human being, someone who has happily mastered all the angles in the game of life.

BODIES See FOUR-BODY THEORY.

BODY/MIND Loose name for all techniques and teachings aimed at producing a conscious interaction between the posture and functions of the body and the conscious attitudes of the person embodied in it.

BODYWORK Any kind of technique that involves direct, hands-on contact with the body, such as massage, acupressure, muscle testing. Includes dozens of techniques, such as Trager Mentastics, polarity therapies, Alexander technique, hakomi, reiki.

BONDING Positive and mutual emotional commitment between people, as ideally should occur between parents and child during infancy. In recovery, a condition necessary for people to see and serve each other's vital dependencies in active trust once the proper BOUNDARIES are established.

BON PO The native religion of Nepal. A form of shamanism concerned with the appeasement or exorcism of demonic forces by means of ritual manipulations, chants, divination, et cetera; supposed to have been purged from the land by the legendary Buddhist wizard PADMA SAMBHAVA, though traces of it still survive in the Nyingma sect of Tibetan Buddhism.

BOOK OF LIFE In the secret teachings of the Rosicrucians and Western alchemy, the record of the successive incarnations of a human being, each page or leaf being viewed as a single lifetime. Called in the Revelation of Saint John the Divine the Lamb's Book of Life, by which the dead are judged (New Testament, Revelation 20:12). But it is also, on a more positive note, the sum total of all the life stories of those who are integrated into the greater, all-encompassing life of the planetary spirit, or humanity itself, conceived as a single person. See also TAROT.

BOOK OF THE DEAD General term for religious manuals containing prayers and instructions for going through the experience of death or describing what happens after it, as in the Egyptian and the Tibetan Books of the Dead (C&B1.8).

B.O.T.A Builders of the Adytum. In modern Hermetics, a revivalist cult established in 1910 by Paul Foster Case as a wing of the GOLDEN DAWN in America; source of symbolic teachings on the Tree of Life and the Tarot.

Adytum (ADD-ih-tum): the sanctuary or inner sanctum where secret knowledge is preserved.

BOUNDARIES   In recovery, the sane limits that define different areas of feeling and relating, so that one's own sense of existence remains intact, free of ENMESHMENT, while one is able to reach out to others or receive them in a self-balanced way. Also, the right distinctions telling how and when and where to share one's experiences, such as knowing not to discuss the agonies of divorce in the supermarket checkout line. Necessary for overcoming the perilous entanglements of codependency.

BRAHMA   Sanskrit, from the root *brih-,* "to swell, expand." In Indian philosophy and religion, the supreme creative principle and the ground of all existence. In the Upanishads (C&B1.5), *Brahma* is continually related to *Atma,* the individual human spirit, with the assertion that *Atma* = *Brahma*: each and every human being is, in spirit, one with the Source. This is not to say, as it is often interpreted, that "You are God," but that the basis of one's self-consciousness is the purely superpersonal ground-consciousness of God as the supreme witness, the all-knowing One, and the Source of all that exists (C&B1, Preface, and E1.4).

BRAHMIN   A priest of the ancient lineage of Indian teachers who recognize Brahma as the supreme principle. In India, an orthodox representative of the prevalent religion of Hinduism. Adj., Brahminical.

BRAIN/MIND   Generic term for theories and studies attempting to understand human consciousness as a result of activities in the brain, or for model making that tries to explain how the entire world as we know it is a creation of our own brains (Pribram's thesis). See also CYBERNETICS.

BRAIN THEORY   A hot item in New Age speculations about the nature of reality as we perceive it—and perhaps construct it. Since the early 1970s, advanced theory in this field has been dominated by a Stanford University neuroscientist, Karl Pribram, who proposed a model of the brain closely allied to theoretical physics and capable of explaining both the normal and paranormal functions of consciousness. According to Pribram, the brain projects the perceived world from given sense-data in the manner of a HOLOGRAM. This implies the activity of consciousness as a reality-structuring power, rather than merely as a faculty for observation and analysis. Pribram's theory (described in C&B4.12) falls in with the paradigm-shift of the NEW PHYSICS. The New Age cliché, "You create your own reality," has apparently been taken quite literally by the theorists on the leading edge in this field. For a brief critique on this outlook, see also OCCULTISM and E2.4.

BRAIN WAVES   Extremely faint though detectable radiations from the human brain, supposed to fall loosely into four groups:

alpha waves: 8–13 cycles per second, 20 millionths of a volt; relaxation, non-focused attention beta waves: about 13–30 cycles per second; conscious attention, critical, anxious

delta waves: .5–4 cycles per second; sleep, "oceanic feeling"

theta waves: 4–7 cycles per second; deep meditation, good memory and facile learning

These frequencies are a matter of great interest in research with BIOFEEDBACK and techniques of meditation. The hard evidence for associating the specific wavelengths with mental states has led to a whole new field of technology, including fancy headgear and brain-tuning devices. The possibilities of the field seem practically limitless and there is plenty of room for SNAKE OIL in the machinery.

BREATHING EXERCISES See PRANA.

BRUJO/BRUJA (BREW-ho, BREW-ha) Spanish, "magician, sorcerer" (masc./fem.). In Western folklore, a practitioner of ancient arts of healing and self-control, especially involving extraordinary states of perception and unusual powers. Famous exemplars occur in the works of Castaneda (C&B4.6).

BRUNTON, PAUL Western philosopher and esotericist (1898–1981), one of the great masters of East/West synthesis, prolific author of explanatory works on highroads and byways of the modern spiritual quest (C&B3.8).

BUDDHA (BOO-dah) Sanskrit, from the root *budh-* (see BODHI). One who attains or realizes the full potential of Enlightenment and achieves the position of complete identification with the mind-state of pure reflection, total detachment, and absolute serenity called NIRVANA. Technically, the title for anyone who attains this state. The proper name for the human being who is most widely recognized for this attainment is GAUTAMA, SIDDHARTHA, or SHAKYAMUNI, a prince of the Indian clan of the Shakya, who lived between 563 and 483 B.C. (or, by another account, between 643 and 543 B.C.).

BUDDHI (BOO-dee) The active power of full-scale integration or synthetic intelligence, exhibited by someone who is awakened to the true nature of mind itself. Attunement to the innermost workings of life; or the blissful awareness of supervitality. Perfect clarity of response, free of approval or disapproval. See also SUPERCONSCIOUSNESS.

BUDDHISM The "ism" of orthodox practice aimed at the act of self-awakening. One of the four great traditional religions of the world, taken up as an alternative religion by many in the West. Originated in India around 600 B.C., then spread to China and Japan. Although purely traditional in its own right, its enormous appeal in the West may be due to the specific options it affords; for instance, the doctrine of liberation by contrast with the doctrine of salvation (E1.4 and 2.4). Another major paradigm-shift attractive to westerners who are dissatisfied with the Judeo-Christian ethic of judgment is the Buddhist ethic of COMPASSION, expressed in the ideal of dedication to the liberation of all SENTIENT BEINGS. Its emphasis on the impermanence of the world, over which we are powerless, rather than the imperfection of the world, in which we are deeply implicated according to the Western view, relieves us of the overwhelming burden to make everything right. Its essential practice consists of observing the neurotic patterns of the mind, overcoming ATTACHMENT, accepting the limits inherent to all human experience, and surrendering to the fragile and transitory nature of existence. It may be pursued by rigorous practice of meditation, chanting, and ritual, or loosely adopted as a kind of philosophical life-style. Its principal aim is the attainment of serenity. More often than not, the ritual and mood of Buddhism attracts new adherents as much as its philosophical outlook. Its rich legacy of humor and paradox is especially evident in the lore of Zen.

BUFFALO   In Native American folklore and myth, a totemic animal representing the permanent presence of the divine-creative powers from which the world originated, analogous to the sacred brahma bull in India, representing BRAHMA, the creator-God. Personified in the figure of White Buffalo Woman, who confers upon humanity the sacred pipe, symbol and instrument of atmospheric communion through the breath.

BUNRAKU   (Boon-RAH-koo) Ancient Japanese art of puppetry created in the eighteenth century, using near life-size puppets. Remarkable for the way the puppeteer, dressed totally in black, stands beside the puppet on the stage and manipulates it with such stealth as to make himself virtually invisible to the audience. Analogy to the guiding efforts of spiritual powers who work inconspicuously through the habit-mechanisms of human behavior. See also HIGHER POWER.

BUSHIDO   (BUSH-ee-doh) Japanese, "the way (do) of the warrior (bushi)." Japanese code of manliness and honor, expressed in mastery of the martial arts and allied techniques of meditation; somewhat comparable to CHIVALRY in the West. Initially based on the high ideal of personal sacrifice and selfless impeccability of action, close in spirit to Zen, but with an emphasis on total fearlessness and "death before dishonor." In recent times it seems to have degenerated somewhat into a macho power trip. Compare with WARRIOR.

C

CABALA (Kah-BAHL-lah) Hebrew, "tradition, legacy." A vast and often shapeless system of mystical knowledge, derived from an ancient stream of Hebraic occultism and largely compiled into its present from by Moses de Leon in the thirteenth century. Consists of a model of creation (TREE OF LIFE), and a complex system of symbols and principles for developing the inner potential of human nature, leading to the stage of conscious service to the divine powers at the source of all creation. Widely used in MAGIC. Spelled in various ways with different connotations: Cabala for its modern and synthetic version, Kabbalah in reference to the Jewish mystical tradition and commentaries on the Torah, Qabalah in magical and ritual use.

CANDOMBLÉ (Kan-DOM-blay) French, "meeting place." Magical and ritualistic religion of Brazil, African in origin, involving mechanistic trance and supplication of spiritual powers, primarily practiced by women.

CANON Loosely, a set of rules or formulas, especially of the kind believed to have been passed down through the centuries by secret groups or spiritual brotherhoods. In specific recent usage, the system of proportional formulas applied in GEOMANCY and sacred geometry—for instance, the mathematical proportions of the Great Pyramid or the geometrical layout of STONEHENGE.

The canon is a tremendous concept in New Age thinking. It represents the belief in a body of sacred knowledge that is as rigorous and consistent as scientific law, though it applies to matters that science does not acknowledge as significant—the numerical ratios of the planetary orbits, for instance. By far the greatest advance in recognition of the canon has come through the study of the proportions of ancient temples and monuments, such as Glastonbury Abbey and the pyramids of Central America. The long-lost Ark of the Covenant (whose canonical proportions are set out in great detail in the Old Testament account of King Solomon's temple) is said to have contained the proportional formulas relating all variations of measure, weight, and number to geometrical rules. By one account, quite famous now in planetary folklore, Saint Bernard of Clairvaux, who ascertained clairvoyantly that the Ark was buried in the stables of King Solomon, created the Order of the KNIGHTS TEMPLAR especially to send a cadre of men to Jerusalem to find the Ark and bring it to France. They did so, and from the canon preserved within it, artisans of the time designed and erected those great architectural wonders, the Gothic cathedrals.

See also GOLDEN SECTION on the astonishing canon of nature.

CAPOEIRA (Cap-oh-EAR-ah). A type of martial art from Brazil.

CASTANEDA, CARLOS American anthropologist (born 1931), key figure in the revival of shamanism, pathfinder in the realm of progressive occultism and mythmaking, author of a series of books introducing the Yaqui Indian Don Juan as the teacher of lost knowledge recast in a modern form. (C&B4.6).

CATHARS (Ka-THARS) From Greek *katharsis*, "purification." A religious heresy of the twelfth and thirteenth centuries, concentrated in communities in the region of southern France. They believed in a radical dualism, or MANICHEAN theology, holding the sensory world to be the creation of Satanic powers; therefore dedicated to keeping themselves pure of its contamination. Although the priesthood of the Cathars was ascetic, living in complete chastity, they maintained a liberal attitude toward the people of their culture, thus allowing the hedonistic society of the ALBIGENSIANS to flourish. Defiantly independent of the Catholic church, they were massacred in the Albigensian Crusade launched by Pope Innocent III. In recent times, the Cathars have curiously come to light in connection with reincarnation. See also MONSÉGUR.

CAUSAL BODY In Theosophy and other esoteric systems, one of the higher or supersensible bodies, supposed to be the permanent vehicle that survives through successive incarnations; probably equatable to the auric egg. See also FOUR-BODY THEORY.

CAYCE, EDGAR (KAY-see) American healer and trance adviser (1877–1945). Sometimes called the Sleeping Prophet, world-famous for his cures and clairvoyant dictations on Atlantis and other matters. Founder of A.R.E.

CELLULAR MEMORY Information stored in the genetic library of DNA, believed to include precise and comprehensive memory of all that a human individual has ever experienced, perhaps extending to past lives and even into the collective experience of humanity at large. See also GENETIC CODE.

CELTIC REVIVAL (E6) (KEL-tik, not SELL-tik) From the Latin word *Keltoi*, reported by Julius Caesar as the name these people applied to themselves. The renaissance of interest in the art, folklore, and religious/mystical beliefs of the ancient Celts, a seminomadic people who occupied vast areas of Europe, from Ireland down to Spain and far eastward into Turkey, from as early as 5000 B.C.; they flourished from about 1500 B.C. to 500 A.D., especially in France, where they were known as the Gauls (hence *Gallic,* a synonym for French). The last remnants of their culture survive in Ireland, Wales, Scotland,

and Brittany (southwestern France). In planetary folklore, the Celts are closely associated with geomancy and the GRAIL MYSTERY.

CENTERING   Any process that serves to assist in concentration or gathering one's emotional and mental forces at a point of rest or balance. See also MEDITATION.

CEREMONIAL MAGIC   Old-fashioned storybook magic, using certain rituals and tools (such as the sword, cup, and pentagram) for the purpose of manipulating the world to one's desired ends, or calling up various kinds of supernatural beings for the assistance or information they can provide. See also MAGIC.

CHAC   Ancient Rain God of the Maya Indians of Central America, equivalent to the Atlantean God Poseidon. Also, title of an excellent small-budget film about a modern Mayan shaman.

CHAKRA   (CHAHK-ruh, not SHAHK-ruh) Sanskrit, "wheel." A vortex or force-center in the nonphysical counterpart of the human body, though it is usually unclear whether the astral or the etheric body is meant; used to be called lotus-flower. See also FOUR-BODY THEORY.

CH'AN   Chinese form of the Sanskrit word *Dhyana,* "flow, momentum." The school of Buddhism that arose in China after the arrival of Bodhidharma in 527 A.D., and specifically the type of mental quieting practiced in that school. Predecessor of Japanese Zen. See C&B1.9.

CHANGE   The aspect of creation through which INFINITY is manifested, by contrast to changelessness, through which ETERNITY is manifested.

CHANNEL 23   The telepathic wavelength that carries information essential to sorting out what is true from what is deceptive on all other wavelengths.

CHANNELING (E7)   The current term for what used to be called mediumship. The offering of one's mind, voice, and body as a vehicle of communication for another being, which may be either a deceased person or a being of superior, other-dimensional nature who seeks to use the channel to make human contact and impart teachings or guidance.

CHANTING   The repetition of words or merely sounds, for the purpose of attaining a state of mental and emotional absorption, as in Gregorian chanting (ritual multivoiced song, unaccompanied by music, introduced into church services by Pope Gregory I around 600 A.D.), or in the practices of the Hare Krishna sect and Nichiren Shoshu.

CHAOS/CHAOTIC PHYSICS   Alternative school of natural science that took shape through the 1970s in a series of startling, almost accidental discoveries by a half-dozen independent researchers—primarily Mitchell Feigenbaum, Benoit Mandelbrot, and Stephen Smale. Concerned with the study of the patterns that inhere within erratic or turbulent phenomena, including everything from leaky faucets to fluctuations in the population sizes of fish colonies. Since the differential calculus used in conventional science does not provide any way to calculate such phenomena, such patterns have largely been dismissed as marginal and insignificant; but chaotic physics is based on a new type of calculation, called fractal mathematics, which allows scientists to detect and map out the hidden patterning within turbulent and nonperiodic events. The remarkable discovery that what appears as "chaotic" is actually stable and structured, though still not predictable, has led to an enormous shift of interest toward this emergent paradigm. In some respects, it approaches ancient and esoteric systems of viewing nature, especially in the way it concentrates on the phenomenon of the INTERVAL or erratic gapping of natural processes.

Chaotic physics differs from the prevailing science of the day in the way it pays attention to ordinary phenomena, most of which are erratic—like the steam bursts produced by a boiling kettle. It is also interdisciplinary, because the simple equations of fractal math can be applied with equal accuracy to everything from economics to heart arrhythmia to weather forecasting. The hidden laws of chaos have been visually translated into computer-generated, "self-similar" images based on fractal equations (the Mandelbrot set, for instance), which are astonishingly elaborate and lyrical in appearance, and somewhat reminiscent of the paisley patterns associated with the psychedelic experience. As it gains acceptance, chaotic physics appears to be an up-and-coming rival of the NEW PHYSICS, and may perhaps even emerge as the modern theory that can redirect us to live in vivid participation with the wonders of nature.

CHARISMA (Kuh-RIZ-mah) From Greek *charis,* "kindness, grace, beauty" > IE root *gher-,* "to desire, want, yearn for." 1. A gift given from God or through divine grace; sometimes considered to be a gift from the Holy Spirit, as in the case of the down-pouring of the holy fire upon the Twelve Apostles at Pentecost (New Testament, Acts 2:4); hence, a spiritual gift or talent. 2. The quality of personal attraction believed to be possessed by someone of high spiritual attainment, which, however, may also be confused with GLAMOR in its spiritual form.

CHARISMATIC (Care-iz-MAT-ik) That which expresses or seeks charisma. Specifically, the name for any fundamentalist sect where the members claim to receive divine inspiration, enabling them to prophesy, heal, and speak in tongues.

CHART Simply a map or design for orientation. Specifically, the natal horoscope or birthchart calculated in astrology: a circular design divided into twelve sections with the SIGNS overlapping the HOUSES, and the planets distributed through them according to their location relative to Earth at the moment of birth.

CHARTRES (Shart) French, place-name for a town near Paris, famous for its thirteenth-century cathedral, an important example of SACRED ARCHITECTURE.

CHELA (CHAY-lah) Sanskrit, "servant." A disciple or devotee of a spiritual master, or someone on the path of a particular discipline; neophyte. An old term much in use in Theosophy but far less common nowadays.

CHI (Chee) Chinese, "life-force." Conceived as a spiritual power animating all of nature and pervading the human form and its organs. In Taoist Yoga and the martial arts, the aim is to concentrate, strengthen, and manipulate chi. Sometimes spelled qi; in Japanese, ki. Compare with MANA.

CHINESE MEDICINE An ancient system of diagnostic and curative teachings believed to originate, for the most part, from the legendary Yellow Emperor, Huang Ti, who lived sometime after 3000 B.C. and supposedly wrote the Chinese medical classic *The Yellow Emperor's Book of Internal Medicine.* Recently, an alternative form of healing that has attracted much interest in the West, including the practice of acupuncture and the prescription of Chinese herbs.

CHIVALRY (SHIV-al-ree) From French *chevalier,* "knight, horseman." In medieval Europe, from about 600 A.D. up to the Renaissance, the code of masculine bravery and honor practiced by the Knights of the Round Table and the TEMPLARS. A Western version of the martial arts, associated with feats of supernatural power (such as slaying dragons) and the idealization of women. See also ARTHURIAN PATH, and C&B2.5 and 3.16.

CHOICE Imperative to the path of free seeking. See E2.4 on the dilemmas of choosing alternative paths. Contrast with CONTROL.

CHORTEN (CHORE-tun) Tibetan, "mound, monument." In Tibetan Buddhism, a square temple with a conical or turnip-shaped top, used for prayer and meditation. Also called a stupa (STEW-pah).

CHRIST/CHRISTOS Greek, from the verb *khreian,* "to anoint"; thus, the one who anoints. A technical term for the supreme God of the SOLAR MYSTERIES, the Savior who assumes human embodiment in the person of JESUS. Thus, a superhuman being not limited to the historical figure of Jesus Christ but viewed esoterically as the Cosmic Christ, the Son of God who incarnates to become united with the Earth. In New Age philosophy, the Earth Spirit, the living medium of planetary wholeness and human convergence, the ideal focus of unity and love in the OMEGA-STATE. Model of the complete integration of the divine and human selves. See also ETHERIC CHRIST.

CHRISTIANITY The historical religion centered on the figure of Jesus Christ; most populous of the traditional religions. Exemplifies the Western paradigm of JUDGMENT.

CHRISTIANITY, ALTERNATIVE (E8) The little-known optional variations of historical Christianity that can provide alternative paths of discovery and devotion for those attracted to the cosmic and mystical aspects of Christ but put off by the dogmas and moral dictates of its conventional form.

CHRISTIAN SCIENCE Neoreligious, quasiscientific movement founded by Mary Baker Eddy (1821–1910) in 1866, based on the concept that God and mind are the same reality, so the power of thought is capable of producing divine or supernatural effects. A reinstatement of biblical Christianity in a quasiscientific form, one of the earliest examples of spiritual technology.

CHRIST MYSTERY   Central concern of the ancient SOLAR MYSTERIES, such as the Mystery Schools of the Druids or the Egyptian priesthood, which preserved teachings about Christ in the mystical and cosmological sense previous to historical Christian doctrines. In the ancient mythologies of these schools, Christ is prefigured as a DIVINE CHILD (Horus to the Egyptians, Mabon to the Druids), who embodies the original purity and perfection of the human race (before the Fall), and who is both the Son of God and the Sun God, destined to come to Earth and unite with humanity, thus empowering it to regain its original perfection.

CHRISTOCENTRIC   Referring to any view of the cosmos or the human condition in which the figure and activity of Christ is taken as the central, all-pervasive factor. The esoteric teachings of two prominent twentieth-century Western masters, Max Heindel and Rudolf Steiner, are Christocentric, for instance, as are the philosophy of TEILHARD DE CHARDIN and the contemporary teachings given out by David Spangler of Findhorn.

CHRISTOLOGY   The science of knowledge of Christ, including all those esoteric teachings that refer to the cosmological and planetary aspects of Christ's mission as the supreme AVATAR, the world-savior, including the problematic issue of the Second Coming.

CHRISTOPHORIC   Adj., referring to a carrier (Greek, *phoros*) of the impulse of Christ, thus representing the unitive spirit of the whole earth and humanity as one organism. Descriptive of those who are dedicated to Christ in a manner independent of conventional Christian teachings and organization. N., Christophore.

CLAIRAUDIENCE   "Clear hearing." The capacity to hear in the range of sound outside the physical limits of the ear. Usually, the instrument of this faculty is held to be the etheric body, which is described as serving as a kind of radio for receiving telepathic signals.

CLAIRSENTIENCE   "Clear sensing." The capacity to see with the natural senses that which is ordinarily not perceptible to them. Many instances are found in the annals of the Western alchemists; for instance, the vision of Jakob Boehme recorded in *Cosmic Consciousness* by Bucke (C&B3.1). Involves full retention and illumination of the sense-impressions of this world by a supernatural light or presence, or both. By many accounts, the PSYCHEDELIC EXPERIENCE offers a glimpse of clairsentience. Adj., clairsentient, synonymous with infrasensory; contrast with extrasensory perception.

CLAIRVOYANCE   "Clear seeing." The capacity to see the human aura or entities of a nonsensory nature, such as disembodied people or spirits working in the atmosphere to produce natural phenomena (DEVAS). Said to be possessed by some people as a natural gift, and developed by others through exercises and meditation. An example of extrasensory perception.

CLEARING   The process of emptying the mind and emotions of negative and disruptive contents, by a variety of methods such as meditation, ritual,
breathing, and use of crystals.

COCREATION   Collaboration by humanity in the ongoing process of
creation, taking it as an event that remains to be completed rather than as an event
over and done by the time humanity wakes up and looks around. The supreme
aim of spiritual development in the ancient *Mysteries,* where the entrants were
prepared to assume the responsibility of fulfilling the design of evolution, taking
up where the Gods left off. An idea inherent to alchemy (E3), rediscovered by
the Romantics (E22), and currently discussed as a key theme, or perhaps the key
theme, of the New Age (E1.4 and E2.4). See also COEVOLUTION, CULTURE,
ATTITUDE.

CODEPENDENCY   An often-fatal disease of emotional confusion,
marked by severe alienation from one's own feelings. Living for and through
others, due to the inadequate development of self-love as a true basis for loving
others. A major concept in RECOVERY.

Variously defined as: (1) the addiction to living for others at the expense
of one's own development; (2) the substitution of adaptation for honest self-
expression; (3) the vicious cycle of using and blaming that arises when we make
others responsible for what we feel and do; (4) the mechanism of controlled/
controlling that locks people into futile dependencies and impossible demands;
(5) abuse and DISCOUNTING disguised in the attitudes and gestures of love,
loyalty, devotion, caretaking, people pleasing. Any combination of the above.
Adjective and/or noun: codependent.

COEVOLUTION   The aspect of cocreation that involves working directly with the processes of nature, to assist or advance them. Esoterically, the
consummation of the alchemical wedding. Conventionally, a basic concept in
ECOLOGY. Also, name of a well-known quarterly based on understanding the
relations between mind and nature according to the teachings of Gregory Bate-
son.

COLLECTIVE UNCONSCIOUS   In the Jungian work, the store-
house of the deep-level formative structures that comprise the framework for all
human awareness and knowledge; the repository of racial and universal information in the form of emotionally charged images called ARCHETYPES.

COLOR THEORY   A system of interpretations about the nature and
relationships of colors, applied to composition in painting or to cures and mood
alteration in healing.

COLOR THERAPY   The use of colors, often in the form of colored
lights, to induce mental, emotional, and physical changes and to cure illnesses.

CO-MASONRY   Variant of the Masonic Order, founded in France in
1893, distinguished by its liberalism and admission of women.

COMMON SENSE   According to A. R. Orage, the last degree of esoteric teaching. As a principle of clear seeking, it should be kept rigorously

distinct from the CONSENSUS-REALITY, or what is often called "conventional wisdom."

COMMUNITY   The most common form of group effort, viewed as a cellular model for planetary organization in some circles of New Age thinking. On the heretical and utopian communities that foreshadowed the New Age, see E1.1.

COMPASSION   In Sanskrit, *karuna*. The primary quality of awareness to be developed in Buddhism, distinguished from love by its impersonal and unattached nature. The most direct and all-encompassing response to the universal suffering of humanity—since it means, literally, to suffer with. The attitude of deep yet unattached participation that counters the human tendency (Luciferic bias) to alienate and isolate, again distinguished from love in that it does not require deep personal commitment to the essence of the other, so seemingly inescapable where love is involved. See also DUKKHA.

COMPULSIVITY   A mood-altering relation to a substance, person, thing, or event that has life-damaging consequences. A primary concept in recovery, where it is viewed as the social norm.

CONDITIONING   The process of learning reactions under the conditions of extreme vulnerability in childhood, when our first responses are formed and the patterns for all later behavior are established. Occurs on many levels, effectuated through IMPRINTING.

CONSENSUS-REALITY   Term coined by Joseph Chilton Pearce (C&B4.9) for the model of reality established by conventional beliefs and agreed upon without question, which excludes the kinds of experiences to be discovered in ALTERED STATES and which prevents us from exploring our innate potential to change and grow.

CONSPIRACY   From Latin, "breathing together." Main theme and frequent obsession of the modern spiritual movement, as seen in many variations of conspiracy theory: the Himalayan masters of Blavatsky and the PLANETARY HIERARCHY of Alice A. Bailey, the Nazi Cult, Great White Brotherhood (E14), Trilateral Commission, oat bran, space people taking over Earth. Historically confirmed in the popular mind by the Kennedy assassination and Watergate. Often referring back to biblical prophecies—for instance, the 144,000 in Revelation who are described as the ones who are selected to survive the Last Judgment. See also CULT.

CONSTELLATION   In astrology, an actual star figure visible in the night skies, associated for thousands of years with mythological beings and events (sidereal mythology). Irregular in extent, not to be confused with the regular geometrical sectors of the SIGNS.

CONTROL   (1) The aim and expression of self-will, basic to the mechanism of manipulation common to both modern science and ancient magic: to get results. Often mistaken for choice, but control implies dictating the result, while in choice there is responsibility for the initial act but not for the outcome. (2) Old-fashioned term for the spirit who takes possession of a medium in the process of channeling.

CONVERGENCE   The state of coming together as an ideal point of harmony, balance, and cooperative vision or action. Synergistic focus. "All that rises must converge," wrote Teilhard de Chardin. See also HARMONIC CONVERGENCE.

CORRESPONDENCES (DOCTRINE OF)   See ANALOGY.

COSMIC CONSCIOUSNESS   General term for the realization of God and the awareness of the all-pervasive design of the universe; the state of omniscience, insofar as it is possible for a human being to experience it. In Eastern religion, SAMADHI. See C&B3.1 and E17 on the two main types of cosmic consciousness.

COSMOLOGY   A description of creation, a complete scenario of how the universe and humanity came into being, such as one finds in *The Secret Doctrine* by Madame Blavatsky. In practical and contemporary terms, a plan or vision of the operative patterns of the human world, including the patterns of nature in relation to the moral and psychological aspects of human behavior.

COSMOS/COSMIC   A term from the sixties, now almost bereft of credibility. In Greek, *kosmos* meant simply "pattern, design," as in the pattern of colors and forms woven into a rug. Thus the cosmos is the order of things, the pervasive design of the world, and cosmic refers to anything that describes, points to, or is included in this design.

COYOTE   In Native American folklore, a TRICKSTER who embodies a baffling mix of mischief and benevolence. An example of the worldwide mythic theme of the erring or meddling Gods, taken up into serious theological speculations in Gnosticism (E13).

CREATIVE VISUALIZATION   The process of using mental images in order to acquire what one desires or produce changes in one's attitude, thus creating one's own reality by the projection of emotionally charged visions. See also VISUALIZATION.

CREATIVITY   From Latin *creare*, "to create" > IE root *kre-*, "to grow, evolve." The ultimate form of self-expression. According to the Romantics, the capacity given to humanity by God in seminal form, which, if developed to its fullest, allows the human being to achieve a stage of God-like activity—that is, to become an agent in COCREATION.

CRITICAL MASS   Term borrowed from nuclear physics, where it refers to the mass of matter that needs to be converted by atomic fission for a chain reaction to occur. In New Age philosophy, a metaphor for the seed-nucleus of human beings who have so changed their lives that they can serve as a catalytic force in global transformation. Compare to HUNDREDTH MONKEY, QUANTUM LEAP.

CROWLEY, ALEISTER English mystic and adventurer (1875–1947), notorious for his experimentations in occultism and sexual magic, key figure in the modern revival of magic, renegade member of the GOLDEN DAWN, originator of an elaborate version of the Tarot.

CRYSTAL DEVA A supernatural being believed to inhabit or work through crystals. See also DEVA.

CRYSTALS (E9) Believed to act as collectors and transmitters of forces not ordinarily in the range of human perception, having various applications, such as healing, controlling dreams, transferring information.

CULT (E10) From the Latin *cultus*, "care, cultivation" > *colere*, "to till" > IE root *kwel-*, "to dwell, care for." Any group organized around a set of principles, a primary belief system, or a leading personality or deity; for instance, the cult of people who believe the earth is flat, or the cult of Kali-worshippers in India. A community in conspiracy with itself, and often at odds with the world at large.

CULTURE The organization of human society according to guiding principles; thus, the cultivation of human potential in the design of group experience. In former times, it was believed that culture was not an accidental development but something intentionally introduced and fostered by certain beings of a superhuman nature—at first, the Gods themselves, then the MANUS or culture-initiators who worked as selfless servants of the Gods in implementing the divine plan amid human affairs. This process, known as culture-initiation, was held to be one of the primary responsibilities of the initiates in the MYSTERIES and is currently being reformulated in New Age thinking (E1.3).

CURANDERA (Cur-an-DARE-uh) Spanish, "healer." In Mexico and South America, a woman, often possessing psychic powers, who heals and gives advice.

CYBERNETICS (Sigh-bur-NET-iks) From Greek *kybernetes*, "helmsman." The study of the workings of the human brain by analogy to the computer, for the purpose of understanding the brain's self-regulating powers, and often applying the knowledge gained in techniques of biofeedback, neurolinguistic programming, and metaprogramming.

CYCLES In the worldview that prevailed before the rise of natural science, repetitive processes believed to operate in a way roughly equivalent to what we now call natural laws; for instance, the planetary cycles in astrology.

D

DAEMON/DAIMON (DAY-mon) Greek, "guiding or advising spirit." In Greek mythology and folklore, a deity who instructs and inspires, the most famous example being EROS, described in Plato's *Symposium* (C&B2.3) as a "mighty daemon" who mediated between Gods and mortals. Psychologically, the inner genius of a person. Adj., daemonic—as in daemonic education, which proposes to draw forth and nurture the unique genius of the child. Not to be confused with DEMON.

DAKINI (Dah-KEY-nee) Tibetan, "sky-walker, sky-dancer." A feminine being of supernatural powers, usually benevolent but often of terrifying aspect, who may resort to impersonating a human being; usually serves in the role of a guide or trickster who instructs or initiates. The classic example appears in the life of Padma Sambhava, the founder of Tibetan Buddhism. Exact equivalent to the FAERY of Irish/Celtic myth and folklore.

DALAI LAMA Tibetan *dalai,* "ocean" + *lama,* "chieftain, high priest." The highest authority in the religious organization of Lamaism, comparable to the pope in Catholicism. The current Dalai Lama, Tyentsin Gyatso, is called the fourteenth, because he is held to be a TULKU in the fourteenth phase of reembodiment. Winner of the Nobel Peace Prize, 1989.

DANCE Mythic image of creation, vividly figured by Shiva and Krishna, the dancing gods of Hinduism, and in many cultures from Native America to Polynesia. Also called the cosmic dance or dance of life, pictured in the twenty-first trump of the Tarot (the World). In Eastern spirituality, often associated with the theme of creation as PLAY. In Gnostic Christianity, the crucifixion, described in the heretical *Acts of John* as a mystic dance performed by Christ to unite his followers with him in vital union. See also SACRED DANCE.

DEAD SEA SCROLLS Ancient manuscripts discovered in 1947 in caves at Qumran near the Dead Sea, Israel. They contain descriptions of the beliefs and practices of a Jewish community of ESSENES that inhabited the area between 250 and 50 B.C.: rites of purification, organization of the community, initiation, the common meal, study practices, the calendar, and some ethical and theological material, including indications of a MESSIAH. Not to be confused with the GNOSTIC GOSPELS.

DEATH AND DYING   A movement and philosophy that seeks to overcome the fear of death and promote an attitude of acceptance toward death as a transition to another kind of life, as it has been considered in many cultures of the past. Often associated with the name of Elisabeth Kübler-Ross, one of its leading pioneers.

DECADENCE   The final phase of ROMANTICISM, centered around 1875, a time when many artists and writers were deeply involved in occult ways of viewing the world. The Decadents were notorious drug-takers and eccentrics who despised and rejected the life of conventional people (especially the bourgeoisie, or affluent middle class of the time) in favor of the terrors and wonders of the INNER LIFE. For instance, they asserted the superiority of the imaginary over the actual, dream over reality, beauty (usually exotic or perverse) over utility. Deeply affected by the European Occult Revival, they resembled the present countercultural New Age in their attraction to the metaphysical and all its trappings. In many cases, they pursued the occult to the extent of losing their minds or their souls in the search for invisible worlds and artificial paradises (E2.3). See also SYMBOLIST MOVEMENT.

DEIFICATION   In Latin, *theo-genesis,* "the birthing of a God." The transformation of a human being into a God, or the raising of ordinary human consciousness to a superhuman state, including psychic powers, awareness of immortality, omniscience. In the ancient Mysteries, the result of INITIATION, though not its final purpose or aim. Called by Dante (in C&B2.7) transhumanization and cited by Bucke (in C&B3.1) as the primary effect of experiencing a moment of cosmic consciousness. In the idiom of the new spirituality, the prospect attending the belief "You are God," which sets New Age thinking apart from traditional religion in which the distinction between God and human is strictly retained (E2.2, E2.4). Associated with all manner of techniques and programs for developing the God within or cultivating the divine potential inherent to human nature. See also DIVINITY, GODSEED.

DELPHIC ORACLE   In ancient Greece, the pronouncements given by the priestess Pythia, a famous medium, in a grotto at the foot of Mount Parnassus. Seated in a chair hung from a tripod above a chasm that gave up intoxicating vapors, she was inspired with prophecies that provided the answers to visitors' questions. Her most famous advice: "Know thyself." Most famous ancient example of CHANNELING.

DELUSION   From the Latin *ludere,* "to play" + the prefix *de,* "away, from"; thus, that which goes away from play. (1) The condition of spiritual ignorance in which the true nature of the self and the world is mistaken, or missed entirely. By strict reference to the Latin root, whatever you can't play with may be a delusion! This accords with the Eastern wisdom that teaches that the nature of all creation is divine PLAY. (2) In recovery, the process of lying to oneself and making it work, or at least maintaining the appearance that it works, usually coupled with DENIAL. Thus, delusion is not just not having fun, it is persisting in what is not pleasurable or good for oneself, while pretending that it is.

DEMON A nonhuman being of malicious or at best mischievous nature. From the Greek *daemon,* originally meaning a benevolent spirit-guide. Applied in historical Christianity wholly in the negative and very inclusively, so that it encompasses any and every kind of supernatural being, such as the NATURE-SPIRITS of Paganism, other than the one Christian God.

DENIAL In recovery, the master mechanism that operates against the natural unfolding of the innate potential for love (of God, self, others). From the esoteric viewpoint, that which is usually called the *unconscious,* can be seen as consisting of two components: the part that is really conscious but held in denial, and the part that is merely latent but subject to conscious development by the methods of genuine occultism. See also AHRIMAN.

DEPROGRAMMING The process of erasing or reversing the attitudes, beliefs, and behavior exhibited by someone who has been indoctrinated into a group or cult that demands rigorous, unquestioning adherence to its belief system. See also IMPRINTING.

DERVISH See WHIRLING DERVISH.

DESTINY From Latin, *de-,* "from" + *sidere,* "star"; something given from the stars or by a higher power, supposed to operate as the preset plan or design of an individual's life. Basically, the expression that results from the full unfolding of one's innate potential. See C&B2, Preface.

DEVA (DAY-vah) Sanskrit, from the root *div-,* "to shine"; hence, "radiant, shining, luminous being." A kind of supernatural being appearing in many forms in Oriental folklore and myth, equivalent to a FAERY in Western culture. Often described as the caretakers of certain processes in nature, such as plant growth or rainfall; thus, spirits of nurturing and growth. Can also appear as tutelary deities, teachers or guides, allies in pathfinding. Adj., devaic (deh-VAY-ik).

DEVIL From Middle English *devel* > Old English *deofol* > Latin *diobolos,* from *dia-,* "against, across" + *bolos,* "throw, assert." The adversary of the good or divine or progressive powers in the universe. A problematic entity in theology and world myth, not just because of the trouble he stirs up, but because it seems to be necessary to distinguish adversarial powers of darkness from adversarial powers of light: SATAN, on the one hand, and LUCIFER on the other. "Devil" itself is a loose term that may be applied to either, though technically it fits Lucifer more closely, because Lucifer is the light-bearing God who opposes the other Light Gods, while Satan, also called AHRIMAN, is definitely an entity of the dark side, the embodiment of cold will or destructive intelligence.

DHAMMAPADA (Dah-muh-PAH-duh) Pali, "track of the truth." The body of Buddhist teachings accepted as the orthodox text in southern India.

DHARMA Sanskrit, from the root *dhri-,* "to establish, hold fast." Curiously, it means both "thing" or "thing done," and "truth, that which holds up as true." Found in both Hindu and Buddhist religion as a term for the path of service appropriate to an individual, the way of doing what is true for that one. In practical terms, duty or obligation to fulfill a particular mission or task. To find your dharma is, quite literally, to do your thing, to serve the cause of truth as you see it. The exact Western equivalent is SERVICE.

DIANETICS From *dia-,* "through" + *noesis,* "mind, thinking." A term coined by L. Ron Hubbard to describe the method used in SCIENTOLOGY.

DIJERIDOO (Dij-ur-ee-DEW) Flutelike instrument made from a tree hollowed out by termites, used ritually by the Australian Aborigines to induce a state of mind for entering the Dreamtime.

DISCIPLINE From Latin *discipere,* "to comprehend, learn." In the old-fashioned sense, rigorous adherence to a prescribed program or set of teachings, such as the strict training of a monk in both Buddhism and Christianity. In modern seeking, the necessary work of mastering knowledge and practices for oneself, not merely by adopting a prescribed set of rules or methods, but more or less by free-form experimentation, often selecting from a number of different options and combining them. See also PATHFINDING and the Preamble.

DISCOUNTING In recovery, the basic and most common deed of trespassing that one human being can perpetrate on another: the act of invalidation, putting someone down by leaving him out, due to the failure either to feel or show compassion. In short, treating someone as if he doesn't count.

DIVINATION Any of a wide variety of methods for finding out what will happen in the future, for investigating events at a distance, or for acquiring answers to questions about situations for which direct evidence or data is lacking. Popular examples: *I Ching,* Runes, Tarot.

DIVINE CHILD A being found in the lore of worldwide religion and mythology, described as a superhuman entity and often associated with the sun: as Horus in Egyptian myth, Aengus in Irish myth. This sun-child is a representative of humanity as a whole, the exemplar of the primal innocence and purity of the human race, who often reappears in a human embodiment to redeem humanity from its division and bondage in sin (delusions and destructive behavior that keep humanity from achieving its true potential). The best-known example is of course Christ, the superhuman being who comes to Earth and assumes embodiment in the man, Jesus, in keeping with the perennial theme of the SOLAR MYSTERIES. See also INNER CHILD.

DIVINE SPARK The individual human essence, spiritual germ, or *monad,* endowed with infinite potential to evolve, viewed as a fragmentary or seedlike emanation of the Godhead.

D I V I N I T Y Godhood or God-essence, by contrast to humanhood. It is usually conceived as something superhuman, though it is believed to inhere in a seedlike way in human nature. The question of just how divinity inheres in human nature is, however, a most subtle and troublesome one. To develop the innate seed of divinity, rather than remain bound within the religious attitude of the divine/human relation, is perhaps the primary mark of alternative seeking (as noted in E1.4). See also GODSEED, HUMAN POTENTIAL.

D . K . Initials of Djwal Khul, "The Tibetan," one of the original masters in Theosophy, channeled through Alice A. Bailey.

D N A See GENETIC CODE.

D O C T R I N E From Latin *docere*, "to teach, instruct." Any traditional or perennial teaching that comes to be embodied in a system and thereby, most often, petrified into a dogma. It implies something taught over many generations, one of the most famous instances being *The Secret Doctrine* of Madame Blavatsky.

D O G D A Y S See DOG STAR.

D O G M A Any teaching enforced in a rigid and compulsory way, such as the dogma of damnation in traditional Christianity, or the dogma of rebirth in Buddhism. See also KARMA.

D O G O N (DOE-gun) A tribe in Mali, West Africa, investigated in the 1930s by the French anthropologists Griaule and Deiterlen, whose initiation into tribal secrets led to the disclosure of the SIRIUS MYSTERY.

D O G S T A R The brightest star in the sky, also called Sirius, about 8.4 light-years from Earth. Played a central role in the religion and agriculture of the ancient Egyptians. In ancient times, the flooding of the Nile was anticipated by observing when Sirius rose with the Sun. Today, the period of hot, sultry weather from the time Sirius rises at dawn (mid-July) to early September is called the dog days due to the prominence of this star. A key element in New Age mythmaking; extraterrestrial guidance and possible intervention are often ascribed to supernatural beings inhabiting this star. See also VEGA.

D O L M E N Breton (Old French) *men*, "stone" + *taol*, "table." In geomancy, a stone construction consisting of two upright slabs and a horizontal slab, making a portal for the sun; used by the Druids for shadow-divinations. Also called cromlech.

D O L P H I N S Water-dwelling mammals known for their swift swimming and playfulness. Believed to be a species with powers of communication more advanced in some ways than the human; they may even possess knowledge of certain processes critical to the ultimate survival of humanity on Earth. Dolphin stories are a part of planetary folklore. See also WHALES.

D O N J U A N Name of the Yaqui Indian wise man popularized in the writings of Carlos CASTANEDA.

D O U B L E An entity believed to exist for each human being as a near-exact counterpart of the physical self, but superphysical and usually invested with all the worst traits of character found in the living person. Perhaps the prototype of the double is the so-called GUARDIAN OF THE THRESHOLD often mentioned in European occultism, but it also seems to be closely related to the NAHUAL in shamanic practices. By some interpretations, the double is the form assumed in lucid dreaming and astral projection. Also called doppelganger and other names, by which it is widely known in European folklore. The extraction and projection of the double is one of the great, troubling secrets of classical occultism. In Robert Louis Stevenson's famous novella, *The Strange Case of Dr. Jekyll and Mr. Hyde,* Hyde is the double of Jekyll. Oscar Wilde's *The Picture of Dorian Gray* is another famous tale based on the double theme, a subject that deeply engaged the morbid imagination of many seekers in the Decadence. Compare with the Jungian concept of the SHADOW.

DOVE (1) In Christianity, symbol of peace attained through the arbitrating and healing presence of the Holy Spirit. (2) In occultism, image of the group-spirit made up of all human beings who have purified their desire-natures (astral bodies) to a degree of selflessness that allows them to experience transpersonal unity (total empathy, telepathic rapport, et cetera). (3) In esoteric astrology, the transfiguration of the Scorpion (emotional-sexual power) into an instrument of healing and grace.

DOWSING In geomancy, the use of a forked twig or metallic rod for detecting the location of water beneath the earth or tracing the flow of telluric (soil-bound) currents.

DRAGON Important image in world mythology. (1) In the case of the Chinese imperial dragon, the symbol of divinity incarnated in material form. (2) In European folklore and Arthurian legend, a supernatural being who embodies the destructive forces of nature, usually overcome in a fierce battle by a valiant knight. (3) In geomancy, the image of the TELLURIC powers of the Earth itself, sometimes called dragon currents. (4) In alchemy, the image of the human metabolism, where matter is destroyed and recreated in a mysterious recycling process (the ouroboros, a dragon or serpent eating its own tail) that is not even fully understood by science today.

DREAM-BODY The form assumed by the conscious self when it passes over into the dream state. It is characteristic of the dream-body that it loosely resembles the physical form of the dreamer but it is usually unable to observe itself. Possibly a manifestation assumed by the DOUBLE.

DREAMTIME In the language of the Australian Aborigines, the "Alcheringa," the "old stone time" or the time when the stones were alive; believed to be a magical dimension of reality, like a dreamworld, that coexists with the world of normal experience; accessible to shamans through their skills in meditation and chanting. Example of the OTHERWORLD.

DREAMWORK The method or exercise of using dreams for self-development, either by recording the progression of one's dreams in a journal and working with the insights that may derive from this, or actually penetrating with self-conscious awareness into the dream process itself, as in lucid dreaming.

DRUIDS   Ancient priesthood of the British Isles, a pure example of a cult of the Solar Mysteries; that is, sun worshipers who possessed an extensive science of astronomy, embodied in Stonehenge. The Druids believed in reincarnation and produced a remarkable lineage of musical seers, or BARDS. Probably named after an ancient word for the oak tree, which they held sacred. See also CELTIC REVIVAL.

DUKKHA   Sanskrit word for "suffering, misery," possibly rendered with a more accurate edge as "frustration." In Buddhism, one of the three primary characteristics of existence, the other two being impermanence (anitya) and the absence of fixed identity (anatta). In a distinct difference from the Judeo-Christian view that we suffer as an effect of having sinned, or even of having inherited the consequences of Adam's sin, Buddhism teaches that dukkha is innate to the nature of existence, without either cause or origin. The challenge of life, then, is to meet it with COMPASSION. Contrast to PLAY in the ecstatic mysticism of Hindu Tantra and in Sufi.

DYSFUNCTIONALITY   In recovery, the state of unwholeness in which the different functions of human makeup (mental, emotional, physiological, sexual, discriminative, et cetera) do not work together in unity, so that all functions become distorted, to a greater or lesser degree, in trying to cover for the others; for instance, the need for sexual contact is displaced by mental preoccupations (working on the computer all night). In short, disintegration and inadequacy to face and meet one's needs; the opposite of integration and wholeness. Often marked by ADDICTION. See also TWELVE-STEP PROGRAM.

E

EARTH CHAKRAS/EARTH TEMPLES In geomancy, a location where the innate, living forces of the Earth are concentrated in a special way due to the natural formation of the land. A place not occupied by actual ruins, yet believed to have the properties of a SACRED SITE.

EARTH CHANGES Term loosely applied to the prospect of immense disturbances of nature, such as earthquakes and POLE-SHIFT. A prime subject of New Age speculation, usually handled in a sensationalistic way. Mentioned in many different prophecies, such as those of Nostradamus and the biblical scenario of the last days. See also VELIKOVSKY.

EARTH MYSTERIES (1) Loosely, a category including almost anything that suggests the unexplained workings of nature, such as Sasquatch and the Bermuda Triangle; or equally puzzling matters relating to ancient lost civilizations, such as the Pyramids, Nazca Lines, et cetera. (2) Specifically, anything relating to the organic vitality of the whole Earth, such as LEY-LINES, dowsing, and other matters in geomancy.

EAST/WEST A neologism from the 1960s for the field of studies and practices that involve a synthesis or comparison of Oriental and Western ideas, philosophies, methods, et cetera. For instance, the NEW PHYSICS, which attempts to blend Eastern mysticism and Western thinking; or the use of transcendental meditation for stress-control among American businessmen. Initiated around 1800 by pathfinders involved in the great transmission (E2.3).

ECKANKAR (Ek-an-KAR) A system of knowledge and practices introduced in 1964 by Paul Twitchell (1908–1971), who claimed to be the 971st member of a lineage going back to Atlantis. Proposes an ancient wisdom applied to soul travel on the ECK current that flows through the universe at large. See also SHABDA.

ECLIPTIC A term in astronomy relevant to astrology: the path of the Earth around the Sun, experienced by us as the apparent path of the Sun around the Earth—called the ecliptic because it is the platelike region of space where eclipses occur when the Sun and Moon are properly aligned. The twelve SIGNS are equal divisions of this path.

ECOLOGY From Greek, *oikos*, "house, dwelling, habitat" + *logos*, "science." Knowledge about the relations between human beings and their planetary habitat, or ecosystem. Theory and practice of planetary resource management; or COEVOLUTION. Expressed on the public scale in the environmental movement—Sierra Club, Friends of the Earth, et cetera. One of the major developments in planetary awareness since the 1960s.

ECSTASY From Latin *ek-*, "out" + *histanai*, "to locate," implying a state of dislocation, out of the body. In accounts of mystical experience, both Eastern and Western, a state of rapture, of total mental and emotional bliss, in which the individual feels utterly released from the ordinary sense of confinement to a physical body and/or to a fixed identity—thus, dis-located. In some Oriental teachings, such as Tantra, believed to be the ground-state of ultimate reality: God is ecstasy. Equivalent to the Sanskrit Ananda. Compare with ENSTASY.

ECTOPLASM In spiritualism, an old-fashioned term for a kind of gelatinous substance exuded from the body of the medium, thus providing a means for discarnate entities to materialize. Supposedly, a superfluous emission of the etheric body. See also BIOPLASMA.

EDUCATION From Latin *e-*, "from, out" + *ducere*, "to draw, extract, conduct": thus, the process of drawing forth (that which is innate). Enabling people to draw upon what they carry within themselves, extracting and expressing the INNATE, rather than filling them with information. A key issue in the New Age, especially concerning education for the discipline of self-actualization.

EGO Latin word for "I." Ambiguous term, formerly used in certain teachings (such as Theosophy) as a name for the higher self or the spiritual essence of human nature, but more lately used as an insult to remind us we are sometimes not who we think we are. At least three distinct usages can be identified:

(1) In Western psychology, the focal point of the self-conscious personal identity, as distinguished (in the Jungian work, for instance) from the greater, transpersonal SELF. Thus, that by which we know ourselves as separate, self-reflecting beings, distinct from the whole-of-being, often equated with God. See also FATHER WISDOM, INDIVIDUALITY.

(2) In its Theosophic use, applied within the fourfold model of the physical-etheric-astral-egoic bodies, the evolving germ of God-potential in human nature, the embryonic or larval state of the DIVINE SPARK. In this usage, usually pronounced EGG-oh.

(3) In recovery, the sane, well-integrated sense of identity that is finally achieved when personal boundaries are established and the God-given capacity for love can be expressed as a free response rather than as a sick need. See also SHAME.

EGYPTIAN RELIGION A frontier of modern spirituality ever since the translation of the Rosetta stone (E2.3). The source of mystical and occult teachings on reincarnation, initiation, magic, healing, and geomancy, taken up in modern times by many societies and revivalist groups who claim lineage from the Egyptian Mystery Schools (C&B4.1). Connected with the enigma of the Great Pyramid and speculations about its construction and purpose. Egyptian civilization at its height is often viewed, idealistically, as the purest example of THEOCRACY that we have on record, though the question of the conflict between the priesthood and the ruling families of pharaohs (who were held to be AVATARS) is problematical, and it was from this culture that the TYPHONIC CURRENT originated. See also HERMETICS.

EL DORADO Spanish, "golden one or place." Originally, a name for the mythical sun kings or golden men of the Incas, supposed to be descended in a lineage of seven regents from Atlantis down to Manco Capac, the primary culture-hero, or Manu, of the Incas. Later, interpreted as a fabulous city of immense riches believed by Spanish explorers of the New World to lie somewhere in the West or Southwest of the United States, or in South America.

Example of the hidden or lost paradise theme. Compare with SHAMBHALA.

ELEMENTS In prescientific ancient wisdom and Greek physics, the four states of matter—solid, liquid, gaseous, thermal—defined simply as Earth, Water, Air, and Fire. Basis of many correspondences under the law of ANALOGY: the four suits in the Tarot, the four worlds in the Cabala, the four bodies in occult anatomy. Loosely, the forces at play in the realm of nature, the realm of the elements, often conceived as inhabited by or embodied in four kinds of NATURE-SPIRITS. In ceremonial magic, the elements are invoked to assist the magician. In alchemy, they are held to be the effluvia or media of extraplanetary forces, which they absorb and distribute by a kind of fluidic conduction. See also AKASHA.

ELEMENTALS Nature-spirits who inhabit the four elements, widely described in folklore as visible to people of former times who lived in close communion with nature; for instance, leprechauns, fairies, and "little people." Specifically, gnomes (Earth), undines (Water), sylphs (Air), salamanders (Fire)—all creatures who figure strongly in ceremonial magic and practices of nature-worship, or Wicca. See also DEVA.

ELEUSINIAN MYSTERIES (El-you-SIN-ee-un) Sacred rites celebrated in ancient Greece in the spring and fall, connected with the Earth Goddess, Demeter, and her daughter, Persephone, who was abducted into the Underworld by Pluto (C&B2.2). By far the best-known of the ancient Mysteries, often cited by C. G. Jung and other modern psychologists who refer to ancient lore in their writings. Represent one version of the rites of death and renewal, especially of the human cognitive faculties, symbolized by grain. Thus, the initiates in this cult were invested with the awareness of how the faculties that enable the soul to know itself also insure its survival after death—as grain, which can be made into bread (life), can also die into the earth and become seed for future grain (rebirth). Named after its locale at Eleusis, a few miles west of Athens.

ELIADE, MIRCEA (MIR-shay El-ee-AH-day) Rumanian-born novelist, mythologist, and historian of religions (1904–1986), one of the greatest modern pathfinders who has attempted to present a clear and comprehensive vision of human spirituality on the world-scale. Author of fifty major works, a good many of them modern classics. A fervent believer in humanity's capacity to develop new approaches and new expressions of spirituality, beyond what is merely inherited from the past (Preamble).

ELIXIR Arabic, "the *(il)* stone *(ixir)*." (1) In alchemy, one of hundreds of names given to the ultimate goal of the work, the philosophers' stone: supreme awareness of the mystery of creation, God-consciousness, including total and perfect immunity to all disease, agelessness. Sometimes identified as an actual substance, able to transmute metals into gold. (2) In a loose sense, any brew or formula, concocted from herbs or gems, that aids in physical or psychic healing. Alka-Seltzer is an elixir, and in fact "Alka-hest" was one of the variant names for the stone.

EMERGENCE POINT In world mythology and especially the lore of the American Indians, such as the HOPI, the opening in the earth from which the tribal ancestors are believed to have emerged.

EMOTIONAL BODY Loosely, another name for the astral body as the seat of personal emotions. More exactly in current usage, the extent of the physical body that is saturated by traumatic imprinting, so that it holds negative feeling; hence the need for "clearing the emotional body." Viewed as an actual part of the nerve-system and cellular makeup, corporeally solid but highly unstable; also viewed as capable of sustaining a high degree of natural ecstatic feeling when cleared.

EMOTIONAL PLAGUE A term coined by Wilhelm Reich (C&B3.15) for the social disease of CODEPENDENCY.

EMPOWERMENT In many disciplines, the acquisition of special knowledge or faculties, gained by going through a specific course of training. In the initiatory science of ancient times, the result of a systematic ORDEAL. Today, loosely understood as the process of claiming one's power, which may be achieved through ritual, meditation, attending a workshop, or undergoing some kind of spiritual test, such as fire walking. In short, the activation of innate potential. See also ORGY, SACRIFICE.

EMPTINESS In Buddhism, the primary quality of all things, including the subjective structures of human consciousness by which we are aware that we exist. Endlessly analyzed and defined in the speculative metaphysics of Mahayana. A good experience of emptiness, as Alan Watts put it, is seeing how your head looks to your eyes. See also VOID, PHENOMENALITY. Contrast with MAYA, the equivalent concept in Hindu metaphysics, and NO-MIND in Zen.

ENABLING In recovery, the act of allowing or assisting another in the acting-out of his dysfunction; for instance, the wife calling the office to make excuses for the alcoholic husband's absence.

ENDOCRINE SYSTEM   Glandular system of the human body (including the thyroid, adrenal, and pituitary glands), which produces internal secretions directly into the bloodstream; believed to be closely associated in its functions with the working of currents through the CHAKRAS, producing definite personality types.

ENDORPHINS   Bodily chemicals, secreted in the brain, which produce euphoria and alleviate pain. Perhaps influential in producing ALTERED STATES.

ENERGY   Taken back to its roots, it means "in the works (Greek *ergon*)." *Ens* is also Latin for "being, entity"; so I think of energy as the workings of entities. In other words, wherever there is activity there are particular beings working within *(en-)* it. To understand what energy really is would then be to know who these beings are.

This is a very old view (see "entheism" under GOD), dating back to a time when people saw or imagined beings working in all phenomena. Due to a facultative shift—which allows us to experience ourselves as distinct, self-conscious beings, apart from what we observe—we no longer perceive or imagine beings (such as the NATURE-SPIRITS) working in all things and processes. We are left to an explanation of energy that is a pure abstraction. Widely used as a euphemism for SPIRIT, though I find it inadequate in any use.

ENLIGHTENMENT   (1) The ultimate goal of spiritual striving in the East, especially in Buddhism, by contrast to salvation, which is the ultimate goal of Christianity (E2.4). The realization of the ultimate nature of reality as identical with the one who seeks it. Variously described as the awareness of the void, self-nature, or Suchness. In Zen, called SATORI. See also BODHI and NONATTAINMENT. (2) Name given to the period of history centered around 1650 when the last vestiges of ancient wisdom were discounted by reason, and the great paradigms of modern society and science were established by such minds as Isaac Newton and Voltaire. See E1.4 on the great paradigm-shift.

ENMESHMENT   In recovery, the state of relating to others without clearly set BOUNDARIES or with no boundaries at all. A primary symptom of codependency.

ENNEAGRAM   (EN-ee-uh-gram) From Greek *ennea,* "nine." In metaphysical and esoteric systems, especially the Gurdjieff work, a model of the principles working in the universe, usually represented as a nine-pointed star with lines connecting every other point. Widely viewed as a profound key to the organization of the universe and human psychology, where it is treated as a system of nine distinct personality types, each with its issues of mental/behavioral fixation. Nineness seems to be an archetypal feature of world-design, often ascribed to the Goddess: for instance, the nine world-generating powers of the

Hindu Devi, the nine daughters of the MUSE, the three times three always associated with the White Goddess, et cetera. Sometimes correlated to the Beatitudes, taken as principles of moral development necessary for encompassing the whole (ninefold) substructure of human potential.

ENOCH (1) Spiritual master in the Old Testament, but especially prominent in the APOCRYPHA; for instance, "The Secrets of Enoch." (2) Occasionally, an alleged source of channeled teachings.

ENSTASY (ENS-tuh-see) Ecstasy experienced while remaining fully within the body and senses. A term coined by Mircea Eliade for altered states achieved in the practice of Tantra. Adj., enstatic.

ENTELECHY (En-TELL-uh-kee) Greek, "the being or agent *(ens)* directing the whole process and bearing it through to the fulfillment of its ends or goals *(telos)*." (1) In esoteric psychology and reincarnation, the immortal entity who assumes mortal personalities and persists, growing and evolving, through a number of successive embodiments, evolving itself into an ever more complex identity and gradually unfolding all the potential inherent to it; the INDIVIDUALITY. See also DIVINE SPARK, SERIAL REINCARNATION. (2) In GOETHEAN SCIENCE, the informing principle, conceived as a being, who carries the growth of the plant from its seed stage to complete flowering; as the entelechy of the oak tree operates through all phases from acorn to full-grown tree, ensuring the consistent unfoldment of the acorn archetype—so that, for instance, fig leaves do not erratically appear where oak leaves should be. (3) In the new physics, the hypothetical biological principle that organizes the genetic lifestream and even directs it toward certain "preconceived" ends. A strong point in the argument that all of nature is conscious and self-monitoring, as demonstrated in the MORPHOGENETIC FIELD. A cumbersome but absolutely essential concept in the occult sciences and esoteric psychology; it explains, for instance, the nature and working of the LOGOS.

ENTROPY A word introduced by the German physicist R. J. E. Clausius, around 1840, in reference to the second law of thermodynamics, developed by the French physicist Sadi Carnot. The process in which the entire universe runs down or runs out of energy, finally arriving at a static condition of heat-death. A primary dogma of materialistic science, now strongly opposed by the paradigm of SYNERGETICS.

ENVIRONMENTAL MOVEMENT See ECOLOGY.

EONICS From Greek *aeon,* "cycle, age." A term coined by Dane Rudhyar (E1.3) for the study of time-cycles, especially the long-term cycles corresponding to the periods of the outermost planets (Uranus, Neptune, and Pluto), which may be taken as being indicative of organic rhythms working in the pattern of historical events and the succession of culture-epochs (PLATONIC YEAR). It is widely believed that the ancient wisdom of many high civilizations, such as China and Egypt, included a vast and sophisticated system of chronology encompassing many cycles of historical and prehistorical development. The clearest evidence of this appears to be in the time-reckoning system of the ancient Maya. Some New Age minds have gone to absurd lengths building vast eonic systems to verify apocalyptic hunches.

EQUINOX (1) The moments of equal day and night *(nox)*, which occur twice a year, on the first day of spring and the first day of fall. In former times, believed to be moments of sacred balance, when an interchange between earthly and cosmic forces could be achieved. (2) Title of a famous periodical published from 1909 to 1913 by Aleister Crowley, exposing many of the secret rites of the GOLDEN DAWN and presenting Crowley's own system of occultism for the New Aeon, or New Age.

ERICKSON, MILTON American psychologist, originator of Ericksonian hypnosis, a powerful transformative method for altering deep-seated habits and overcoming the automatic nature of many human responses. See also NEUROLINGUISTIC PROGRAMMING.

EROS Greek, usually translated as "love," though the Greeks have other words for love as well: *philos* (deep affection, as in "philo-sophy": love of wisdom) and *agape* (soul-love). Eros seems to have meant something encompassing a mix of sexual passion, willpower, and sensual pleasure. In his dialogue *The Symposium* (C&B2.3), Plato defines it as a daimon, a mighty spiritual agent that mediates between the divine and the human. In older, pre-Platonic mythology, Eros was the God of the creative impulse, not merely sexual, but cosmological. In Orphic religion, for instance, Eros is identical with the Cosmic Christ, the God of Love, who is the sonlike emanation of the Creator. After Freud, Eros became associated with the sexual drive—libido, pure and simple.

EROTICISM (E11) A long tradition of religious and mystical practices in which sensual intoxication is taken as a path to rapturous attunement to God, and sexual union may even be practiced as a sacramental rite. Rooted in the belief that God is PLAY and the ultimate form of play for human beings is sexual ecstasy. See also TANTRA and GODDESS REVIVAL.

ESALEN (ESS-ah-len) An institute established in 1961 by Michael Murphy and Richard Price as an open forum for experimentation in spiritual development, now famous for its work in East/West studies and HUMAN POTENTIAL. Located on the California coast below San Francisco and named after the Indians who originally inhabited the region.

ESOTERIC From Greek *esoteros*, "inner." Pertaining to the study and development of the potential forces inherent to human nature, such as the capacity for expanding the range of the physical senses, or enhancing the powers of the brain.

ESOTERICISM/ESOTERICS The field of spiritual studies and practices directed toward evolving the INNATE, the innermost potential of the human soul; theory and practice of soul evolution. Thus, a kind of spiritual midwifery. The term is also applied to the study of whatever is viewed as essential for the moral and cultural advancement of humanity—especially in the "primordial tradition" of Rene Guenon and Frithjof Schuon.

ESOTERIC PSYCHOLOGY The field of knowledge defined by special language and diagnostics for understanding the innermost workings of the human soul, usually set apart from ordinary psychology by its peculiar idioms and terms. It includes, for instance, FOUR-BODY THEORY and speculations concerning the functions of the various CHAKRAS.

ESSENCE Latin, "beingness." The core of human nature, the pure potential of who one really is or what one really is capable of becoming. In Theosophical idiom, the MONAD, a spark of divinity capable of evolving to an infinite degree (E2.4). Strongly distinguished in the Gurdjieff work from personality, which is viewed as an external construct, whereas essence is the internal and autonomous core of our being, even the germ of immortality. In Christian language, the human spirit. In Buddhism, its existence is denied according to the doctrine of anatta (lack of fixed identity), since the Buddha-nature is described, paradoxically, as an awareness without anyone who is there to be aware. See also INNATE.

ESSENES From Greek *Essenoi,* probably from Aramaic *hasen,* "pious, holy." An ancient religious sect of which little is known, though ruins of one settlement on the shores of the Dead Sea in Israel became world-famous due to the discovery of the Dead Sea Scrolls. Known for their ritualistic way of life and a kind of obsession about purity. A highly secretive group who believed in an Apocalypse and the coming of a MESSIAH, apparently distinct from the tribal hero of the Jews.

EST Initials for Erhard Seminar Training, a crash program for radical change of personal attitudes and behavior, introduced by Werner Erhard in the early 1970s. In Latin *est* means "it is."

ETERNITY The perfect and perpetual design that informs all things in the universe; not so much a dimension of endless time, as the dimension of all-pervading order and mathematical organization that endures through time without change. For instance, see GOLDEN SECTION. Contrast with INFINITY.

ETHER (1) In modern physics, a problematic concept generally held to be invalid after the Michelson-Morley experiment of 1887, which proved that the so-called ether did not exist because it could not be detected by physical instruments. Previous to that, it was believed to be an elastic medium filling space and supporting the planets as well as providing the "water" for electromagnetic radiation to make "waves." Discarding of the hypothesis of the ether led to Einstein's Theory of Special Relativity in 1906, in which the quasi-material plenum of ether is replaced by the FOUR-DIMENSIONAL SPACE-TIME CONTINUUM. However, the enigmatic notion of empty space, that specter of the ether, continues to haunt modern physics. (2) In ancient wisdom and many systems of occult knowledge, the pervasive medium of life-forces that operates all through nature, imbued with inherent intelligence that allows it to shape and direct growth processes. Recently rediscovered in the concept of MORPHOGE-NETIC FIELDS, or etheric fields. (3) An anesthetic discovered by a Philadelphia dentist around 1840, formerly used in operations before more effective painkillers were developed. Treated by William James as a stimulant to altered states (C&B3.2).

ETHERIC BODY   In four-body theory, the meshlike configuration of subtle currents that form a counterpart to the human body, consisting of an outer weave of thousands of fiberlike strands (including the main strands of the MERIDIANS described in Chinese medicine) and an internal structure consisting of the seven (or perhaps more) CHAKRAS, described in Yoga manuals. Also called life-body, the basis of vitality as well as the instrument of the corporeal intelligence and organic self-regulation, somehow related to the DNA structure and genetic code.

ETHERIC CHRIST   Christ understood as the planetary spirit, the being who focalizes in itself all the evolutionary potential of humanity on Earth and actually "indwells" and superanimates all human and organic life; the core-dynamic of the pattern that connects all living things into a single weave; the master cell in the organic weave of planetary life-forces; the Solar Logos on Earth. According to some interpretations, the form of Christ to be encountered in the SECOND COMING.

ETHERIC WEB/PLANETARY WEB   The immense weave of vital and organic forces uniting all life-processes on Earth and accessible through the human faculties of feeling, thought, and imagination. A concept developed by Alice A. Bailey before it passed over into the popular idiom. Initially expressed in a grave and eloquent way by Chief Seattle, around 1854: "This we know . . . the earth does not belong to man, man belongs to the earth. All things are connected, like blood which connects one family. Whatever befalls the earth befalls the children of the earth. Man did not weave the web of life—he is merely a strand in it. Whatever he does to the web, he does to himself." Key idea in New Age philosophy of holistics, central to the new paradigm of GAIA, and major subject of study and exploration in geomancy. See also PLANETARY GRID.

EURYTHMY   A form of dance and exercise, developed by Rudolf Steiner, supposed to assist in developing the fine dynamics of the etheric body; also used in the curing of mental and physical disabilities, and in dramatic performances. Distinct from the system of musical gymnastics (comparable to modern aerobics) called eurythmics, developed by the Frenchman Émile Jacques-Dalcroze in 1903. From Greek, *eu-*, "healthy, good for you" + *rhythm.*

EVANGELICAL   From Greek *evangelos,* "messenger." Fundamentalist sect often fanatically devoted to spreading the message of Jesus Christ, using powers of mental persuasion and emotional appeal but distinct from CHARIS-MATIC methods.

EVIL From ME *ivel* > IE base *upo-,* "beneath, under." That which is beneath one's true potential or, in the extreme, undermines that which is above it. Loosely, the destructive or counterevolutionary tendency in evolution, which works against the organic perfection of the whole. A problematic theme in world mythology and religion, as well as in New Age philosophy which, to a great extent, unfortunately discounts and dismisses its existence. See also SATANISM.

EVOLUTION Conventionally, the Darwinian theory of evolution of species, asserted by materialistic science against the paradigm of creation, which is put forth in worldwide mythology and religion. In the new spirituality, it always means the evolution of consciousness, involving the paradigm of participation, in which consciousness as we experience it is held to be a dynamic process working all through nature and the universe, so human beings may be viewed as conscious agents critically located within the entire process. See also COCREATION, DIVINE SPARK, INVOLUTION.

EXORCISM From Latin, *ex-,* "out" + *orgia,* "working"; literally, an "out-working." The process of driving out demonic forces or actual beings believed to possess someone. An example of the sensational side of occultism, widely popularized through novels in the genre of the occult thriller and the 1974 film *The Exorcist.*

EXTRASENSORY PERCEPTION (ESP) The capacity to see and hear things or entities that lie outside the normal boundaries of sense perception. TELEPATHY, or thought transmission, is an example of ESP. Seeing disembodied beings, such as ghosts, is another.

EXTRASENSORY POWERS Loose term for any kinds of abilities that lie beyond the limits of the ordinary, pregiven senses, such as remote sensing, teleportation, psychometry. Contrast with INFRASENSORY.

EXTRATERRESTRIALS Beings who come from beyond *(extra)* Earth *(terra),* such as those believed to travel in UFOs, or spirit-guides from other regions of the universe, such as Sirius or the Pleiades, or from other dimensions of space and time, parallel worlds, et cetera. Compare with ANCIENT ASTRONAUTS.

F

FAERY/FAIRY   In Irish and Celtic myth and folklore, a supernatural being of terrible powers who usually assumes a human form to wreak havoc or confer favors. A denizen of the Otherworld. Originally such beings were objects of awe to mere mortals, but in our times they have become belittled into wispy imps, "little people," leprechauns, and the like. The Oriental equivalent is the DAKINI.

FAIRY TALE   In world folklore, a narrative used to illustrate spiritual questions or express the natural symbolic workings of the human psyche, often in a form suitable for children but always revealing to adults who are able to see life imaginatively.

FAITH   Goes back to the IE root *bheidh-,* "to urge, to be convinced." The power of conviction that can lead to urgent or significant action, to be distinguished from belief, which involves the desire to adhere to something that cannot be proven, or often even tested. Although the two words are often used synonymously, I make a case for contrasting them in the Afterword.

FAITH HEALING   The curing of physical and mental illnesses by supernatural powers, usually through prayer or calling upon divine forces; often demonstrated in public meetings of high emotional intensity.

FAKIR   (Fah-KEER) Arabic *faqir,* "poor man." Crudely, a Moslem who lives by begging. In the deeper sense, someone who has given up everything for the spiritual quest. Equivalent to the Hindu YOGI, an ascetic usually known for exhibiting paranormal abilities in feats of magic, such as remaining buried alive for days and healing severe wounds without medical treatment.

FALL   The dominant paradigm of Western religion, drawn from the myth of Adam and Eve in Genesis, which implies that human nature is intrinsically flawed: There is something really wrong with us and we have to make up for it by redemption or salvation. Associated with the belief system that places God in an inaccessible realm as an object of faith, at best, but not as a genuine subject to be encountered directly by the human subject. This paradigm also generates the historical structure of time-bound affliction, expressed in the triple curse of Jehovah: give birth in pain, earn thy bread, and die. It leads inevitably to the scenario of the LAST JUDGMENT, which compensates for the Fall and produces a final restoration of part of the human race to perfect union with the Godhead, while others are cast off into the infernal regions. Compare with MAYA, the contrasting paradigm of the East (E2.4).

FALLEN SOPHIA In Gnosticism, the thirtieth emanation of the all-creative God-wisdom, whose spiritual anguish to please the Creator causes her to produce from herself the realm of the material elements (inhabited by humanity), below and outside the realm of Divine Fullness (PLEROMA). May be interpreted as that aspect of the divine, all-creative Mother Wisdom that is totally interfused with the realm of the senses. In the Gnostic gospels, sometimes called the Whore of Wisdom. She whom Christ comes to Earth to redeem and claim as feminine ally and counterpart. In human embodiment, Mary Magdalen. See also MOTHER WISDOM.

FATHER WISDOM The creative intelligence active throughout the universe that makes it possible for all entities to become self-knowing and self-sufficient; hence, the divine-creative basis of self-awareness, self-reflection, originality, independence, individualization, conscience, freedom, choice, judgment, boundaries, linear temporality, and ego. See also PATRIARCHY.

FÁTIMA (FAH-ti-muh) A village in West Portugal, location of a famous shrine dedicated to the Virgin Mary, who appeared there in six miraculous apparitions to three shepherd children in the spring of 1917. Six months later, as promised, the Virgin appeared again, this time before a crowd of 70,000, and performed the miraculous feat of causing the sun to dance and radiate a play of rainbow lights. Classic case of an APPARITION.

FAUST Philosopher and occultist of European legend (C&B2.8), associated with the historical figure Magister Georgius Sabellius Faustus (1480–1540), reputed to be a notorious sorcerer. Known for making a pact with the Devil, selling his soul in exchange for boundless wealth, magical abilities, sexual gratification, and physical immortality. Exemplar of the dominant myth of technological society: the self-seeking hedonist, disillusioned with God, who forsakes humanity by choosing power over love and knowledge over responsibility.

FELDENKRAIS METHOD In bodywork, a method developed by Moishe Feldenkrais, an Israeli physicist and judo expert, for relearning how to express one's fullest potential through the physical body; consists of gentle and subtle movements.

FENG SHUI (Fung-SHWAY) Chinese, "wind and water." Chinese name for GEOMANCY.

FIBONACCI SERIES (Fib-oh-NAHTCH-ee) A special numerical sequence first identified by Leonardo Fibonacci, an Italian mathematician of the twelfth century, consisting of a series of numbers formed by the sum of the two preceding numbers: 1, 1, 2, 3, 5, 8, 13, 21, 34, 55, et cetera. Appears in hundreds of amazing instances throughout nature, in the branching of plant stems and the arrangement of flowers, in the breeding patterns of rabbits and bees, even in the quantum multiplication of electrons. Widely applied in geomancy and in the tradition of the sacred CANON, where it is taken as evidence that superhuman intelligence operates as a consistent ordering principle throughout nature (argument by design). See also GOLDEN SECTION.

FIELD THEORY   In physics, the conceptual framework in which material objects are viewed as configurations of an all-encompassing field, rather than as separate things in empty space. Characteristic of modern physics since Maxwell, who developed the field equations that were eventually adapted and advanced by Einstein for his RELATIVITY THEORY. In the new physics and holistics, a model of organic totality, often compared with the Buddhist concept of the VOID.

FINDHORN   (FINNED-horn) An unusual community founded in northern Scotland in the early 1970s by Eileen and Peter Caddy and Dorothy Maclean, based in part upon collaboration with the NATURE-SPIRITS of the place, so that it was possible for the members of the community to get miraculous results in growing plants and vegetables at an ordinarily barren site. Source of certain spiritual teachings, especially through one-time member David Spangler.

FIREWALKING   A method of producing sudden and radical changes in one's attitudes and behavior by walking barefoot over a bed of hot coals without getting burned. A shamanic practice in some ancient cultures, recently revived.

FLAT EARTH   Theory proposed by the Reverend J. A. Dowie, a Scottish faith healer, in 1895, and accepted by several thousand people who formed a cult, the remnants of which still survive in Zion, Illinois. Compare with HOLLOW EARTH.

FLOAT TANK   An enclosure filled with water for suspension of the body in a state of near gravity-free relaxation, to induce mental calm and concentration or to explore ALTERED STATES. Also called isolation tank.

FLOWER ESSENCES   See BACH FLOWER REMEDIES.

FLYING SAUCERS   See UFO.

FOLK-SOUL   The spiritual being who oversees and protects a race or nation, often described as indwelling the souls of the people, who act as its members or cells. In old Theosophical thinking, this entity is responsible for the unique racial and linguistic features of a people; that is, the ghost in the gene pool. Sometimes conceived as ancestral spirits (among the Chinese) or as actual Gods who express themselves through the collective-genetic makeup of the people (as in the Celtic clans). Often said to become focused in special individuals; for example, Walt Whitman as a personification of the American folk-soul. Sometimes called nation-souls and identified with specific ARCHANGELS. A matter of much concern in early Theosophical/Anthroposophical teachings, but now almost entirely forgotten.

F O O L In the Tarot and in esoteric teachings of magic, the image of the highest degree of human potential; the exemplar of purity, innocence, and spontaneity. Figuratively, someone who is fully trusting of the moment, and capable of opening to its fullest possibility due to knowing that everything in the universe, from molecule to star, responds directly and cooperatively to the way one perceives it. In the Western Mystery Tradition, Parzival (C&B2.5) is known as the Holy Fool (Preface to the Essays). In Castaneda, the "master of intent" who practices the high risk of "controlled folly." In our idiom, the spirit of discovery, the free and often bumbling seeker.

FORTUNE, DION Assumed name of Violet Firth Penry Evans (1891–1946), English occultist and key figure in the modern revival of magic, as well as an outstanding example of a WESTERN MASTER. Author of several sane and solid works on modern occultism and founder of the Fraternity of the Inner Light.

FOUR-BODY THEORY A doctrine found in many esoteric systems, probably derived from the model of the four ELEMENTS taught in the Mystery Schools and common to alchemy and Greek/Arabian physics. Inconsistent in its modern forms, but more or less like this:

physical body: senses, mineral realm—Earth
etheric body: vitality, plant realm—Air (Atmosphere)
astral body: emotions, desires, animal nature—Water
egoic or causal body: spirit, will, EGO—Fire

Each of the "higher bodies"—etheric, astral, and causal—is described as interpenetrating the physical, as well as expanding beyond it, with the causal or egoic body pervading the other three and encompassing them all in the auric egg. In esoteric psychology, the interaction of the bodies explains changes of consciousness; for instance, when we sleep, the astral and egoic bodies separate from the etheric and physical; when we die, the etheric separates from the physical. The astral body, which becomes independent in astral projection, may be identical with the DREAM-BODY. The etheric body consists of a complex mesh, which is mapped out by the system of meridians in acupuncture and an infrastructure where the chakras are located, though these are shared as common formations with the astral body. See also OCCULT ANATOMY.

It is interesting to note that in most systems of occult anatomy, the etheric body, the seat of vitality, is also the seat of memory. Its plastic and retentive capacities enable us to perform learned actions automatically, such as knitting or typing. My favorite description of the four bodies is: you crave raspberry ripple with your astral body, then you drive to the ice-cream parlor with your etheric, you experience shame in the ego as you go in the door, and you taste the flavor with your physical body, which is then stuck with the messy job of digesting the stuff.

FOURTH DIMENSION   In the traditional seven-dimensional model of occultism, the central and balancing dimension, where the three dimensions of space and the three dimensions of time coexist, interfused in an ambiguous and inseparable manner. The dimension we normally inhabit, though we are unaware of its actual properties—thus, the purpose of some occult training is to awaken the faculties for perceiving that we are already in the fourth dimension, though we continue to act as if we're in the third.

FOUR-DIMENSIONAL SPACE-TIME CONTINUUM   Name given in relativity theory to the fourth dimension we inhabit, where the properties of space and time are continuous and inseparable. See also SPACE-TIME.

FOURTH WAY   Alternative name for the Gurdjieff work, drawn from a passage in P. D. Ouspensky's *In Search of the Miraculous,* where Gurdjieff describes a fourth way of spiritual attainment, distinct from the three traditional paths he defines as the ways of the fakir, monk, and yogi.

FREEDOM   Essential to independent seeking in the modern quest, since the seeker who faces the wide variety of options available today must choose intelligently among them, rather than adopt a single path merely because it's the only one available or because tradition and authority impose it upon him. According to the Russian existentialist Nicholas Berdyaev, freedom existed even before creation. Since it precedes the unfolding of the universe from the Godhead, the problems of good and evil, right and wrong, so often involved in human choice, cannot be attributed to the Creator, but rather to freedom itself. As the ground of choice, freedom is observed on the spiritual quest through the principle of Free Approach stated in E2.2. See also INTENTION.

FREEMASONS   A fabled brotherhood supposed to have been in possession, from very ancient times, of the geometrical and mathematical knowledge necessary for the construction of sacred buildings and monuments (CANON), such as the Gothic cathedrals. Claims the usual lineage of masters, one of whom was Hiram Abiff, master builder of the Temple of Solomon, around 950 B.C.; though the Grand British Lodge was only founded in 1716. A SECRET SOCIETY whose members are rumored to be influential agents working behind the scenes in many areas of human endeavor, especially science and politics. For instance, Masons are said to have played a key role in drafting the U.S. Constitution and determining the symbology of the dollar bill (E1.4). To this day, Freemasons are organized locally in lodges where their symbolic knowledge and rituals are preserved. Often associated or confounded with the TEMPLARS and the ROSICRUCIANS.

FRIENDS, SOCIETY OF   Religious group originating in England around 1650, under George Fox. Commonly known as Quakers, they call themselves Children of Light. Associated in America with William Penn, who founded a Quaker community at Philadelphia in 1682. Known for their pacifism and Quaker meetings, where the members sit in silence and await the inspiration of the INNER LIGHT.

F U H S I (Foo SEE) Mythical Chinese ancestor, half monkey, half angel, attributed with discovering the eight primary HEXAGRAMS of the *I Ching* (C&B1.1) inscribed on the shell of a tortoise that suddenly emerged from the Yellow River after a flood, and with instructing the Chinese people in the basic arts of survival. Example of a MANU.

FULL LOTUS See LOTUS POSTURE

FUNDAMENTALISM Loosely, any type of traditional religion that insists on authority over discovery (E2.1) and perpetuates the belief that the revelation of the Divine has come through specific people in the past (such as Moses and Mohammed) and cannot be either altered or improved. In Christian fundamentalism, for example, the Bible is held to be the supreme authority in all human affairs and God's revelation is viewed as over and done, except for a final showing at the Last Judgment. Variants and splinter-groups are legion, but principally divided into CHARISMATIC and EVANGELICAL sects. Fundamentalism is a belief system that stands in radical opposition to the Gnostic heresy of human divinity, or developing the God within (THEOGENY), which has been widely adopted, and adapted, in New Age circles (E2.4)—leading some fundamentalists to view the New Age as a Satanic movement.

G

GAIA/GAIA HYPOTHESIS (GUY-uh) Greek, "mother-goddess-earth." (1) Loosely, a name for Earth conceived as a living being, an animate entity with a consciousness of its own, in which human beings are included as cells. Thus, Earth as our living habitat and mother organism. This view is believed to accord with the experience of Mother Nature common to many peoples in the past and still preserved today among the cultures of certain native groups, such as the American Indians and the Australian Aborigines. (2) More specifically, in ecology, a theory proposed by Lovelock and Margulis, stating that organic life on Earth actually monitors and controls the processes of the atmosphere. Although this hypothesis has not yet been either widely accepted or understood, the name has been adopted for the living totality of the Earth as a self-regulating entity—a great step toward PLANETARIZATION for the popular mind. See also etheric fields under ETHER.

GANGES (Gahn-JEEZ) Sacred river of India, along whose banks SANYASSINS have gathered for thousands of years, to bathe and meditate, especially at the holy city Benares (Ben-NAR-ess).

GAUTAMA (Gow-TAH-mah) From Sanskrit *gau,* "world" + *-tama,* a superlative suffix; thus, "supreme in the world." Common title of the historical Buddha, who lived as a prince in India during the sixth or seventh century B.C. See also SIDDHARTHA and SHAKYAMUNI.

GELLER, URI Israeli psychic (born 1946), known for astonishing psychic powers he first exhibited at the age of seven: making watches stop or reverse, making things appear and disappear, and especially the feat of bending spoons with his mind. Claims to be directed by outer-space intelligence. A well-known example of the UNEXPLAINED, typical of sensationalistic pop occultism.

GEMATRIA In the Cabala, the interpretation of words by assigning numbers to the letters and computing the results.

GENETIC CODE The system of information contained, like a vast miniaturized Library of Congress, in the chromosomal units of the human body, consisting of protein and DNA (deoxyribonucleic acid), as well as the messenger or transcribing acid, RNA. Since the structure of DNA (a double helix of interweaving strands of threadlike genetic material) was worked out by J. D. Watson and F. H. C. Crick in 1953, the genetic code has been the center of enormous speculation and fantastic experimentation—especially with the technique of recombinant DNA, in which single strands of genetic material are separated from two different substances and combined in a new helix to form a third, human-made substance. This has led to claims of humanity's capacity to play God—but what about playing with God, instead (E2.4)? The genetic code— that is, DNA and RNA in action—is believed to be the source of the infinite self-regulating intelligence of the body, including the neurochemistry of consciousness and stretching through time and generations. It has even been proposed as the biochemical repository of God-consciousness (the "Word made flesh" or Shabda-Brahman in Hindu physics and Tantra), perhaps to be accessed through occult training or the use of drugs to enter altered states. See also PSYCHEDELIC EXPERIENCE.

GEODESIC (Gee-oh-DEE-sik) "World-line." (1) Mathematical term coined by Riemann and Einstein for the most efficient (or force-economical) path of interaction between two events in SPACE-TIME. Imagined as spiraling, for instance, in the corkscrew trajectories of tracer bullets fired between two moving fighter planes. (2) Mathematical norm applied by Buckminster Fuller in his science of SYNERGETICS, especially in the construction of geodesic domes, using lightweight bars for efficient curvature in long spans.

GEOMANCY (E12) From Latin *geo-*, "earth" + *mans*, "calculate." (1) In a limited sense, divination by means of lines and figures drawn in the earth. (2) More widely in current use, a vast system of knowledge and practices based on the theory that the earth is an intelligent and sentient being whose natural processes are permeated by supersensible fields and currents that conform to consistent mathematical and geometric laws, not recognized by modern science, though they were carefully plotted and manipulated in ancient methods of technology and mathematics that are now being widely revived (C&B4.7). The study and application of the CANON of divine proportions, including the golden section and the Fibonacci series, especially in the analysis of sacred architecture. Includes the subgenre of archeo-astronomy.

GESTALT THERAPY (Gesh-TALT) German, "pattern, whole." Method of attaining emotional wholeness by viewing life-situations not as problems, but as meaningful designs that reveal the innermost concerns of the individual. Originated in 1912 by Kurt Koffka and Wolfgang Köhler and developed by Fritz Perls.

GLAMOR/GLAMOUR A term of special significance in modern seeking, referring to the allure of pretensions and self-delusions that tempt anyone on the path of expanding his inner potential. Its diverse forms—spiritual glamor, psychic glamor, sexual glamor—are all variations of the basic delusion in which spiritual talents are perverted into tools of deceit and manipulation. Where glamor comes into play, deceit and exploitation often arise and personalities may be placed before principles. Curiously, the word *glamor* is merely the Scottish variant of *grammar,* telling us that the term was originally applied to those who could read and write. This goes back to the medieval belief that writing or spelling was equivalent to casting a spell. Medieval manuals of ceremonial magic, which contained instructions for calling up demonic forces, were called grammars, or grimoires. See also DELUSION.

GLASTONBURY A small market town in Somerset in southwestern England, site of the ruins of an abbey that legend connects with Joseph of Arimathea (Air-uh-muth-THEE-ah), the man who embalmed the body of Jesus (New Testament, John 19:38). Joseph is supposed to have collected the blood of the Savior in the HOLY GRAIL and eventually taken it to England, where he founded the first Christian monastery at Glastonbury. Called in Celtic folklore *Ydris-widrin,* "city of glass," and held to be the geographic location of the mystical realm of AVALON. A sacred site of enormous importance in the Celtic Revival and geomancy.

GLASTONBURY ZODIAC An immense configuration of shapes roughly resembling the images of the Zodiac, believed to be inscribed in the landscape around Glastonbury by means of natural features and human-made details, such as roads and embankments. Discovered around 1910 by Katherine Maltwood.

GLOBAL VILLAGE Term coined by Marshall McLuhan (C&B4.4) in reference to the unification of the world into a kind of tribal intimacy by the media. An example of the New Age theme of PLANETARIZATION.

GNOSIS (No-sis) Latin, "knowledge," tracing back to the IE root *jna-,* as in the Sanskrit *jnana,* "spiritual knowledge." Direct and intimate knowledge of God and the workings of superhuman intelligence in the world. The way of knowing God as it is known to itself, rather than merely through faith or mental inference. An ancient discipline of finding God within and actually evolving toward Godhood, rather than remaining separate from and merely in relation to God without or above. Contrast with FUNDAMENTALISM.

GNOSTIC GOSPELS The general name for a collection of rare documents dating from the second century A.D., later discovered in the twentieth century in places where they had been hidden to preserve them from destruction. At present, still being translated and interpreted by scholars, though gradually becoming more accessible to the layperson. They present startling approaches toward an alternative path of Christianity. See also NAG HAMMADI GOSPELS.

GNOSTICISM (E13) (NOS-tis-sizm) A lost system of philosophical and cosmological teachings, of unknown origin, including a vast and complex scenario of mythical events in which deviant powers intervene in human evolution and Gods make mistakes—a touchy point that compelled the early Church fathers to eliminate all traces of Gnosticism from the Bible, as far as possible. Most of the known sects of Gnosticism were eliminated by the fourth century as the Catholic church came into power and consolidated itself with the Roman Empire. Currently, Gnosticism is undergoing a revival of sorts, perhaps as a compensatory response to the rise of fundamentalism.

GOATS   In classical times, for some strange reason, associated with the INITIATES or more evolved members of the human race, who are responsible for imparting the directive impulses that guide and inspire human culture through the centuries. For instance, the emblem of the MANU is the goat's head, or the more complex image of the goatfish in the constellations. In classical Greece, the tragedy was, literally, the "goat *(trag)* song *(odoi)*," by some accounts, because the secrets known to the initiates about the deepest issues of human karma and evolution were translated into dramatic form by the Greek playwrights, such as Sophocles, who was rumored to have been an initiate.

Riddle asked of every candidate in the Mysteries: "How are initiates similar to goats?" Answer: "In both cases, long after they've gone, you still know they were around."

GOD   From the IE root *ghau-,* "to call forth, invoke." The Supreme Being, usually conceived as the Creator of humanity as well as the entire extrahuman universe, who somehow exists as a superintending presence in the world, even though not ordinarily evident to human awareness in the way other beings and things are evident.

How God is present in the world and especially for or within human consciousness is the great religious issue of the ages. Responses to it have been formulated as:

Monotheism: belief in a single and Supreme Being who oversees human affairs in some way and is generally held to stand in a direct personal relationship to the believer;

Deism: belief in a God who does not appear by direct revelation and remains in complete detachment from the universe;

Theism: belief in a God who pervades the world, though rather impersonally, and is sympathetic to human concerns;

Pantheism: belief in a God who pervades the world not as a personality but an animating spirit, present as much in trees and the wind as in human consciousness;

Polytheism: belief in many Gods of various potencies and roles, as in Hinduism;

Entheism: belief that God is infinite intelligence existing in a boundless variety of beings *(ens)* who animate all things from atom to star—that is, all *en* ergies are really *en*tities expressing the infinite life-activity of God;

Atheism: the belief that God as a Supreme Being, whether Creator or an all-pervading presence, simply does not exist;

Agnosticism: the belief that it is impossible to know, one way or the other, if a God exists—which may be a matter of despair or indifference.

Among modern seekers, the two great issues still seem to be whether God is to be felt and known personally (Jesus Christ) or impersonally (Buddha), and whether our relation to God is to be based on direct contact (Gnosis) or blind belief (fundamentalism). Another huge enigma is how God can act as a superintending presence, sometimes taking a role in the direction of human affairs, causing things to happen or preventing them from happening. RELIGION, generally, promotes the belief in having a relationship to God, while Gnostic and alternative paths promote the adventure of becoming God, or at least God-like. (For my commentary on Gods in diapers, see E1.4.) In both cases, however, the question of how we communicate with God is crucial. In Christian doctrine, Jesus Christ is the human/divine hybrid, the mediator between us and the Creator; though the question of how to communicate with the mediator remains problematic. Likewise, in Gnostic teachings the theory of theogenic transhumanization is nowhere fully and clearly set out, and the question remains, If we become elevated to the status of God, how does this change our relation to the rest of the human species? See also MYSTERIES (E16) and COCREATION.

G O D D E S S / G O D D E S S   R E V I V A L   (E 1 1)   The study of the divine in its feminine aspect, often looking back to the fertility cults of prehistory and stressing the high role of women and female deities in all cultures of the world. An emergent paradigm-shift increasingly supported by archaeological findings, which attests to the deep and pervasive influence of matriarchal structures in high cultures of the past, such as the one unearthed at Catal Huyuk in central Turkey. A popular front within the New Age, encompassing a variety of teachings and techniques aimed at restoring sensitivity for the lost values of woman, nature, and earth, reinventing matriarchy, and reevolving the Mother Wisdom. Closely identified with GAIA, the environmental movement, and the dawning of planetary conscience. May be viewed in counterpart to the revival of EROTICISM.

G O D H E A D   In theology and esoterics, a term applied to God as the Source of all creation, including the creation of humanity. The plenum or matrix of the divine sparks who plunge into a long process of involution (descent through the planes) so that they can eventually undergo an evolution in which new and infinitely differentiated aspects of the original, unmanifest potentiality of the Godhead come to expression—or so goes the Theosophical scenario. The question of whether this Source, usually described as existing far beyond us in eternity, is to be directly experienced or is to be discovered within us somehow, perhaps inhering as the ground of our very self-awareness, is one of the great religious issues. In Gnosticism, the Pleroma; in Tantra, the realm of pure sensation. See also FREEDOM.

G O D O T (Guh-DOE) The mysterious person who never arrives yet controls all the action in the famous Samuel Beckett play *Waiting for Godot,* a masterpiece of the "theater of the absurd." Modern parody of the belief in a God who never shows and never delivers. Made up from "God" + "aught" (zero, naught); thus, the God who ought to come but who comes to naught.

G O D S E E D In esoterics, the divine potential of humanity, usually held to be more present in our capacities for love and compassion than in our intellectual powers, and subject to infinite unfolding by various practices of AWARENESS and SELF-ACTUALIZATION. Monadic essence, divine spark, the innate transcendental basis of HUMAN POTENTIAL. A term coined by Jean Houston, whose efforts toward a modern-day revival of the Mysteries extend the concept of human potential into the concept of divine potential (E1.4). See also CHRISTOLOGY.

G O D - S E L F Pun on "God's elf," the Godling or INNER CHILD, epitome and promise of the divine potential in us all. See also HIGHER SELF.

G O E T H E A N   S C I E N C E (GUR-tee-un) Alternative method of science derived from the work of the German poet and philosopher J. W. Goethe (C&B2.8), whose scientific studies have largely been ignored or discounted by the establishment. Proposes an option to Newtonian optics and mechanics, with an emphasis on the organic totality of nature, as in Goethe's model of the archetypal plant. Taken up by Rudolf Steiner as the basis for his method of spiritual science. Forerunner of holistics, currently being rediscovered and reformulated in theories about MORPHOGENETIC FIELDS and IMPLICATE ORDER.

G O L D E N   D A W N The most famous occult society of the late nineteenth and early twentieth centuries, founded in 1887, which included prominent artists and writers (such as the Irish poet W. B. Yeats) among its members. Based on the attempt to reinstate a system of spiritual teachings and initiation supposedly derived from Rosicrucian/Hermetic and Cabalistic traditions of ancient lineage, carried down to modern times by "secret chiefs." Key organization in the modern revival of mystical and supernatural belief systems. See also Aleister CROWLEY and MAGIC.

G O L D E N   S E C T I O N The most famous and widely used proportion in the CANON of ancient geometry as applied to sacred architecture: the ratio formed when a line (of any length) is divided at a point where the smaller section of the line is to the larger section as the larger section is to the whole line. Defined by the mathematical ratio of $1:1.618$, a constant (sometimes called the phi-function) that appears in many forms in nature and generates the expanding logarithmic spiral, perfect and consistent, to be seen in the pattern of seashells, animal horns, the seed rows in the heads of sunflowers, and thousands of other instances. Used extensively in the design of Greek temples, Egyptian pyramids, sacred art of the Renaissance, et cetera. Called the divine proportion. See also FIBONACCI SERIES.

GOOD LOOKING Term of praise and delight used by enthusiastic seekers when prize knowledge or transformative insight has been attained by wise persistence in asking the right questions. The result of good seeking. See the Preamble for my own revelation on this.

GOTHIC CATHEDRALS Huge, high-spired churches built in Europe from the twelfth through the sixteenth centuries, with stained-glass windows and elaborate sculptures supposed to incorporate a complex system of symbols expressing secret knowledge of human evolution. Variously described as the work of Masons (or Freemasons), Rosicrucians, Templars, and alchemists. The most famous is CHARTRES, outside of Paris. For a famous legend concerning their construction, see CANON.

GÖTTERDÄMMERUNG (Gert-er-DAM-er-rung) German, "twilight of the Gods." (1) End-of-the-world scenario in Nordic and Teutonic mythology. (2) An early variation of reggae popular in the Bavarian Alps in the mid-1930s.

GRACE That which is given freely *(gratis)* by God or a superhuman agency, without having to be earned; especially, freedom from suffering or punishment. Apparently, an out devised in the Christian faith for avoiding the victim scenario of the FALL.

GRAIL/GRAIL MYSTERY From ME *graal,* Latin *gradalis,* "dish, platter." Literally, the cup used for Communion at the Last Supper; also said to have been used to collect the Holy Blood from the body of Christ when it was taken down from the cross. Described in medieval legend as having been taken to GLASTONBURY and hidden in a well. In Western culture and literature, a vast body of legend—part myth, part history—has grown up around this sacred article, which has become a powerful symbol of redemption and a key theme in the Western Mystery tradition, especially in the Celtic Revival. Concerning the Grail Question, see the Preface to the Essays.

GRAPHOLOGY See HANDWRITING ANALYSIS.

GREAT PYRAMID OF GIZA A monumental relic of sacred architecture located across the Nile from Cairo, Egypt. Subject of immense research in the effort to determine its geometric proportions and their significance (canon), not to mention its original purpose. Believed to have been merely a pharaoh's tomb by most historians and archaeologists, though the esoteric explanation makes it out to be a huge initiation chamber. See also KING'S CHAMBER.

GREAT WHITE BROTHERHOOD (E14) Most common name for an age-old organization of highly evolved beings believed to oversee and guide the evolution of humanity, supposed to have existed up to around 400 A.D. in a worldwide network of Mystery Schools. Traditionally, the great, world-encompassing organization of the initiates of the various regional Mysteries, from Ireland to Egypt, from China to Oceania, supposed to go back to a superhuman core group formed in Lemurian times. Obviously, a major item in planetary folklore and New Age mythmaking. Updated in the Himalayan masters described in the works of Madame Blavatsky, and the planetary hierarchy of Alice A. Bailey (E1.2). Also called the White Lodge or Mother Lodge.

GREAT WORK In alchemy, the euphemism often applied to the supreme aim of all alchemical practice: COCREATION, active and conscious collaboration in the ongoing process of creation, which was viewed by the alchemists as a product of divine intelligence, but left unfinished.

GREEN-CHILI ENEMA Old folk remedy from New Mexico, commonly prescribed for those suffering from terminal SELF-IMPORTANCE.

GREENHOUSE EFFECT In ecology, the process in which chemical emissions (primarily from automobiles and coal burning) cause an unnatural buildup of the carbon dioxide layer in the atmosphere, with the result that solar radiation is trapped in excessive quantities and local temperatures increase—perhaps leading to the melting of the polar ice caps, a rise in the sea level, and other catastrophic EARTH CHANGES. Along with the ozone hole, this is considered to be one of the gravest ecological dangers facing the planet.

GREEN POLITICS Alternative political movement, originated in West Germany by Charlene Spretnak and Petra Kelly in 1979, now worldwide. Emphasizes progressive values in ecology, human-scale management of government, and nonviolence.

GRIMOIRE (Grim-WAHR) French, medieval variant of *grammar*. In the black arts, a book containing formulas for calling up and controlling demonic beings. A manual of ceremonial magic. See also GLAMOR.

GRIS-GRIS (Gree-gree) French, "gray-gray." In voodoo, charms in the form of herb bags used for warding off evil influences.

GROSS BODY In FOUR-BODY THEORY, old Theosophic term, rarely used anymore, for the lowest vehicle, the physical body.

GROUNDING What you have a gross body for. Also the act of getting grounded; that is, coming back to practical issues and common sense, over against the tendency to intellectualize and fantasize, to go into one's head, to indulge in wishful or magical thinking. Due to their appeal to the imagination and the wiles of personal mythmaking, a great many New Age concerns can turn into escapist delusions, but in the discipline of pathfinding, this danger can be averted by solid grounding: getting down to basics.

GUARDIAN OF THE THRESHOLD In the Mysteries and their latter-day offspring, the occult societies of the eighteenth, nineteenth, and twentieth centuries, a monstrous being met by the seeker about to cross the threshold into the realm of secret spiritual knowledge. By some interpretations, a composite of the individual's worst character defects, the monstrous manifestation of the

SHADOW or even the hideous embodiment of the DOUBLE, encountered by the seeker in the crucial moment of self-confrontation at the culmination of the PSYCHODRAMA. Known as the concierge in France. Dramatically described in the famous occult novel *Zanoni* (1847), by Edward Bulwer-Lytton.

G U I D A N C E   One of the deepest perennial issues facing humanity, now assuming new dimensions in the New Age, when hundreds of alternative paths of self-initiation are accessible. The goal of free seeking is to become self-guiding. Ideally, this is possible if one learns how to be directed by life itself, taking all methods and techniques of self-development as provisional and tangential, rather than as definitive paths that dictate the way one lives. See Preamble and E1.4. Compare with INTERVENTION.

G U I D E   Any being, either human (alive or dead) or extrahuman, who instructs and directs a person in spiritual growth, or assists in seeking answers to certain questions.

G U I D E D   M E D I T A T I O N   A process of concentrating on feelings and images while being taken through it by another person, usually for the purpose of accessing feelings and changing them. Contrast with ACTIVE IMAGINATION.

G U N A   (GOO-nah) Sanskrit, "quality, trait." In Yoga and Indian metaphysics, a principle or tendency informing all things and processes, expressed in the threefold formula: *rajas* (impulsion, initiation)/*tamas* (resistance, phase of balancing-out or stasis)/*sattva* (harmony, integrity, formal perfection). Example of the universal TRIAD, found in many variations in esoteric psychology and physics.

G U R D J I E F F ,   G E O R G E   I V A N O V I T C H   Assumed name (?) of an influential and somewhat notorious occultist ([1866?]–1949), who originated a school of spiritual discipline, the Gurdjieff work, and established a commune called The Institute for the Harmonious Development of Man at Fontainebleau near Paris, in the 1930s. Known for his adaptation of SACRED DANCE as a modern method of self-development. Emphasized the basic message that we are asleep and need to exert super-efforts to free ourselves from the bondage of pure automatism. Introduced to America through the efforts of A. R. Orage (E1.2).

G U R U   (GOOR-rue) Sanskrit, from the root *gur-*, "to raise, lift up." Spiritual teacher, preceptor, mentor, MASTER.

G U R U - D I P   A variation of sheep-dip. A murky substance exuded in great lumpy masses by maniacally devout followers (sheep) of gurus.

G Y P S I E S   Slang, from a shortening of the word *Egypt*. A mysterious nomadic tribe believed to have come to Europe from India in the fifteenth century, though their origins may trace all the way back to the Jews who remained in Egypt after the Exodus of Moses, as their name indicates. Known for fortune-telling, psychic powers, flamenco music, and dangerous passions. Sometimes attributed with transmission of the Tarot.

H

HAIKU (High-KOO) A form of poetry in Japan, formally defined around 1850, consisting of a brief three-line unit of seventeen syllables (5-7-5) used to express startling perceptions, often toned with humorous or poignant emotion; now adopted as a verse form in other languages, not always preserving the syllable count. Example: "From a bough / floating downriver / insect song" (Issa). Used as a technique of mindful spontaneity in ZEN.

HAIR (1) Unconventional Broadway musical that opened in 1968, celebrating the hippies and the AQUARIAN AGE. (2) In many traditions, a symbol of spiritual purity and power, worn long by holy men in India, warrior kings of ancient Iceland, and knights of the Holy Grail, to name but a few.

HAKOMI (Hah-KOH-mee) Japanese, "how one stands in relation to the many things in the world." Technique developed by Ron Kurtz for tapping into the innate wisdom and healing power of the self, and unlocking memories that block the way to personal growth, primarily by letting the body reveal what it knows.

HALL, MANLEY PALMER Vastly learned American scholar of esoteric and mystical traditions (born 1901), founder of the Philosophical Research Society in Los Angeles, author of the massive encyclopedia *The Secret Teachings of All Ages,* astrologer, and Orientalist. Notable for his well-balanced appreciation of both Eastern and Western spirituality.

HARE KRISHNA SECT (Hahr-ray KRISH-nah) Devotional group dedicated to the worship of the Hindu God KRISHNA, known for their public displays of chanting in the streets. Established in America in 1965 by Swami Prabhupada Bhaktivedanta.

HARMONIC CONVERGENCE A term coined by Jose Arguelles in his book *The Mayan Factor* (1986), referring to his estimate of the end date of the calendar system of the ancient Aztecs, which he set in August 1987, though noting that the calendar of the Maya extends this to a later date (2013), so he takes the interval between the two as a transitional time of massive global reorientation. Exemplifies an attempt to define the APOCALYPSE in terms of contemporary historical and societal trends. Arguelles's scenario, based upon a monumental system of analogies and correlations, proposes the ancient Maya as a magical race of technocratic wizards who disappeared at will into another dimension, and may return to intervene in human affairs due to the timing of a cosmic beam (originating at the galactic center) that is now sweeping over our Solar System. Thus, an instance of an INTERVENTION scheme. Received brief media attention and comic-strip coverage in August 1987.

HASIDISM   (Hah-SID-izm) Sect of Judaism founded in Poland around 1750 by Baal Shem Tov, stressing a live, active relationship to God, preserved and celebrated in song and dance, and a sense of wonder and magic in relation to all things. An alternative path within Judaism (E2.1).

HATHA YOGA   (HAHT-tah YOH-gah) Sanskrit, from the root *hath-*, "to oppress, control by force." One of the six Yogas in ancient Indian tradition. Specifically, the practice that employs strenuous exercises in the form of postures (ASANAS) supposed to assist the practitioner in maintaining health, improving stamina, and attaining mental and emotional composure. Often accompanied by pranayama (see PRANA).

HEALING   Goes back to IE *kailo*, "solid, sound, unbroken," the same root as the word "whole." To be healed means not only to be whole, but to participate in the whole. One of the pervasive main themes of the modern spiritual movement (E1.3), evident both in the variety of therapeutic practices, such as acupuncture and bodywork, and in the widespread belief that humanity is in danger of destroying itself and must be healed of madness and all its consequences. Its enormous spectrum is expressed in clichés that range all the way from healing the planet to healing the inner child. Fundamentally based in the Western paradigm of the FALL, positing a situation of dire loss and destruction that requires human correction.

HEALING ARTS   From OE *hal,* "sound, healthy, whole." Curing disease or correcting dysfunction by alternative methods, generally understood in the new spirituality as a mere facilitation of the individual's process of becoming at one with life and achieving full attunement to the earth and to God. Within the overall philosophy of HOLISTICS, a large number of methods of alternative healing, applicable to specific mental and emotional and physical disorders, have emerged. Their success depends a great deal upon ATTITUDE.

HEBREW ALPHABET   Symbolic system of twenty-two letters, correlated to the cards of the TAROT, also used extensively in the practice of ceremonial magic.

HEBREW MYSTICISM   See CABALA, MYSTICISM.

HEINDEL, MAX   Assumed name of Louis von Grasshoff (1865–1919), founder of the Rosicrucian Fellowship in Oceanside, California, in 1907, supposedly on direct orders from an "elder brother." Author of the *Rosicrucian Cosmo-Conception* (1910), a late syncretic extension of Theosophy and Anthroposophy, with emphasis on Western occultism, healing, astrology, and Christology.

HELL A problematic theme in world mythology. Totally absent in some religions, but strongly emphasized in the Christian scenario of the LAST JUDG-MENT. An inevitable adjunct to the paradigm of the Fall: If all of fallen humanity cannot ultimately be restored to perfect union with the Godhead, then the unredeemed group must have someplace to go. According to the existential humorist Jean-Paul Sartre, "Hell is other people." Stated with rather more relativistic flair and a dark dose of Slavic humor by the Russian philosopher Nicholas Berdyaev: "The 'wicked' create hell for themselves, but the 'good' create hell for others" *(The Destiny of Man)*. See also UNDERWORLD.

HEMLOCK SOCIETY Organization founded by Derek Humphry to support the option of voluntary euthanasia for the terminally ill. Named after the poison voluntarily drunk by the Greek philosopher Socrates (C&B2.3).

HERBOLOGY (Ur-BALL-uh-gee) The use of herbs in curing and pre-venting disease, as in the Bach flower remedies.

HERMETICS (Her-MET-iks) From Greek *Hermes,* equivalent to the Egyptian Thoth: the God of writing, calculation, and the sacred arts. Loosely, the body of technical and inspirational teachings believed to be derived from the secret schools of the Egyptian Mysteries. Specifically, the corpus of thirteen manuscripts introduced into Europe in the fifteenth century, which opened the way to independent spiritual seeking in the West, especially through disclosure of the THEOGENIC IDEA. See C&B2.9 and E2.2. Loosely equatable with EGYP-TIAN RELIGION.

HEXAGRAM In the *I Ching* (C&B1.1), the six-leveled composite of broken and solid lines in sixty-four variations, used for divination and ethical guidance. Curiously, this has been correlated to the GENETIC CODE, which also consists of a sixty-four-unit system of codons, or chemical units, which transcribe and direct the entire array of life processes.

HIERARCHY From Greek *hiero-*, "sacred" + *archos,* "ruler." Loosely, any ruling group endowed with spiritual or mundane authority that operates according to ranks, such as the grades in the Roman Catholic church or the U.S. Army. Specifically, in the esoteric teachings of Dionysius the Areopagite (E8), the vast community of spiritual beings who served as God's architects and artisans in creating the world, conceived as consisting of nine levels or three threefold choirs—and sometimes claimed to have its living extension in the PLANETARY HIERARCHY. See also PLEROMA.

HIEROGLYPHIC WRITING Ancient pictorial script of impor-tance in retrieving lost knowledge. Of primary interest in modern spiritual work are the Egyptian hieroglyphs, first deciphered from the ROSETTA STONE in 1821, and Mayan/Aztec hieroglyphs, still largely untranslated, though believed to contain profound secrets of ancient psychic and technical knowledge.

HIEROPHANT From Greek *hieros,* "sacred, holy" + *phanein,* "to appear, manifest"; thus, the one to whom or through whom the SACRED is manifested. (1) In the Mysteries, the supreme leader who conducts the process of initiation and presides over the final critical stage of IMPRINTING. (2) Also, specifically, the fifth Major Trump of the Tarot.

HIGHER POWER   In recovery, the one (or sometimes anyone) who knows better than oneself how one's life works. A nonreligious concept of spiritual assistance, availed through the admission of complete powerlessness. In the practical philosophy of the recovering person, responsibility is taken for making choices but the outcome is left to one's higher power—an attitude that effectively disengages the control mechanisms of the personal ego. It is generally held that each person has his own higher power, not to be confused with the HIGHER SELF.

HIGHER SELF   A loose term in wide use, referring to that part of every human being that is supposed to exist independently of the conscious ego, though in some cases it appears to be merely a projection of that ego toward a glorified and inflated version of itself. The divine or eternal aspect of the mortal person, often held to be endowed with spiritual powers, such as the capacity for guidance and healing, pure and continuous contact with God, or access to other dimensions—a definition rooted in early Theosophical teachings, and ultimately derived from the Oriental concept of ATMA. "Contacting your higher self" is a New Age cliché. See also EGO, DIVINITY, GODSEED, INDIVIDUALITY, SELF.

HIMALAYAN MASTERS   In Theosophy, the elder brothers of the race, having their abode in remote recesses of the Himalayas, described by Madame Blavatsky as overseeing and directing human evolution from a plane of supersensible awareness and using telepathy to communicate with their chosen agents (E1.2). Best-known prototype of the planetary hierarchy. The question of the attitude of the masters regarding INTERVENTION is a tricky one.

HINAYANA   (Hin-ah-YAHN-ah) Sanskrit, "little raft." The southern branch of traditional Buddhism, which emphasizes ethical purity and direct absorption into the emptiness of Nirvana, without dwelling on the importance of the historical Buddha or conventional sainthood. Contrast with MAHAYANA.

HINDU   Sanskrit, name for the people dwelling in the region of the Indus River, or migrating from that region. Commonly referred to as Indian (not to be confused with the Native American Indian, or Amerindian).

HINDUISM   A polytheistic Eastern religion. Consists of a popular form centered largely on the worship of KALI, and a distinct and separate body of ancient teachings, not familiar to the masses, but widely influential in the transmission of Eastern spirituality to the West—for instance, the VEDAS, the UPANISHADS, the BHAGAVAD GITA, and the Brahminical philosophy and cosmology adopted by Madame Blavatsky and other Western proponents of occultism.

HOBBIT   A dwarflike creature who inhabits an imaginary realm called Middle Earth, as described in the novels of J. R. R. Tolkien and celebrated in a huge cult movement in the late 1960s. See also INKLINGS.

HOLISTIC A term originally coined by Jan Christiaan Smuts (1870–1950), prime minister of South Africa and progressive social thinker, for cooperative unity of different spheres of activity, viewing the parts in relation to the whole. Also called the holistic paradigm. A basic theme of the new spirituality (E1.3), especially prominent in the healing arts (holistic medicine). Umbrella term for any way of thinking that is not confined to analytic division but keeps in view the whole as being greater than the sum of its parts. Invoked in the cause of interdependence and opposed to the control system of modern science and power politics. In current use, sometimes spelled *wholistic*. Compare with SYNERGETICS.

HOLLOW EARTH Theory proposed in 1818 by J. C. Symnes in a letter sent to Congress and the heads of major universities. Later described in a famous occult novel, *Vril,* by Edward Bulwer-Lytton, as well as in H. G. Wells's *The Time Machine,* both of which describe the physical Earth as hollow. In a variant form, eventually picked up by the Nazis and accepted by Hitler, who commanded an experiment at Rugen Island in the Baltic Sea in 1942, hoping to verify that the surface of the Earth is in actuality a hollow sphere, with the sun at the center and human beings inhabiting the inside of its huge curvature. Good example of an OTHERWORLD scenario, occasionally picked up by psychics or endorsed by channelings (Oahspe). Sometimes cited as the origin of UFOs.

HOLOGRAM From Greek *holos,* "whole" + *gram,* "write, inscribe." (1) Technically, a device theoretically proposed by Dennis Gabor, a Nobel Prize laureate, in 1947, and later constructed through the application of laser technology. A ghostlike three-dimensional image produced by the intersection of two laser beams when one is reflected off a photographic plate that contains a likeness or prototype of the image to be produced. One really remarkable property of the hologram is that if it is broken, any fragment of it will reproduce the entire image, intact. (2) By adaptation, taken as a hypothetical example of how the human mind or brain can project the three-dimensional appearance of the real world. For instance, the hologram is used as a model for the reality-structuring function of human consciousness in BRAIN THEORY. (For a critique of this hypothesis, see E2.4.)

Adj., hologrammic. Also called holograph; adj., holographic.

Through the concept of the hologram/holograph, modern science and neuropsychology seem to have come upon a model of how we create our own reality. The hologram is imagined as comparable to the seed-form of the whole universe, the active core-design that is capable of projecting the entire structure it contains, as the acorn of an oak tree projects the entire structure and growth process of the tree, extending through both time and space. This is a heady concept, but a very important one in the spiritual outlook of modern science and psychology. It is big news, yet the hologrammic paradigm, for all its novelty, appears to be nothing more than a reformulation of the ancient concept of the Logos, or WORD. See also IMPLICATE ORDER, and contrast with CHAOS.

HOLY GRAIL   In Old French *San Graal,* which makes a pun: it means, literally, "sacred dish," but phonetically it sounds like *Sang Real,* "true blood." The pun expresses the secret understanding that the Grail is not merely the cup in which the Blood of Christ was collected, but the very Blood itself. This alludes to the Gnostic/alchemical interpretation of the Grail, in which the blood shed by Christ at the Crucifixion has the effect of a magical effluvium imagined to spread like a homeopathic dose through the atmosphere of the entire planet. See GRAIL/GRAIL MYSTERY.

HOLY MAN   Western term for a saint or *sanyassin.* As a term of respect or reverence, it seems fairly consistent in use, whereas holy women have been called everything from white goddesses to whores. Contrast with SACRED PROS-TITUTION.

HOMEOPATHY   (Home-ee-AH-puh-thee) From Latin *homo,* "same" + *pathein,* "feeling." Alternative system of medical diagnosis and treatment developed by German doctor Samuel Hahnemann (1755–1843), which applies the principle of curing like by like, using high dilutions of herbs and minerals that, in larger doses, produce the very symptoms they are used to cure. The mysterious key to the homeopathic remedy lies in the dilution of the medicament used to the point where all its detectable chemical properties are eliminated. This method was possibly derived by Hahnemann from the principle of PROJECTION known to the alchemists. Diagnosis and prescription rely on a careful considera-tion of the life history and habits of the patient. A remarkably successful example of alternative medicine.

HOPI   Shoshonean dialect, "peace, harmony." A small tribe of Pueblo Indians living on three barren mesas in northeastern Arizona, known for their intense reverence for the Earth, their spiritual purity, and certain prophecies concerning the disordering of nature due to human arrogance and wrongfully applied intelligence. Recognized internationally as guardians of the spiritual wisdom of Native America.

HOPI PROPHECIES   Teachings of the Great Spirit, Massau'u, brought into modern form in 1948 by Hopi elders, stating, among other things, that nuclear war (the "Gourd of Ashes") is inevitable before the way of total harmony can be reestablished.

HOROSCOPE   From Greek *horos,* "hour" + *skopein,* "see, observe." In astrology, a chart, usually circular, including the rising sign and the sun sign and showing the positions of planets, stars, and astronomical directions relative to the place of birth at the moment of birth. Primary device used in astrology for interpretation of character and life events. Also called birth chart, natal chart, nativity. See also HOUSE, SIGNS.

HOSPICE   A place for the terminally ill to experience DEATH AND DYING in an atmosphere of peace and noninterference.

HOUSE   In astrology, one of twelve divisions of the circular chart called the horoscope, in which each section is supposed to correspond to an area of life activities and concerns, such as finance, travel, relationships, profession. House systems in current use derive for the most part from medieval attempts to divide the heavens surrounding the Earth into a well-proportioned grid.

HUMAN DIVINITY The ultimate degree of human potential, as proposed in the Hermetica (C&B2.9 and E2.2). The essential Gnostic heresy, which opposes it to the doctrines of fundamentalism (whether Buddhist or Christian, Islamic or Judaic). The result of initiation in the Mysteries, though not the ultimate goal. See also GODSEED, THEOGENIC IDEA.

HUMAN POTENTIAL Recent term for the concern to discover and evolve the inner capacities of the human being to their highest level—first, by relating the inner self to God, and then by expressing personal creativity in external roles and activities that reflect the spiritual endowment of the whole person. Places the value of the human being as a free agent and instrument of God—that is, as an embodiment of DIVINITY—over against its mere function or role adapted solely for survival or social integration.

The human potential movement, which took shape in the mid-1960s and is often associated with ESALEN, can be seen as the flowering of a long-term, three-phase paradigm-shift, reflecting a change in the way humanity defines being human: from creature in medieval times, to personality in the Renaissance, to human potential in the 1960s. As noted in E1.4, as soon as the concept of human potential is introduced, it raises the issue of indwelling divinity, God-in-us, and how the divine potential inherent in human nature might also be developed. In the new spirituality, the concept of human potential establishes the broad framework within which many approaches to SELF-ACTUALIZATION can be introduced.

HUMANISM As just noted, this is the Renaissance prototype of the human potential movement. Historically, it is the worldview that emerged during the period of European history from 1250 to 1600, asserting that the individual person has a deep intrinsic value, regardless of social role or material status. The rise of humanism in the Renaissance is an example of a PARADIGM-SHIFT, displacing the worldview of the Middle Ages, when the individual was looked upon as a creature of God, subject to the preordained laws of creation, and not as a self-determining personality who could become, ultimately, a law unto him- or herself. Shakespeare, for one, represents the great breakthrough into humanism.

HUMANISTIC Adj., referring to any philosophical view or personal attitude that accepts the inalienable dignity and value of the human individual as a basis for all actions and considerations. When called secular humanism, it refers to a view deeply opposed to FUNDAMENTALISM and all other religious doctrines that locate the sanction for human activity and the ultimate validation of the personality outside us in a superhuman source, rather than in the rich potentiality of human nature itself.

HUMANISTIC PSYCHOLOGY Loosely, the school of modern psychology that attempts to understand the value and meaning of personal experience for the one who has it, rather than by external analysis or clinical/scientific definition of how the person functions, or is supposed to function.

HUMANITY According to Gurdjieff, Rudolf Steiner, Teilhard de Chardin, and other teachers of progressive occultism, the superevolving part of organic life on Earth, ultimately or potentially capable of developing (through the enigmatic functions of individual self-consciousness and memory) into a being who can assume responsibility for the ongoing process of creation—or at the very least one who can serve as a responsible caretaker for planetary life in its given form. The ancient and common purpose of the Mysteries and all legitimate schools of spiritual training was just this: to prepare humanity for its work of divine service in COCREATION. When this is achieved through the harmonious collaborative union of humanity with nature, it is called the ALCHEMICAL WEDDING. When it is achieved through the actualization of the Godseed innate to human nature, it is called the THEOGENY. According to the Sufis, a source of sympathy for God. According to the Hindus, a population of odd, fleeting entities who inhabit the dream of Vishnu. According to itself, a great riddle. On the troubling issue of human nature and the possibility or impossibility of ever changing it, see ROMANTICISM (E22).

HUMANKIND A way of referring to humanity as a single family unit.

HUNA (HOO-nah) See KAHUNA.

HUNDREDTH MONKEY Term coined by Lyall Watson in 1979, referring to the behavior of monkeys on the Japanese island of Koshima: When masses of sweet potatoes were dumped by researchers on the beach, the monkeys did not at first know how to eat them, but eventually a few monkeys started dipping them in the ocean to remove the sand and then eating them in the sight of the others—so that eventually, when the hundredth monkey began doing as the first ones had done, all the monkeys on the island and on all the neighboring islands began doing the same thing, simultaneously, without each one having to go through a long process of trial and error. Now widely taken as verification of the notion of CRITICAL MASS in evolutionary processes at the behavioral level.

HYPNOTHERAPY/HYPNOTISM In modern times, the outgrowth of the work of Friedrick Anton Mesmer (1734–1815), an Austrian doctor who introduced methods for manipulating what he called the vital fluids churning about in the field of animal magnetism of the human body. Mesmer was sensationally effective in producing outrageous effects in his subjects, and he proved the efficacy of hypnotism in healing. Age-old practices of Yoga may be viewed as techniques of self-hypnosis. Mesmer's work was followed up by Baron von Reichenbach, who claimed to have discovered a mysterious force called od, later called ECTOPLASM, to be seen in the auras of mediums and hysterics. These ideas and manipulative techniques were adopted by Eliphas Levi and converted to the revival of MAGIC at the dawn of the twentieth century. Currently in wide use as techniques of self-help and attitude correction.

I

"I AM" MOVEMENT Esoteric cult founded in 1934 by Guy and Edna Ballard, centered on the ascended masters, especially Saint Germain; emphasizes ascension by transforming the causal body into pure light; known for its decrees, or loud verbal incantations, used to dispel evil influences; associated to this day with Mount Shasta in northern California, where the Ballards' initial contact with Saint Germain is said to have occurred. Attained an immense popularity for a few years, enlisting thousands into faith in the Great White Brotherhood; later revived in the teachings of Mark L. and Elizabeth C. Prophet, cofounders of the Church Universal and Triumphant, a self-declared organ of the GWB dedicated to a revival of the Mysteries for the salvation of humanity.

I CHING (Yee CHING) A Chinese system of divination, very ancient in origin, consisting of sixty-four patterns called hexagrams. Widely used since the 1960s for consultation in making ethical and practical choices. Originally cast with dry yarrow stalks, now commonly thrown with coins. C&B1.1.

IKEBANA (Ee-kay-BAH-nah) The Japanese art of flower arrangement, often taken up as an esthetic discipline in the practice of Zen.

ILLUMINATI Latin, plural of *illuminatus,* "one who is unusually bright." Occult society formed in 1776 by Bavarian scholar Adam Weishaupt, in an attempt to implement the progressive ideas of the Enlightenment by means of secret, elite-controlled group efforts. Often cited as an example of an occult CONSPIRACY.

ILLUSION From Latin *illudere,* "to mock, play with." Ill-using, the perversion of what is basically true and appropriate by using it wrongly or playing it badly, against its real purpose. See also DELUSION, MAYA.

IMAGERY Loosely, almost any sort of mental picturing. Applied in certain forms of meditation where VISUALIZATION is the goal.

IMAGINATION The capacity to produce mental images, often charged with emotional force, that are completely independent of any sensorial stimuli. In Romanticism, the primary evidence and expression of the God-like, cocreative power inherent to the human soul. See also INNER LIFE.

IMAM (Ih-MAHM) From Arabic *amma,* "to go before, precede." In Islamic religion, a prophet, guide, or founder of a spiritual LINEAGE.

IMMANENCE In theology, the INDWELLING of the Godhead within the world, by contrast to the doctrine of transcendence, which places God elsewhere, removed from the realm of tangible access. In Hinduism, asserted as the all-pervasive presence of Vishnu, the World Dreamer, within the consciousness of the entities he dreams. In Buddhism, asserted in the doctrine of the VOID. In Ch'an and Zen teachings, indicated as the SUCHNESS. According to this principle, there is no reality superior to the one we can experience right here and now; also, no heaven and hell located in some other dimension beyond the one we inhabit. Adj., immanent, applied to many instances of cosmic consciousness (C&B3.1) and spontaneous God-contact, such as experienced in mysticism and especially in Tantra. Primary point of difference between traditional religions and alternative paths (E2.3). See also SECOND COMING.

IMMORTALITY Deathlessness of the physical body or, more often, of the conscious soul. From the earliest accounts, ascribed solely to great kings and heroes, many of whom were considered to be descended from the Gods by THEOGAMY; also held to be the privilege of the initiates, due to having undergone the process of immortalization in the Mysteries. Among the enlightened Greeks of Plato's time, held to be attainable in rare instances by philosophical effort. In Christianity, granted to everyone by a kind of blanket coverage, but dependent upon developing a personal relationship to Christ, as emphasized in fundamentalism. See also SPIRITUAL DEATH.

IMPERMANENCE In Buddhism, one of the three primary traits of existence. It involves us in a typical damned-if-you-do-or-don't situation, since it is the cause of suffering (DUKKHA) through loss, if we accept it, and through alienation, if we attempt to deny it. See also the contrast between INFINITY and ETERNITY.

IMPLICATE ORDER Term coined by modern exponent of the new physics, David Bohm, for the nonobvious dynamic pattern that informs and directs all processes in nature. Exact equivalent to the WORD in ancient cosmological teachings.

IMPRINTING (1) In the ancient psychology of the Mysteries, the process undergone by the neophyte who suffers through the ORDEAL or PSYCHODRAMA to the point of becoming scared near to death and extraordinarily vulnerable. It is said that in this condition the etheric body separates unnaturally from the physical, a condition that allows for the etheric body to be imprinted with new patterns. Imprinting was generally accomplished by chanting, group meditation centered on the neophyte, the use of music, and sometimes the application of psychotropic drugs—but only after long years of preparation. In the Egyptian

Mysteries, the rite of imprinting—which amounts to an actual rebirth of the human soul at the level of its divine potential—is said to have been performed in the sarcophagus of the KING'S CHAMBER.

Admittedly somewhat difficult to understand (because we lack confident knowledge in the workings of occult anatomy), the ancient technique of imprinting has been rediscovered in our time in connection with the use of psychedelic drugs, or neurotransmitters, for reprogramming the nervous system.

(2) In contemporary use, the process of acquiring fixed attitudes and behavioral habit mechanisms by the impact of early impressions, emotional trauma, and sociocultural indoctrination. The imprints so acquired may be modified through neurolinguistic programming and temporarily suspended in altered states.

INCA Ancient high civilization of Peru with its capital at Cuzco, based on sun-worship and held in native myth to have been established by a lineage of seven kings who came from Atlantis after its destruction. Discovered and ruined by Francisco Pizarro, a Spanish adventurer, in 1527.

INCARNATION (1) Loosely, the process by which a spiritual entity free of physical embodiment takes on tangible form, and especially human form. (2) Specifically, the Incarnation: the embodiment of the cosmic being, Christos, in the human body and personality of Jesus of Nazareth, believed in conventional Christianity to have occurred at the moment of Mary's Immaculate Conception, but in Gnostic and alternative Christian traditions, believed to have occurred at the moment of Jesus's baptism in the Jordan by John the Evangelist and to have ended at the Resurrection. See also ADVENT.

INCOMPLETION One of the most radical and deeply guarded secrets in Western occultism. In alchemy, it appears in the theory that the universe is a vast handiwork that superhuman beings have left in an unfinished state. The alchemists, who were consecrated to the task of divine service in completing the work left undone by the Gods, insisted that humankind must learn first to imitate nature, then to surpass it—but never to suppress it. This was also the goal *(telos)* of the Mysteries, and it now comes to new expression in the modern quest through the ideals of COEVOLUTION and COCREATION. Profoundly associated with the mytheme of intervention, since the meddling of a rebellious or trickster God in human affairs (such as the serpent, Lucifer, who tempts Eve in the Garden of Eden), often results in the grave situation where human beings have to restore the original perfection that was disrupted or was never fully actualized. This complex doctrine of incomplete and deviated creation was widely taught in Gnosticism. See also FALL, FREEDOM.

INDIVIDUALITY Loosely, that which results from the evolution of God-essence or divine potential through a long process of learning and becoming; the aim of incarnation, undergone by the DIVINE SPARK or fragmentary germ of the Godhead, so that God, which is originally all-one, may come to know itself in an infinite variety of ways, through many ones. Specifically, in the old

Theosophical idiom and esoteric psychology, the aspect of the reincarnating ego that continually grows and gains through the experience of successive life cycles, so that ultimately it becomes evolved enough to maintain and express active Godhood on Earth. This Theosophical notion of the human individuality is usually described as the threefold articulation of the Monad: "Atma-Buddhi-Manas." Though this old lingo is now largely forgotten, the concept survives in the New Age cliché of the HIGHER SELF.

INDIVIDUALIZATION   In the technical language of Theosophy, the long-term process by which a human being, considered as a spark from the Godhead, progressively comes to differentiate itself, to develop its own history and karma, its own original gifts and specific lasting attributes, so that it is eventually able to serve as a complete articulation of the greater whole, while remaining distinct and unique unto itself. In short, the process required for the infinite perfection of DIVINITY. In the esoteric account of human evolution, individualization began with the Fall and is necessarily attended by problematical side effects, namely pain, labor, and death—the triple curse described in Genesis 3:16–19.

INDIVIDUATION   In current usage, especially in the Jungian work, the process of developing a conscious relationship between one's separate personal ego and the universal SELF, conceived either as God or the human totality, humanity as a whole. Following indications from his studies of alchemy, Jung often identified the principle of individuation with the Christ, viewed as the being who actively mediates between the totality-image of God and the self-conscious personal ego. The result of individuation is to become more and more oneself, more and more unique and original in one's personal ESSENCE and self-expression—even though, paradoxically, this uniqueness is solidly grounded in the awareness of total self-sameness with all others. On the crucial distinction between the awareness of being someone unique and the awareness of being no one special, see C&B1 and 2 for prefatory remarks on Eastern versus Western spirituality.

INDO-EUROPEAN   Abbreviated IE. Designation of the largest language family, including Greek, Sanskrit, Avestan, Germanic, and Celtic languages. Source of many English words, as a random look at a dictionary will show: grain, from Old French *grein* > Latin *grana* > IE root *ger-*, "to become ripe." The common root of Greek and Sanskrit was established by Jakob Grimm in 1822, a breakthrough in EAST/WEST studies that has led to our current understanding of the worldwide framework of religion and spirituality (E2.3).

INDWELLING   The immediate presence of the Godhead in the world and in the human soul, which implies the accessibility of its divine potential for cultivation and expression through alternative paths of spirituality. A primary theme of the New Age. Specifically in Tantra, the inherence of the root-potential of creation in pure sensation. See also SACRED.

INFINITY   The source of perpetual change, the root-potential of boundless variation and originality, expressed in endless and ever-new variations on the enduring design of ETERNITY, which itself is changeless. "Eternity is in love with the productions of time" (William Blake).

INFINITY SYMBOL In the form of a figure eight: Western counterpart to the YIN/YANG.

INFRASENSORY That which occurs or is manifest within the senses. Describes a type of mystical experience or altered state in which a spiritual or supernatural presence reveals itself by breaking directly into the ordinary senses and perfusing them. Contrast with EXTRASENSORY. See also CLAIRSENTIENCE.

INITIATE As a noun, someone who underwent the full course of training in the Mysteries, and who thereby became elevated to a superevolved or God-like state, gaining powers of knowledge and extraordinary faculties that allowed him to assume responsibility for teaching and guiding the human race, and specifically for initiating culture. In the Western Mystery tradition, a master or Manu. Loosely, in modern terms, any individual whose degree of inner development and dedication to the ultimate welfare of humanity and the planet qualifies him as a teacher who can introduce progressive impulses and impart knowledge and practices useful for the moral and cultural evolution of humanity.

As a verb, *to initiate (into),* to start someone on a spiritual path by firsthand contact with a master or by putting him through a course of training and education. To start anew (East) or to start something new (West). See also GOATS, ORGY.

INITIATION The methodology of the ancient Mysteries (E16): long and intensive training with the aim of elevating the one who undergoes it to begin (initiate) living a new, higher life, often described as being on the level of Godhood, above and beyond the state of ordinary mortals—hence, the initiates of former times were viewed as incarnate Gods by ordinary people. In the classical sense, may be viewed as threefold: method, goal, and practice. The method was a long preparation culminating in the psychodrama and imprinting, which resulted in transhumanization (THEOGENY). The goal or aim (Greek *telos,* for which those on the way to it were called *telestes,* "bound for the end") was service in the divine mission of cocreation. The actual practice was culture-initiation and spiritual guidance of the human race, according to the racial and regional needs where the Mystery Schools were located (Egypt, Ireland, Tibet, et cetera). Also, faculties such as thought-reading, thought transmission, mathematical and musical knowledge, power over nature, conscious dreaming, direct communication with superhuman beings, and other outrageous talents, may be considered as sensational side effects gained through initiation and used by the initiates as appropriate to the fulfillment of their tasks. See also SELF-INITIATION.

INKLINGS An English literary-philosophical group with strong esoteric interests, formed early in the century and consisting of J. R. R. Tolkien, C. S. Lewis, and Charles Williams, early prominent authors of occult fiction.

INNATE What is inmost and original, unique to each being. That which makes each one of us special: the seed of the Godhead in us, considered as infinite potentiality for difference, which does not preclude our sameness with others and is in fact grounded in it. The basis of true individuality and creative talent. In modern initiation, the central and most significant concept to be understood if one is to enter upon the path of self-initiation through a course of independent seeking. That which is stimulated and unfolded through the learning process that unfolds in the context of LIFE ITSELF. See also VIRGIN.

INNER CHILD   The essence of humanity in us all, the pure and inexhaustible source of human potential. In recovery, the true self as the one who experiences the precious sense of all life's richness in early childhood and needs to rediscover that sense in order to fulfill the possibilities of adulthood. "Healing the inner child" is a powerful theme of the modern spiritual quest, reflecting the Christian paradigm of the Fall, which states that we have lost our original innocence and need to be restored to it. Equates almost directly with the divine child as the archetype of the human spirit. See also ADULT CHILD.

INNER GAME   Recent term referring to the possibility of taking any and every activity—from skiing to shopping—as an exercise in self-awareness, a game of self-reference in which the way one plays it reveals attitudes about oneself and the world. For example, the inner game of tennis.

INNER LIFE   The life of imagination, fantasy, personal MYTHMAKING. In Romanticism in its final phase, the Decadence, this was set over against the outer life of convention and mundane bourgeois desires, posing a violent contrast between the imaginary and the actual that led many of the Decadents to choose degeneration through drugs and weird fantasies as an outrageous rebellion against the deadening grind of the outer, ordinary life (E2.3).

INNER LIGHT   Loosely, the presence of God as higher intelligence within the human mind; source of illumination, peace, acceptance. Specifically, the human ability to contact God directly, as understood in the Society of FRIENDS. See also WHITE LIGHT.

INNER WORK   Any study or discipline for developing the innate, especially whatever allows an individual to discover and unfold the full potential of his relationship to himself, as a centering for all other kinds of relating. In Eastern ways, often accomplished by surrendering the relationship to oneself for the relationship to God; that is, finding yourself by finding God. But in Western ways, inner work involves the cultivation of one's personal essence, rather than attainment of impersonal or transpersonal selfhood. This is accomplished through unfolding one's original gifts, such as imagination, sensitivity, the sense of beauty, dreams, fantasies, inspirations—in short, through creative INDIVIDUATION.

INTEGRAL YOGA   System of Yoga developed by Sri Aurobindo, emphasizing the link between the ordinary personality and the superconscious.

INTEGRATION   The process of combining all the parts of oneself into a functional whole, bringing together head and heart, intellect and love, pleasure and suffering, openness and boundaries, innocence and discrimination, et cetera. Opposite to DYSFUNCTIONALITY.

INTENT   In Castaneda, the power that operates mysteriously within all acts of human perception and establishes us in relation to both the known and unknown without our knowing (ordinarily) how it does so. Thus, its mastery implies the ability to alter totally and at will the given realm of perception and, in effect, to discover other worlds; for example, shifting the ASSEMBLAGE POINT.

INTENTION   The conscious formulation of motive, which serves as the basis for taking responsibility for one's action though it does not extend to control of the outcome. In esoteric psychology, that which distinguishes the human as such, though subject to deviations (E4, E13): when separatistic, the LUCIFERIC bias, when controlling, the AHRIMANIC bias. A crucial concept in the understanding of free will and the human capacity for choice. Contrast with MAGIC.

INTERNAL DIALOGUE   The act of talking to oneself, which is fairly constant in human consciousness, since we only know what we are thinking through hearing it as silently sounded language in our heads. Stopping the internal dialogue, briefly or for longer periods of time, is the aim of many methods of meditation.

INTERSPECIES COMMUNICATION   The art or science of communicating with members of other species, such as birds or DOLPHINS.

INTERVAL   (1) One of the most important theoretical and practical concepts in occultism, basis of many techniques for developing higher awareness or special powers. It signifies the hidden potentiality that lies in the often unobserved transition between two states; for instance, the interval between conceiving a gesture of your arm and actually performing it. In occult theory it is believed that hidden forces can be tapped by working consciously upon the interval. The two most common intervals are the moment before falling asleep and the moment before waking up. Few of us can observe exactly what happens in these intervals—but if we could, life might become very different. See also CHAOS.

Cosmologically treated by Pythagoras, a Greek mathematician of approximately 500 B.C., in a model correlating the distances between planets to musical chords: music of the spheres. Widely applied in the GURDJIEFF work, where the "mi-fa" interval in the seven-tone octave is taken as designating the point in any sequence of thoughts or actions where a break occurs and a "super-effort" can be applied, producing extraordinary results.

(2) In SACRED MUSIC, the sound-gap between tones or octaves, supposed to be able to produce special effects upon consciousness, resonate the higher bodies, or induce healing.

(3) In esoterics, the period of time between incarnations, or LIFE-INTERVAL.

INTERVENTION Worldwide mytheme often entertained in scenarios of modern spirituality—for instance, the intervention of extraterrestrials to save the world from doom. Illustrated in world mythology in countless instances of Gods descending to assist humanity by specific acts of SERVATION; also, in many stories of Gods meddling in human affairs where they have no business, as in the case of the Luciferic and Ahrimanic aberrations. In modern-day mythmaking, often associated with the end-of-the-world scenario, the classic instance being the Last Judgment described in Revelation. Often revived in channeling when "off-planet" entities give direction and make predictions. A serious issue of the new spirituality, calling for a deep look at the question of GUIDANCE (E1.4).

INTROSPECTION Looking within, either to examine one's innermost thoughts, feelings, and motives, or to clear the mind for a sudden moment of awakening to the true self, experienced to be identical with God and the entire universe, as in SATORI.

INTUITION Knowledge that comes direct and unmediated, without the need for rational thought or even inspired guessing; usually held to be a crucial aspect of CREATIVITY, as in creative intuition.

INVOLUTION In the idiom of Theosophy, the descent of spirit into matter, involving the darkening of consciousness in the divine spark, the seed of human divinity, as it takes on increasingly dense sheaths of materiality. Technical term for VEILING, the necessary condition for individualization.

IRIDOLOGY The diagnosis of human ailments and psychological states from the deposits of pigment in the eye, where the organs of the body are mapped out.

ISHVARA (Ish-VAHR-ah) Sanskrit, "lord." In Hinduism, designation of the Supreme Being as a personal entity. See also PERSON.

ISKON International Society for Krishna Consciousness, more commonly known as the Hare Krishna movement.

ISLAM Arabic, "submission," from the verb *salama,* "to be resigned." The traditional religion of the Moslems, with Allah as the supreme deity; or the land and culture where this religion predominates.

ISSA (EE-sah) Lord Issa, a yogi-saint identified by some with Jesus of Nazareth, who is believed to have traveled to the East during his "lost years" from age twelve to thirty.

I-THOU A term introduced by theologian Martin Buber (1878–1965) for the attitude of relating to other people or even inanimate things as another subject, rather than as an object or "it." This approach preserves not only the equality of the two subjects in relation, but it also values the relation-between as something to be respected in itself. Developed by Buber as a paradigm of the dialogue between God and the human self, which in turn becomes the model for all relating. The formula for intersubjective contact, fostering love.

J

JAGUAR   In the myth and ritual of Central and South America, a symbol of occult power, often of an evil slant. The supreme title in the ancient Maya and Aztec priesthoods; also, the NAHUAL of the jungle sorcerers. *Balam* in the Maya tongue. Comparable to the panther as the animal familiar of the Greek God of Ecstasy, Dionysus.

JAIN/JAINISM   From Sanskrit *Jina*, "victor," name of an Indian prophet of the sixth century B.C. who founded an alternative religion to Hinduism, rejecting Vedic scriptures and caste. Noted for the principle of *ahimsa*, harmlessness to all things, demonstrated by some Jains wearing gauze masks so they do not breathe and kill microscopic organisms in the air. Previously one of the world's great religions, now a small sect numbering about two million. Revived in America by Guruved Shree Chitrabhanu, 1975.

JATAKA   (JAH-tahk-ah) In Buddhism, a famous collection of folktales that describe previous incarnations of SIDDHARTHA as a variety of animals.

JEHOVAH   Also called Yahwe or Jahve. Monotheistic God of the ancient Hebrews, who viewed him (definitely masculine) as their special tribal deity, yet able to prevail over the entire world. Expanded form of the mystical and unpronounceable name Yod-he-vau-he (YHVH) in the Cabala. Mischievously equated with Satan by Madame Blavatsky, following clues left by the Gnostics.

JEHOVAH'S WITNESSES   A religious group of fundamentalist Christians who claim to have existed since Abel, the first witness of Jehovah, the supreme monotheistic God of the Old Testament. Founded in 1881 by C. T. Russell, and strongly oriented toward ARMAGEDDON and the SECOND COMING. Known for its members, who go door-to-door to seek converts (working toward a quota of 144,000) and distribute pamphlets.

JESUS   English variant of the Hebrew name Jeshua, the historical person associated with the human embodiment of Christ. In Christian religion, the personification of God on Earth. In fundamentalism, the single and supreme instance of the personhood of God, and as such considered to continue living in our midst. In esoteric Christianity, the hybrid of human/divine, Jesus/Christ; that is, the human being who receives and incorporates the God-being in the Incarnation. Viewed humanistically, not the unique example of a man who incorporated a superhuman God, but simply the Jewish teacher and religious rebel who has influenced the world more than any other spiritual figure with his message of forgiveness, love for one's enemies, and seeking the kingdom of heaven within oneself. See also ISSA, MAGDALEN, MESSIAH.

JIN SHIN DO   A variant of ACUPRESSURE.

JIVA   (JEE-vah) Sanskrit, "personal soul." The human soul in embodiment, generally viewed as a state of oppression and enslavement. See also MOKSHA.

JOURNAL/JOURNALING   The method of using a diary for self-evaluation, accessing the questions and issues of personal existence and exploring the inner life. Developed principally by Ira Progoff.

JUDAISM   From *Judah,* a tribe in the Old Testament. The religion and culture of the Jews or Hebrews. One of the major world religions, numbering about eighteen million.

JUDEO-CHRISTIAN ETHIC   A belief system dominant throughout the world, derived from the moral theology of the Old and New Testaments of the Christian Bible, based mythologically on the FALL, emphasizing obedience to the commandments of God and punishment of transgression in an end-of-the-world scenario, the APOCALYPSE.

JUDGMENT   In theology and religion, the process of working out what is right or wrong, good or evil, in human affairs—a task fundamentalism assigns to God, requiring that humanity accept the God-given sanctions and prohibitions. A basic paradigm of the Western worldview, contrasting radically to the doctrine of compassion for all sentient beings in Buddhism. In modern seeking, judgment is a problematic issue that often comes up as seekers look critically or disbelievingly upon the paths chosen by other seekers and judge them for their choices. In short, a major problem of ATTITUDE. Mythologically dramatized in the scenario of the Last Judgment. See also NONATTACHMENT.

JUNG/JUNGIAN WORK   Carl Gustav Jung, Swiss psychologist (1875–1961), student of Freud who later became the founder of his own school and author of a huge body of writings. Founder of ANALYTICAL PSYCHOLOGY, world-class mythologist, cautious and diligent seeker into the realms of parapsychology and the occult, ambitious revivalist of alchemy and Gnosticism. Originator of key concepts in modern depth psychology—collective unconscious, archetype, animus/anima, projection, individuation, shadow, synchronicity—referred to as the Jungian work.

JUNGIAN/SENOI   In dreamwork, the synthesis of the teachings and methods of Jung with the practices of the Senoi natives of Malaysia, who are known to use dreams actively in the organization and management of all aspects of their life and culture.

K

KABALA/KABBALAH See CABALA.

KAHUNA (Kah-HOO-nah) The way of the HUNA, Hawaiian for shaman. An ancient tradition of Polynesian shamanism, including a body of sophisticated teachings on self-empowerment, purification from evil and negative influences, and activation of potentials in the higher bodies.

KALACHAKRA (Kah-lah-CHAHK-rah) Tibetan, "wheel *(chakra)* of time *(kala)*." In Tibetan Buddhism, an important body of teachings written down in the tenth century, concerned with the mysterious process of the succession of the Bodhisattvas, by which the transmission of the original impulse initiated by Gautama Buddha is ensured of surviving through time.

KALI (KAH-lee) Hindu Goddess, immensely popular among the masses in India; often pictured as a frightful, all-devouring witch with feral eyes, blood streaming from her mouth, and a garland of human skulls around her neck. In Tantra and esoteric Hinduism, the image of Time, which like a mother gives birth to all things and beings, but also consumes them. As the Black Goddess, the one who destroys egotistical limitations and illusions and gives access to the secret realm of INFRASENSORY vision. Especially in Tantra, the image of the ground-potential of creation, often realized in a state of violent ecstasy.

KALI YUGA (KAH-lee YOO-gah) Sanskrit *Kali,* "Dark Goddess," associated with time and eternal night, and *yuga,* "time cycle, age"; hence the Age of Kali. In the tradition of the Brahmins there is a complex system of time-reckoning that gives the Kali Yuga a duration of 432,000 years. Its exact starting point is a matter of much dispute, but the death of KRISHNA, the Eighth Avatar of Vishnu, in 3102 B.C. may be taken as a likely margin. Described as a time of deep delusion when active communion with God is difficult. In Western terms, the age of total materialism, when even spiritual values and principles are degraded into shallow forms of gratification or mere pretenses. See also SPIRITUAL MATERIALISM.

KALKI (KAHL-kee) In Hindu mythology and Brahminical religion, the tenth and final Avatar of Vishnu, yet to come, usually pictured as a riderless white horse bearing a banner upon which the future fate of the world is written. Key image in the Hindu myth of the Apocalypse.

K A M A S U T R A Sanskrit, "scripture *(sutra)* of desire *(kama)."* A kind of marriage manual giving explicit instructions on the art of sexual intercourse, supposed to have been written by Vatsyayana anywhere from the first to the twelfth century A.D. Probably leaked from the oral traditions of sacred intercourse in Hindu TANTRA. Revived by hippies in the 1960s in the cause of free love. See also EROTICISM (E11).

K A R A T E Japanese, "empty hand." A form of martial art originally developed in Okinawa when bearing weapons was forbidden to the native population; imported to Japan around 1920.

K A R M A Sanskrit, from the root *kri-*, "to do, enact, perform." Your act, the way you perform in the game of life, as well as the inherent law of responsibility by which whatever you have done, in this life or another, will return in a form that requires you to own up to it and live out the consequences. This is not moral cause-and-effect in the strict sense of action-reaction or deed-retribution. Karma is not a victim game. Rather, it is an educational process of learning responsibility and choice by suffering the consequences of blind, repetitive behavior. Even viewed as an educational process, however, karma can be a tricky proposition, since the lessons it entails must be discovered by mastering a kind of emotional logic, rather than rational logic. For instance, the emotional logic in "you rejected me, so I don't need you anymore" is not rational but is certainly effective, and as common as day in human affairs. To fathom this kind of logic one has to undergo it fully and become, as it were, the subject in one's own learning experiment. Only then can karma be mastered and the lesson converted from a compulsory act into an optional course of action. Perhaps the best-known term from Indian teachings, by now become pure street-slang, so we often hear reference to "good karma" and "bad karma" and the classic bumper sticker, "My karma ran over my dogma": a way of saying that what you're actually doing (karma) will always show up what you believe you're doing (dogma).

K A R M A P A Sanskrit, "man of action." In the Kargyu (Black Hat) sect of Tibetan Buddhism, a common title for a master or lineage-holder, going back to a primary TULKU in the sixteenth century.

K A T C H I N A (Kah-CHEE-nah) Shoshonean, from *ka*, "respect" + *china*, "spirit." Among the Hopi and Pueblo Indians of the southwestern United States, a spirit-helper or guide, often represented by a doll or mask. Ancestral spirit who ensures the fruitfulness of the earth and gives power to one who ritually impersonates it.

K I See CHI.

K I N G ' S C H A M B E R Central cell in the Great Pyramid of Giza, Egypt, containing a stone sarcophagus believed to have been used for the process of imprinting during the TEMPLE SLEEP of ancient initiation, as described by Peter Tompkins, Manley Palmer Hall, Rudolf Steiner, and others.

K I R L I A N P H O T O G R A P H Y A method of photography for capturing the color patterns of the human aura or the aura of plants; sometimes in the former cases used to diagnose physical and psychological states or even to read past lives. Uses film laid on a plate where the object to be photographed is pressed as a current of 75,000 to 200,000 pulses per second passes through it. Developed in 1939 by Russian electrician Semyon Davidovitch Kirlian and his wife, Valentina.

K I V A (KEE-vah) Among the HOPI, a round ceremonial structure with an entrance by a ladder through a hole in the top, used for sacred rites and gatherings of the elders.

K N I G H T S T E M P L A R See TEMPLARS.

K O A N (KOH-ahn) In Zen, a kind of brainteaser or unanswerable question intended to break the tendency for conclusive thinking and open the mind for spontaneous enlightenment. "What is the sound of one hand clapping?" is the koan used by J. D. Salinger as the epigraph for his novel *The Catcher in the Rye.*

K O E S T L E R , A R T H U R (KEST-lur) Hungarian-born British novelist and free-lance occultist (1905–1983), tireless investigator of parapsychology, world political enigmas, the creative process, and historical riddles. Especially notable for his great study *The Act of Creation,* and his lucid, coolheaded investigations of parapsychology.

K O K O P I L A U / K O K O P E L L I (Ko-ko-PEE-lau, Ko-ko-PELL-lee) In Native American folklore and especially among the Navajo and Hopi, the hunchbacked flute player, a phallic God and spirit of fertility who enlivens the corn and grains. Possibly the Amerindian equivalent to Pan.

K O K O R O (Ko-KORE-oh) Japanese, "heart-mind." The quality of inner rest, peace, harmony, Enlightenment, localized in the center of the chest. See also SERENITY.

K O R A N (Ko-RAHN) Primary sacred text of Islam, said to have been dictated by an angel to Mohammed.

K R I S H N A (KRISH-nah) Sanskrit, "black." In Hinduism, the eighth Avatar of the supreme deity Vishnu, believed to have been in human embodiment around 3100 B.C. In the classic Indian teachings of the Bhagavad Gita (C&B1.6), Lord Krishna, embodied in human form, delivers a sublime message concerning the human soul and its mission on Earth. Mythologically, the supreme example of a dancing God, a playful, even erotic, deity who appears as a fluteplaying cowherd in Hindu folklore and in the magnificent love-poem of Jayadeva, the *Gita-Govinda,* or Song of the Cowherd. His love affair with the mortal woman Rahda is the consummate example of EROTICISM in world literature.

K R I S H N A M U R T I , J E D D U Unusual Hindu teacher, a kind of antiguru, known for his reductive method of using dialogue to take the listener back to a direct, intuitive sense of truth, independent of rational thought and language.

Also known for the Krishnamurti Affair: After being chosen at the age of thirteen by the Theosophist C. W. Leadbeater to be the next embodiment of Christ as MAITREYA, the World-Teacher, Krishnamurti eventually rejected the role and withdrew into seclusion in 1939, disclaiming any knowledge of the Theosophical MAHATMAS and declaring his personal conviction that truth-seeking is a journey through a "pathless land." After enduring long years of soul-struggle and near-psychotic disturbance, he emerged as a teacher of rational discourse and a champion of free seeking, who became world-famous for his lucid, often startling talks and dialogues. Lived from 1887 to 1986.

K U K U L K A N (Koo-KOOL-kan) Maya name for QUETZALCOATL, chanted in mass ceremonies at Chichén Itzá in the Yucatán, Mexico.

K U N D A L I N I (Koon-dah-LEE-nee) Sanskrit, "spiral power" or "serpent power." In Indian Yoga and especially in Tantra, an internal force of the human body, believed to be stored in a coiled-up form at the base of the spine. According to the old tradition of Kundalini Yoga, raising this power through the inner force-centers (or chakras) of the body produces a series of extraordinary states, awakening hidden faculties and eventually, when it is raised into the head, liberating the yogi from all bondage to the physical body and material world.

K U N G F U Chinese, "task, work, exercise." Generic name for any kind of physical exercise useful for meditation and body/mind coordination; also a variant of the martial arts.

K U T H U M I (Koo-TOOM-mee) One of the best-known of the Theosophical MAHATMAS, introduced by Madame Blavatsky and later identified as a source of channeled information by various psychics.

L

LABYRINTH From Latin *labor* + *intus,* "into": the place of entering into labor, birth, or rebirth. At sacred sites, such as Chartres, Glastonbury, and Knossos on Crete, a maze constructed of earth-walls, ruts, tiles, or underground windings, believed to have been used in initiations as a place of ordeal and initiation through the PSYCHODRAMA. These constructions, found worldwide, have been interpreted as imitating the convolutions of the brain. They are also closely related to SACRED DANCE, for which they may have provided a sort of ground plan.

In our times, the analogue of modern seeking—a quest that twists and winds, yet exhibits an amazing design, the kind of pattern produced as the seeker responds, moment by moment, to the lessons and opportunities for self-revelation posed by life itself. Also, an analogy for the many and various aisles of the spiritual supermarket.

By a second derivation, labyrinth comes from the ancient Greek word *labrys,* "the double-headed axe." In Cretan myth, the maze of Daedalus, where Theseus found and slew the Minotaur, was known as the place of the double-headed axe—this being, apparently, the weapon of slaughter or sacrifice that the hero used. But deep research into Mediterranean culture of five to seven thousand years B.C. (reported by Marija Gimbutas) turns up the curious notion that the double-headed axe may have been a visual pun: At the earliest stage it appears to have been more common as the image of a butterfly! Now the butterfly itself—in Greek, *psyche*—is the earliest symbol that we have for the immortal human soul. It was also an emblem held sacred to the Great Goddess or Mother Earth. Somehow the butterfly is deeply connected with the labyrinth, as much as the double-headed axe. These two images, one so masculine and the other so feminine, appear to spring from an ancient unity of some kind. In any case, the butterfly motif suggests that the meandering design of the labyrinth may have been derived, by some wild transposition, from tracking the flight of that elusive and beautiful creature.

LAMA/LAMAISM   (LAH-mah, LAH-muh-izm) From Tibetan *blama,* "chieftain, high priest." A priest in the religion now called Tibetan Buddhism, which began in the eighth century as a small cult centered on the legendary sage PADMA SAMBHAVA, who came from India and converted the populace of the wild mountainous regions of Nepal to Buddhism. Noted for its elaborate ritual, its rigid hierarchical organization, and its extraordinary tradition of TULKUS. See also BON PO.

LANGUAGE   A vast signal system common to all seekers, in one form or another. Generally dismissed as mere words by the uninitiated, it is held in high regard in many ancient teachings and esoteric systems, some of which even claim that it conceals the very secret of creation.

According to the alchemists, the mysterious "stone" that is ignored and despised, though it holds the secret to the Great Work.

According to esotericists who see the proof of divine intelligence in natural phenomena, language is the repository of the formative and generative forces in nature; that is, the laws that operate in the formation and articulation of language by human beings are active under different guises in all processes of nature that exhibit design and continuity (as seen in the FIBONACCI SERIES, GOLDEN SEC-TION, and so forth).

According to the Christian Gnostics, including Saint John the Divine, the originating impulse of creation: "In the beginning was the Word (LOGOS) . . ."

According to some modern speculations, the "Word made flesh" in the biochemical dimension of DNA, an immense code language, which directs and perpetuates all life processes and which, if it could be accessed directly, might allow the infinite evolutionary intelligence of countless eons to become operative at the level of ordinary consciousness.

The role of language—here distinguished from mere speech—seems to have been very crucial in spiritual work in the past, though it is far less so today. Perhaps our appreciation for its occult power is confounded by the unresolved question of how language relates to thinking. Is it possible to think nonverbally, or is thinking merely a form of subvocal speaking? This is certainly a difficult question to answer, but in practice I have found one thing to be consistently true: One only thinks as well as one can express one's thinking in words. See also MIND.

LAO TZU   Chinese, "ancient youth." Famous and lovable Chinese sage who lived around 600 B.C.; author of the *Tao Te Ching* (C&B1.2).

LAST JUDGMENT   Judeo-Christian mytheme, also called Armaged-don; an end-of-the-world scenario or Apocalypse in which Christ appears out of the skies to judge the world, separating the sinners from the do-gooders and annihilating the world as we know it, in a massive spiritual war to vanquish Satan for a thousand years. Depicted by Michelangelo on the ceiling of the Sistine Chapel at the Vatican. An example of INTERVENTION. Compare with SECOND COMING.

LAYING ON OF HANDS The practice of healing or dispelling evil forces by physical touch, practiced in many of the early Christian communities but also common in pagan and shamanic folk traditions.

LEFT BRAIN The half of the brain neurologically linked to the right side of the body, supposed to mediate the functions of reason and logical thinking; the verbal and analytic half. Contrast to RIGHT BRAIN.

LEFT-HANDED PATH A somewhat old-fashioned term for those beliefs and practices based on the intention to separate and dominate, thus verging on SATANISM. Loosely, the black arts of invoking spirits, casting spells, engaging in sexual Yoga, and in general using special powers to control and deceive. Sometimes attributed to those SINISTER fellows, Brothers of the Shadow, emissaries and instruments of EVIL, though the designation is so broad it could easily be applied to any devious and manipulative act, such as the tactics of a good lawyer.

LEMURIA (Lee-MURE-ee-ah) A lost continent said to have existed before Atlantis, in the Pacific Ocean. Named after the lemurs (monkeys) of Madagascar, believed to be the last remnants of the Lemurian race. Also called Mu. Described in the teachings of Theosophy and Anthroposophy, where it falls into a sevenfold time-scheme of immense ages: Polarian, Hyperborean, Lemurian, Atlantean, and ours, the so-called POST-ATLANTEAN, with two others to come before the next PRALAYA. This chronological system, an example of EONICS, was apparently borrowed by Madame Blavatsky from some of the most closely guarded teachings of the Brahmins, who have been miffed ever since.

LEVI, ELIPHAS (El-LIE-fuss LEV-ee) Assumed name of Alphonse Louis Constant (1810–1875), French Catholic occultist, a self-declared magus and master of the arcane sciences, who played a vital role in the European revival of MAGIC.

LEVITATION The act of raising the body from the ground by supernatural means in defiance of gravity, attributed to Hindu yogis and some Western saints and recently revived as an entertainment during afternoon tea by disciples of Maharishi Mahesh Yogi, founder of transcendental meditation.

LEY-LINE In geomancy, a pathway of invisible forces believed to be generated by the Earth itself, either as electromagnetism or organic currents pulsing through the planetary organism (GAIA). According to planetary folklore, the term originally occurred to a pioneer geomancer, Alfred Watkins, while watching the track made by a snail crawling across the table of a pub in Cornwall.

LIBERATION Fundamental concept in Eastern spirituality: freedom to be or complete mastery of being, often described as reached through the total elimination of ATTACHMENT. The state of the Buddha or a master who lives in complete freedom from all illusions concerning the nature of existence, self, time, suffering, et cetera. Release from the vicious and bewildering conflict of SAMSARA. In extreme, the rejection of the world and all it offers. A dominant paradigm of the East, standing in contrast to the fundamental theme of SALVA-

TION in the West. Regarding this contrast, a good question is: With the shedding of all attachment, what happens to commitment? See also NONATTAINMENT.

LIFE AFTER DEATH The continuation of consciousness and possibly even some type of bodily existence after death. Posited in many ancient teachings and now inferred from the testimony of NEAR-DEATH EXPERIENCES.

LIFE-FORCE An idea common to all ancient religions, metaphysical systems, and existing "primitive" tribal folk. In Sanskrit PRANA, in Chinese CHI, and universally MANA or its variants; found in countless variations, such as *huaca* (Incan), *wakan* (Sioux), and *orenda* (Iroquois), especially among Native American Indians and other peoples who still retain the empathic sense of inhabiting the living weave of nature. In current idiom, vitality not exclusively bound to the body, biochemical intelligence, the enwombing sea of the ETHERIC WEB. See also DNA and SPIRIT.

LIFE-INTERVAL The period of existence passed between two human lifetimes or physical embodiments on Earth. Described in the ancient Mysteries, especially the Orphic Mysteries, as a journey through the planetary spheres, a kind of pilgrimage in which the wandering soul encounters lessons and tests on other planets, with the ultimate aim of gathering new forces to bring to Earth upon the next cycle of embodiment.

LIFE ITSELF The ultimate teacher. This proposition is a little tricky, because it seems that we do not know how to learn from life itself, so first we have to learn how to learn! This may be done through any alternative path or way of seeking that one chooses, given the understanding that the path or teaching or technique is, in and of itself, viewed as provisional. The Buddha, for instance, compared the teaching of Buddhism to a raft, to be discarded when one has crossed to the other shore. Applying this same slant to the whole activity of seeking, all techniques of self-realization can be viewed as tangential to what life itself can show us. To paraphrase the old cliché "not an end but merely a means"—each path is not an ending but merely a meaning.

LIFE-PATH The course of activities that develops when the lessons and skills gained on any spiritual path or paths are directed back to LIFE ITSELF, rather than retained as specific practices that keep the seeker narrowly identified with the path where he acquired them. See Afterword.

LIGHT (1) In ancient religions and many occult teachings, the pure active intelligence of God or superhuman beings; the living radiance of the SOLAR LOGOS, biochemically alive and intelligent, which both conceives (male aspect) and sustains (female aspect) all things in creation. Also, the habitat of spirit-beings, such as devas and angels, or the invisible legions of the celestial hierarchies. (2) In modern physics, a field of electromagnetic radiation described in complex and exquisite mathematical formulas, which do not, however, tell us anything about how it is able to grow poppies and tomatoes. (3) In relativity theory, the medium whose velocity—186,000 miles per second—sets the limit to all events in the four-dimensional space-time continuum. See also PLASMA.

LIGHT WORK Loose term for visualization with the use of light in meditation and healing.

LIGHT-YEAR The distance light travels in a year at a constant rate of 186,000 miles per second: about 5,880 trillion miles. The Sun is nine light-minutes away, the distance across the Solar System about eleven light-hours, and the distance to the nearest star, 4.3 light-years. See also ALPHA CENTAURI.

LILA (LEE-lah) Sanskrit, "divine play." In some teachings connected with the worship of the Lord Krishna, the divine diversion or play of appearances dreamed up by the Gods for their amusement. Ecstatic quality of the VEILING. See also PLAY.

LINDISFARNE (LIN-dis-farn) (1) Island off the northeast coast of England, site of a Christian monastery built in 635 by Saint Aidan. (2) New Age educational movement founded by William Irwin Thompson, dedicated to collaboration in evolving a true planetary culture.

LINEAGE In Eastern spirituality, usually refers to a succession of teachers or masters, such as the twenty-eight Indian patriarchs, culminating in Bodhidharma, who brought Buddhism from India to China. Based on the tradition of long-term TRANSMISSION of spiritual techniques and teachings by oral means, person to person. Most of the gurus and swamis who have come to the West since the 1960s claim position in a lineage. In Western spirituality, this method of literal, hand-me-down succession from teacher to pupil is superseded by a different kind of continuity: the progression of Western masters who periodically reappear through SERIAL REINCARNATION in successive historical epochs, bringing in new impulses and directive teachings according to the changing needs of humanity.

LINGAM (LING-gum) Sanskrit word for the male sexual organs. Compare with YONI.

LOCH NESS MONSTER A serpentine creature believed to inhabit a lake in Scotland. According to some alleged sightings, it measures thirty to sixty feet long and is apparently quite docile, even timid. The first mention of it on record occurs in the writings of Saint Adamnan, bishop of Iona, 565 A.D. A well-known example of the UNEXPLAINED, the kind of thing that draws sensational interest in occult and psychic phenomena.

LOGOS (LOW-gose) Greek, "word, pattern, design, intelligence." Primary concept in all ancient religion and cosmology. The blueprint of creation, endowed with the dynamic force to evolve itself through planes and hierarchies, thus parenting all forms and entities. Variously conceived as masculine (Father Wisdom, Shiva) and feminine (Sophia, Shakti, Virgin). Currently, it is being rediscovered and redefined in the concepts of implicate order, morphogenetic fields, holograms, and so forth, although these attempts, so prominent in the new physics and high-rise brain theory, do not really get us inside the living, accessible dimension of the Logos. It looks as if CHAOS has a far better chance. See also SOLAR LOGOS, WORD.

LOGOTHERAPY   A method of therapy developed by European psychologist Viktor Frankl, partially from his experiences in the death camps of World War II; emphasizes the human capacity to find meaning in all events, no matter how difficult.

LONGEVITY/PROLONGEVITY   The extension of life and physical health beyond what is normal, or believed to be normal. Pursued in ancient times through a wide variety of natural cures and exotic techniques, including the TAO OF SEX. In recent times, brought to public attention due to astounding discoveries in biochemistry since the plotting of the structure of DNA by Watson and Crick in 1953—although no reliable biochemical remedy for aging has yet been developed.

LOTUS POSTURE   In Yoga, the most common seated position for meditation, in which the legs are crossed and the feet are locked onto the thighs, sometimes with the soles upward. In this posture, the body forms a perfect triangle.

LOURDES   Resort town in the Pyrenees in southwestern France, site of a holy well known for miraculous cures, attributed to the Virgin Mary, who appeared there to an invalid girl, Bernadette Sourbiros, in 1858. Compare with FÁTIMA.

LOVE   Attraction toward what "co-laborates" (works with) or "co-ludes" (plays with). Recognition of the divinity in another, and commitment to support its unfoldment. Whether love is the most problematic thing in human experience, or whether it is in fact the universal solvent of all our troubles, remains a riddle. One thing is sadly evident, however: The dynamic of love, fundamental to the principle of INDIVIDUATION, is often and surprisingly overlooked in the presentation and application of many spiritual programs being promoted today.

Sometimes cited as proof of God's presence in the world, even moving the stars (in Dante's final vision, C&B2.7); viewed in the long legacy of European Romanticism as a tragic, troubling contradiction between passion and devotion (C&B3.16); defined with eloquent brevity by Scott Peck as participation in the spiritual growth of another person (C&B4.11); but more often, it seems, confounded with CODEPENDENCY. From IE root *leubh-,* "desire, attraction," which may be interpreted to mean that love is attraction, yes, but to the ESSENCE of another human being. Contrast with COMPASSION.

LSD-25   D-lysergic acid diethylamide tartrate, a synthetic chemical produced from the extract of ergot (fermented rye), said to have been accidentally discovered by Swiss chemist Albert Hoffmann in April 1943; later to become a cause of much delight and confusion among God-seekers and thrill-seekers of the 1960s. See PSYCHEDELIC EXPERIENCE.

LUCID DREAMING   Wide-awake dreaming, the events of which are retained in full memory upon waking. Primary aim of dreamwork.

LUCIFER From Greek, "light-bearer." In Gnosticism, a superhuman benefactor of humanity, equatable to the Serpent in the Garden of Eden who promises Adam and Eve, "Ye shall become as Gods, knowing good and evil" (Genesis 3:5). Thus, the primary proponent of the Theogenic idea (E2.2). In occult psychology, the superhuman agency who cooperates in the bias of human intention toward pretending and separation, thus promoting selfishness rather than genuine self-love; by contrast to AHRIMAN, who cooperates in the bias toward denial and controlling. See also MEPHISTOPHELES.

Adj., Luciferic (or Luciferian). Applied to the Gnostic proposition that human evolution underwent a number of interventions when superhuman beings ventured to meddle in the divine experiment, as it were. In one instance, the Luciferic beings departed from the divine plan and introduced egotism prematurely into human development. As a result, we are implanted with Luciferic tendencies, not actually human in origin though they have long since become innate to human nature. To be Luciferic is to separate ourselves wrongly and ego-centeredly from the rest of humanity, to isolate, self-glorify (or self-martyrize, thinking we're better than everyone else), and to indulge in selfish passions and pretenses, especially an overinflated idea of our own spiritual development.

LUMINOUS FIBERS In Castaneda, tendrillike emanations or rays of force rooted in the region of the abdomen, which become visible to the seer and are instrumental in the performance of supernatural feats of courage or plain tomfoolery.

M

MABINOGION (Mab-in-oh-GEE-un) In the Celtic Revival, a collection of fantastic tales in Welsh mythology, closely related to the folklore of King Arthur, containing many vivid descriptions of the OTHERWORLD. The name is of doubtful meaning, but it may be understood either as "youthful adventures" (of the Welsh folk heroes described in the stories) or "magical workings *(ogio/ orgia)* in honor of the Divine Child *(Mabin/Mabon* in Welsh)."

MACHU PICCHU (MAH-chu PEE-chu) Magnificent temple-fortress of the ancient Incas, fifty miles northwest of Cuzco, Peru, in the high Andes. Site of pilgrimage for New Age seekers such as Shirley MacLaine in *Out on a Limb.* Also, theme of a poetic sequence by Chilean poet Pablo Neruda. Curiously, one of the most spectacular sacred peaks in the Himalayas is called by a similar name, Machapuchare. See also ANDES MASTERS.

MACROBIOTICS From Greek *macro-,* "big" + *bios,* "life." Nutritional philosophy originated by Julius Hensel, an organic chemist and nutritionist, in 1884; later developed by Georges Ohsawa and extended by Michio and Aveline Kushi, proposing a special diet of grains and vegetables to achieve optimal balance of YIN/YANG.

MACROCOSM Greek, "great design." Age-old idiom for the universe at large, Earth and its cosmic environment, the greater design in which we live and move and have our being. Contrast to MICROCOSM.

MACUMBA (Mah-COOM-bah) A form of spiritualism prevalent in Brazil, combining elements of African tribal magic with South American folklore; noted especially for its reverence of the Black Goddess, *Iemanja* (YAY-man-jah).

MADONNA Honorific name for the mother of Jesus, said in Christian doctrine to have received the seed of the Christ child by immaculate conception. In Catholicism and orthodox practices, her worship is called Mariolatry, and she is often elevated close to the status of God. Since the early 1500s, the subject of famous apparitions. In Greek or Eastern orthodoxy, she is called *theogenetrix,* which may be interpreted esoterically as she who gives birth (genetrix) to the divine (theo) within the human. In the Goddess Revival, she is portrayed as a key image of nurturing and matriarchal values. Embodiment of the SOPHIA, to be contrasted carefully with Magdalen. See also MOTHER WISDOM.

MAGDALEN   According to the Gnostic gospels, the woman who was the closest human companion and spiritual ally to Jesus Christ. Also viewed as the human embodiment of the FALLEN SOPHIA, to be distinguished from the Madonna, the actual mother of Jesus who personifies the VIRGIN. In the widest sense, the eternal soul mate or consort of the Christ, the missing counterpart in the Christ Mystery and the compensation for the sexual one-sidedness of the Incarnation. Poetically, perhaps, the tragic human embodiment of the MUSE. In folklore and mythology, an epiphany of the Black Goddess or Black Virgin, a being who represents the mystical dimension of sexuality and the powers hidden within the INFRASENSORY realm. In France, Sainte Marie-Madeleine, patron saint of lovers.

MAGI   (MAY-jeye) Traditional name for the three kings who visited the Christ Child. Plural of MAGUS.

MAGIC   (E15) From Greek *magike*, "sorcery, working with hidden powers," tracing back to the IE root *magh-*, "to strengthen, to increase in power." In the naive, folkloric sense, the use of charms and spells or the manipulation of supernatural forces. In the esoteric sense, the activity or ritual of concentration that leads to the *mag*nification of any effect; hence the power to produce effects in accord with predetermined intent. A complex control-system, previously the equivalent to what modern scientific technology is today.

MAGIC MUSHROOMS   Colloquial term for the psychedelic mushrooms scientifically identified as *Psilocybe* (Sill-oh-SIGH-be), known for their effect of producing a state of clarity and ease, often rendering the world in a wonderful comic light.

MAGICK   Spelling of magic introduced by Aleister CROWLEY, to distinguish it from the trivialities of card tricks and pulling rabbits out of hats. Also widely used by advocates of the magical revival and Wicca.

MAGNETISM   (1) The power of spontaneous attraction, supposed to be susceptible to infinite amplification, so that whatever one desires can be drawn to oneself. (2) Old-fashioned, eighteenth-century name for mediumship and psychic phenomena in general.

MAGUS   (MAY-juss) Old Persian name for a magician, a high priest possessed of unusual power and knowledge, especially concerning the will of the Gods and the "big world," or macrocosm. Adept, initiate, hierophant, practical master of occult powers. Also, the title of a best-seller by John Fowles, a good example of occultism in modern fiction.

MAHABHARATA   (Ma-ha-BAHR-rut-tah) National epic poem of India *(Bharat)*, a massive arrangement of verses (220,000 lines) passed down as stories through a long oral tradition, describing events that occurred at the time of the Lord KRISHNA, around 3100 B.C., including the exquisite dialogue between Krishna and Arjuna known in excerpt as the Bhagavad Gita (C&B1.6).

MAHARISHI MAHESH YOGI (Maha-RISH-ee Ma-HESH Yoghee) Indian guru (born 1911) and originator of TM (TRANSCENDENTAL MEDITATION), who came to national attention in 1967 when he was adopted as the official guru of the Beatles (C&B4, Preface).

MAHATMA (Ma-HAHT-mah) Sanskrit, "great spirit." (1) General name for anyone of high moral and spiritual attainment, such as Mahatma Gandhi. A title rather than a proper name. (2) In Theosophy, the title specifically applied to the Himalayan masters described by Madame Blavatsky; thus, an executive in the PLANETARY HIERARCHY.

MAHAYANA (Mah-ha-YAHN-nah) Sanskrit, "large raft." The northern or metaphysical branch of traditional Buddhism. Noted for its extensive and subtle teachings on human suffering, the development of compassion, and the acceptance of total transience through embracing the doctrine of PHENOMENALITY. Also associated with the doctrine of the Bodhisattva. Contrast to HINAYANA.

MAITHUNA (My-THOON-ah) Sanskrit, "intercourse, coitus." (1) Specifically, the posture of union in SEXUAL YOGA, in which the woman traditionally assumes the superior position. This corresponds to Indian and Tibetan icons that present consorting deities as the image of universal creation. The image represents pure consciousness, which is static (male), and self-manifesting consciousness, which is dynamic (female). (See also YAB-YUM.) (2) In a wider sense, sexual intercourse practiced as a sacramental rite or conjugal meditation, in which the partner may be conceived as a deity for the purpose of ultimate unification with that deity—this being a primary doctrine of TANTRA. (3) Sanskrit name for the constellation of the Twins (Gemini).

MAITREYA (My-TRAY-yah) (1) Sanskrit, "fortunate friend," a name for the next or future Buddha, supposed to appear at an unknown time after the departure of the last historical Buddha, Gautama. (2) The name given in the later Theosophy of Alice A. Bailey to the World-Teacher who occupies a central position in her scheme of the planetary hierarchy. (3) In Western occultism, a Bodhisattva who is said to reincarnate continuously, three times a century, by assuming a TULKU in someone around the age of thirty-three, in order to prepare for a final and full incarnation, about 4400 A.D., as the fully incarnated Maitreya Buddha, leader of a spiritual community who will bring forth from themselves, through the generative power of the WORD, a magical race of beings capable of leading humanity toward the next incarnation of the Earth.

MANA/MANNA From IE root *man-*, "mind, intelligence." A word found universally in many variants, from Polynesia to Tibet; also mentioned in the Old Testament as the heavenly food fed to the Israelites in the wilderness.

Vital intelligence, the supernatural power that animates all things, from stones to stars; generally conceived of as being independent of material forms, which it enters and leaves at will. May be helpful or inimical to human beings. Added as a prefix to the names of culture-heroes and Gods who teach and guide, such as Manitou and Manibhozo among the American Indians, Menes in ancient Egypt, and the MANU in the Western Mysteries.

MANDALA (MUN-duh-luh) Sanskrit, "circular design." A device used to calm the mind and bring all attention, mental, emotional, and physical, to a point of complete rest—a kind of bull's-eye for the attention. May be merely a geometrical design or a figurative one, an icon containing pictures of Gods or Buddhas, such as the Tibetan TANKA.

MANAS (MAH-nas) Sanskrit, "power of mental picturing." In Theosophy, the fifth principle or next faculty to ripen in human evolution: the capacity to imagine what is true, rather than rely solely on sensorial evidence; the cocreative power of IMAGINATION. In short, creative imagination—not only the capacity to imagine what is real and true, but to generate it. Called by Rudolf Steiner spirit self: that part of human identity that is self-generated through the spiritual/creative powers of imagination. In Castaneda, the principle of autonomous awareness by which we are able to experience the world as a separate reality.

MANICHEANISM (Man-uh-KEE-un-izm) Ethical/esoteric philosophy of radical dualism proposed by Mani, a Persian heretic who lived around 250 A.D. A melding of Gnostic and Zoroastrian features with Christianity; posits a battle between light and dark, stressing Christ as a redeemer who releases humanity from material bondage by providing us with light-bodies as replications of the resurrected body. Believed to be the basis of the heretical theology of the CATHARS. N., Manichee (MAN-uh-kee); adj., Manichean (Man-uh-KEE-un). Noted by Ezra Pound in one of his *Cantos*: "And they called us Manicheans/Wotever the hellsarse that is."

MANTRA (MAHN-trah) Sanskrit, same root as MANAS. A verbal formula or mere sound (like AUM), to be repeated silently or chanted aloud as in prayer, for the purpose of achieving different states: serenity, joy, detachment, attunement to God, power over external obstacles, et cetera.

MANU (MAH-noo) Sanskrit, same root as above. In Blavatsky and esoteric Brahminical teachings, a superhuman being (who may or may not assume human form) responsible for carrying over the seeds of culture and evolutionary progress from one time-cycle to another. The supreme culture-initiate, whose symbol is the ARK. Corresponds to many figures found in worldwide mythology: FU HSI in China, Manco Capak in South America, Manibhozo in North America, Noah in the Bible, et cetera.

This is a concept crucial to any serious understanding of what occultism and the Mysteries legitimately were, in their prime. Perhaps even more significantly, knowing the function of the Manu enables us to pose a number of difficult questions as to what now might replace it. For instance, who is there today to guide humanity and impart progressive impulses for cultural and historical development, as the Manus formerly did? On the question of who originates practical directives for cocreation, see E2.4.

MARANATHA (Mar-en-NAHTH-ah) From Aramaic, "O Lord, come." Used as the name of the coming Lord or the Christ of the Second Coming as conceived according to a long-standing Biblical tradition.

MARTIAL ARTS Practices of physical prowess and self-defense, primarily Oriental in origin, that involve rigorous mental and emotional training and are usually based on a philosophy of harmony with the universe. Including T'AI CHI, kenpo, KARATE, CAPOEIRA, tae kwan do, judo, AIKIDO, sumo, and variations from other cultures. See also WARRIOR.

MASONIC LODGE/MASONS See FREEMASONS.

MASTER From ME *maistre* > Latin *magister* > *magnus,* "great," from IE root *meg-,* "great, of the whole." As a verb, to achieve the fullest degree of competence in something (mathematics, law, sculpture, sailing). As a noun, a person of such achievement, which may be seen as a feat of doing or a feat of being. In European tradition, someone versed in full and comprehensive knowledge and technique of a skill or craft, such as stonework or weaving. In the guild system, the highest of three grades of proficiency, the preceding two being journeyman and apprentice. Esoterically, an initiate trained to transmit practical skills and progressive knowledge in a particular field, such as architecture or music. Hesse's *Magister Ludi,* the "Bead Game Master," is one remarkable example in modern fiction.

In more common usage today, applied almost exclusively to someone who has attained a state of being (rather than doing) variously called self-realization, God-consciousness, Enlightenment, or liberation; often believed capable of transmitting or inspiring the identical state in others. See also SPIRITUAL MASTER.

MATRIARCHY (MAY-tree-ark-ee) The foundation and direction of human culture, both material and spiritual, by women. See also EROTICISM, MOTHER WISDOM, PATRIARCHY. Adj., matriarchal (May-tree-ARK-ul).

MAYA (MY-uh) Sanskrit, from the verb-root *ma-,* "to measure." Often interpreted as "illusion," but more correctly translated as "apparition." Maya is, literally, the power by which the infinite and eternal Source measures itself out in the form of finite and transient phenomena. Thus, Maya is not an illusion, any more than the shrinking of objects in three-dimensional perspective is.

In Hindu philosophy and religion, Maya is the dynamic of self-veiling by which the One Source, or supreme unmanifest BRAHMA, assumes visible and animated form in a kind of cosmic picture-show, an apparition quite real in figure and activity though not substantially existent. This is proven by a simple comparison: just as you would be deluding yourself to imagine that the house that appears to shrink as you move away from it is actually, substantially shrinking, so you are deluding yourself if you imagine that what appears before you in the form of the world is substantially present. In Buddhism, this apparitional quality of all that exists is vividly described in the twelve similes of NAROPA. Maya is used ambiguously to describe both the process and effect of VEILING, as in the dreaming of Vishnu. Unfortunately, it is widely abused as a derogatory reference to the "cheap trick" of transitory existence, the illusionary aspect of existence. But a surefooted Hindu would say, "Since it is all Maya, there can be no illusion!" Compare with IMMANENCE and INDWELLING. See also FALL, the contrasting paradigm (E2.4).

MAYA INDIANS AND CULTURE, (MY-uh) The indigenous people of Central America whose remnants now live in Yucatán, Guatemala, and Honduras. Origins unknown, they are believed to have attained a high civilization directed by a priesthood of prodigious occult powers, the cult of the BALAM. One of their great surviving spiritual testaments is the POPOL VUH (C&B2.12). They disappeared inexplicably around 900 A.D.

MAYAN CALENDAR A complex system of time-reckoning involving several overlapping cycles, mathematically exact in its determination of planetary movements, though it derives from a time long before astronomical science as such was known to exist. Recorded in a complex hieroglyphic code, using a system of dots and bars for numerical notation, inscribed on standing stones found in the jungle all over Yucatán, Guatemala, and Honduras. See also APOCALYPSE.

MAZDA In ancient Persian and Zoroastrian religion, the supreme God of light and goodness, who was opposed by the spirit of darkness, Ahriman. See also ENERGY.

MEDICINE In Native American spirituality, spiritual power or whatever can be achieved with it, such as the ability to heal, contact totem animals, see visions, cooperate with natural forces; or healing substances like herbs and "power meat." Especially good if it is "big." Probably an idiom used by the early settlers for the MANA spoken of by the native peoples under a variety of names. Interestingly, from the OE *metan,* "to measure," from the IE root *ma-,* same as MAYA. By this derivation, medicine can be interpreted as an extract of the root-power that produces the world.

MEDICINE LODGE Meeting-place for the assembly of tribal elders, where spiritual matters were decided; or the assembly itself, conceived as a sacred body of ancient lineage.

MEDICINE MAN/WOMAN See SHAMAN.

MEDICINE WHEEL In geomancy, a stone circle constructed by American Indians at an unknown time, probably as a device of spiritual technology for reflecting and grounding the harmony of the Macrocosm on the Earth; distributed through the region of the northern Rockies into Canada; now known to incorporate alignments to the Sun, Moon, and stars, similar to those of Stonehenge, the Great Pyramid, and other ancient monuments now being subjected to serious and minute analysis in ARCHEO-ASTRONOMY.

MEDITATION Any way of achieving focus, concentrating attention in the middle *(media)*, or CENTERING. Any practice for achieving inner serenity, mental and emotional composure, clarity, and balance, or access to contents of the innermost realm of consciousness, which are not available to the ordinary state of attention. May be performed in silence or through chanting; often employs a mantra, mandala; may be achieved through concentration with a group. Its supreme goal is SAMADHI.

MEDIUM In Spiritualism, one who offers him- or herself as the instrument through which a departed soul or otherworldly entity can speak and sometimes act. Old-fashioned, nineteenth-century term for someone who does CHANNELING.

MELCHIZEDEK (Mel-KIZ-uh-dek) The title (not a proper name) of the High Priest of the SOLAR MYSTERIES on Atlantis, variously claimed as the initiator of ancient and latter-day lineages of occult teaching. In the Old Testament, a mysterious figure who appears to Abraham (Genesis 14:18) and serves a kind of mass, using a chalice sometimes identified with the Grail.

MENHIR (MEN-heer) Breton/Welsh, *men,* "stone" + *hir,* "long." A rough pillar or spirelike stone, usually called standing stone, found throughout France, England, and Ireland, believed to have been erected by the Druids; used to mark ley-lines and identify SACRED SITES in geomancy.

MENTAL PLANE Old Theosophical term for the realm where ideas and mental images exist independent of the physical senses, like a field of radio waves detectable to a receiving crystal (i.e., the mind itself).

MENTAL SCIENCE The systematic use of the mind to produce changes in character or even external circumstances. An outgrowth of NEW THOUGHT, a movement of the nineteenth century that emphasizes positive thinking and self-determination. Originated in America by Phineas Parkhurst Quimby (1802–1866), a clockmaker who took up Mesmerism and developed it into an autosuggestive method he called the Science of Health and Happiness. Close relative of Mary Baker Eddy's Christian Science and Ernest Holmes's Science of Mind. Prototype of contemporary schools of prosperity awareness; also influential in some schools of PARA-CHRISTIANITY.

MEPHISTO/MEPHISTOPHELES In European literature and folklore, a diabolical figure who acts as emissary for the DEVIL or may be the Devil himself, and who tempts human beings with the promise of unlimited power, knowledge, pleasure, and physical immortality, as in Goethe's *Faust* (C&B2.8). Sometimes appears in American folklore as a salesman of SNAKE OIL.

MERIDIANS In Chinese medicine, lines of subtle force running in patterns along the length of the body, having vital points located on them; channels for the flow of the life-force or CHI.

MERLIN An important figure in the Celtic Revival, a great magician and trickster, who may actually have lived at the time of King Arthur, around 550 A.D. Supreme prototype of the European shaman or WIZARD. Described as having disappeared (perhaps due to the spell cast by a woman) into a kind of state of suspended animation, with the implication that he will reemerge at some future time—example of the RETURNING GOD/HERO.

MESCALINE A psychedelic drug synthetically produced from the extract of the mescal plant, known for its vivid hallucinatory effects.

MESSIAH From the Hebrew *mashiah* > Aramaic *meshiha,* "annointed," translated into Greek in the New Testament as Christos. In the old prophetic tradition of the Hebrews, the one who is promised to come and deliver the Israelites from their trials. Ironically, though the name was later transferred to Jesus Christ, the Judaic religion of that time and ever since has consistently denied that he is the expected one whom their tradition anticipates, and even Jesus himself attempted to throw off the Messiah role. See also SECOND COMING.

MESSIAH COMPLEX The paranoid delusion that compels someone to believe he can save the world, or at least a chosen segment of it, often leading him to recruit others into messianic cults such as the Manson family and the Jonestown cult.

METAPHYSICS The systematic study of what is beyond *(meta-)* the physical, especially beyond what is evident to the normal senses by which we perceive the physical world. From the time of Aristotle up to the middle of the nineteenth century, the term applied to all philosophical systems that dealt with purely intellectual matters, especially those that attempted by pure thinking to arrive at sure knowledge of the first principles of things. With the ENLIGHTEN-MENT, metaphysics fell into disrepute and the so-called positive sciences rose to prominence, but in the last half of the twentieth century it has come into vogue again. The term is now applied widely and very loosely to anything having to do with the spiritual, occult, esoteric, Hermetic, mystical, paranormal, or supernatural, as in "metaphysical bookstore."

METAPROGRAMMING A term coined by John Lilly for the technique of altering, eliminating, or manipulating our preestablished attitudes and beliefs, the "programs" that determine how we view the world and how we behave. Compare with the ancient technology of IMPRINTING.

MIASMA In radionics, a kind of virus or blight of an elusive, quasi-material nature. In homeopathy, an inheritable disease pattern running through generations.

MICHAEL (ARCHANGEL) (MEEK-hy-el, or Meek-HAY-el) One of the seven primary Archangels of traditional Christianity, often associated with the sun. By some calculations, the overseer of a time period that began in 1879 and lasts until 2229 A.D. Now and then cited as a source of channeled material. See also FOLK-SOUL.

MICROCOSM Greek, "little design." Age-old idiom for the human form as a miniaturized expression of the great design of creation; as contrasted to MACROCOSM.

MIDDLE WAY   In Sanskrit, *Madhyama-Pratipad.* The path that steers between extreme indulgence and extreme denial, as taught by the Buddha.

MILAREPA   (Mill-ah-RAYP-ah) In Tibetan Buddhism and Himalayan folklore, the most famous example of a yogi-saint, known for his ecstatic verses or songs (1052–1135). Also, a member of an important lineage, which includes NAROPA.

MILLENNIAL/MILLENARIAN   Pertaining to the end of an age, especially a period of a thousand years (millennium). In mythology and culture studies, concerned with the end of the world, expecting or demanding the APOCALYPSE. In sociology and the background of the New Age movement, the designation of heretical sects who believe in the end of the current social order and the sudden enstatement of a new paradigm (E1.1).

MIND   Now here's a tough one. On a wild guess, it may be just a side effect of memory. Derives from the ME *mynde,* going back to OE *(ge)mynde,* "memory." Sure, you can remember without thinking, but can you think without remembering?

Mind is the observing awareness, that by which we are capable of being onlookers. But mind also involves us in that which we observe, and it may even engage us in cocreating what is observed. Used one-pointedly in a state of total, relaxed attention, it can be the instrument of impeccable discernment *(prajna),* even the revelation of spontaneous enlightenment (BODHI)—so the Eastern teachings affirm. Yet for some reason mind is inclined to become enmeshed self-referentially in its own mechanisms, like an elaborate garden tool designed to plow, plant, weed, and water but which malfunctions and ends up performing weird operations on itself. At its best, mind is the bright frontier of the new physics, the dazzling hypothesis of holographic brain theory, the unwobbling pivot of Buddhist and Zen practice, the central principle of New Thought and many self-transformational techniques.

Mind is also the supreme trickster, the monkey slave of MAYA, perhaps the device Vishnu uses to conceal himself in the hide-and-seek game of his Dreaming. The most difficult thing to understand about mind is how it can be so impotent—no amount of thinking about something will make it happen or undo it—yet so omnipotent as well, for mind, operating in the dynamic of ATTITUDE, seems to shape and project everything we see and do. Mind is delusion, mind is the source and substance of Enlightenment. Mind is all, and nothing at all.

Perhaps the Zen masters have the last word on it. In the doctrine of NO-MIND they assert that mind is the Void, by which they mean to say that mind is nothing as such, nothing in itself, but "mind" is the name we give to the process of total interreflection that brings all things into relation with each other—as a mirror placed in the corner of the room will present you with different views of yourself and the room as you move around, though there is nothing as such "in" the mirror. See also NONATTAINMENT, VOID.

MIRACLE Any act or event believed to occur in defiance to the laws of nature or the limitations of human comprehension. From Latin *mirus,* "wonderful" > IE root *smei,* "to smile, be surprised." Thus, whatever makes you smile in surprise may be considered a miracle.

MIRACLES, A COURSE IN In para-Christianity, a basic work in the form of thirty-three lessons, teaching a total reorientation to life on the basis of the principles of nondivision and forgiveness. Received by channeling through Helen Schucmann.

MISSING YEARS OF JESUS See ISSA.

MOBY An obsession with something that ultimately cannot be verified by experience, which may end up consuming the one obsessed with it. A monstrous belief system or groundless fantasy that keeps a person locked in desperate searching or bound to futile faith. From the main animal in the novel *Moby-Dick* (1851), by Herman Melville.

MOHAMMED/MAHAMMAD Prophet and founder of Islam (570–632), formerly called Mohammedanism by non-Muslims. Said to have received the Koran by dictation from the Archangel Gabriel.

MOKSHA (MOCK-sha) Sanskrit, "liberation." In Buddhism and Hindu Yoga, the supreme goal of spiritual practice, transcendental relocation of consciousness out of this world, releasement from all bonds of ATTACHMENT.

MONAD (MOE-nad) Specifically, in Theosophy and some Cabalistic and alchemical teachings, the original divine seed or germ-plasm of the human soul, equivalent to the DIVINE SPARK. More loosely, the unit of individuality or dynamic essence, treated as the metaphysical counterpart to the atom in dozens of occult and philosophical systems from Pythagoras to the moderns. Adj., monadic (Moe-NAD-ik).

MONISM The belief that there is one principle at the basis of the universe, even though it may assume a dualistic manifestation—as in the single TAO, consisting of YIN and YANG, in Taoism; contrasted to the view that posits more than one single principle operating in creation, as in the Persian myth of the opposition of Ahriman to Ohrmazd, in MANICHEANISM, and in Gnostic heresies that describe autonomous counter-forces warring against the supreme will of the Creator. Adj., monistic.

MONSÉGUR (Mon-say-GOOR) Ruins of a hilltop fortress in southwestern France near the foot of the Pyrenees, believed to have been the last holdout of the Cathars who were brutally massacred in the Albigensian Crusade early in the thirteenth century. Recently a sacred site for those who identify themselves with the members of that late medieval heresy.

MOONIES Members of the Unification church founded by the Korean messiah Sun Myung Moon in 1972. Emphasizes the fulfillment of the Second

Coming in Korea, with rites of mass marriage and "blood cleansing" to overcome the sin of Adam and Eve. Good example of a modern CULT.

MOON WARS According to Rudolf Steiner, founder of Anthroposophy, a prolonged battle fought in the upper atmosphere of the Earth from 1840 to 1879, between the host of the Archangel Michael and a degenerate faction of the angelic hierarchy, who lost and were cast out into the planetary atmosphere, where they assumed the form of parasites who incorporate themselves into the etheric bodies of human beings and inspire them to heinous antievolutionary crimes, such as scientific materialism, genetic engineering, and terrorism. An example of occult MYTHMAKING.

MORMONISM The Church of Jesus Christ of Latter-day Saints, founded in 1830 by Joseph Smith, who received a revelation concerning the lost tribes of Israel. Taken from the name *Moroni,* claimed by Smith to be a prophet of the fifth century who buried the testament of the sect on gold tablets in Palmyra, New York. Its primary scripture is The Book of Mormon. A minor religion centered in Salt Lake City, Utah, with its own ethical and financial practices, including polygamy.

MORPHOGENETIC FIELD Term coined by biologist Rupert Sheldrake for collective intelligence (like that of a beehive or ant colony), which informs and directs the life-activity of all its members. Compare with FOLK-SOUL.

MOTHER LODE The treasure of all human potential sustained and nurtured in the womb of the VIRGIN. The prize at the heart of the labyrinth.

MOTHER LODGE See GREAT WHITE BROTHERHOOD.

MOTHER WISDOM The creative intelligence active through the universe that supports and guides the interdependence and mutual activity of all beings; hence, the divine-creative agent of relating, consistency, generosity, sacrifice, unity, wholeness, collaboration, and generic as opposed to individual existence. The all-nurturing intelligence of the VIRGIN, which makes nature grow and provides the universal features of human nature, such as basic needs (to love, belong, care, accept, et cetera). Imagined, revered, and embodied in the worldwide pantheon of Mother Goddesses such as Anahita, Chicomecoatl, Cybele, Danu, Diana, GAIA, Hathor, Isis, Ishtar, Kuan Yin, Pachamama, SHAKTI, SOPHIA, Tara, and Tlazolteotl, to name a few. Culturally manifested in matriarchy.

MU (1) In Ch'an and Zen teachings, nothing, void, perfect awareness. See also WU. (2) Alternative name for Lemuria. (3) A strong, musky tea, highly favored by Zen monks.

MUDRA (MOO-drah) Sanskrit, from the root *mud-,* "to be happy, rejoice." A ritual gesture of the hand or body, often seen in Oriental art and sculpture, as in figures showing the Buddha with one hand raised in the gesture of granting peace or dismissing fear. Also, trancelike motions, or convulsive-ecstatic poses and hand gestures, often performed in a convulsive manner by someone receiving a direct transmission of spiritual power from a master (shak-tipat).

MUSCLE TESTING See BIOKINESTHESIOLOGY.

MUSE (Myooz) From the Greek *mousa,* tracing back to the IE root *mendh-,* "captivating, drawing all attention": the root of "mental." In ancient times, a Goddess of special inspirational powers, who inbreathes or infuses the power of creative expression into the artist, poet, or dancer; associated in mythology and folklore with the number three or its square, nine. She is the divine source of poetic language, often invoked by the ancient poets before reciting their verse, in order to make themselves selfless mediums for the Muse herself to sing. In Greek myth, there were nine Muses who ruled over the various arts, all of them born from a single and supreme Muse, Mnemosyne (Nuh-MOSS-suh-nee), "supreme memory." See also MAGDALEN, MIND.

MYSTERIES (E16) (1) From the Greek verb *muien,* "to speak through pressed lips, to communicate in secret." Extensive teachings about the creation of the world and the interaction between the Gods and humanity, preserved and disseminated through cult-centers of spiritual training, associated with specific planets and celestial beings, and differing in character according to the race and geographic location of the people they served. Of many varieties, such as Orphic, ELEUSINIAN, Hibernian, Druidic, Dionysian, Mithraic, and dozens more. The Mysteries were the universities of spiritual training of former times. (2) In modern times, detective stories and tales of the unexplained or supernatural, belonging to a genre created by Edgar Allan Poe, a dipsomaniacal poet and leading figure of the DECADENCE.

MYSTERY SCHOOLS Regional centers where the Mysteries were perpetuated. Ancient institutions for spiritual education and INITIATION.

MYSTICISM (E17) Same root as MYSTERIES. The path of seeking direct contact with God or the divine by reaching a state of inner attunement so pure and deep that one becomes identified with God. The quest for immanence, the indescribable and ineffable union with the God within, the deep and consummate ecstasy of INDWELLING.

MYTHMAKING Going a step beyond this collaboration, mythmaking is a kind of cocreation, working from the raw materials provided by myth. A lot of this goes on in New Age circles, though it is not often grounded in a solid understanding of worldwide mythemes and their implications. Myths of INTERVENTION, for instance, are common in the planetary folklore of the new spirituality, as in Arguelles's scenario (Harmonic Convergence) of the Maya as technological wizards who may come back and save us from the perils of the current global crisis. The fundamentalist vision of Armageddon is an archaic example of intervention, but we cannot call this mythmaking, because it is taken up unmodified from its biblical version. However, if we were to add UFOs to the Last Judgment, that would be mythmaking. In Tom Wolfe's book *The Right Stuff,* the reentry of John Glenn's space capsule into the atmosphere is accompanied by a mysterious display of firefly-like sparks that Wolfe links to a ritual performed by Australian Aborigines down on earth at that very moment—a touching example of creative mythmaking.

If it is true, as the Romantics intuited, that imagination is the faculty through which the divine comes to expression in the human, then exercising the imagination must be a crucial part of our spiritual development. But everything depends on how we play at making up creative fictions, and how we relate them to the actualities of our lives. In the era of the Decadence, when Romanticism reached its final throes, many artists and writers asserted the superiority of the INNER LIFE over the realm of conventional affairs, which at its most extreme resulted in the undertaking of dangerous quests into the occult, the unconscious, and the underworld of drugs. To take our own inventions literally, and thereby lose the clear distinction between what is actual and what is invented, is certainly a dangerous game—or it may just be a silly game. Mythmaking is a great part of the new spirituality, for which the guidelines have yet to be worked out. On the dangers of mythmaking, see E2.3 concerning the spiritual extravagance of the Decadence, and the Afterword, where I cite David Spangler's wise comment on New Age pretending.

"In our time, and in our time alone, the power of the actual and the power of the invented are most nearly matched." Lukas Crozius, occult historian.

The question is, how to find the seam?

MYTHOLOGY The language or study *(logos)* of myth (Greek *mythos,* story); the explanation of how humanity tells its own story, down through the ages. Expressed in countless narratives and sacred scriptures, folktales and tall stories, which can be synthesized into consistent and recurrent *mythemes* (myth themes)—a term coined by Mircea ELIADE, who taught that the basic function of myths is to illustrate paradigms. One of the growing fronts of the new spirituality is independent myth study, which has been greatly stimulated by the last talks of Joseph Campbell, collected under the title *The Power of Myth.* By exploring for oneself the worldwide repertoire of mythical adventures and images, often describing the actions of the Gods, each individual has the opportunity to collaborate in humanity's ongoing quest for meaning and purpose.

N

NAG HAMMADI GOSPELS (Nahg Ha-MAHD-dee) A collection of thirteen bound manuscripts discovered by an Arab peasant in huge clay jars in December 1945; named after the place where they were found, the ancient town of Chenoboskion, at the foot of the mountain Gebel et-Tarif, in the district of Nag Hammadi, near the Nile River about sixty miles north of Luxor. Commonly known as the GNOSTIC GOSPELS.

NAGUAL/NAHUAL (Nah-HWAL) (1) In anthropology, an animal that appears in dream or trance as a projection of the power of the dreamer. Totem animal, familiar, like the black cat who accompanies the witch in European folklore. (2) In Castaneda, the Unknown or someone who is able to enter and draw upon the secret resources of power it contains. See also ANIMAL GUIDES.

NAHUA/NAHUATL (Nah-HWAH, Nah-HWATTLE) Aboriginal culture and pictographic language of the pre-Aztec peoples of Mexico, adopted by the Aztecs. Source of sacred teachings of Meso-America. Primarily an ancient oral language, recorded in hieroglyphic form. See SACRED LANGUAGES.

NAROPA (Nah-ROPE-uh) In Tibetan Buddhism, a famous master of Tantric philosophy and practices (1016–1100), known for undergoing extraordinary ordeals of magical training with his master, Tilopa (TILL-oh-pah), as well as for his twelve similes describing the apparitional nature of existence: "A magic spell, a dream, a gleam before the eyes, a reflection, lightning, an echo, a rainbow, moonlight upon water, cloud-land, dimness before the eyes, fog, and apparitions—these are the twelve similes of the PHENOMENAL." Namesake of the Naropa Institute, a Buddhist university founded in 1974 by Chogyam Trungpa in Boulder, Colorado.

NASRUDDIN (NASS-rude-een) In Sufism, a famous trickster featured in many humorous teaching stories illustrating the paradoxical and unpredictable nature of reality and the surprising presence of the divine within the ordinary.

NATAL CHART/NATIVITY See HOROSCOPE.

NATIVE AMERICAN SPIRITUALITY (E18) Comprehensive

term for the mythology, folklore, religious rites, and sacred teachings of the native peoples of the Americas (especially North). Characterized by reverence for nature, strong belief in ancestral spirits, and a long oral tradition of storytelling, dance, and ritual, including the practice of SHAMANISM.

NATURAL HEALING   The curing of illness without recourse to conventional medicine, drugs, or surgery. According to the holistic paradigm as applied to medicine, the body itself, being one of the wonders of nature, is able to heal itself if given the right enhancement through the medicaments and practices of natural healing.

NATURE MYSTICISM   In Romanticism, the attitude or mood of communing with nature, by cultivating a pantheistic sense of God or getting in touch with one's own innermost thoughts and feelings through allowing them to be reflected in the mirror of natural processes. Early form of the back-to-nature movement. Exemplified in the poetry of William Wordsworth.

NATURE-SPIRITS   Playful, ethereal spirit-beings (including devas and elementals) who animate the processes of nature, such as the leafing and blossoming of plants, the misting of waterfalls, the rooting of tubers; the little people and fairy folk of European lore. Believed to have been visible to humanity in former times through a natural clairvoyance, which eventually faded out due to occlusion by other faculties (calculation, conceptual-analytic thinking, literacy). Degraded by the Christian church to the status of demonic forces. See also PAGAN.

NATUROPATHY   (Nat-chur-OP-uh-thee) The system of treating diseases and maintaining health exclusively by the use of natural forces (sunlight, water) or medicines compounded from plants. Adj., naturopathic (nat-chur-oh-PATH-ic).

NAZCA LINES   (NAZ-cah) Huge pictographs of animals and patterns of long, straight, intersecting lines inscribed in an area covering 250 square miles on the floor of the high desert in southern Peru, and visible only from the air; interpreted by some as evidence of extraterrestrial contact. See also EARTH MYSTERIES.

NAZI   (NAHT-zee) German, short for *Nationalsozialistische Deutsche Arbeiterpartei*: German National Socialist Workers' Party. Organization founded by Adolf Hitler in 1919, described in some accounts as the front for a Satanic cult (C&B4.2). Noted for its nefarious doctrine of the superiority of the ARYAN race, and its glorification of the SUPERMAN, a concept robbed from Romanticism.

NEAR-DEATH EXPERIENCE   The experience of almost dying or, in the extreme, dying briefly and returning to life, as reported in many cases of clinical death in which the patient miraculously revived. Originally studied and interpreted by William James (C&B3.2), now the subject of a number of national institutes and research programs.

NEOPHYTE (NEE-oh-fite) From Greek *neos,* "new" + *phyein,* "to produce, grow, evolve." An evolutionary newcomer, a beginner in spiritual development, especially one who wishes to enter into training for INITIATION. A term left over from the Mysteries.

NEOPLATONISM (Nee-oh-PLAY-tun-izm) Revival and extrapolation of the teachings of Plato by later philosophers, especially Plotinus (Plo-TINE-us) of the third century A.D. A nonethical system of speculative mysticism, based on a monistic doctrine stating that all things in the universe, including the human being, are produced by emanations from a single source to which the human soul (located between pure ideas, above, and matter, below) can ultimately be reunited by attaining SUPERCONSCIOUSNESS. Basic to the philosophy of HERMETICS.

NEOTERIC New, recent, newly discovered or invented.

NETWORKING New Age slang for organization of group efforts, or the process of linking up people according to common issues or visions, often carried out on a global scale (E1.3). May be considered the social groundwork for full PLANETIZATION.

NEUROLINGUISTIC PROGRAMMING (NLP) A method of using words and mental exercises to change ingrained behavioral responses, overcome phobias, and erase chronic destructive patterns of feeling and thinking so that new patterns of behavior can emerge. Developed by R. Bandler and J. Grinder from the advanced therapeutic work of Milton Erickson and Virginia Satir.

NEUROLOGIC Term coined by Timothy Leary for the innate operative intelligence of the human nervous system, encoded in the DNA. Described in terms of a complex set of eight circuits, encompassing all processes of consciousness and evolution from the cellular level up to intergalactic dimensions.

NEW AGE (E1) A time period of uncertain beginning or duration, supposed to be marked by massive changes in human society and spiritual reorientation for the individual. The era of the modern spiritual movement, when many people are seeking a new awareness of themselves and the world at large; sometimes equated with the AQUARIAN AGE. Contrast to NEW TIME.

NEW BIOLOGY Current attempt to reformulate biology and the science of evolution according to the holistic paradigm; for instance, by application of theories describing MORPHOGENETIC FIELDS and IMPLICATE ORDER. See also HUNDREDTH MONKEY.

NEW GAMES Noncompetitive group sports, developed in 1966 by Stewart Brand, George Leonard, and Rose Farrington.

NEWGRANGE Sacred site in Ireland, thirty miles north of Dublin, of what may possibly be the oldest megalithic structures in the world: huge aboveground PASSAGE-GRAVES with long tunnels oriented to the rising of the sun at the winter solstice, believed to date back as far as 7000 B.C. Typical of ancient groundworks found at SACRED SITES all over the world, for which there is no satisfactory conventional explanation, either of their purpose or their construction. In geomancy, they are interpreted as huge timing devices that served not only to keep track of seasonal and ritual cycles of activity, but also to represent the union of Earth Mother and Sun Father in the sacred marriage of the Solar Mysteries, eventually to result in the birth of the Divine Child.

NEW JERUSALEM   Image from the REVELATION of Saint John the Divine, representing the world restored to perfection at the end of time. Mystical utopia in William Blake's poem of the same name. A mytheme expressive of global unity and harmony, thus a blueprint for the perfect society, the terrestrial community of spiritually enlightened members (E1.1).

NEW PHYSICS   Current attempt, gaining form and credibility since the early 1970s, to reformulate modern scientific theories (especially quantum physics and relativity theory) into a "physics of consciousness," capable of explaining not only the events of the natural, atomic, and subatomic worlds, but also the interaction of the human mind with those realms. Its philosophical basis lies in the prospect of a paradigm-shift from observation (human outside nature, looking on; or human against nature) to participation. Often closely aligned with brain/mind research; draws strongly upon parallels between Eastern spiritual/metaphysical teachings and Western theories: for instance, by paralleling the VOID of Buddhism with the field of modern relativity. Also called paraphysics. Contrast with CHAOTIC PHYSICS.

NEW THOUGHT   Philosophical movement aimed at using the powers of the mind to create optimal life-situations, founded by Phineas P. Quimby late in the nineteenth century. The historical precedent of positive thinking and other philosophies of SELF-HELP and self-improvement, which count on changing reality by changing the way one thinks about it, such as Christian Science. See also MENTAL SCIENCE and PARA-CHRISTIANITY.

NEW TIME   In recovery, the time of rediscovering life and recreating one's experiences on new terms—even to the point of altering the meaning and effect of the past by living through the pain inherited from it—which begins with the commitment to a TWELVE-STEP PROGRAM for overcoming addiction and dysfunctionality. Derived from AA (Alcoholics Anonymous), where the new time begins with the date of sobriety. New timer: someone in recovery.

NICHIREN SHOSHU   (NISH-she-rin SHOW-shu) A sect of Japanese Buddhism derived from the teachings of the thirteenth-century monk Nichiren, centered on the conception of the "Pure Land" of Amitabha (Ah-me-TAH-bah), the Buddha of Supreme Light. Members are known for monotonous chanting believed to bring them anything they want: *Namyo Myoho Rengekyo*, "Adoration to the Lotus Sutra of Perfect Truth."

NIRVANA   (Nir-VAH-nah) Sanskrit, from *nir-*, "out" and *vana*, "blown"; literally, "blown-out." In Buddhism, the state of final and complete cessation of all cravings and expectations that arise with the conditions of mortal existence; the ultimate transcendence of the human condition achieved by the Buddha. Complete removal from the realm of transient doings, ordinary human affairs; the state of complete and serene detachment in which all desire is extinguished, all forms of distraction dispelled, all involvement canceled. Perfect and complete immersion in the Void. LIBERATION, the ultimate way out, "getting off the wheel (of rebirth)." When it coincides with conscious passage through death, it is called para-Nirvana. See also BODHISATTVA.

NOETICS (No-ET-iks) From Greek *nous,* "mind, intelligence." The study of how consciousness works, both upon itself and in relation to the external world. Loose term for the study and discipline of consciousness as a direct instrument of cocreation. A cognitive discipline often associated with the new physics and BRAIN/MIND studies.

NO-MIND Chinese *wu hsin,* "empty heart" or "heart of emptiness." In Zen, the mind freed of the snares of conceptual thinking, so that it remains in spontaneity rather than losing itself in the act of groping toward logical conclusion or definition. See also WU.

NONATTACHMENT In Buddhism and other Oriental paths based on the paradigm of LIBERATION, the imperative to let go, to become completely free of any response or attitude that binds one to the world of transient things.

NONATTAINMENT Fundamental but often forgotten principle of Buddhism, derived from the oral testimony that Gautama, upon being asked what he gained by entering Nirvana, replied, "Absolutely nothing." Expresses the Eastern viewpoint on the essential paradox of seeking the ground of one's own being (finding yourself): The SELF-NATURE is identical with pure and unconditional being, so it is not to be gained or attained—though whatever stands in the way of its direct realization must be removed. Yet even this process of removing illusions that stand in the way of realizing the self-nature is itself described as illusory! According to the Ch'an master Huang Po (C&B1.10), the self-nature is not gained in the moment of Enlightenment, nor is it lost under the conditions of illusion. This implies the radical technique expressed in the *bodhicitta* (Bow-dee-CHIT-ah): "I will become Enlightened by ceasing to seek to be."

Also stated as the identity of Nirvana and SAMSARA, a radical teaching that is (to my continual amazement) usually overlooked by modern-day practitioners of Buddhism and Zen, perhaps because if understood, it would discourage new recruits. Put in simple language: "What you are seeking is you who are seeking it." This is the supreme truth in Ch'an and Zen teachings, expressive of how the self-nature, VOID, Buddha-mind, is always present, invariable and inviolable, like the depths of the ocean, which are not added or removed by the play of cloud-shapes reflected on the surface. See also EMPTINESS. See also WU.

NONCONFORMITY A precarious ideal that emerged briefly in the 1960s and was soon forgotten, yet remains significant as an expression of the deep issues of ORIGINALITY and CHOICE, essential criteria for right seeking.

NOOSPHERE (NEW-oh-sphere) According to the Catholic philosopher Teilhard de Chardin, the planetary envelope of Earth considered as a medium for thought activity; serves as a kind of womb-sheath or ETHERIC WEB for the superorganic growth of human society. An important concept for developing a concrete vision of planetization.

NOSTRADAMUS (Noh-stra-DAHM-us) French astrologer and physician (1503–1566), known for his prophecies, which were written in a long sequence of four-line poems, very obscure and open to multiple interpretations. Noted in his time for having saved thousands from the bubonic plague by effecting a miraculous cure.

NOTHINGNESS See VOID.

NOUVEAU PREACH The kind of fanatical talk, aimed at impressing or converting others, that often comes from someone who has just discovered a "new religion" or gotten seriously bitten by the bug of "ancient wisdom."

NOVA A star that explodes due to extreme heating up of its atmosphere. Usually attributed to a binary or two-star system in which the atmosphere of the larger star is caused to vaporize in a violent flash; thus, the supreme example of the lumination of matter, or matter turning into light. Compare with SUPER-NOVA.

NOVALIS Assumed name of Friederich von Hardenberg, (1772–1801), German poet and aphorist, key figure in the Romantic movement and precursor of the DECADENCE. Known for his theory of magic idealism, positing the imagination as the primary power not only in coloring but actually in creating human experience; thus, probably the first on record to state that we create our own realities. See E2.4, however, for a careful rewording of this principle. See also RAPHAEL-NOVALIS IMPULSE.

NUMEROLOGY The system of interpreting character and events through the meaning attached to numbers, based on the idea of their vibrational quality.

NUMINOUS (NEW-min-us) Adj., in mythology and the history of religions, that which is charged with spiritual or supernatural power. Something radiant and overwhelming, which breaks upon the mind and emotions in the moment of direct contact with the divine. N., numinosity (New-min-OSS-uh-tee). From the Latin *numen,* "divinity, sacred object." See also SACRED.

NYINGMA (NING-mah) In Tibetan Buddhism, one of the three main sects, called the old, unreformed sect due to its close association with the indigenous shamanism of Nepal, BON PO.

O

OAHSPE (Awe-ASS-pee) The so-called Kosmon Bible, compiled tele-pathically by John Newbrough in 1881, presenting a fantastic scheme of cosmic and terrestrial evolution. Example of an Otherworld scenario, including the HOLLOW EARTH.

OCCULT/OCCULTISM (E19) From Latin *ob-*, "toward, about" + *celare*, "to hide, conceal": thus, that which tends toward being hidden—to be distinguished from that which is deliberately concealed.

Specifically, the practice of cultivating hidden or nonobvious forces. First used in the modern sense by the French revivalist Eliphas LEVI, and adopted by the English Theosophist A. P. Sinnet around 1881, when it was all the rage among the European intelligentsia. Once adopted, the term came to be applied to the entire repertoire of practical psychology and transformational techniques common to the ancient wisdom of antiquity. As the standard name for the traditional sciences of inner development, occultism has become pitifully cheap-ened and wrongfully maligned in our time, when it is likely to be associated with everything from Ouija boards and candle burning to the horrors of the Jones-town cult.

The last genuine representative of classical occultism was Rudolf Steiner, a spiritual teacher exceptional for his emphasis on special training to ensure the moral integrity of those who seek to penetrate the occult. As the study and mastery of the hidden or unacknowledged forces operating in the natural world and in the human mind and body, occultism has been largely superseded by the new physics, brain/mind theory, neurolinguistic programming, and a myriad of easy-access self-transformational techniques, including the recent device of SUB-LIMINAL TAPES. Occultist (AWE-cul-tist): someone who practices and imparts occultism.

OCCULT ANATOMY The description of the human body, including the brain, according to theories not accepted by conventional anatomical and medical experts—including, for instance, the CHAKRA-system believed to interpenetrate the physical torso, or the function of the glandular system (especially the pineal and pituitary glands) as an instrument of consciousness. See also FOUR-BODY THEORY.

O C C U L T A T I O N   (Awe-kul-TAY-shun) The blotting from view of one planet by another, or of a star by a planet, or, most often, of a star or planet by the Moon.

O C T A V E   A structure or pattern of forces, analogous to the eight notes in the musical scale, often applied in occultism to explain the formative processes of the universe and especially applied to the concept of the INTERVAL. See also SEVEN, LAW OF.

O D / O D FORCE   (Owed) A mix of psychic and vital force, defined by Baron von Reichenbach (1788–1869), one of the pioneers of hypnotism and paranormal studies; also called ECTOPLASM.

O F F - P L A N E T   Slang for an extraterrestrial or any entity from a different or alien dimension.

O G A M / O G H A M   (OH-em) In the Celtic Revival, a form of writing consisting of groups of slashes, or strokes, laid out along a central stem-line, usually inscribed on stone pillars or along a stripling of wood. Technically called early Irish linear script, believed to be a kind of secret alphabet. Also, perhaps used for notation of musical scales among the Celtic bards. See also TREE-ALPHABET.

O M   Shortened form of AUM.

O M E G A - S T A T E   In the writings of Teilhard de Chardin, the final unification of humanity into a single entity or PERSON, a huge multicellular organism in which every single human being is a cell-unit conscious of the whole to which it belongs. Believed by some to be already embodied or at least prefigured in the CHRIST as the indwelling Planetary Spirit, provisional center of the living, loving, self-regulating wholeness humanity has yet to attain. According to Teilhard, this state lies "not above, but ahead"—that is, in the direction of the future, toward what he calls the ultrahuman. From *omega* (Oh-MAY-gah), last letter of the Greek alphabet. "I am the Alpha and the Omega . . ." (Revelation, 22:13). Supreme example of how planetization works, organically and societally.

O P T I O N   P R O C E S S   Method developed by Barry Kaufman for determining what actually motivates a person and clearing the motivation of its negative bearing so that new choices can be recognized. Based on the core principle that we wrongly use unhappiness for self-motivation.

O R A C L E   In antiquity, a medium consulted for answers to questions and predictions of events; a prophet or anyone who reveals information not accessible by ordinary means. From Latin *orare*, "to speak, pray." Currently revived in the phenomenon of channeling. The most famous is the DELPHIC ORACLE.

O R D E A L / O R G Y   In the Mysteries, the elaborate ritual of trial and testing undergone by all those seeking initiation, achieved through a systematic process of traumatization (PSYCHODRAMA) leading to the re-imprinting of the etheric body during the near-death experience of the three-day TEMPLE SLEEP. Also said to have required the confrontation with the Guardian of the Threshold, and other supernatural dangers, apparently replaced in modern society by the mere struggle for survival.

Also called orgy (ORE-gee), from Greek *orgia,* "secret rites, power-workings." Not a sexual free-for-all, but the training undergone to achieve spiritual empowerment. Also called labor, as in the Twelve Labors (Orgies) of Hercules, which describe a specific stage of initiation in the twelvefold system of the SOLAR MYSTERIES, enabling the initiated to become totally identified with the Sun God. In classical writings, *orgy* sometimes refers to the mental and physical exertion of initiation, and sometimes to the ecstatic, superhuman results of such exertion, such as in the raving, dancing, snake-charming, and animal dismemberment exhibited by the Dionysian cults.

ORGONE (Org-OWN) The basic life-force pervading the universe, from atom to galaxy, and specially concentrated in human biology as a plasmatic agent that pervades the body and can appear as a bluish flame. Discovered and named by Wilhelm Reich and used for healing in the Reichian work. Orgonomics (Ore-go-NOM-iks): term coined by Reich for the study and management of orgone.

ORIGINALITY The mark of good finding. A result of the discipline of right seeking: to become a source unto oneself. Stated theologically, God, the All-One, seeks to become infinitely evolved as Each-One in us. In Western spirituality, becoming original is the primary result to be achieved through the process of INDIVIDUATION. It matures in the sense of knowing how one is different, having a special mission to fulfill or a unique gift to offer (C&B2, Preface).

ORION (Ore-EYE-un) The prominent constellation of the Northern Hemisphere, visible through the year except for June and July, when the Sun passes over it. Appears as a huge figure cartwheeling through the sky, marked by the striking alignment of the three stars in its "belt," which point downward and left to SIRIUS. According to the latest efforts to map out the astrography of the universe, this is the constellation that defines the region of the galactic spiral arms inhabited by our solar system. By extension, it can be taken as the namesake for our entire galaxy: Orion Galaxy. Identified with Osiris in Greek and Egyptian mythology, where it is called the Starwalker. See also ANDROMEDA.

OSIRIS (Oh-SIGH-russ) Greek form of Egyptian Asar, the most prominent deity in Egyptian religion and mythology. A type of Sun God celebrated in the Solar Mysteries, equivalent to Christ as a "dying God" who becomes the Judge of the Soul in a typical scenario of the UNDERWORLD.

OTHERWORLD In world mythology and religion, an other world that mysteriously coexists with one normally present to us. In the Celtic Revival, the refuge of departed Gods and dead heroes, a dangerous, alluring realm of ordeal and supernatural bounty that intermingles with the ordinary realm of the mind and senses, like a fogbank eating away the landscape and then dissolving to reveal it again—or perhaps the landscape dissolves with it! Especially prominent in the folklore of the Celtic Revival, such as the MABINOGION. Revived by Rod Serling as the "twilight zone." Actually encountered as a "wall of fog" in Castaneda. Not an other world beyond the senses—the astral plane, dream world, the realms of the other planets, et cetera—rather, a world not beyond but within this one (i.e., INFRASENSORY), interpenetrating it, and accessed by tricking the senses.

O U I J A   B O A R D   (We-jah) Made-up word consisting of the French and German for "yes," *oui* and *ja:* a yes-yes board. A board with letters and numbers for spelling out messages by moving a pointer (planchette) under the direction of psychic forces, often believed to be spirits of the dead.

O U R O B O R O S   (You-ROW-bore-ose) Gnostic/alchemical image of the serpent swallowing its own tail, used in alchemical manuals as a specific symbol of the activity of the human digestive system in the breakdown (catabolism) and reconstitution (anabolism) of proteins. Also, as a general symbol of INFINITY in its dynamic function of inexhaustible recycling and reprocessing.

O U T - O F - B O D Y   E X P E R I E N C E   Detachment of consciousness from the physical body in full awareness, either in sleep or awake, voluntary or not; usually explained as being due to release of the astral body. Compare with ASTRAL PROJECTION.

O V E R S E L F   Term coined by Paul Brunton for the higher self, the Atman of Indian philosophy (C&B3.8).

O V E R S O U L   In Transcendentalism, the universal self, realized by merging self-consciousness into God-consciousness; the pure subject, or the indwelling presence that integrates all functions of consciousness; the root of genius and the mystical sense of oneness-with-all-things. A term introduced by Ralph Waldo Emerson (C&B2.10) as a translation of *Atman* in Indian philosophy (C&B1.5), and later converted by Nietzsche into his concept of the *Übermensch,* "SUPERMAN," made notorious by the Nazis, who modified it to fit their creed of Aryan racial supremacy—one of the most famous and unfortunate instances of "Password" on record.

O z   (1) Retirement home for over-the-hill masters whose powers are failing them. (2) Code name for any source of channeling that defies identification. (3) Trickster God who uses cosmic pranks to expose spiritual DELUSION.

O Z O N E   H O L E   In ecology, one of the gravest dangers facing the environment. A hole in the thin sheath of allotropic oxygen (O_3) that serves as a protective shield against the dangerous effects of ultraviolet rays. Due to the slow dissipation of certain human-made chemicals, especially the gases released by aerosol propellants, the ozone layer (located from six to thirty miles in altitude) appears to be disintegrating, with large holes growing at an alarming rate over the South Pole and certain temperate regions, such as Switzerland.

P

PADMA (PUD-mah) Sanskrit, "lotus."

PADMA SAMBHAVA (PUD-mah Sum-BAHV-ah) Sanskrit, "Lotus-born One." Legendary founder of Tibetan Buddhism, supposed to have lived historically around 750 A.D. as an Indian sage and outrageous wildman of profound learning and extraordinary magical skills. His initiation by a DAKINI with high-tech apparitional powers, recorded in *The Tibetan Book of the Great Liberation,* is one of the most sensational spiritual adventures in Eastern lore. By an interesting East/West parallel, it equates very closely to ordeals in the Otherworld described in such Western classics as the Mabinogion.

PAGAN (PAY-gun) From the Greek *paien,* "to pasture, tend flocks." Adj. and n., the people of the countryside, who lived with flocks of animals. Later, in Christian times, used to describe all people who were not specifically Christian, especially if they believed in many Gods (polytheism) and were involved in the worship of the forces of nature. Once Christianity came to power and asserted the singular supremacy of the Sun God Christ (expropriated from the Solar Mysteries), the familiar, sometimes nurturing, sometimes menacing NATURE-SPIRITS of paganism were driven underground into the psyche, where they eventually appeared as the demons of the Middle Ages. An attempt to rectify this harmful psychic inversion occurs in the revival of WICCA.

PAGAN (Pa-GAHN) A spectacular site in Burma on the Irrawaddy River, filled with the ruins of over a thousand Buddhist temples.

PALENQUE (Pah-LEN-kay) A sacred site in Chiapas, Mexico, occupied by Mayan temples, one of which contains a bas-relief that has been interpreted as evidence that the Gods of the past were actually visitors from outer space (ANCIENT ASTRONAUTS).

PALI (PAH-lee) Scriptural language in which the works of Southern or Theravada Buddhism are written. Differs slightly in spelling from Sanskrit, the sacred language of Northern Buddhism; for instance, *dharma* in Sanskrit, *dhamma* in Pali. Pali Canon: The collection of Buddhist texts setting forth the doctrines of HINAYANA Buddhism.

337

PALMISTRY The art of reading the lines of the hand in order to predict the course of life or interpret personal experiences.

PAN From Greek *paien*, "to pasture, tend the flocks." In Greek myth, the supreme Nature God, half man, half goat, humorously depicted as a merry beast of drunkenness and debauchery. An example of a phallic or priapic God, a crude personification of the masculine aspect of Eros, as worshiped in the SOLAR-PHALLIC religions of Asia and the Mediterranean. Called the Arcadian God, associated with the Peloponnesus (Pell-uh-puh-NEE-sus), the large peninsula forming the southern part of Greece. Compared to Socrates by Aristophanes at Plato's famous dinner party (C&B2.3). Degraded by Christianity into the figure of the Devil. See also EROTICISM (E11).

PANSPERMIA "All-seeding." Theory first proposed by the Swiss chemist Svante August Arrhenius (1859–1927), who stated that life on Earth originated from templates or microscopic spores deposited in the atmosphere by a donor planet or passing comet. Possibly supported by the discovery of organic molecules in a meteorite that fell in Orgueil, France, in 1864. Later adopted and amplified by Watson and Crick, discoverers of the structure of DNA. Later still transposed into STARSEED.

PANTHEISM From Latin *pan-*, "all, inclusive" + *theos*, "God": the belief that Gods or divine powers pervade all things and all processes, especially the workings of nature. See also NATURE MYSTICISM, NATURE-SPIRITS.

PARA-CHRISTIANITY My neologism for a movement "alongside of" *(para)* Christianity, dedicated to a humanistic and nondogmatic reformulation of Christian principles and their application to the urgent needs of society and the individual. *Para-* implies going beyond or surpassing the given limits of orthodox Christianity. Exemplified in the work of Scott Peck (C&B4.11), for one. Derived to some extent from NEW THOUGHT in the nineteenth century, and now amplified by association with recovery.

PARACLESIAN SPIRIT (Para-CLEES-yun) In alternative Christianity, the group-spirit, the comforting, healing power that lives organically in the communal effort of people dedicated to the free unfoldment of human potential. In Russian mysticism and theology, the principle of *sobornost*, "solidarity, communal feeling," and in modern times in America, the impulse that informs group activity in RECOVERY. Another name for para-Christianity, seen in the common spirit that informs the work of such para-Christian teachers as Emmet Fox (inspirational thinking based on nondenominational Christian idealism), the "Course in Miracles" (guidelines for applying the Christian principle of forgiveness), Scott Peck (community-building), John Bradshaw (family recovery, generational healing), and Jean Houston (Christian Mystery teachings in modern form.)

From *Paraclete*: Greek *para-*, "superior, beyond" + *kalein*, "to call, summon, comfort." Originally, the *Parakletos* or "Comforter" promised to be sent by Christ in the New Testament (John 14:16), and usually interpreted as manifesting in the descent of the "tongues of flame" upon the circle of Apostles on Pentecost, ten days after the Ascension. Source of the higher, transpersonal bonding of those committed to group effort toward the unfoldment of human potential and personal healing, the spirit of anonymity.

PARADIGM (PARE-uh-dim, or -dime) From Greek *para-*, "alongside of, beyond" + *deiknynai*, "to show, reveal": thus, something that shows us what is beyond. A pattern for events or the unfoldment of events, a developmental model or comprehensive scheme. One of the most important concepts in the worldview of the new spirituality, originally introduced by Thomas Kuhn in his book *The Structure of Scientific Revolutions* (1962). Usually applied to indicate an overruling system of thought or valuation that is more or less invisible to those who live by it; for instance, the current scientific model of the world that assumes that consciousness and even human feeling are merely the effects of material-chemical processes is the paradigm of materialism. On the exercise of tracking paradigms, see Classics and Basics, Preface.

PARADIGM-SHIFT The shift from one worldview or belief system to another and all that goes with it, such as vast historical changes and the emergence of new, unprecedented questions for society and the individual. For instance, the shifts from viewing the human being as creature (medieval paradigm) to viewing it as personality (Renaissance) to viewing it as cocreator. On the current paradigm-shift, see E1.4, and on the problem of conflicting paradigms, see E2.4. Compare with QUANTUM LEAP.

PARALLEL LIFE A theory in New Age thinking and science fiction, proposing that we live different lives simultaneously but in distinct realms, sometimes with weird and comic overlapping, as in the novel *Slaughterhouse Five* by Kurt Vonnegut. May be viewed as an alternative theory to PAST LIVES. (See also OTHERWORLD.)

PARALLEL UNIVERSE In fantasy and theories of occult physics, another universe (or many) like our own in which we may exist in a mirrorlike reflection of this world, but with fine differences, thus affording an infinite number of possible variations on what we experience in the present moment. In actuality, the ANDROMEDA GALAXY, taken as the parallel and counterbalancing realm to our own.

PARANORMAL Anything beyond or outside what is considered normal, whatever that is. Loose term for all manner of psychic phenomena, including telepathy, UFOs, channeling, et cetera. See also UNEXPLAINED.

PARAPHYSICS Alternative name for the NEW PHYSICS, especially when referring to extrapolations of physical theory, such as quantum mechanics, into theories of consciousness.

PARAPSYCHOLOGY The study and evaluation of processes and events associated with the unexplained potentials of the human mind, "beyond psychology" as it is conventionally understood. This includes such phenomena as precognition, lucid dreaming, telepathy, psychokinesis. Originated with the "Ghost Club" at Trinity College, Cambridge, in 1851, and assumed scientific form in the Society for Psychical Research, founded in 1882 in England; now developing into a legitimate branch of academic study.

PAROUSIA (Par-oo-SEE-ah) Greek, "the arrival of a higher being, or a higher state of being." In the New Testament, the word used to describe the Second Coming.

PARSI Persian for "Persian." A member of the ancient sect of Zoroastrianism (see ZOROASTER), which settled in India after the period of Moslem persecutions in the eighth century. Known to seekers of the 1960s for the sensational entertainment of the Towers of Silence near Bombay, where the Parsis leave their dead exposed atop high columns to be eaten by wild birds.

PARZIVAL / PARSIFAL / PERCEVIL / PERCIVAL (PAR-suh-full) One of the knights in Arthurian Romance who, although not officially a member of the Round Table, succeeds in obtaining the HOLY GRAIL by his own efforts rather than the traditional methods of initiation and blood inheritance. *The* key figure in the Western Mystery tradition, who represents the paradigm-shift from transmission to self-initiation. The primary representative of the Western hero who discovers a unique destiny through the trial and error of independent seeking, leading to INDIVIDUATION (C&B2.5). For a comparison between Parzival and Siddhartha, see the Preface to the Essays.

PASSAGE-GRAVES Name given to ancient structures in Western Europe, especially in Ireland, in the form of hollowed-out mounds with long, narrow passageways usually aligned to the rising of the Sun at winter solstice. Evidence of the SOLAR MYSTERIES in which the sun-ray was imagined as entering the uterine passageway of the earthworks and penetrating to the womb of the Earth, thus indicating the marriage of Sun and Earth and the birth of the Solar Logos as the DIVINE CHILD. A matter of immense interest in geomancy. See also SACRED SITES.

PAST-LIFE REGRESSION The process, often facilitated by bodily manipulation and guided imagery, of accessing memories of former lives, thought to be stored in the body, either in the genetic code, or in regions of the subconscious mind not normally accessible to conscious reference due to emotional blockages.

PAST LIVES Former embodiments as a human being on Earth, often believed to go back into the remote, prehistorical ages of Atlantis and Lemuria; less often described as having occurred on other planets. See also REINCARNATION.

PATANJALI (Paht-TAN-jah-lee) Indian teacher of Yoga, author of the first systematic text. Probably lived around 200 B.C.

PATH From the IE base *penth-,* "progress, a way of going." Any way of self-discovery; any method of teaching that leads to increased self-awareness and deeper participation in life; any technique of practical and/or theoretical use in exploring and evolving human potential. Not the where, but the way of getting there. At worst, a serious distraction from being here. Specifically, a spiritual path is a way of progressing toward a richer and keener awareness of how we are all involved in the dynamic of life as intricate parts of a vital, all-encompassing whole. On the difference between a spiritual path and a spiritual trip, see the Afterword. See also LIFE-PATH.

PATHFINDING   In the new spirituality, a discipline required of every seeker due to the overwhelming array of options now available (spiritual supermarket). See Preamble.

PATHWORKING   A technical term in the Western Mystery tradition for the method of using imaginal processes to get to actual experiences: for instance, a course of meditation on the symbols in the Tarot or the system of the Cabalistic Tree of Life, which leads to the awakening of inner potentials or psychic powers and may often produce outer effects in the form of specific events, challenges to growth, or odd coincidences (SYNCHRONICITY). Loose term for any consistent method of self-actualization.

PATRIARCHS   Loosely, leaders and authorities in the cultural system of male dominance. Specifically, the twenty-eight Indian patriarchs, stretching from Gautama to Bodhidharma, who were instrumental in the oral, person-to-person TRANSMISSION of Buddhism from India to China.

PATRIARCHY   The domination and direction of human culture and society by men, as opposed to matriarchy. Probably originated historically at the time of the never-yet-explained "discovery" of patrimony—the role of the male seed in human propagation. The institution of the male of the species as supreme, all-ruling, life-bearing, and authoritative, considered by many people to be nearing its end—its final stage being marked by the appearance of the death-bearing phallic seed-cones of nuclear warheads, tragic end of the FATHER WISDOM.

PEAK EXPERIENCE   Term coined by Abraham Maslow for moments of spiritual ecstasy or creative outpouring recorded in the lives of artists, mystics, athletes, and other exceptional people; applied to the new paradigm of HUMANISTIC PSYCHOLOGY from 1956 onward, stressing the possibilities of personal transformation and creative breakthrough.

PENDULUM   A device, usually consisting of a crystal on a string, used in divination to detect hidden currents and obtain simple yes or no responses, according to the way it rotates.

PENTAGRAM   A five-sided figure, usually in the form of a star. An ancient symbol of human personality and a teaching device used in the Mysteries to describe the five principles or stages required to transform the animal nature or creaturehood of humanity into true humanhood. Inverted, it presents the abstract figure of a goat's head and is generally taken to represent the exploitation and glorification of the animal drives and erotic forces, as encouraged in SATAN-ISM. Compare with the ENNEAGRAM. See also GOATS.

PERENNIAL PHILOSOPHY   Term coined by German philosopher Gottfried Leibniz (1646–1716) for the worldwide and age-old belief in the active INDWELLING of God in all beings and natural processes. Title of a breakthrough book in East/West studies by Aldous Huxley (C&B3.13).

PERSON/PERSONALITY   In esoterics and old-school occultism, the mortal identity, contrasted to the immortal identity, or individuality. There is much confusion about this term, which in some teachings is taken as the artificial or learned mechanism of the external self, opposed to ESSENCE (as in the Gurdjieff work). In other teachings it is taken as the multitoned instrument of the divine self (as in the Sufi teachings of Hazrat Inayat Khan and the existential theology of Nicholas Berdyaev, a modern Russian philosopher).

The question of how GOD, as the Divine Presence, is actually present to us or with-and-in us is complicated by the associated question of whether this presence is personal or impersonal. Or both. In Taoism and Buddhism, the spiritual principle informing the universe is viewed impersonally, and never referred to as God. In Hinduism, it is viewed rather ambivalently, as both the impersonal *Brahma* (universal creator) and the personal or person-centered *Purusha* (world-soul). In Christianity, God is viewed as a divine-creative spirit who becomes accessible through personal embodiment in Christ, the Second Person or SON PRINCIPLE. In esoteric Christianity, Christ is viewed as the principle of organic growth in both human nature and external nature—even as time personified! For instance, see OMEGA-STATE, in which a divine "person" is the growth-focus for the becoming of all human persons.

Troublesome as it is, this concept of how the divine makes itself known to us "in person" (E24) seems inevitably to underlie the question of what the human being itself is, as person. From Latin *per-*, "through" + *sona*, "mask," in reference to the masks worn by actors in Greek tragedy.

PEYOTE   (Pay-OH-tee) Native cactus plant of the southwestern United States and Central America, used by the indigenous peoples as a sacrament for communing with supernatural beings and achieving the VISION QUEST; eaten in the form of dry buttons; nonhabit-forming, sometimes nauseating.

PHALLIC RELIGION   In eroticism, the worship of the sexual powers of the male or of the forces streaming through the penis, believed in ancient times to be generated directly from the Sun, rather in the way the radio waves streaming down a car aerial are derived from the radio station where they originate. Also called priapic, from the Roman God of the phallus, Priapus, a variant of the Indo-European Manu, Prajapati. See also SOLAR-PHALLIC.

PHARAOH   (FAIR-roe). From Egyptian *pr'o*, "great dwelling." In ancient Egypt, the embodiment of divinity on Earth in the social system of THEOC-RACY. As distinct from the priesthood, consisting of men and women of a high degree of initiation, the pharaoh (and, by extension, his family) was held to be a living God, the Egyptian equivalent to a TULKU. The breeding and interbreeding of the pharaonic line was carefully controlled by the priesthood, who eventually attempted to usurp the role of the royal family, thus resulting in the downfall of Egyptian culture.

PHARAONIC SCIENCE (Fare-uh-YON-ic) The massive body of teachings and practices associated with the pharaohs of ancient Egypt, although actually maintained and transmitted by the priesthood. Includes the system of theocracy, the mysteries of the Great Pyramid, the sacred code-system of hieroglyphs, and arcane methods of initiation described theoretically in HERMETICS. See also EGYPTIAN RELIGION.

PHENOMENAL/PHENOMENALITY Important concept in Eastern thought, and especially Tibetan Buddhism, stating that reality as we normally experience it is a mere play of appearances, transitory and insubstantial. This view is formulated with great finesse in the doctrine of the VOID and described in the famous similes of NAROPA. Correlative to the concept of Maya, the self-veiling power of pure, unmanifest Being. See also SUCHNESS.

PHENYLETHYLAMINE (PEA) (FEE-nal-ETH-ul-AM-een) An enzyme related to amphetamines, found in chocolate, known as the love chemical because ingesting it supposedly simulates the sensation of being united with the one you love. May have been the chemical agent operative in inducing the ALTERED STATE of momentary God-ecstasy enjoyed by the Aztec royalty who were exclusively allowed to ingest cacao in its raw form.

PHILOSOPHERS' STONE The ultimate goal of alchemy, not only a substance, but a state of awareness rooted in the experience of vital contact with the dynamic forces operating in the endless creativity of nature. The fountainhead of cocreation, direct access to which endows the alchemist with full capacities to participate in cocreation. See also LANGUAGE.

PHILOSOPHY Greek *philos,* "love" + *sophia,* "wisdom, knowledge of the primary matters." Systematic questioning of the meaning and purpose of human existence. Literally, "loving to know." Western philosophy is generally held to have begun with the classical Greeks, for whom philosophical questions were tackled with the same relish some people today apply to solving brainteasers.

PHRENOLOGY (Fren-NOL-oh-gee) From Greek *phrenos,* "upper middle of the chest, seat of the heart-intelligence." The art of reading character from the features of the face or contours of the head; generally taken as an old-fashioned belief system easily ridiculed and proven unscientific by those who favor other belief systems. Might be more convincing if we read the chest instead. See also SCHIZOPHRENIA, THYMUS.

PILGRIMAGE A long journey to a holy site, for the purpose of worship or spiritual atonement.

PINEAL GLAND (PIN-e-al, or Pi-NEE-al) A small, cone-shaped organ in the forebrain, somewhat obscure in function. In OCCULT ANATOMY, the physical correspondence to the third eye, hence a seat of paranormal faculties, especially thought-transference. Symbolically represented in the headgear of the Egyptian Pharaohs, the uraeus, a serpent extending from the forehead.

PISCEAN AGE The Age of Belief, the era of human history and spiritual-cultural development characterized by widespread reliance upon religious authorities, and an emphasis on the dogmatic, fundamentalist view that revelation of the divine to the human is over and done. According to such a view, the relationship between God and each individual is normatively fixed, not subject to being evolved or changed. Often contrasted with the AQUARIAN AGE, described as a time in which direct access to divinity supersedes mere belief, and the divine potential in each of us can be freely explored and endlessly evolved. The beginning and duration of both ages is a matter of some obscurity, though they may be determinable by a chronological framework based on the PRECESSION OF THE EQUINOXES.

PITUITARY GLAND (Pit-TOO-uh-terry) A small, oval endrocrine gland attached by a stalk to the base of the brain; secretes hormones important to body growth and metabolism. In OCCULT ANATOMY, believed to be the physiological counterpart to a subtle organ, the crown chakra, seat of paranormal faculties and superconsciousness.

PLANE Level or state of awareness. In the old-fashioned sense, another "place" in the universe, like Oz, Shambhala, or Toontown. Understood more correctly as a dimension of consciousness, accessible here and now as consciousness is adjusted or tuned (like the dial of a radio), rather than a remote locale elsewhere in space and time.

PLANETARIZATION/PLANETIZATION In the first spelling, a term used by Dane Rudhyar in *The Planetarization of Consciousness* for the state of human development when individuals unite in a sense of living as cellular components in the greater organism of the Earth, fully conscious of their relationship to the larger entity in which they are incorporated. Comparable to planetization, proposed by Teilhard de Chardin as the process that unfolds as humanity evolves toward the OMEGA-STATE. A main theme of the New Age (E1.3), replete with enormous implications. Compare with the GLOBAL VILLAGE of Marshall McLuhan; also GAIA, the concept of planetization as applied in ecology.

PLANETARY Of or concerning the entire world, the encompassing network of social and biological relationships on the Earth, taking the Earth itself as a living entity, and human society as a conscious instrument through which the entire planet can become SELF-conscious.

PLANETARY GRID In geomancy, a worldwide network of power lines defined by the location of sacred sites. According to the studies of some Russian researchers, it consists of a vast icosahedron (twenty-faced polygon), with ancient groundworks like Stonehenge and the Great Pyramid located at its apexes.

PLANETARY HIERARCHY   In the works of Alice A. Bailey, the latter-day organization of the Great White Brotherhood, described as a vast bureaucracy with the masters in executive positions, and below them, initiates and disciples who work within a system of "rays" to implement specific aspects of the "plan" on Earth. An elaboration of Madame Blavatsky's scenario of the HIMALAYAN MASTERS. Typical of the conspiracy theories that show up, now and again, in New Age thinking (E1.3).

PLANETARY SPHERES   Ancient scheme of the Solar System taught in the Mysteries; a massive system of interpenetrating spheres or resonance-shells, corresponding to the orbits of the planets, where the human soul goes through a kind of pilgrimage during the LIFE-INTERVAL between death and rebirth. A ninefold extrasensory realm, corresponding by an old analogy to the realm of the Nine Hierarchies in esoteric Christianity.

PLASMA   (1) In astrophysics, superhot ionized gas circulating in a vast field in interplanetary and interstellar space. Main subject in the new field of plasma physics. (2) In biology and medicine, the fluid part of human blood. (3) In alchemy, the living medium of the terrestrial atmosphere, considered as a biologically active solution in which the human form is deposited as a spore. The biochemical substance of light, implied in the colloidal theory of light in GOE-THEAN SCIENCE.

PLATONIC YEAR   See PRECESSION OF THE EQUINOXES.

PLAY   A paradigm in religious and metaphysical teachings of the East. In Hinduism, the world is produced from the dreaming of Vishnu, a kind of hide-and-seek game in which the supreme Lord who is dreaming us plays at being us so that he can delight in countless ways of rediscovering himself. In Tantra, the universe is a kind of side effect of the erotic play of Shiva and Shakti, a pair of Gods intertwined in blissful intercourse who give off shuddering waves of ecstasy, which unfold into the various planes of natural and creaturely manifestation. In Sufism, the consciousness of being at one with God is awakened in the heart-center by the sensation of a dreamy, ecstatic dance, incited through meditation and whirling.

In the East, play is a major paradigm for the creative process, according with the basic notion that God is pure bliss, or ANANDA. This stands in strong contrast to the Buddhist view that all existence is suffering, a state of intense frustration; though the Buddhists do affirm that Nirvana, attained by clearing out this exasperating muddle (SAMSARA), is a state of total serenity and imperturbable bliss. However, the Hindu idea of bliss as cosmic play is far more dynamic and world-engaging.

In the West, suffering seems to have been emphasized over play. For instance, in Christianity the suffering of Jesus Christ is dramatized to a melodramatic pitch, although the Gnostic gospels give quite different glimpses of a Savior who danced and laughed, even viewing the Crucifixion as a joke. By contrast to the Hindu/Sufi interpretation of play as a divine diversion (God entertaining itself), there is Shakespeare's notion that "All the world's a stage," expressing a view of play as a moral-dramatic process rather than an apparitional one. One Western philosopher, the Romantic idealist J. C. F. Schiller, proposed that the "play-impulse" was essential for the human personality to balance and reconcile the opposing thrusts of material and spiritual concerns. In our own time, David Spangler wisely sees play as a necessary phase of creative experimentation in the inceptive unfoldment of the new spirituality. See Afterword.

PLEIADES (PLEE-ah-deez) In Greek myth, the seven daughters of Atlas, the supreme ruler of Atlantis; and in Hindu myth, often equated with the seven wives of the RISHIS. In astronomy, a bright group of six stars (one daughter being "lost," according to the myth) in the constellation of the Bull. In New Age mythology, often described as the location of certain superhuman entities, or star-beings, who may visit Earth by supernatural means or transmit information telepathically to human recipients, for the guidance of human affairs.

PLEROMA (Pluh-ROAM-uh) In Gnosticism, the realm of the divine-creative Hierarchies, the supreme fullness, ground of existence, womb of creation; from which the FALLEN SOPHIA became alienated by her attraction to the lower sense-worlds.

PLUMED SERPENT See QUETZALCOATL.

POETRY From the Greek *poien*, "to create." Creative speech. High-compression LANGUAGE, the most intimate and generative form of human communication. Viewed by the Romantics as the form of communication through which humanity rises to its full-blown God-like potential. See also MUSE.

POLARITY The condition of harmonious interplay of opposites; dynamic interdependence, such as the polarity of the sexes. By contrast to duality.

POLARITY THERAPY General term for various kinds of health care and healing practices that seek to balance the forces and organs of the body. Originated by Randolph Stone after sixty years of studying human diet, pastimes, and behavior; based on his concept that each person exhibits an "energy anatomy," which can be adjusted to perfect symmetry.

POLE-SHIFT A change in the location of the poles of the Earth, due to a shift of the axial orientation of the planet to the surrounding heavens. Frequently cited in EARTH CHANGES as an event that happened before or is about to happen. See also VELIKOVSKY.

POLTERGEIST German, "playful ghost." A petty spirit known for pranks, house-haunting, and disruptive behavior.

POLYTHEISM Belief in the existence of many *(poly-)* gods *(theos)*. An aspect of paganism, reintroduced in the Celtic Revival and Wicca. See GOD for other -isms.

POPOL VUH (POE-pull VOO) Maya, "book of the people." A great classic of Western spirituality, taken from the oral tradition of the Quiché Maya. A mythological account of creation, filled with supernatural events and magical adventures (C&B2.12).

POST-ATLANTEAN Theosophic idiom for the era in which we are now living, said to have begun after the sinking of the last islands of Atlantis, around 9500 B.C. Said to be marked off by the precession of the equinoxes and sometimes calculated as consisting of seven sub-ages, culture-epochs, or Platonic Months of 2,150 years each, of which ours is the fifth beginning in 1413. See LEMURIA for the preceding sequence.

POTALA (Po-TAHL-lah) The vast palace in Lhasa, Tibet, where the Dalai Lamas lived from 1694 until the Chinese invasion of 1959. The Vatican of Tibetan Buddhism.

POWER Conventionally, the most acceptable substitute for love. Essentially, the ability to achieve full expression of the INNATE. Paradoxically, that which often appears in its rightful form when the desire for it is completely surrendered. Tragically, often confounded with CONTROL.

POWER ANIMAL Any kind of animal encountered in a dream (nahual) or produced by visualization as a means to focus and define one's own power or a specific faculty. See also ANIMAL GUIDES.

POWER OBJECTS In anthropology and shamanism, totems and all kinds of articles (stones, trees, feathers) believed to be invested with supernatural power, used as instruments for the transmission of psychic forces. Objects invested with MANA.

PRAJNA (PRAHJ-nah) Sanskrit, from *pra-*, "ahead, before" + *jna,* "knowing, perception." Perception in the awakened state that sees all phenomena with crystal-clear accuracy in their relation to the ground-state of ultimate reality, pure essence, or VOID. In Buddhist psychology, the application of compassion to perception; the skill of reading the intent of human actions with impartial clarity. Spiritual discernment.

PRALAYA (Prah-LIE-uh) Sanskrit, from *pra-*, "through" + *laya,* "dissolution." The interval between two phases of manifestation, conceived as a pause or sleep phase of the creation process. Old Theosophical term taken from the Brahmanical scenario of the "Days and Nights of Brahma." During the nights, Brahma sleeps, and there is complete cessation.

PRANA (PRAH-nah) Sanskrit, "life-force, vital power," especially that which comes from the Sun. In Yoga, the pervasive vitality of the human body, which may be intensified to an infinite degree by certain practices such as pranayana (Pra-nah-YAN-nah), breathing exercises and postures used to manipulate and intensify prana, preparatory to reaching levels of higher consciousness.

PREBIRTHING A method that uses deep breathing to access memories of experiences undergone in the time previous to birth (specifically, in the interval between one incarnation and another).

PRECESSION OF THE EQUINOXES The long-term movement

of the Vernal Point—the position of the Sun against the background of the constellations at the moment of the spring equinox, March 21—in an east-to-west direction across the sky, encompassing a total cycle of about 26,000 years (the so-called Platonic Year). This is a movement located on the orbital plane of the Earth due to the slow wobbling of the Earth on its polar axis, like a top slowing down. Apparently, it was known to the ancients before it was historically identified by Hipparchus, a Greek astronomer, around 150 B.C. It may have been used to establish the framework for a grand scheme of twelve Precessional Ages or Platonic Months (Piscean Age, Aquarian Age, et cetera) of 2,150 years each, marked off by the slow backshift of the Vernal Point through the CONSTELLA-TIONS. As a cosmic time frame, this system might be useful in defining the age we live in, though an adequate revision of the ancient scheme has yet to be worked out. See also EONICS.

PRECOGNITION   Knowing things before they occur.

PRIMAL THERAPY   Method of reliving deep-rooted experiences and releasing the pent-up forces of emotional trauma, developed by Arthur Janov (The Primal Scream).

PROBATION   From Latin probare, "to test, prove." In the old systems of spiritual training and latter-day secret orders such as the GOLDEN DAWN, the stage when the moral and mental integrity of the seeker is tested before entering the course of initiation.

PROGRAMMING   The process of acquiring attitudes and belief systems in early years, due to influences in one's upbringing, traumatic experiences, and education. See also IMPRINTING.

PROJECTION   (1) In the Jungian work, the enactment of a psychic complex in external attitude or behavior, as in the projection of the fear of one's father upon someone who resembles him. (2) Loosely, perceiving and responding to a situation or person as you expect or wish it to be, rather than as it actually is. (3) In alchemy, the final stage of manifestation, also called magnification, when the powers of concentration acquired during the work are totally committed to achieving a specific aspect of cocreation.

PROPHECY   The act of foretelling events, looking into the future, predicting what is to come; attributed to the Old Testament prophets, the Magi, NOSTRADAMUS, Fátima, and numerous New Age channels.

PROVIDENCE   The state of active supervention in the world, by which God provides for human needs. A belief system strongly emphasized in New Thought and para-Christianity, and more recently in recovery. Also, an issue of great spiritual anguish in the West, as in the case of Parzival (C&B2.5), who went through a period of hating God for his apparent lack of providence.

PSYCHE   (SIGH-key) From Greek psyche, "soul"; also "butterfly." That by which we are attuned to the innermost SELF, often defined as the feminine aspect of the self, source of dreams, imagery, moods, feeling, and fantasy. Realm of the imaginal, giving access to the deeper, undefined potentials of the INNATE but also supporting illusion and self-deceit. In the ancient paradigm, the realm where memories of the Gods lingered, like after-impressions of things seen in a strong light. In the medieval paradigm, the realm of erratic and uncontrollable demonic forces on the one hand, or precious but intangible ideals (expressed in allegorical form as Modesty, Valour, Chastity, et cetera) on the other. In the Renaissance idiom, the realm of personal wit, imagination, and genius. In the modern idiom, a realm of immense confusion due to the lack of an exact method to determine if what arises in the psyche is exclusively of the psyche's own making or if it appears through an external intervention (as a virus may invade the body where it does not normally abide). And if it is both, how do we distinguish between the two?

PSYCHEDELIC DRUGS Mescaline, psilocybin, peyote, LSD. Used to expand consciousness and produce sensory enhancement; catalysts of chemical ecstasy; sacramental tools for accessing the OTHERWORLD. Previously used worldwide in their natural form for sacred rites such as the Dionysian orgies; recently used in synthetic form on a mass scale—a situation that supports the definition of KALI YUGA as the time in human religious experience when all the sacraments become profaned.

PSYCHEDELIC EXPERIENCE In the 1960s, the experience of taking LSD as an experiment in self-initiation and a conscious act of revolution, using the chemical aid to break away from the CONSENSUS-REALITY and enter a world of expanded horizons and mystical beauty where all things become possible. In some cases, treated as an analogy to the death experience (C&B4.3); in others, as a "magical mystery tour" (Beatles, 1967) into euphoria and childlike wonder. Characterized by seeing atmospheric wave-patterns ("paisley"), radiant colors, or actual hallucinations; also by hearing one's thoughts audibly, by detecting low-frequency "whispers," or plunging into the "sound of silence" (Simon and Garfunkel, 1965)—all due to the chemical alteration of the normal boundaries of audio-visual perception. Possibly, a result of gaining direct access to the GENETIC CODE through biochemical alterations produced by the drug.

PSYCHIC Loosely and crudely, anything connected with the feelings and perceptions that are not commonly granted as evidential or objective, such as a "psychic flash" about what's happening to a friend who is out of touch in another country. More precisely and profoundly, anything pertaining to the realm of inner feeling and imagination through which a person becomes cocreative with his or her experiences—as when listening to a piece of music, you enter sympathetically into its mood and message, making a creative connection to be lived out in some kind of personal attitude or expression. To be psychic is to be attuned to life's subtler rhythms and moods, to be empathetic with the surprising and open-ended flow of events.

PSYCHIC FAIR A bazaar for the bizarre, where people gather to offer card-readings, crystal charms, astrology, et cetera.

PSYCHIC POWERS Literally, "soul powers." Loose term for any unusual faculty, such as precognition or telepathy.

PSYCHIC SELF-DEFENSE Any method or attitude for protecting oneself against negative or invasionary influences of a psychic nature (such as harmful thoughts entertained by another person). Name of a modern classic by Dion Fortune.

PSYCHIC SURGERY A shamanic method practiced widely in Brazil and the Philippines, in which the healer operates without tools to remove bodily growths and repair damaged organs. One of the more controversial of the healing arts.

PSYCHO-CYBERNETICS Method of self-programming or transforming one's self-image, introduced by Maxwell Maltz, a plastic surgeon who observed that making his patients physically beautiful, as they requested, did little or nothing to change the way they felt about themselves. One of dozens of contemporary methods for reprogramming behavior and changing ATTITUDE.

PSYCHODRAMA From Greek *psyche*, "soul" + *drama*, "work." (1) In the Mysteries, the method of ORDEAL, using fear and awe to induce emotional trauma for imprinting the astral and etheric bodies with the higher knowledge and paranormal faculties to be acquired through initiation. The technique of transformative imprinting, common to all the Mystery Schools, requiring the initiate to undergo a deliberately induced near-death experience. One of the most important concepts necessary for understanding the efficacy of ancient psychotechnology. See also TEMPLE SLEEP, STEREOTYPE. (2) In modern self-help and alternative therapies, the group theater of transformation, in which participants act out feelings, attitudes, and beliefs in improvised situations, with the aim of achieving cathartic release and emotional rebirth.

PSYCHOIMMUNITY The state of physical immunity to disease and infection achieved by psychic methods, such as visualization, self-hypnosis, BIO-FEEDBACK, and general strengthening of the inner structure of the etheric body, especially in the region of the THYMUS. A new frontier of the healing arts, often associated with the problem of AIDS.

PSYCHOKINESIS OR PK (Sigh-koh-ki-KNEE-sis) In parapsychology, the demonstration of mind over matter by moving objects at a distance, slowing or stopping clocks, bending spoons, et cetera, solely through concentration and visualization.

PSYCHOMETRY (Sigh-KAHM-et-tree) The method of tracing or reconstructing events by laying hands upon objects; for instance, investigating the events of Roman times by reading the impressions received psychically from a bracelet of that era. Sometimes applied in geomancy as a kind of psychic archaeology.

PSYCHOSYNTHESIS "Soul unification." A syncretic method developed by Robert Schultz and Roberto Assagioli, combining Eastern and Western techniques for integrating the conscious ego to the SELF and the self to the world at large.

PSYCHOTECHNOLOGY Term coined by Marilyn Ferguson (C&B4.12) for any and all systems and methods of consciousness-raising and self-transformation. With reference to the traditions of spiritual training in the past, such as the methods applied in the Mysteries, it is called sacred technology.

PSYCHOTRONICS The practical application of mental and psychic powers; psychic technology.

PUER ETERNUS (Pwhere A-TURN-us) Latin, "eternal child, eternal youth." In Jungian psychology, the complex of attachment to, or identification with, unending youth, euphoria, innocence, and magical thinking—a symptom of the inherent human need to recognize the INNER CHILD.

PUJA (POO-jah) Sanskrit, "ceremony of reverence." Any act or attitude of devotion, such as placing flowers upon the altar of a deity or watching the "Tonight Show" on a regular basis.

PURPLE (1) Color at the ultraviolet end of the spectrum, favored by some New Agers as expressive of high spiritual empowerment (violet ray). (2) Slang term used when someone lapses into irrational talk full of psychic absurdities.

PURPOSE A mixed blessing, a rare prize, and a troubling obsession. It seems that the search for purpose cannot help but be a struggle, though living *from* purpose, once it's found, ought to be a pleasure! The story of Parzival provides the main Western model for the dilemmas involved in finding one's purpose (C&B2, Preface). Purpose is a primary concern of seeking in the West, contrasted to the East, where purposeless surrender to the flow is the aim, as seen in cultivation of pure spontaneity in Taoism and Zen. *Tao* means simply "process," which stands in direct counterpoint to *purpose.* The ancient Mysteries of the West were strongly purpose-oriented, or "teleological": *telos* being the Greek term frequently applied to the end or goal of initiation. Perhaps the perfect compromise would be to live from purpose but act as if you had none.

The distinction between living from purpose and living for purpose is, by the way, essential.

PYRAMID Greek, "fire in the midst." A geometrical solid of four equal triangular faces and a square base, with a slope angle of fifty-one degrees and fifty-two minutes, close to one-seventh of the 360. Specifically, stone structures found in Egypt and Central America, considered to be tombs by archaeologists but more likely to have been used as chambers for the TEMPLE SLEEP necessary to the ordeal of spiritual initiation. See also GREAT PYRAMID.

PYRAMIDOLOGY The study of the geometrical and mathematical design of pyramids to decode information concerning the structure and dynamics of the Earth and the Solar System, as well as religious and historical events crucial to the spiritual development of humanity. Also, the use of pyramids for therapy, healing, meditation, and preserving food or other materials.

PYTHAGORAS (Puh-THAG-or-us) Greek philosopher, mathematician, and free-lance initiate (ca 582–ca 507 B.C.). Known for founding an occult school of mathematics, one of the best-known examples of a Mystery School in Western/European tradition; originator of Pythagorean Brotherhood, an esoteric school founded at Croton, in southern Italy—cited by many latter-day groups as the source of their secret teachings, especially the CANON of mathematical principles applied in sacred architecture. Typical case of a SECRET SOCIETY with historical continuity extending into modern times.

Q

QABALAH/QABALLAH See CABALA.

QUANTUM LEAP (1) In modern physics, a jump in the intensity of activity at the atomic level due to an electron shifting from one orbital shell to another. (2) In New Age idiom, a sudden, exceptional advance in growth or awareness, such as a radical change in one's personal attitude or a massive social transformation, such as the shift from a competitive to a cooperative society. Typical of a PARADIGM-SHIFT—for instance, on the personal level, the sudden leap from seeing oneself in a victim role to seeing oneself as a warrior. Compare with HUNDREDTH MONKEY.

QUANTUM MECHANICS/QUANTUM THEORY (1) Specifically, the branch of theoretical physics that deals with the structure and activity of subatomic particles. Established in 1900 when Max Planck proposed that energy is not infinitely divisible but is composed of consistent elemental units, called quanta; elaborated by Einstein in 1905 by the definition of light-quanta, or photons. In itself, the *quantum* (from Latin *quan*, "how much" > IE *kwo-*, "what or who") is a discrete unit of atomic force, first defined by Planck. Basis of modern particle theory, consolidated in its present mathematical form by Paul Dirac in 1927, though brought into question in the same year by Werner Heisenberg's principle of UNCERTAINTY. (2) In the new physics, the model of how consciousness works in interaction with nature. In short, the framework applied in alternative physics to develop a dynamic theory of COCREATION.

QUARK Made-up word found in James Joyce's *Finnegans Wake* from the Latin *qua*, "what," and "quirk": so a quark is what quirks or puzzles. Borrowed by the physicist Murray Gell-Mann to describe the threefold set of hypothetical master particles from which all other atomic particles are derived. Example of how the perennial TRIAD shows up in physics, as much as it does in metaphysical system-building.

QUEST From Latin *quaerere*, "to seek, ask, inquire," same as the root of *question*. The act of seeking, either for oneself or for one's purpose (see C&B1

and C&B2, Prefaces). Typically, it involves entering upon a PATH of experience that does not necessarily lead to a fixed and final goal, because the very process of traversing the path evolves into an ongoing act of self-discovery. The quest is a developmental and educational process, which in our time calls for the discipline of PATHFINDING, due to the enormous array of options that face the seeker. Through questing, one comes to a sense of purpose as well as a state of enlightenment regarding one's relationship to God, to self, to others, and to the events of one's time. One image of the quest is the LABYRINTH (see Preamble). In the Western Mysteries, the quest (usually of the hero or demigod) represents in story form the process of individuation. See also VISION QUEST, SERVICE.

QUETZALCOATL (KETZ-ahl-KWAT-ul) Aztec, "feathered serpent." In Central American myth, the divine teacher and initiator of the Toltec civilization; example of a MANU. One of the many RETURNING GODS in world myth, though a special and peculiar case who was equated by the Aztecs, either through deception or mistaken identity, with the conquistador Hernán Cortés, who subdued them and annihilated their civilization. Good example of myth taking revenge on history.

QUICHÉ (KEE-chay) Guatemalan Indians descended from the ancient Maya. Through their tradition the marvelous epic of the POPOL VUH has come down to us.

R

RABELAIS, FRANÇOIS (RAB-uh-lay) (1483–1553) French doctor and author of *Gargantua and Pantagruel,* a comic masterpiece of bawdy excess. Example of a WESTERN MASTER who passes off occultism and deep cultural instruction as an amusement; from whom Aleister Crowley pirated his "Law of Thelema": "Do what thou wilt."

RADHA (RAHD-dah) In Hindu eroticism, the supreme love mate of Krishna, the dancing God.

RADHA SOAMI (RAHD-dah SWA-mee) Sanskrit, "Lord of the Soul." A devotional movement founded in the late nineteenth century by Shri Dayal, stressing meditation on the cosmic sound-current (SHABDA) and special dietary rules.

RADIESTHESIA (RAY-dee-ess-THEE-see-ah) Literally, the feeling *(esthesia)* of *radi*ations. Loosely, any technique using the mind, body, or specific tools (such as a pendulum) to detect radiations not acknowledged by conventional science, such as the vibrations generated by an underground water supply. More specifically, mental or mechanical manipulation of biological processes, using special detection machines to monitor bodily currents believed to radiate from the nervous system like a magnetic field from a magnet.

RADIONICS (Ray-dee-ON-iks) Another term for radiesthesia, but especially referring to the direct stimulation of unknown or supersensible currents as well as the detection of them.

RAINBOW Symbol of the covenant between God and humanity (Old Testament, Genesis 9:12). Biblical image taken up by D. H. Lawrence in his novel of modern love, *The Rainbow,* and converted into a symbol of the many-hued passion uniting woman and man—a good example of the transposition of religious feeling into the realm of personal intimacy typical of Romanticism.

RAMAKRISHNA (RAH-mah-KRISH-nah) Indian saint from Bengal (1836–1886), one of the first spiritual masters known to the West. Noted for his belief in the unity of all religions, his reformist view of Hinduism, and his ecstatic devotion to the Great Mother, KALI, in her loving aspect.

RAMANA MAHARSHI (Rah-MAHN-ah Ma-HAR-shee) Indian master of Arunachala, Madras, (1879–1950) known for his radical method of directing the seeker back to the self. Introduced to the West through the writings of Paul Brunton in 1935 (C&B3.8).

RAMAYANA (Rah-ma-YAHN-nah) Sanskrit epic poem by Valmiki, describing the adventures of Prince Rama, an Avatar of the God Vishnu. See also MAHABHARATA.

RAPHAEL-NOVALIS IMPULSE A term coined by Rudolf Steiner, in reference to the Renaissance painter Raphael Santi, said to have been John the Baptist in a previous incarnation, and to have lived again as the German Romantic poet NOVALIS. (In esoteric shorthand, the linking of names with a hyphen indicates the continuity of an impulse working progressively through successive lives.) Meant to indicate an emergent potential for directing one's life according to the truth embodied in what one invents, rather than the truth one derives from actual events. The power of cocreation expressed through the genius of moral invention, or moral imagination as Steiner called it. Pretending or make-believe as a transformational tool. In esoteric terms, the full maturation of manas. See also MYTHMAKING and E2.3 on the glorification of the INNER LIFE in the Decadence.

RAPTURE (1) Ecstasy, bliss, complete surrender to joy. In some Eastern teachings and among the Christian mystics such as Saint Teresa, the feeling that comes from experiencing ultimate unity with God; the sensation of total, all-consuming pleasure—ANANDA, God-ecstasy. In Tantra, the ground-sensation of actual corporeal existence. (2) In fundamentalist Christianity, a special term for the state of the blessed, the chosen ones who are lifted up to heaven with Christ in a rapturous moment of escape from damnation at the LAST JUDGMENT.

RATIONAL EMOTIVE THERAPY A method of self-actualization developed by Albert Ellis, stressing rational management of the emotions.

RAY See SEVEN RAYS.

READING Common term for the process (often a dialogue) in which one individual interprets the attitudes, emotions, health, or even the entire life-situation of another, or responds to questions by means of psychic powers or certain tools; for instance, astrological reading, Tarot reading, psychic reading.

REBIRTHING A technique that uses expansive breathing (guided by a therapist) to deepen the conscious awareness of body, mind, and emotions, and sometimes to afford access to memories of past lives in order to release their emotional hold and become open to a complete sense of renewal, facing life on totally fresh terms, with previous mental and emotional habits eliminated. Originated by Leonard Orr and Sandra Devi.

RECOVERY (E20) Regaining one's true self. The task of seeking and restoring that which has been lost, denied, or damaged, both in the outer personality and the innermost self, due to inadequate or abusive treatment during childhood. Closely associated with the work of overcoming one or another kind of ADDICTION. Since the late 1960s, a group-supported self-help movement dedicated to fostering self-integration and sanity, following the pattern of the TWELVE-STEP PROGRAMS. Involves the work of reparenting and healing the inner child.

REDEMPTION The process of making up what has been lost or repairing what has been damaged. A main theme in Western seeking, closely associated with the paradigm of the FALL. In Gnosticism and alchemy, the moral imperative to restore our distorted and incomplete world to the full actuality of its potential. In recovery, the act of claiming and developing the lost potential that was not actualized in the first place due to basic needs having been unfulfilled in childhood. In short, the belief that we must be fixed before we can truly and fully be at one with life, contrasting with the Eastern view that our innate oneness with all things merely has to be found (E2.4).

REFLEXOLOGY In the healing arts, the treatment of diseases and maintenance of good health by application of pressure and massage to key points in the body, such as the soles of the feet, which are supposed to be connected to the involuntary functions (breathing, digestion); thus, the stimulation and balancing of these functions by working on the accessible pressure points (reflex points).

REICH, WILHELM Austrian-born radical psychoanalyst (1897–1957), who departed from the method of his teacher, Freud, into daring explorations of human sexuality and healing. Discoverer of ORGONE, author of practical textbooks on "human physics," which were banned in his time (C&B3.15). Originator of the Reichian work, encompassing new approaches to psychoanalysis *(Character Analysis)*, sexual theory *(The Function of the Orgasm)*, sociological theory *(The Mass Psychology of Fascism)*, bioenergetics, and extensive studies in the bodily and planetary dynamics of orgone.

REIKI (RAY-kee) A technique of bodywork for manipulating and balancing the ki, or CHI.

REINCARNATION (E21) The appearance of the same entity over and over again in different lifetimes, due to the capacity of the human soul to reembody itself—either voluntarily or by the compulsion of cyclic forces: through love or necessity. See also SERIAL REINCARNATION.

REJUVENATION Restoring to youth, as in the practices of Taoism and alchemy, based on the belief that the human body can be maintained in a condition of perfect health and youth, or even that the aging process itself can be totally arrested. See also LONGEVITY/PROLONGEVITY.

RELATIVITY THEORY The most famous theory of modern physics, proposed in two phases by Albert Einstein (1879–1955): Special Relativity (1905), stating that the velocity of LIGHT is invariant for all observers; and General Relativity (1916), stating that gravitation is a local effect of mass on the curvature of SPACE-TIME. Introduced a new paradigm, presenting the picture of a universe integrated into a holistic field, but nonhierarchical and without absolute mechanical laws (as in Newtonian physics, the paradigm it replaced). In the new physics, often interpreted by analogy to the psychological outlook of Eastern mysticism, because of the way it restores the observer to the realm of nature. Relativity means relative to when and where the observer is located in the weavework of space-time.

RELIGION   Literally, the act of binding (*ligio,* as in "ligament") to what came before (*re-,* as in "reverse, rewind"). Thus, the process or method of binding-back to a former condition or time and making what happened then the basis for what one does now; for instance, preserving the past by enacting a ritual to commemorate it, such as the Sacrament of Communion in the Catholic Mass. See E2 on traditional religions.

RELIGIOUS SCIENCE   A movement founded in 1938 by Ernest Holmes, also called Science of Mind, stressing the positive use of the mind for moral and material self-improvement. Adapts the message of Jesus Christ to the idiom of New Thought. An example of PARA-CHRISTIANITY. Compare with CHRISTIAN SCIENCE.

REM   Rapid Eye Movement. Observed to occur during sleep as an indication of dreaming.

REMOTE VIEWING   Observing things at a distance, without the aid of any instruments other than the human mind and whatever psychic powers may be latent in it. One of the hottest areas of research in parapsychology, of great interest to the government for its military and intelligence potential; for instance, in locating nuclear submarines.

REPARENTING   In recovery, the process of doing for oneself what one's parents were not able to do, such as developing a sense of self-respect, meeting vital dependencies, and in general fostering a strong and healthy relationship to oneself and the world in those areas where this relationship was not adequately supported and nurtured by one's parents.

RESURRECTION   Raising from the dead. A mytheme found in dozens of instances in world mythology, its earliest form illustrated in the cyclic return of the vegetation Gods of the Middle East (Attis, Tammus, Adonis, Osiris). In both esoteric and orthodox Christianity, the act of corporeal revitalization after death, performed by Christ and manifested in the Resurrection Body, which then (in the esoteric view, exclusively) serves as a kind of master cell or seed-nucleus imbued with regenerative powers available to heal and harmonize the entire ETHERIC WEB of the Earth. Contrast with SPIRITUAL DEATH.

RETREAT   Either the act of secluding oneself for the purpose of introspection and spiritual growth, or the place where such seclusion is sought. One may go on a retreat to an ASHRAM, a holy site (such as Lourdes), or the wilderness. The purpose of a retreat may be to gain serenity, study a certain subject or art, or improve one's health and sense of well-being. Compare with VISION QUEST.

RETURNING GOD/HERO In worldwide mythology, a theme expressing the belief that certain Gods and heroes who have died or disappeared will eventually return: such as King Arthur of the Round Table, Quetzalcoatl in the Toltec/Aztec myth, and the best-known example, Christ, supposed to reappear at the end of time in the grand scenario of the Second Coming. On returning mortals, see REINCARNATION.

REVELATION (1) In the old-fashioned sense, anything taught or shown directly by a superhuman power or God, such as the revelation received by Moses on Mount Sinai. More commonly today, a life-changing insight or any personal realization of vast and radical implications. (2) Specifically, the last book of the orthodox Christian Bible, a Gnostic/Cabalistic text of deep symbolic significance, presenting the scenario of the end of the world, or Apocalypse, and the Second Coming of Christ.

RIDER-WAITE DECK Most popular version of the Tarot, designed by Pamela Coleman Smith under the direction of Arthur Waite.

RIGHT BRAIN Generic term for the functions of the right lobe of the brain, which controls the left side of the body; believed to be nonverbal, intuitive, and "feminine" by contrast to the left brain.

RILKE, RAINER MARIA (RILL-kuh) German lyric poet (1875–1926), author of *The Duino Elegies, The Sonnets to Orpheus,* and profound personal reflections on human suffering, solitude, creativity, and love (C&B3.3). See also TURNINGS.

RINPOCHE (Rim-POH-shay) Tibetan, "precious, venerable." A term of respect applied to a man of high attainment in Tibetan Buddhism.

RISHI (RISH-shee) Sanskrit, from the root *dris-,* "to see." In ancient Indian religion, a wise man or seer of high attainments, especially supernatural powers such as direct vision of and intercourse with the Supreme Being, Brahma. Traditionally cited as the head of a LINEAGE of spiritual masters stretching from prehistorical times down to the present. In Hindu mythology, one of an original group of seven Rishis whose wives are often associated with the seven stars in the constellation of the Pleiades. Exact counterpart to the Western Magus.

RISING SIGN In astrology, the zodiacal SIGN located on the eastern horizon of the birthplace at the moment of birth, indicating the path of self-evolvement or the kind of growth process necessary for bringing personal identity to mature definition.

RITE/RITUAL Any act that serves to establish or affirm a relationship between a person and whatever he believes in; for instance, prayer is a rite of communication with God, as voting is a rite of democratic conviction.

RNA See DNA.

ROERICH, NICHOLAS (ROW-rik, or RUR-rik) (1874–1947)

Russian-born mystic, author, occultist, and luminist painter, self-declared representative of the Great White Brotherhood, husband of Helena Roerich (Agni Yoga), key figure in the planetary folklore of the twentieth century. Established the Pax Cultura for international peace in 1929, explored the Himalayas and Gobi extensively in search of Shambhala and evidence of ISSA.

R O L F I N G   A form of bodywork using intense massage of muscles and tissues to achieve total restructuralization. Originated by Ida Rolf, a biochemist, who viewed the body as a plastic medium whose natural flexibility, lost due to muscular tension, can be restored by structural integration.

R O M A N T I C I S M   (E22) European-rooted artistic, literary, spiritual, and political movement, lasting roughly from 1775 to 1840, with enormous repercussions throughout the rest of the world, right down to our time. A movement led by a small band of artistic geniuses and moral renegades, who proposed a number of fantastic possibilities for humanity without leaving a clear and coherent program for how to achieve them. In many respects, the forerunners of the new spirituality. See also TRANSCENDENTALISM.

R O O T   R A C E   In Theosophy, old-fashioned term for racial strains going back to Atlantis, from which all current peoples of the earth have originated.

R O S E N C R E U T Z ,   C H R I S T I A N   (ROSE-en-croitz) Half-mythical, half-historical person, supreme master of the Western Mystery tradition. Often attributed with an impressive string of incarnations: as Cain (who slew Abel); as Hiram (the master builder of the Temple of Solomon, ca 950 B.C.); as Lazarus of the New Testament; as an unnamed master around 1250 A.D.; as Christian Rosencreutz (supposed to have founded the current Rosicrucian Order in 1459); as the count of SAINT GERMAIN, also known as Prince Ragozcy of Transylvania (1710–?). One of the most famous characters in planetary folklore.

R O S E T T A   S T O N E   Basalt slab found in the Nile delta in 1799 and deciphered by the French genius Jean-François Champollion in 1821, thus providing the initial clues to the meaning of the Egyptian hieroglyphs and opening the way for the retrieval of ANCIENT WISDOM. Crucial factor in the Great Transmission (E2.3).

R O S H I   Japanese, "revered master." Honorific title of a Zen master.

R O S I C R U C I A N   M A N I F E S T O E S   Three documents (*Fama Fraternitatis, Confessio rosae crucis,* and *Chymical Wedding of Christian Rosencreutz*) released to the public in 1616 in southern Germany, declaring the existence of the secret society of the Rosicrucians and its aim to establish a utopian state by implementation of its ideals and occult principles. Cause of a huge political scandal at the time. Also, the beginning of the decline of European occultism, due to public exposure of what had previously been secret, conspiratorial efforts. See also SECRET SOCIETIES.

R O S I C R U C I A N S   An occult organization, having its prototype in the

Mystery Schools of ancient Egypt, said to have been reformulated around 1250 for the purpose of guiding and educating humanity as it advanced into the trials and troubles of the modern age. Their symbol is a cross covered with fresh-bloomed roses—referring to the mystery of the Resurrection, in which they are said to participate in a special, intimate way. A society of WESTERN MASTERS, often described as working behind the scenes as agents in leading humanity through crucial phases of its development; for instance, in the framing of the Declaration of Independence, designing the dollar (E1.1), initiating such scientific advances as the steam engine, and the "accidental discovery" of LSD. See also Max HEINDEL and A.M.O.R.C.

ROUND TABLE Archetype of the Solar Mysteries: a circle of twelve units or rays, represented by twelve warrior-priests who embody the twelve different efficacies or virtues of the SOLAR LOGOS. In the Celtic Revival and the ARTHURIAN PATH, the order of knights associated with King Arthur.

RUMI (Roo-mee) Short for Jalal ed-Din Rumi, Persian Sufi and poet supreme (1207–1273), known for his ecstatic surrender to the wonderful and paradoxical anguish of life. Good example of a Sufi master: half saint, half trickster, dreamer, and drunkard, infatuated with God, all too human.

RUNES From Middle English *roun* > Old English *run,* "a secret letter" > the IE root *reu-,* "a hoarse or whispered sound." In the singular, a letter of an obscure alphabet found inscribed on stones in Scandinavia, the British Isles, and some parts of Europe. In the plural, the secret alphabet itself, a kind of hieroglyphic system used in the Celtic, Nordic, and Germanic cultures from prehistoric times. Said to have been received by the God-man Woden when he underwent the ordeal of hanging for nine days and nights on the WORLD-TREE. The script of a magical language, consisting of sixteen to thirty or more characters, used for divination. Popular item in the Celtic Revival.

RYOANJI (Ree-oh-AHN-jee) Japanese, temple of the "dragon's repose." Famous Zen temple with a garden of rocks and raked gravel, in Kyoto, Japan.

S

SACRED From Latin *sacer*, "holy" > Sanskrit root *sac-*, "to be power-ful" (same as in *sacrifice*). Holy, divine, to be revered because it embodies or expresses a power beyond the human realm. Rediscovering the sacred is a main theme of the new spirituality (see Afterword), approached by one angle through mythological studies revealing how the sacred was understood and expressed by many cultures in the past. See also SHAKTI.

SACRED ARCHITECTURE In geomancy, the tradition of con-structing temples and churches, such as the Gothic cathedrals, according to a standard set of ratios, geometrical figures, and mathematical formulas (CANON)—so named in the belief that these formulas have been handed down to humanity by divine beings. See also ARCHEO-ASTRONOMY.

SACRED ART A vast area of world art, including far more than the well-known examples of stained-glass windows illustrating scenes from the Bible. Encompasses many different genres of art, down through the ages, in which occult and spiritual themes and images are represented. Although modern art, for the most part, is conspicuously lacking in the sacred, it was widely and outrageously portrayed in the art of the SYMBOLIST MOVEMENT, a brief prefigu-ration of the New Age that flourished at the end of the nineteenth century in Europe.

SACRED DANCE A tradition found in many cultures throughout the world, from the hula of Polynesia to the crane dance of ancient Crete to the Sun dance of the American Indians. The use of ritual movement, usually including music and song, to affirm participation in the great dance of creation. Also, mythic image represented in the Hindu icons of Krishna and Shiva dancing, in the twenty-first Trump of the Tarot ("The World"), and countless other instances. Revived in some modern occult schools, notably the GURDJIEFF WORK.

SACRED LANGUAGES Languages originating in prehistorical times, many of which are now "dead": Sanskrit, Prakrit, Pali, Avestan, Egyptian hieroglyphs. Believed to have been given to humanity by the Gods and used, at first, exclusively for religious purposes. Latin and biblical Hebrew are two examples of dead languages still in use in religious services. Curiously, Aramaic, spoken by Christ, was merely a local Palestinian dialect, not a sacred language. Other languages, like those spoken by the American Indians, are still sacred, orally alive, and have in some cases never yet been converted into written form (E18).

SACRED MUSIC The tradition of using music to contact the Gods or raise oneself to a higher level of consciousness, or to express experiences and inspirations of a spiritual and transcendental nature; for instance, in Hinduism, where the basic forms of musical composition are contained in the Vedas, ancient religious texts supposed to have been received by inspiration from the Gods. In European tradition, often connected with the God Apollo and the ninefold MUSE.

SACRED PROSTITUTION Important concept in worldwide EROTICISM. An age-old tradition in the Orient, where sexual intercourse was treated as a rite of unification between man and God(dess), or as a means for the male to be initiated into awareness of psychic/spiritual realms, as in the case of Gilgamesh (C&B2.1). Also common in Egypt, the Middle East (especially in the cults of the Great Mother, represented by Aphrodite, Cybele, Astarte, Mylitta), and the Mediterranean (in the cult of Eros and Aphrodite at Corinth). In the form of temple prostitution, probably developed as a formalization of fertility rites from the time of universal matriarchy. Perpetuated in the practice of SEXUAL YOGA.

SACRED SITES In geomancy, general term for any place on the earth where power is concentrated, either due to the special geographic and telluric potency of the landscape, or due to its having been the location of a temple or sanctuary in the past. Examples: Chartres, Glastonbury, medicine wheels, pyramids, Palenque, Newgrange, Stonehenge (all defined).

SACRIFICE From Latin *sacer,* "powerful" + *facere,* "to make": thus, "to make powerful." The process by which the will and power of the Gods is transferred to human beings, accomplished in ancient times by prayer and ritual. Exact equivalent to the modern term empowerment. See also TRANSFERENCE.

SAGE From Latin *sapere,* "to know" > IE base *sap-,* "to taste." Someone who possesses (or has tasted) spiritual wisdom, especially concerning human nature and the principles necessary to live in accord with the truth.

SAINT GERMAIN A mysterious and fabulous personality, reputed to be the greatest of the WESTERN MASTERS, whose existence is actually confirmed by some historical evidence—for instance, diaries and letters of members of the European aristocracy during the time of Marie Antoinette. The leading figure in the occult brotherhood of the Rosicrucians, attributed with immense wealth, extraordinary knowledge, and the capacity to remain forever young. See also Christian ROSENCREUTZ.

SALVATION   From Sanskrit *sarva,* root of "save," "salvage," "safe." Literally, the process of making whole, completing that which is unfinished or restoring that which is lost. In Christianity and the Western Mystery tradition, the ultimate goal of human striving, in contrast to the view prevalent in Eastern teachings, where Enlightenment or liberation takes its place. See E2.4 on the crucial distinction between these conflicting paradigms. See also SERVICE.

SAMADHI   (Sah-MAH-dee) Sanskrit, from *sam-,* "unite" + *adha,* "foundation, root, source"; thus, to be united or identified with the root of all existence, God, the Ground, the Source, et cetera. In Yoga, the ultimate state of spiritual perfection in which the individual self is absorbed into the All. According to Patanjali, may be of two kinds: without "seed" or content, as a state of total and selfless absorption in God, knowing nothing; or with "seed," as in Dante's vision of the Divine Rose, an instance of cosmic consciousness, knowing everything at once. See also SUPERCONSCIOUSNESS.

SAMSARA   (Sahm-SAHR-uh) Sanskrit, from *samsri-,* "wandering, passing through." In Buddhist teachings, the inevitable state of confusion and blind, repetitious behavior suffered by all SENTIENT BEINGS who have not yet realized the nature of their own minds and thereby gained the release of Enlightenment. The endless cycle of death and rebirth, a no-win situation in which pleasure and pain mutually reinforce each other. Usually contrasted to Nirvana, though in the paradoxical doctrine of nonattainment, Nirvana and Samsara are described as one (E30).

SAMSKARA   (Sam-SCAR-rah) Sanskrit, from *samskri-,* "script, inscription." In Buddhist psychology, the karmic script that determines all human activities and attitudes; the set of automatic predispositions that result from actions done in former lives; the script of one's life, which is mechanically, compulsively performed until one is able to erase it—or, by Western standards, CHANGE it.

SANSKRIT   From *sanskrita,* "perfect," with the implication that it comes from a superhuman source, the Gods. One of the oldest SACRED LANGUAGES of the world, originally used by the ancient Hindus to preserve their religious doctrines and the mythology of the Aryan people. The main Indo-European (IE) language instrumental in the transmission of Eastern philosophy and religious teachings to the West (E2.3), so that today hundreds of words coming into common usage, from ASHRAM to ZEN, are pure Sanskrit or derivatives from it. Likewise, a great many common, nonesoteric words go back to Sanskrit roots; for instance, *please,* from Middle English *plaisen* > Latin *placere,* "to calm, soothe" > IE root *plak-* "flat, smooth." See also INDO-EUROPEAN.

SANTERÍA   (Sahn-teh-REE-uh) Spanish, "worship of the saints." Modern folk religion originated in Cuba by African slaves who identified the Roman Catholic saints with their own tribal Gods. Includes the practice of casting spells and animal sacrifice. Large followings in Miami and New York.

SANYASSIN (Sun-YASS-sin) Sanskrit, "one who renounces." Someone who gives up the ordinary involvements of life to become totally dedicated to self-realization or to follow the path designated by a spiritual master. Compare with SEEKER.

SARMOUN DERG (SAHR-moon Durg) Secret order of Arabian teachers, cited by Gurdjieff as the source of his access to a secret lineage of Arabian/Sufi wisdom, including sacred dance.

SASQUATCH "Giant" in the language of the Salish Indians of British Columbia. A huge, elusive, apelike creature spotted in the northwest U.S. and around Mount Shasta, California, believed to be a leftover from a previous stage of human evolution. Also called Bigfoot due to the size of its tracks. Often compared to the Abominable Snowman of Tibet.

SATAN From Hebrew *satan*, "enemy, adversary." The arch-foe of human evolution, who opposes everything that leads to individual fulfillment and the ultimate happiness of the human race; the epitome and active agent of separation and devolution toward a subhuman state of physical and moral slavery. Identical with AHRIMAN, to be distinguished from Lucifer, or the Devil. The spirit of DENIAL.

SATANISM The belief and practice of taking sides with Satan; that is, opting for power over others by separation from the common lot of sharing and suffering. The ultimate power trip, enacted through final and complete dissociation from the rest of humanity, except to exploit it through CONTROL. An age-old tradition that is said to have originated among the Turanian culture of Atlantis and assumed its present form in the TYPHONIC CURRENT of Egypt, around 2500 B.C. Revived in the late nineteenth century in certain circles of the DECADENCE and in contemporary America in the Church of Satan, founded by Anton Sandor Le Vey in 1966. See also PENTAGRAM.

Can be classified in three degrees: first, dedication to total control of others through sexual magic and black occultism, including human sacrifice—that is, the actual practice of EVIL; second, exploitation and manipulation of others through the use of suggestion and latent powers; third, hedonistic self-seeking, glorification of personal passions and selfish desires, worship of the animal instincts, with a strong dose of harmless blasphemy into the bargain. See also E1.5.

SATCHITANANDA (SAHT-chit-uh-NAHN-dah) Sanskrit for the triple unity of being at one with the truth of God *(sat)*, living in the full light of unconditional awareness *(chit)*, and enjoying the state of complete, imperturbable bliss *(ananda)* that results from this. In Yoga, complete spiritual attainment. Also, the name of a yogi who was famous during the 1960s, Swami Satchitananda.

SATORI (Sah-TOR-ree) Japanese, "sudden illumination." In Zen, the experience of sudden and complete awareness of the SELF-NATURE, the essence of one's own mind seen to be identical with the Buddha-mind. Described in many famous incidents as happening by accident or triggered by a quick, totally unexpected sensation, such as when the monk coming back from the well at night looks down at the moon reflected in the water just as the bottom of the wooden pail drops out. Sudden Enlightenment. An Eastern variety of COSMIC CONSCIOUSNESS.

S A T S A N G   Sanskrit, a gathering of the community *(sangha)* of all those who are dedicated to realize the ultimate truth of being *(sat);* in short, any religious gathering for ritual observance or to receive teachings, practices, et cetera.

S A T T V A B U D D I E S   Slang applied to the BODHISATTVAS by those who know them in the deep intimacy of being treated as if they were their equals.

S C H I Z O P H R E N I A   (Skits-oh-FREH-nee-uh) From Greek *schizein,* "to cut, cleave" + *phren,* "mind" (conceived by the Greeks as located in the chest). Split-mindedness, a condition of radical disintegration of the human ego, due to its capacity to imagine itself as more than one entity. Multiple identity, a condition apparently suffered by many Romantics, who saw it as an ordeal of madness for advancing into new dimensions of artistic and creative intensity.

S C I E N T O L O G Y   Movement founded by L. Ron Hubbard (1911–1982), originally presented in fictional form, proposing a method to erase all previous behavioral and attitudinal imprinting and free the individual into a state of God-like empowerment, or being "clear." Also called DIANETICS.

S E A S O N S   In former times, considered as moments for humanity to commune with higher powers and undergo a renewal of soul-forces. See also EQUINOXES, SOLSTICES.

S E C O N D   C O M I N G   In traditional Christianity, the promise made by Christ to return to Earth; thus, a second advent as a follow-up to the original Incarnation. Though indicated only by the briefest clues in the words of Christ himself, the theme was taken by early Christians as a fulfillment of the Hebrew scenario of a world ending, or LAST JUDGMENT, set at some time in the indefinite future, with Christ cast in the role of the wrathful judge of the world, damning all the sinners. Renewed and reformulated today as a mytheme of the New Age, expressing a general sense of IMMANENCE, the possibility of divinity awakening in all of us, the feeling that we stand on the threshold of a new era in which some vast and radical change in human affairs may be accomplished. Often explained by a complex visualization of the convergence that may result as humanity approaches a state of organic and unified awareness, in which all individuals can experience themselves as cells in a single organism whose totality of life-forces is concentrated in a specific being, the Christos, understood as the Planetary Spirit, or ideal focal point of PLANETARIZATION. A major theme of the New Age, as well as a huge obsession among Christian fundamentalists. See also RESURRECTION.

S E C R E T   C H I E F S   Variation on the theme of spiritual masters in its conspiratorial form, cited by the founders of the GOLDEN DAWN as the authorities behind their efforts.

SECRET SOCIETIES The name given to small local groups that appeared in Europe from 1600 onward, claiming to be latter-day extensions of the Mystery Schools of antiquity. Also called occult brotherhoods, such as the Rosicrucians, Masons, and the Golden Dawn. Now discredited for the most part, or else accepted as totally conventional and unmysterious—as the Masons are classed, in mainstream America, practically along with the Rotarians and the PTA.

SECT From Latin *sequi,* "follow." Any group organized around a body of beliefs or practices and most often self-defined as followers of a spiritual leader, guru, or master. Often, a sect is a lesser part or *sect*ion of a large-scale religion: for instance, the Vaishnavas, or Krishna-worshipers, are a sect within orthodox Hinduism. See also CULT.

SEEK/SEEKER From IE root *sag-,* "to track down, trace." V., to search for truth on one's own, and to explore the creative expression of it with others. To enter a PATH or engage in a QUEST. N., someone who is on a path of self-discovery, a course of self-actualization that includes all the knowledge earned and all the skills gained along the way. Someone open to learn what life itself has to teach, especially concerning how to unfold the INNATE. (See introductions to C&B1 and C&B2). See also GOOD LOOKING, SELF-RELIANCE.

SEER Someone possessed of extraordinary powers of perception or vision into other worlds; thus, an accomplished seeker.

SELF The core and ground of human identity, the permanent base of moment-to-moment awareness, ultimately equated in many spiritual teachings with the Supreme Being itself, God, as in the ancient formula of the VEDAS:

Atma = Brahma

The individual human entity capable of saying "I" (Atma) is identical with the infinite and all-encompassing ground-state of awareness, the One, the Source, Supreme Being, God the All-Self (Brahma).

In New Age thinking, the person viewed as who he or she really is, the "true self" with all pretenses and externally learned mechanisms stripped away. Also, the source of universality, the sense of awareness that everyone is like everyone else ("no one special"), by contrast to the sense of INDIVIDUALITY. Specifically, in Jungian work, the image of wholeness or "totality-image" as the basis of what we call God. In Buddhism, paradoxically, the "no-self": the presence of the all-observing Buddha-mind as no particular identity, rather as the ground of all perceiving and all that is perceived, like a mirror reflecting all appearances.

SELF-ACTUALIZATION In humanistic psychology, the term coined by Abraham Maslow for the process of living up to one's full potential as a unique human being who embodies or represents the capacities universally innate to human nature. The optimum of psychological health and INTEGRA-TION.

SELF-GUIDANCE A primary option in modern seeking, perhaps expressed in its most radical form by French existential philosopher Jean-Paul Sartre, who wrote: "For every human being, each act unfolds as if all humanity had its eyes upon him and were guiding itself by what he does." Also called self-direction, the process of learning rather than obedience, as explained in E2.1.

SELF-HELP Any method or attitude useful to the individual in developing inner potential and/or proficiency in skills for coping with the outer world; includes dozens of kinds of do-it-yourself spiritual practices such as meditation, creative visualization, bodywork, hypnosis, Yoga. Also, title of a book by Scottish journalist Samuel Smiles, published in 1859 (curiously, the same year as Darwin's *Origin of Species*), which went through many editions and was translated into more than twenty languages. Today, a common genre of best-seller, frequently concentrating on diet and exercise.

SELF-IMPORTANCE According to Castaneda, the most difficult obstacle to be faced by the warrior on the path of developing complete openness and clarity of intent. See also SOBRIETY.

SELF-INITIATION In modern Western spirituality, the paradigm of independent seeking, exemplified by the figure of PARZIVAL (C&B2.5). The process of developing one's innermost potential by learning from life itself, using methods and techniques at most as guidelines and provisional tools, over against the traditional way of complete identification with a pregiven teaching and program for self-realization. See also LABYRINTH.

SELF-NATURE In Buddhism, Taoism, and Zen, the innermost simple ESSENCE of anything or anyone, realized by eliminating all that distracts from it and all attachments to it. Also called Buddha-nature.

SELF-REALIZATION Loosely, the path or task of discovering one's true nature, including both who one is and what belongs originally and innately to oneself. A term initially coined by English Romantic poet and philosopher Samuel Taylor Coleridge around 1795, and then brought into use for specific application to spiritual seeking by Swami Yogananda, one of the first spiritual masters to come to the West.

SELF-REALIZATION FELLOWSHIP Movement for teaching Yoga and Vedanta in the West, founded by Swami PARAMAHANSA YOGA-NANDA.

SELF-RELIANCE Emersonian principle of independence, typical of rugged individualism in American Romanticism (C&B2.10). Serves as a valuable criterion for right seeking, by directing the seeker back to the INNATE.

SENOI (Sen-NOY) A tribe of twelve thousand living in the central mountains of the Malay Peninsula, unique for using dreams in the determination of their social and moral practices. See JUNGIAN/SENOI.

SENTIENT BEINGS In Buddhism, ordinary human beings who are limited to perceiving intermediately through their senses, which give them a separatistic and distorted view of the world, rather than immediately through the Buddha-mind, to which the original nature of all things is directly and primarily evident. Usually contrasted to the Buddhas or Bodhisattvas, sentient beings are misled by the evidence of the senses and suffer profound confusion in SAMSARA due to their inability to grasp the true nature of the PHENOMENAL, which is that all things and beings are mere reflections in the One Mind, while in reality there are no separate things and events to be reflected. Imagine a mirror with an image in it, such as a tree—but no tree in front of the mirror to cast the image. Such is the way the Buddha-mind holds in mirrorlike clarity the image of a world that does not exist outside of the beholding awareness in which it is reflected. See also COMPASSION.

SEPHIRA/SEPHIROTH (SEF-ir-rah, SEF-ir-roth) Hebrew, "number, cipher." In the CABALA and MAGIC, a point of emanation or the emanation itself, supposed to operate in forming all aspects of creation; principles, code-symbols in the world-system of ancient wisdom.

SEPHIROTH/SEPHIRA Hebrew, "cipher, number." In the Cabala and magic, centers of creative emanations, nodal points in the dynamic pattern of the universe, where God-powers are concentrated. Specifically, points on the diagram of the TREE OF LIFE, taken to represent psychic/astral planes or potentialities of inner development.

SERENDIPITY A word coined in English around 1750, from the Sanskrit name for Sri Lanka, *sarandvipa,* in reference to a Persian fairy tale in which a prince and his entourage set out for that country and, while on the way, undergo a series of wonderful distractions and detours. Happenstance, a course of fortunate accidents—or the easy, accepting attitude that goes along with them. The main desideratum of seeking in the Western way, equatable to a happy, haphazard jaunt through the labyrinth. Contrast with SERENITY.

SERENITY The state of complete peace and tranquillity achieved by those who accept life unconditionally, on its own terms, which are shifting and unpredictable; therefore a state of deep calm, which is, however, not static but perfectly flexible in its spontaneous adjustment to whatever happens. The main desideratum of seeking in the Eastern way.

SERIAL REINCARNATION The process of living a succession of human lives in chronologically sequent historical time, attributed to the WESTERN MASTERS, who are supposedly able to direct the course of their incarnations by conscious intent and to locate themselves strategically in different historical eras and cultures according to the progressive impulses they wish to impart.

SERVATION   Technical term in comparative mythology for the action in which Gods serve humanity by imparting knowledge or teaching skills. A mytheme that appears in thousands of instances, such as the giving of fire by Prometheus in Greek myth, or the giving of the sacred pipe and its ritual by White Buffalo Woman in the folklore of the Plains Indians. Proper function of the MANU, exemplified in Fu Hsi and Thoth, among countless others.

SERVICE   Commitment to cocreation, including the salvation of humanity and healing of the Earth. The particular and unique task of fulfilling one's destiny. To be distinguished from DHARMA in Eastern spirituality: not a duty assumed but a free choice rooted in love, determined by no other principle than the creative vision of the one who undertakes it. The ideal of Western spirituality, expressed in the Grail Question asked by Parzival of his uncle Amfortas, the wounded Grail King, who represents suffering humanity: "How can I serve thee?"

SETH   Entity channeled by Jane Roberts from 1963 to 1984. Source of a massive volume of teachings in esoteric psychology. See also CHANNELING.

SEVEN, LAW OF/SEVEN RAYS   In some esoteric teachings, such as Theosophy, a system used for describing everything from human psychology (sevenfold anatomy, septenary constitution of man) to cosmic evolution (Seven Planes, Globes, Rounds, et cetera). An archetype or mytheme in numerical form, representing the consistent pattern by which unmanifest spirit translates itself into manifestation. Widely and stupefyingly applied, for instance, in the works of Alice A. Bailey.

SEXUAL YOGA   In Tantra, the practice of ritual postures and mental/emotional concentration involving the use of sexual intercourse as a form of meditation (MAITHUNA), with the aim of imitating the original polaric model (SHIVA/SHAKTI) of creation, and returning to the ecstasy of pure being or reunification with God. See also TAO OF SEX.

SHABDA   (SHUB-dah) Sanskrit, "primal sound current." In the ancient teachings of Hindu Tantra, the vibratory power of pure sound conceived as the originating and shaping force in all creation. The generative sound current that produces all phenomena, all life-forms and entities.

SHABDA-BRAHMAN   (SHUB-dah-BRAH-mun)   The   infinite ground-potential of the universe; the Godhead conceived as a boundless wellspring of pure sound, expressed in the mantra *aum*.

SHADOW   In the Jungian work, the dark side of one's personality, a composite of all one hates and denies, which often appears by PROJECTION in the person and actions of someone else. Compare with DOUBLE and GUARDIAN OF THE THRESHOLD.

SHAKERS   Heretical religious sect, established in America in 1774 by Ann Lee, an Englishwoman taken by the members to be the second embodiment of Christ on Earth. Remembered today for the simplicity and stark elegance of their furnishings. See E1.1.

SHAKESPEARE See BACON/SHAKESPEARE.

SHAKTI (SHAHK-tee) Sanskrit, from the root *sac-*, "to be powerful," same as the root of *sacred, sacrifice.* In Hindu and Buddhist cosmology and psychology, the root-power that materializes the universe, conceived as feminine, by contrast to the power that observes the universe, the passive but all-witnessing consciousness called Shiva in Hinduism, and Buddha in Buddhism. The supreme Goddess, or Devi, source of the Mother Wisdom, often depicted as dispensing the formative forces of creation in the form of letters or discrete sound-units (i.e., increments of SHABDA). See SHIVA/SHAKTI. When transmitted directly from a master, by either touch or gaze, this root-power is sometimes released in a massive jolt called shaktipat.

SHAKYAMUNI (Shah-kyah-MOON-nee) Sanskrit designation of the historical Buddha, as a sage *(muni)* belonging to the clan of the Shakyas, a group of landowners in Central India, sixth century B.C. See also GAUTAMA, SIDDHARTHA.

SHAMANISM (E23) (SHAH-man-izm or SHAY-man-izm) Russian (Tungusic dialect) *shaman,* from Prakrit *shamana,* "monk, ascetic, one who exhausts the life-forces in supernatural feats." Perhaps the oldest form of practical spirituality in the world, originating in the time of Ice Age people, going back as far as 35,000 B.C. The practice of trance and bodiless travel to other dimensions, or the subjugation of evil forces and the casting of spells through intense feats of concentration and superelevation of the vital forces. Virtually a worldwide practice.

SHAMBHALA (Shahm-BAHL-lah) A mythical kingdom often associated geographically with the remote interior of the Gobi Desert; said to be a kind of secret headquarters for the spiritual powers who oversee the course of human evolution. The oldest indications of it appear in Tibetan folk religion, but in recent times it has been taken up into the popular mythology of the New Age movement. Compare with AVALON.

SHAME (1) In mythology and esoteric psychology, the negative side effect of the gift of Lucifer, who endowed humanity with the God-like ego-sense in a premature way—out of wanting us to become like Gods, so the story goes, before giving us the chance to become truly human and thus have a solid grounding for the Godseed to mature. (2) In recovery, the sense of being a mistake, in contrast to guilt, which is the sense of having made a mistake. The primary emotion of not being enough, not good enough, flawed, imperfect, which stifles and suffocates all efforts to evolve our true potential, and comes to expression in "shame-based" reactions, such as the feeling of not deserving (love, success, recognition, you name it). Contrast with AWE.

SHAPE-SHIFTING In shamanism, the act of transforming oneself into an animal or other nonhuman creature, or, less often, into another type of human being. Often attributed as an evil capacity to witches and such, but more appropriately viewed as the playful act of the TRICKSTER. Occurs in a famous scene in Castaneda's second book, *A Separate Reality,* as well as in a little-known instance featuring Christ as the shape-shifter, in the Gnostic "Acts of John."

SHEATH   Old-fashioned term for a body (physical, etheric, astral, et cetera) as a vehicle of manifestation and expression.

SHINTO   Japanese, from Chinese *shin-,* "spirit" and *tao,* "way." The indigenous folk religion of Japan, a combination of nature and ancestor worship, characterized by stark and beautiful ceremony. The state religion of Japan until 1945, when the emperor Hirohito, still considered at the time to be a direct descendant of the Gods *(kami),* was forced to renounce it along with his divinity.

SHISHTA   (SHISH-tah) From Sanskrit *shish-,* "to remain, to continue." In the teachings of the ancient Brahmins, the special group of superevolved souls who carry over the fruits of evolution from one cosmic cycle to another. Adopted by Dane Rudhyar as the term for an evolutionary avant-garde or "seed-group" in his theory of planetary cocreation (E1.3).

SHIVA/SHAKTI   (SHEE-vah/SHAHK-tee) In Hindu Tantra, the image of God and Goddess in sexual union, taken as a model of the polaric forces at the root of creation. In Hindu myth, the act of primordial intercourse said to produce all things and beings in the universe—not through actual procreation, however, but purely by the emanation of the shuddering fields of sexual bliss thrown off from the bodies of the interlocked lovers. The supreme MAITHUNA, image of the Godhead as a sexual act. Pictured in Tibetan Buddhism as the union of Buddha (the static, passive, observing awareness) and consort, or SHAKTI (the active, dynamic, manifesting awareness), as in the common icon of the YAB-YUM.

SHROUD OF TURIN   A mantle imprinted with the silhouette of a human body and face, believed to have been the cloth in which the body of Jesus Christ was wrapped when taken down from the cross. Kept in a vault in a cathedral in Turin, Italy, and rarely displayed to the public, though it has been made accessible for various scientific tests to establish its authenticity—with contradictory results, of course.

SHUNYATA   (Shun-YAHT-tah) Sanskrit, "voidness," from *shunya,* "void, empty." In Tibetan and Mahayana Buddhism, the primary concept for the fundamental nature of all things as VOID. See also EMPTINESS.

SIBYL   (SIB-ul) In ancient Greek and Asia, a divinely inspired ORACLE, a woman who prophesied, often in a state of intoxication from herbal fumes or terrestrial vapors. Ancient medium or channel.

SIDDHARTHA   (Sid-DART-tah) Sanskrit, from *siddhi-,* "power, attainment" + *artha,* "goal, purpose." A designation of the historical Buddha as one who has attained a specific purpose (namely, Enlightenment) and all the powers that derive from it. The historical person of the Buddha is sometimes called Prince Siddhartha, as in the novel *Siddhartha* by Hermann Hesse. See also GAUTAMA, SHAKYAMUNI. See the Preface to Part II, "The Essays," for a comparison between Siddhartha and Parzival.

SIDDHI/SIDDHA   (SID-hee, SID-hah) Sanskrit, "perfected." In

Yoga and Eastern occultism, spiritual power *(siddhi)* to perform extraordinary feats, such as shrinking and enlarging the physical body without limits, telepathy, telekinesis. Or one who possesses such powers *(siddha)*.

SIDEREAL ASTROLOGY The lesser-known school that uses the actual constellations, which are visible groupings of stars, rather than the signs, which are geometrical sections on the orbital path of the Earth. Highly developed in India, where it has been consistently studied and practiced for over five thousand years and where it is used to this day to decide material affairs and arrange marriages.

SIGN In astrology, one of the twelve divisions of the orbital path of the Earth, each being 30 degrees in extent and measured by the apparent passage of the sun along the ECLIPTIC in thirty-day intervals. For example, the sign Aries corresponds to the extent of the sun's motion from March 21 to April 22 each year. Described in psychological language as personality types or Sun signs. Featured in newspaper columns and read by millions, though the idea that all people can be categorized accurately into twelve distinct types has never (yet) gained acceptance in conventional psychology. Technically, a sign might best be defined as an INTERVAL in the "time spectrum" of the year, loosely comparable to a color band in the spectrum of visible light—a difficult concept to develop, however, due to the inadequacies in our current understanding of TIME.

SIKHISM (SEEK-izm) From Hindi *sikh,* "lion, warrior." Religious movement founded around 1500 by Guru Nanak in opposition to the caste system of traditional Hinduism. Established as a military caste important in protecting India against the invasions of the Muslims. Segregated in the area of the Punjab, northern India, with satellite communities throughout the world, totaling about 16 million adherents.

SIN Falling short of one's true potential, missing the mark, being less than one could be or, at worst, not even being who one is. The failure of HUMAN POTENTIAL. A dominant paradigm in Western spirituality, by contrast with ILLUSION in the East. Being a sinner is not the same as suffering illusion.

SINISTER Latin, "left." Belonging to the "left-hand side," the way of darkness or evil. An age-old prejudice perhaps explained by the left side of the body being linked (as we now know) to the right side of the brain: hence, intuitive, nonverbal, beyond reason, "feminine," wily, WYRD, mysterious. Exemplified in Castaneda's "left-side awareness," and in the Aztec God of occult power, Huitzilopochtli, "Hummingbird on the left."

SIRIUS From Greek, "scorching." Brightest star in the sky, at a distance of 8.4 light-years. Most important star in ancient Egyptian cosmology and religion. Called the DOG STAR, identified with Isis. In recent times, claimed to be the home base of various superhuman entities who contact the Earth through mediums for the purpose of providing guidance and instruction. Also called Musa.

SIRIUS MYSTERY A peculiar matter brought to light by two

French anthropologists in the 1930s: In the folklore of the DOGON, an African tribe in Mali, there is evidence of extensive knowledge of the orbital cycle and physical properties of Sirius and its invisible white dwarf companion, the existence of which was only verified scientifically in the early 1980s, although the Dogon have apparently known about it for centuries.

    SITAR   (SIT-tar) (1) Hindu lute with main and sympathetic strings, recognizable by its gourdlike resonators. Known for its odd, stringy-whiny sound, which can be quite erotic. Achieved popularity in the 1960s through the Indian master musician Ravi Shankar, who tutored George Harrison of the Beatles. (2) New Age idiom for a near-miss mystical experience: "Close, but no sitar."

    SKEDADDLE   Slang term for a UFO lift-off.

    SNAKE OIL   Quick-fix metaphysics, fraudulent spiritual practice. It was the snake in the Garden of Eden who tempted Adam and Eve with the THEOGENIC IDEA, "Thou shalt be as gods, knowing good and evil," and snake oil is the sticky, slippery stuff that seems to fulfill the promise—not too bad for instant gratification, but it wears off quickly and often leaves unpleasant aftereffects.

    SOBRIETY   (1) In recovery, complete freedom from addiction to alcohol and drugs, as well as from the destructive emotional mechanisms of SHAME and CODEPENDENCY. The optimum state of human potential, in which an individual can exercise choice without assuming control and feel self-worth without confusing it with self-importance. (2) In Castaneda, the basis of impeccability, source of the clarity and precision exhibited in all the actions and attitudes of the true spiritual WARRIOR.

    SOLAR LOGOS   The intelligence of the Sun, conceived as a dynamic field of activities (or IMPLICATE ORDER) informing all life and within the bounds of the Solar System. In world myth and esoteric teachings, often conceived as an indwelling presence or divine person: Vishvakarman in Hindu myth, Hunab Ku among the Maya, Christos in Christianity, to name but a few. See also TRANSFERENCE.

    SOLAR MYSTERIES   From ancient times up to the Advent, the special body of spiritual teachings and training undertaken in preparation for the coming of the Christos, conceived as a superterrestrial Sun-Being. Thus, a generic term for the ancient Solar religions—such as Druidism, centered on the advent of Mabon, the divine Sun-Child, and Brahminism, with its emphasis on the Solar Logos Vishvakarman, as the cosmic prototype of the perfect human ego—which were actually pre-Christian forms of cosmic Christianity in which the Christos was recognized under diverse guises and names. Ancient mythological basis of the GRAIL MYSTERY.

    SOLAR-PHALLIC   Another name for the Solar Mysteries, but with a special emphasis on those teachings where the Sun God was identified with the mysterious workings of the male generative forces, as in the sexual cults of southern India and the Mediterranean. A term briefly popularized and enormously perverted by Aleister Crowley, who applied it to his experimentations with the TYPHONIC CURRENT. See also PHALLIC RELIGION.

SOLSTICE Literally, the moment when the Sun *(sol)* stands still *(stasis),* or appears to halt and reverse its movement. Not directly visible, for it is not the Sun's motion across the sky in the course of the day that halts; rather, the gradual side-shift of the Sun northward during the summer and southward during the winter, relative to the local horizon. The *sol-stasis,* or momentary standstill of this motion (called declination in the technical language of astronomy), occurs twice a year, on June 21 and December 21: the summer and winter solstices, celebrated in ancient times as moments of special religious import, when the connection between the Earth and the surrounding universe is renewed and recharged. Likewise for EQUINOX.

SOMATIC From Greek *soma,* "body." Referring to the body and senses, as in somatic therapy, a technique for healing the relation between the conscious mind and the physical senses.

SON PRINCIPLE In esoterics and ancient cosmologies, the projection of the Supreme Being (Father, Source) as the vital breath, filled with patterning power, that brings the universe into creation. For instance, in Egyptian cosmology, Ra is the Supreme Being who does not, however, act to create the world, but projects itself through Khephera, the Scarab God, vehicle of the divine-creative breath, or Logos. The SOLAR LOGOS conceived as a PERSON, superhuman but capable of human embodiment. In modern esoterics, the principle of Love-Wisdom, that which animates and unifies the Earth as a whole.

SOPHIA (So-FEE-ah) Greek, "wisdom." A divine feminine being, Mother Wisdom, who grants knowledge concerning all aspects of the spiritual growth of the human being from its present embryonic state to a condition of God-likeness. Female counterpart to the Son Principle and mother of the INNER CHILD. See also FALLEN SOPHIA.

SORCERY From Old French *sorcerie, sorz,* "lot, chance," from Latin *sors,* "lot, share (set apart)." Age-old name for the path of separation, the acquisition of knowledge and power exclusive of any connection with ordinary human affairs. As its derivation shows, sorcery is almost identical with SATANISM, because to choose a "lot" or a "share, set aside" is to participate in matters set off from the ordinary lot of humanity, intentionally divorced from the unity of human experience. Essential to premodern religion and science is the belief that all of nature, including human nature, is part of a grand, organic design—but sorcery sets itself off from all this and may even work against it. The quest for knowledge, power, and immortality for their own sake, as in the legend of FAUST (C&B2.8). More loosely, comparable to OCCULTISM: the exploitation of the hidden powers working behind processes normally taken for granted as automatic; thus, getting to the little-known sources of things, such as sense-perception, memory, or the automatic mechanisms of sleep and waking. This benevolent, explorative, and non-Satanic type of sorcery is propounded in the works of Castaneda, for example.

SOTHIS CALENDAR Oldest known calendar in the world, dating from 4241 B.C., based on a 1,460-year cycle, named after the Egyptian Goddess Isis.

SOUL Traditionally, the middle term in the trinity of body-soul-spirit; thus, the mediating agent, which is conscious both of a permanent, transcorporeal life in the spirit, and a transient life in the realm of the senses, bound to the body. Ideally, that which unifies and harmonizes the other two. In the psychology of modern self-development, the principle and faculty of self-awareness, which enables us to work on ourselves, to evolve. Also, the capacity to feel in kinship with the human race; the species-sense. See also FOLK-SOUL, PSYCHE.

SOUL DEATH Loss of capacity to identify with the human race, or to respond sympathetically with ordinary folk, as seen in the plight of Harry Haller, the antihero in Hermann Hesse's novel *Steppenwolf.*

SOUL-MAKING A term proposed by Jungian psychologist James Hillman, for the discovery and cultivation of inner resources of imagination and feeling, taken from English Romantic poet John Keats: "Call the world, if you please,/The veil of Soulmaking."

SOUL MATE Someone ideally suited to be a companion in the sharing of the one's development, both spiritual and personal; often believed to have been an intimate companion in former lives.

SPACE PEOPLE Loose term applied to beings from beyond the Earth, who are usually conceived as benevolent onlookers from more advanced civilizations in our galaxy, another galaxy, or, less often, another dimension altogether.

SPACE-TIME A mathematical invention proposed late in the nineteenth century by Hermann Minkowski, friend and teacher of Einstein. A theory of union supported by obscure equations but evidential to common sense in the fact that it takes, say, three hours (a certain interval in time) to get from Boston to New York City (a certain distance in space), these two factors being always inseparable. Often described as unimaginable to the ordinary mind and nonsensorial in character, so that it remains more or less beyond the experience of the ordinary person. See also TIMESPACE, FOURTH DIMENSION.

SPICY RUBBER PEOPLE Slang term for space people or walk-ins, known to exude the smell of old inner tubes spiced with paprika.

SPIRIT From Latin *spiritus,* meaning literally "breath"; exact equivalent of the Greek *pneuma,* also meaning "breath," with many parallels in other languages, such as Ahau, the Mayan hieroglyph of the BLOWGUNNER, Sanskrit Atma, and the Hebrew Ruach, the vitalizing breath by which Jehovah created

Adam (primordial humanity) from the dust. Thus, what gives and sustains the breath of life. Now loosely used to mean God, the power that informs all things, the superhuman/supernatural agency working in all events, conceived as an intelligent and purposeful being or process.

SPIRITUAL DEATH Loss of essence or annihilation of the divine spark, the potential for immortality and God-fullness. Although many people believe that the immortality of the spirit is an inalienable right, not to be lost or eradicated under any conditions, certain teachings indicate that it can be at risk. Warned against by Christ in the paradoxical remark, "To those that have will be given, and to those that have not shall be taken away even that which they have"—a theme dramatically developed in the message of Gurdjieff. Also, the AZTEC myth of the dying Sun that must be fed by tearing out human hearts may be interpreted as an omen of the danger of spiritual death (loss of heart, i.e., self-essence, spiritual core).

SPIRITUALISM (1) Historically, the movement of the late nineteenth century characterized by a great interest in the beyond, communication with the spirits of the departed (carried on into the time of World War I, when many people in Europe hoped to contact their sons who had died in the war), séances, table-knocking, et cetera. Consisted of diverse groups who disagreed on points of doctrine concerning reincarnation and Theosophical ideas. (2) Loosely, the quasi-religion concerned with invisible beings, sometimes linked to UFOs and extraterrestrials, believed to influence human affairs from beyond.

SPIRITUALITY The cultivation of whatever inspires and motivates the human individual to develop its inner potential for self-AWARENESS, to deepen its basic sense of humanity and its vision of the unitary evolution of all people, to explore and actualize its capacities for love, compassion, honesty, wonder, innocence, imagination, and creativity, and ultimately to express the selfless intent of service in all its actions.

SPIRITUAL MASTERS (E24) (1) In the traditions of Western occultism, the so-called elder brothers, or more evolved members of the human race, who are believed to live a selfless existence of service, guiding and inspiring humanity or directing human progress from behind the scenes; such as the Himalayan masters of Madame Blavatsky. (2) Conventionally, teachers from the East who have attained an exceptional state of God-realization and are believed to be able to foster the same condition in their followers. See also WESTERN MASTERS.

SPIRITUAL MATERIALISM A term coined by Tibetan teacher Chogyam Trungpa in his book *Cutting Through Spiritual Materialism,* for the attitude of neurotic neediness that causes a person to see spiritual progress as a goal-oriented process to be pursued in the same manner as a pay raise or a condo in Aspen, rather than as a risky, open-ended experiment in truth-seeking.

SPIRITUAL SCIENCE (1) Alternative term coined by Rudolf

Steiner for the teachings of Anthroposophy, which he originated, and specifically for those aspects of his work that propose to treat matters usually considered nonscientific (afterdeath, reincarnation, Avatars, spiritual hierarchies) by a consistent method of thinking. (2) Name sometimes applied by Mary Baker Eddy to her system of Christian Science.

SPIRITUAL SUPERMARKET   Slang term for the typical American phenomenon of too many choices in the realm of spiritual seeking and self-actualization. I prefer LABYRINTH.

STAND-IN   An alien entity who gains immediate access to Earth by taking up residence in the body and personality of an ordinary human being, either coexisting with its host or entirely eclipsing it. Compare with WALK-IN.

STARSEED   A term invented in 1973 by Timothy and Joanna Leary, referring to the concept of PANSPERMIA; that is, the seeding of planets with DNA material carried by comets, causing life to spring up in many solar systems throughout our galaxy (for some comets pass among different stars in their orbits), so that human beings may be conceived as having a genetic makeup in common with other interstellar species. Later adopted in some New Age circles to define a kind of spiritual pioneer, an evolutionary seedling.

STARWALKER   The image of the redeemer God, Ausar-Osiris, Egyptian prototype of Christos; depicted in many hieroglyphs and examples of temple art as a visualization of the constellation ORION.

STEREOTYPE   In modern culture, especially since the introduction of movable-type printing by Gutenberg (around 1537), the primary device for IMPRINTING, transferring information and modeling human behavior, both individually and socially. Modern counterpart to the ARCHETYPE, which works from within outward in the same way that the stereotype works from without inward.

STONE   See PHILOSOPHERS' STONE.

STONEHENGE   One of the world's greatest sacred sites and evidence of the Solar Mysteries, the ruins of a circular megalithic temple on Salisbury Plain in southern England, believed by some to have been a prehistoric site of worship for the DRUIDS. The mecca of geomancy.

STRESS   The condition of being overwhelmed by excessive demand or emotional intensity, or both, common in modern society. Whereas the root meaning of AWE indicates that the feeling of being overwhelmed was a primary and natural response in former times when human beings experienced direct contact with divine or supernatural forces, in modern times the capacity for awe has apparently been occluded by stress. Alleviating it is the common aim of many techniques of healing and bodywork. First investigated by Dr. Hans Selye in the 1930s and diagnosed in his book *The Stress of Life* (1956), in which he declared it to be fatal. Approaches to stress management have been proposed by Herbert Benson, a Harvard cardiologist (*The Relaxation Response*, 1975), and in the practice of transcendental meditation.

S T U P A   Spire or turnip-shaped dome of a Buddhist temple; equivalent to the Tibetan CHORTEN.

S U B C O N S C I O U S   The part of consciousness that continually operates in the background of taken-for-granted functions like memory and association, yet without showing itself; employed by the conscious mind rather like an automobile is used by the average person who knows how to operate it but not how it works. In basic practical occultism (E19), the storehouse of latent potential, available for cultivation to an enormous or even infinite extent. Generally agreed to be not merely a submechanism of the rational mind, but a strong dynamic field in which the element of feeling operates powerfully—for instance, in the controlling mechanism of certain attitudes, such as thinking one doesn't deserve something, in which case the thinking is interfused with feelings of shame, inadequacy, et cetera, and the subconscious disposition determines how one acts in spite of what the conscious mind intends.

S U B L I M I N A L   M I N D   Below *(sub)* the limits *(limin)*—of ordinary consciousness, that is. Another name for the subconscious mind.

S U B L I M I N A L   T A P E S   Cassette tapes used for PROGRAMMING the subconscious/subliminal mind, to produce sudden and effortless changes of attitude and behavior, such as aggression in business affairs, inner serenity, sexual confidence, or quitting smoking.

S U B T L E   B O D Y   See CAUSAL BODY.

S U B U D   Spiritual movement founded around 1925 by Mohammed Subuh, a man who entered a permanent state of superconscious ecstasy after being struck by "slow lightning" while strolling in the fields of his native Indonesia. Known for group gatherings (latihan) in which inspirational moods are generated.

S U C H N E S S   Sanskrit *Tathata,* Chinese *Chen Ju.* Fundamental concept in Zen Buddhism for the perfection of things as they are, just so, simple and complete unto themselves, impermanent and impossible to duplicate or replace. The revelation of EMPTINESS in pure appearance. Its closest Western counterpart is the NUMINOUS, although this implies the revelation of the divine through a sensory form whereas in the Suchness there is nothing beyond, nothing divine or transcendental that is revealed, but simply the sound of wind in the grass, the waters shaking the moon (E30). See also PHENOMENAL.

S U F F E R I N G   In Sanskrit, DUKKHA. One of the great mysteries of human experience, declared by Buddha to be the fundamental nature of all existence. Basis of the Eastern principle of liberation (from suffering), in contrast to the Western principle of salvation (making something fruitful and serviceable out of the suffering and, in so doing, getting beyond it). Contrast with PLAY.

S U F I / S U F I S M   (E25) (SUE-fee, SUE-fizm) Arabic translation of the Greek *sophia,* "wisdom, divine-feminine awareness," also a pun on the Arabic word *suf,* "wool," referring to the Sufi habit of wearing wool. By another derivation (Hazrat Inayat Khan), from Arabic *saf,* "pure"; free of all distinctions, unconditional. A devotional path centered on "the Beloved" as an image of God, with whom union is sought through selfless ecstasy. Known to the West through its great mystical poets, such as RUMI.

SUN SIGN   In astrology, the section of the orbital path of the Earth occupied by the Sun at the time of birth, supposed to indicate a set of typical character traits, impulses, and attitudes. See also SIGN.

SUPERCONSCIOUSNESS   A term applied to COSMIC CONSCIOUS-NESS as a norm, rather than an exception. The next stage of human awareness, beyond ordinary self-consciousness. Equivalent to SAMADHI in Indian Yoga; also described in the philosophy of the Western initiate Plotinus.

SUPERMAN   (1) An unfortunate term, especially because of its association with the Nazis. In modern context, it always refers back to the *Übermensch* of the late Romantic philosopher Nietzsche: "Behold, I teach you the Superman. Man is something to be overcome." In this striking language, from *Thus Spake Zarathustra,* Nietzsche was presenting a dramatic synopsis of the THEOGENIC IDEA, which had been sensationally exposed by the Romantics. A more accurate, well-tempered paraphrase might be: "Behold, I teach you the Ultrahuman. The human is something to be surpassed." This expresses the Romantic belief that humanity can overcome the given limits and predictable habits of human nature and develop its innate potential for divinity, or superhumanhood. "Ultrahuman" is actually the term used by Teilhard de Chardin to describe what humanity is becoming as it evolves toward the Omega-state of planetization. See also OVER-SOUL. (2) American folk hero endowed with supernatural powers.

SUPERMIND   In the teachings of Sri AUROBINDO, the activation of total spiritual potential through the descending current of KUNDALINI along the psychic centers (chakras) located in the infrastructure of the human etheric body. Not merely a mental state, but a condition of total, vital integration, perfect marriage of spirit and matter, as in the ALCHEMICAL WEDDING.

SUPERNOVA   The complete dematerialization of the matter of a star at the final stage of its evolutionary cycle—though it also may be the condition for a new cycle of multiple star-births. Occurs rarely in our galaxy; observed more frequently in other galaxies. Most famous historical example: the Crab Nebula of 1054, still visible in the constellation of the Bull. Most recent and spectacular example: Supernova 1987A, on 24 February 1987, in the Larger Magellanic Cloud.

SUPERSTITION   The belief in things standing *(-stition)* over *(super)* oneself or beyond one's rational understanding or acceptance. According to Rudolf Steiner, of two kinds: positive superstition, such as believing in the existence of ghosts, and negative superstition, such as not believing in the existence of ghosts.

SWASTIKA   Ancient symbol of the fourfold elemental power of the

Solar Logos—the solar wind, or plasma, or AKASHA, which radiates into the four realms of Earth, Air, Water, and Fire—found in many cultures, from Polynesia to Siberia. Adopted by the NAZIS as the occult symbol of their aim to conquer the world.

SWEAT LODGE In Native American spirituality, a hut designed for spiritual retreat, with heated rocks or wet wood to produce steam for purification and healing; helpful in achieving the VISION QUEST.

SWEDENBORG, EMANUEL Swedish scientist, philosopher, and occultist (1688–1772), who became a mystical visionary at the end of his life and produced many descriptions of spiritual realms beyond human perception, which he claimed to perceive directly. Hoped to found a new religion for educating humanity in the true nature of the Second Coming. Enormously influential in the magical/occult revival of the DECADENCE at the end of the nineteenth century.

SYMBOLIST MOVEMENT Artistic-literary movement in Europe around 1875, influenced by many occultists of different stripes who mingled with the prominent writers and painters of the time, introducing spiritual teachings such as Theosophy and Hermetics. See also DECADENCE and E2.3.

SYNASTRY (Sigh-NAS-tree, or SIN-es-tree) "Matching stars." In astrology, the comparison of birth patterns for the purpose of interpreting relationships.

SYNCHRONICITY (Sink-ron-ISS-i-tee) Happening at the same *(syn)* time *(chronos)*. Term applied by C. G. Jung, in collaboration with physicist Wolfgang Pauli, to an "acausal connecting principle" between events that occur at the same time and express a shared value or meaning, but are not evidently linked by mechanical cause-and-effect. Jung poses a cross-shaped model ("quart-ernio") in which synchronicity figures as one of the main principles of the universe, opposed to "causality" on the horizontal arms of the cross, with "inde-structible energy" at the apex, and "space-time continuum" at the base.

SYNERGETICS (Sinner-JET-iks) Name coined by Buckminster Fuller for his theoretical and practical system of planetary physics, a kind of reformula-tion of sacred geometry in modern terms.

SYNERGY (SINNER-gee) From Latin *syn-,* "together" + *ergon,* "force, work." The power of working together, especially in the combination of the energy of two systems in such a way that the total is more than the mere sum of the two. Thus, a fusion that multiplies the forces individually inherent to the beings, systems, or elements fused. Key principle in holistics, opposed to EN-TROPY.

SYSTEMIC Adj., pertaining to the Solar System as a whole.

T

T'AI CHI (Tie CHEE) Chinese, "supreme power." (1) In Chinese folklore and medicine, a method of exercise for maintaining health and raising vitality, consisting of balletlike movements in imitation of the natural gestures of certain animals and birds, originally conceived in a dream by fourteenth-century Taoist Chang San-Feng. (2) In the martial arts, a technique of self-defense consisting of yielding movements designed to exhaust the opponent; usually called t'ai chi ch'uan. (3) Name for the emblem of YIN/YANG, the supreme principle of polaric unity, usually represented as a half-red or -white, half-black circle divided by an S-shaped line.

TANKA (TAHN-kah) In the religious art of Tibetan Buddhism, a painted scroll decorated with a panorama of the various Buddhas or a geometrical design for meditation (MANDALA), similar in function to an altarpiece in Christian iconography.

TANTRA (E26) (TAHN-trah) Sanskrit, from the root *tan-*, "to spread, weave"; often translated as "continuity." Radical path of Eastern spirituality, supposed (by one account) to have been orally transmitted by Gautama Buddha with the express instructions that it be kept secret by a select few and only made known to the world at large in the time of greatest spiritual darkness, the KALI YUGA. Proposes the use of sex and the physical senses in the service of spiritual development, according to the fundamental principle that the Godhead is present in pure sensation. Tantracist (TAHN-tra-sist): Western term for one who practices Tantra. Tantrika (Tahn-TREE-kah): Sanskrit term for one who practices Tantra, specifically when the worship of woman as embodiment of divine-creative power (SHAKTI) is implied.

TAO/TAOISM (DOW, DOW-izm) Chinese, "the way, process, pure spontaneity"; literally, "peach." Ancient philosophical outlook said to have originated with the sage Lao Tzu around 600 B.C. (C&B1.2). Teaches supreme serenity by cooperating with the spontaneous flow of nature and time. Advocates passivity and contemplation, historically contrasted to the pragmatic ethics of

Confucianism, whose adherents vastly outnumber those of Taoism today. A way of acceptance, ease with self, and gentle but courageous engagement with life that has proved immensely popular in the West. See also TE.

TAO OF SEX The application of Taoist principles to sexuality, by using the sexual act as a form of meditation and as a means of generating high vitality and fostering REJUVENATION. Chinese equivalent of Tantra, roughly.

TAROT (E27) (TAR-oh) From Old Italian *tarocco* > Arabic *taraha*, "remove, keep out," probably in reference to its being considered esoteric, to be kept out of the hands of ordinary folk. A deck of seventy-eight cards representing a complete system of cosmological and psychological symbology, to be used: (1) superficially, for fortune-telling; (2) psychologically, for the analysis and evaluation of personal experiences; (3) esoterically, for delving into the realm of the master-complexes, or ARCHETYPES, encountered on the path of personal development and deeply penetrated in the work of occultism.

TE (TAY) Chinese, "virtue." Capacity for straightforward action from the heart. Indicated in the title of Lao Tzu's classic, *Tao Te Ching* (C&B1.2) "the book *(ching)* of the virtue *(te)* of pure spontaneity *(tao)*." Also, the ethical ideal of the Confucian *Analects* (C&B1.4). Exact equivalent to the Latin *virtu*—considered by the TROUBADOURS as the mark of individual essence, the signature of personal authenticity. Right action, not so much in terms of what is done, but how it is done. Impeccability.

TEA CEREMONY In Zen, a traditional ritual of self-awareness using the brewing and sipping of tea as an exercise for attaining complete presence of mind, ease, and elegance of gesture.

TECHNOCRAT One who leads or rules by virtue of special or technical knowledge. Hypothetically, a master of the ideal control-system of planetary management, someone who proposes to enforce technological supremacy. One who masters by technical skill and elite knowledge, especially when used to manipulate nature, rather than cocreate with it through devout imitation, in the manner of the alchemists. The FAUST-type, prominent agent in "general systems theory" and other schemes of technocratic planetarization, which have been deeply criticized by some New Age theorists.

TEILHARD DE CHARDIN, PIERRE (TAY-yar duh Shar-DAN) Unorthodox French Catholic philosopher and geologist (1881–1955), who proposed a Christocentric vision of planetary wholeness. Now widely influential in the teaching of holistics and cocreation, though his works were banned by the Catholic church during his lifetime. See also OMEGA-STATE, SECOND COMING.

TELEKINESIS (Tell-uh-kin-NEE-sis) "Far-off movement." Movement of physical objects without contact or apparent physical cause. Adj., telekinetic (Tell-uh-kin-ET-ik).

TELEPATHY (Tell-LEP-ah-thee) From Greek *tele-*, "far off" + *pa-*

thein, "to sense/feel/perceive." The act of direct communication from one person to another by transmission of thoughts; thought-transference in the old-fashioned lingo of the nineteenth-century salons of Spiritualism. Nonvisual; may occur through tonal hearing (clairaudience).

TELEPORTATION (Tell-uh-port-TAY-shun) Transportation (usually instantaneous) of an object from one location to another without evident material means, as when they "beam up" the crew in "Star Trek."

TELLURIC (Tell-LURE-ik) Adj. In geomancy, pertaining to earth-bound radiations or close-to-ground forces in the atmosphere, often said to emanate strongly from sacred sites where ancient ruins are found. Includes the base pulsation of the entire planet, supposed to be measurable at a rate of 7.83 cycles per second.

TEMPLARS / KNIGHTS TEMPLAR (TEM-plar) A military and religious order established in Europe around 1120 for the purpose of protecting the roads traveled on the way to the Crusades, but also believed to have other, more mysterious purposes, such as the guardianship of special knowledge inherited from the secret cults of ancient Egypt, or from the Freemasons. Said to have been familiar with Eastern-type practices of occultism, such as Tantra. Perhaps served as cover for an order of warrior-initiates, invested with exceptional physical and spiritual powers. Decimated in a conflict with the Catholic church, which charged them with anti-Christian practices of paganism and Satanic magic and had their last Grand Master, Jacques de Molay, burned by the Inquisition in 1314. See also GOTHIC CATHEDRALS.

TEMPLE SLEEP The three-day state of near-death, deliberately induced in the Mysteries at the final stage of the PSYCHODRAMA, when the astral and etheric bodies, lifted out of their usual connection with the physical, received the imprinting of higher knowledge and paranormal faculties—thus allowing the initiate to reawaken in a God-like state of illumination and empowerment. Common to many of the Mystery Schools, as known from the evidence of PASSAGE-GRAVES, mound-chambers, and pyramidal crypts such as the King's Chamber at Giza.

TENOCHTITLÁN (Tay-noch-tee-TLAHN) Ancient sacred capital of the Aztecs, now covered for the most part by Mexico City. Captured and sacked on 30 June 1520 by Cortés, who was erroneously taken by the natives to be QUETZALCOATL, whose reappearance was foretold in sacred prophecies of the Toltecs.

TEOTIHUACÁN (Tay-oh-tee-wa-KAHN) Aztec, "city of the Gods *(teo)*." Ancient sacred capital of the pre-Aztec civilization of the Toltecs, thirty miles northeast of Mexico City. Site of the spectacular Pyramids of the Sun and the Moon.

TESLA, NIKOLA (TESS-lah) Yugoslavian engineer and inventor (1856–1943), dandy, eccentric, and would-be occultist. Worked in America from 1884 onward as a pioneer in high-tension electricity and radio transmission. Given to grand schemes such as lighting the world by a system of wireless electricity. Designed the power station at Niagara Falls; invented hundreds of electrical and radio devices, many of which are now in wide use. Proposed the use of alternate current (now adopted), against direct current, as promoted by Edison (now rejected). Died in obscurity, leaving a massive body of patents and theoretical writings, which are believed by some present-day experts to contain solutions to the most baffling and crucial scientific problems facing humanity.

THELEMA (Theh-LAY-mah) Greek, "will." Main principle in the magical philosophy of English occultist Aleister Crowley, which he pirated from RABELAIS: "Do what thou wilt shall be the whole of the Law." Key theme in the *Book of the Law,* channeled by Crowley's wife, Rose, during their honeymoon in Cairo in 1904.

THEOCRACY (Thee-AHK-ruh-see) Rulership by the Gods *(theos),* the original form of government in all the high cultures of the ancient past. Described in world mythology in hundreds of accounts, as well as in many historical records, and persisting right down into modern times in the concept of the Japanese emperor as "Son of Heaven." Described by historians as divine kingship. Theocrat: one of the original rulers of the great civilizations (Chinese, Egyptian, Celtic) who were believed to be incarnate Gods, or God-human hybrids, or their descendents: pharaohs, emperors, shahs, et cetera; or someone who believes in the government of society by such beings.

THEOGAMY (Thee-OG-ah-me) The mating *(gamos)* or marriage between a God and a human being, widely described in classical mythology, such as the birth of the Trojan hero Aeneas from the union of his mortal father, Anchises, with the Goddess Aphrodite. Adj., *theogamous* (Thee-OG-ah-muss). The God-kings of ancient high civilization, such as the Egyptian pharaohs, were held to be the progeny of theogamous unions, or else interbred from stock originally sprung from a superhuman source, the most famous instance being given in the Old Testament, Genesis 6:2, "That the sons of God saw the daughters of men that were fair; and they took them wives of all whom they chose."

THEOGENIC IDEA/THEOGENY (Thee-oh-GEN-ic, Thee-AWE-geh-nee) The coming-to-birth *(geny)* of a God *(theos),* especially the raising of a human being to a God-like status through initiation. The actualization of DIVINITY in human form, widely understood in the past as the result achieved by participation in the Mysteries. The ultimate example of cultivating and fulfilling human potential. Called by Dante transhumanization (in the *Paradiso* [C&B2.7]), disclosed in the Hermetica (C&B2.9) as the primary goal of independent spiritual work (E2.2), and cited by Bucke (C&B3.1) as the effect of experiencing cosmic consciousness. Emphasized with wild-eyed enthusiasm by the Romantics, such as William Blake ("Therefore God becomes as we are, that we may be as he is") and Emerson ("The simplest person, who in his integrity worships

God, becomes God"), echoing the age-old teaching of Eastern spirituality, that "No one who is not himself divine can successfully worship a divinity" *(Gandharva Tantra)*. Also called DEIFICATION, the method of supreme empowerment in the Mysteries, though not the aim *(telos)*, which was COCREATION. Today, probably the main bone of contention between traditional religions and the new alternative paths (E1.4).

THEOSOPHY   (E28) (Thee-OS-suf-fee) The wisdom *(sophia)* about or concerning God *(theos)*. (1) Specifically, a movement founded in 1875, dedicated to universal brotherhood and the dissemination of an enormous system of spiritual teachings called the Wisdom Religion by its founder, Madame Blavatsky. (2) In a general sense, the perennial tradition of esoteric teachings propounded by the centuries-long progression of masters and saints who have attempted to educate humanity in the ways of God, but outside the limits of conventional religious dogma. The PERENNIAL PHILOSOPHY viewed in its psychological and cosmological aspects, including reincarnation, cyclic evolution, the role of the hierarchies, planes, mahatmas, adepts, Avatars, and a cast of millions.

THERAVADA   (Ther-uh-VAHD-uh) Sanskrit, "path of the Elders." The branch of Buddhism prevalent in Ceylon, Thailand, Burma, and Laos, noted for its intellectual simplicity and dedication to ethical concerns. See also HINAYANA.

THETA WAVES   See BRAIN WAVES.

THIRD EYE   A nonphysical organ located in the center of the forehead just above the line of the brows, usually identified with the PITUITARY GLAND; supposed to be developable into a "higher organ" for ESP and telepathic command. Called in Yoga the *ajna* center or brow chakra.

THOTH   (Toth) Egyptian God of Wisdom, equivalent to the Greek Hermes, source of the metaphysical teachings contained in the Hermetica. Key figure in the Egyptian Mysteries, an agent of servation who instructs humanity in hieroglyphic writing, medicine, astronomy, geometry, and dice shooting. Criticized by Socrates in Plato's dialogue *Phaedrus* (C&B2.3), as being far from a benefactor, because the skill of writing he provided must inevitably cause memory and innate retention to atrophy.

THOUGHT FORM   Vibratory impression or shape assumed by a thought; for instance, a thought of great inspiration might take the form of a cathedral. In Theosophical literature, title and subject of a classic work by Leadbeater and Besant.

THUNDERBIRD   In Amerindian folklore, the image of divine intelligence as a winged fire-spirit coming from the Sun, equivalent to Horus in the SOLAR MYSTERIES of Egypt, and incorporating the idea of the Logos as cosmic sound (SHABDA).

THYMUS   (1) A gland found in human beings and some animals, consisting of a knot of lymphoid tissue in the middle upper chest, whose exact purpose is unknown, though it plays a role in infant development, possibly affecting growth by regulating the assimilation of the mother's milk. Usually atrophies by puberty. (2) In occult anatomy and bodywork, an important center for harmonic integration of physiological processes. Often described as a proto-chakra, the bud of a new etheric center that underlies and supports the immune system; thus a crucial organ in developing PSYCHOIMMUNITY. *Thymus-thumping:* the practice of rapping lightly on the thymus with one's knuckles—right in the area where the voice will change tone if you hum while you're rapping—believed to calm the nerves and tone the etheric body as a whole.

TIBETAN BUDDHISM The special form of Buddhism that evolved in Nepal after the conversion of the country by its half-legendary, half-historical founder, Padma Sambhava, in 757 A.D. Brought to the West in a vast migration beginning in the late 1950s when the Chinese invaded Tibet (C&B4.5). Consists of three main sects or lineages: the *Kargyu,* the *Gelugpa,* and the *Nyingma.* Noted for its theories of the Void and phenomenality, presented in a complex intellectual scheme consisting of dozens of categories and sub-categories for defining the functions of the mind and senses. Also known for its high pomp and hierarchical lineage, consisting of a succession of TULKUS believed to be the direct emanations of Bodhisattvas. Its teachings include a great deal of material on Tantra, ritual, visualization, and esoteric psychology, elaborately expounded in the sacred books of the Tanjur (225 volumes) and the Kanjur (108 volumes). Also called LAMAISM and VAJRAYANA.

TIME The invisible dimension we inhabit, which is present *to* us in a different way than we are present *in* the dimension of visible space, although both space and time are given in some kind of union, leaving us unaware of how the union occurs, or if they may occur somewhere in disunion, independent of each other (a state denied in RELATIVITY THEORY). Perhaps the most mysterious thing in the world, the next frontier to be crossed by passing the "time barrier"—which might require a "time program" at least as sophisticated as the space program. One of the most difficult areas of occult research, requiring an exact understanding of what happens in the INTERVAL and how memory works. A realm to be described by precise laws of "time physics," yet to be discovered, but perhaps known to the alchemists who sometimes described themselves as caretakers of time, or to the latter-day sorcerers in Castaneda, who are able to reconstruct past moments of time by entering altered states. May be lost or even stolen, as in the film by George Harrison and Terry Gilliam, *Time Bandits.* Might be explored, yet remains largely ignored. Variously described as SPACE-TIME, TIMESPACE, ETERNITY, and CHANGE. May be circular, linear, or in droplets: Time doesn't flow, it drips.

TIME TRAVEL The possibility of mobility in time, comparable to mobility in space—which is not the given case, since we are normally unable to move around, in more than one direction, in time. Believed possible through occult development, as suggested by some episodes in Castaneda. A favorite issue in science fiction.

TIMESPACE   Human equivalent of SPACE-TIME; time's pace or time's innate rhythm, the time-patterning of the innate and natural unfoldment of human potential. Complete continuity of growth at the proper pace of sanity.

TOLTEC   (TOLL-tek) "Artisan." (1) Obscure civilization of ancient Mexico. Believed to have predated by many centuries the Aztecs, who came in around 1150 A.D. and took over, although the Toltecs may have had their revenge by passing on to their conquerors the myth of the return of QUETZAL-COATL, whom the Aztecs identified, disastrously, with the Spanish conquistador Cortés. (2) In Castaneda, the culture that produced the master sorcerers of the old lineage.

TONAL   (Toe-NAHL) The world of reason and intelligible order, the realm of the known and knowable, as defined in the "sorcerer's explanation" in Castaneda. Contrast to NAHUAL.

TOTE   N., in Western occultism, slang for a TULKU.

TRADITION   From Latin *tradere,* "to deliver." (1) In a general sense, that which is passed down from the past, delivered by those who preceded us, rather than discovered by those who are here, now. On this contrast, see E2.1. (2) Specifically, in modern esoterics and New Age revival of ANCIENT WISDOM, the wellspring of guiding principles and inspiring impulses, perennial and invariant though expressed in many different ways, which remains independent of the cultural and religious trappings it may assume. Applied in this sense specifically to the school of thought founded by French esotericist Rene Guenon.

TRADITIONAL RELIGIONS   The great world-religions, all Eastern in origin, including Christianity, Islam, Buddhism, Hinduism, Confucianism, and Judaism. Usually adopted as a matter of inheritance, rather than chosen through a process of free seeking, these belief structures currently dominate human affairs on the world-scale (E2.1).

TRANCE CHANNEL   Someone who serves as the instrument of communication for a disembodied or even nonhuman entity, usually by going into a state of semi-unconsciousness so that he does not know what occurs while the transmission is taking place. See also AIRTIME.

TRANSCENDENCE   From Latin *trans-,* "over" + *scandere,* "to climb, scale." In the old Oriental sense, the act of overcoming the given limitations of the human mind and senses to enter into a state of direct communication with God, Tao, the divine, BRAHMA, et cetera. In the modern conventional sense, outgrowing one's personal limitations and needs by expanding toward a more conscious participation in the whole of life, and becoming appreciative of the larger design of things, above and beyond mere personal issues. See also TRANS-PERSONAL.

TRANSCENDENTAL MEDITATION   (TM)   Movement   and

method established in 1959 by Maharishi Mahesh Yogi, who claimed to represent a lineage of masters going back to the Vedic RISHIS. Teaches the practice of inner centering to overcome stress, through the use of a personal mantra. Proposed as a scientific method of mental self-management, rather than a religious philosophy.

TRANSCENDENTALISM   A philosophical movement of the nineteenth century, formally established in Concord, Massachusetts, in 1840 and centered on Romantic poet and essayist Ralph Waldo Emerson (C&B2.10). Also associated were Nathaniel Hawthorne, Henry David Thoreau, and Herman Melville. American counterpart to Romanticism, stressing radical individualism, self-reliance, social reform (in association with the cooperative community of Brook Farm [E1.1], for instance), and personal mysticism. Deeply antimaterialistic and strongly influenced by Eastern teachings such as the Bhagavad Gita and the Upanishads.

TRANSFERENCE   (1) Generally, the aim and result of sacrifice, as practiced in all cultures of the past, where prayer and offerings were used to effectuate a hand-over of power from the Gods to humanity. Thus, the transmission of actual power, or the means to acquiring divine sanction. (2) Specifically, in the Solar Mysteries, the Advent of Christ to Earth, conceived mythologically as the birth of the Divine Child from the union of the phallic sunbeam of the Divine Father and the earth-womb of the Divine Mother, commemorated in the PASSAGE-GRAVES. This union effectuates the transplantation of the Solar Logos from the Sun to the Earth. (3) Specifically, in the Jungian work and other forms of psychotherapy, the process in which the patient projects upon the analyst the positive and negative emotions to be worked through in the process of analysis or therapy. At first established to provide trust and context for effective dialogue; later dissolved when the patient is able to take responsibility for the PROJECTIONS.

TRANSIT   In astrology, the passage of a planet as it actually occurs in the skies relative to the fixed positions of the planets in the birthchart of an individual. Used to interpret or predict the course of current events; for instance, the transit of Mars (actual motion in the skies) over Mercury (in the birthchart) denotes a time when the individual is prone to get involved in heated arguments or to speak rashly.

TRANSMEDIUM   Fancy term for a channeler who goes completely "under," into a sleeplike state, while channeling.

TRANSMIGRATION   Reincarnation from one species to another, as from a dog into a human or vice versa.

TRANSMISSION   In most Oriental spiritual lineages, such as Zen and Tibetan Buddhism, the passing-on of spiritual knowledge, firsthand, from the master to the pupil—who then becomes a master in his or her own right. Often formalized into a rite of EMPOWERMENT and preserved in a succession of teachers or masters (lineage). A highly selective process; for instance, Gautama Buddha, although he delivered sermons on Enlightenment to thousands of people, only achieved direct transmission to three of his disciples. Contrast with TRANSFERENCE.

TRANSPERSONAL Adj., a term that became popular in the late 1960s, referring to a wide variety of studies and inner disciplines for achieving an expansion of self-awareness beyond the limits of personal rules, issues, attitudes, and postures.

TRANSPERSONAL PSYCHOLOGY Loose, comprehensive term for various approaches to self-actualization that direct the individual to the "deep self," stressing universal concerns and the exploration of inner creative potential. Compare with HUMANISTIC PSYCHOLOGY.

TREE-ALPHABET In the Celtic Revival, a code-system consisting of a wide and variable set of analogies in which certain trees (such as the ash, yew, alder, and oak) are viewed as embodiments of natural and supernatural principles and influences; expressed in a vast set of correlations (planetary, curative, magical, musical, inspirational). Described at length in a famous modern classic, *The White Goddess,* by Robert Graves.

TREE OF LIFE In magic and the Cabala, the master scheme upon which all theory and practices are based. A design consisting of ten points (SEPHIRA) linked by twenty-two lines, taken as a model of the creative emanations from the Godhead. Used for elaborate metaphysical speculations, psychological exercises, and ceremonial magic. Compare with BOOK OF LIFE.

TRIAD A form found universally in world religions and spiritual teachings, such as in the Christian Trinity (Father–Son–Holy Spirit) and in the formula of the three GUNAS (Rajas-Tamas-Sattva) in Indian Yoga psychology. Appears in endless variations in world religions, mythology, and metaphysics: body-soul-spirit, space-time-matter, et cetera. See also QUARK.

TRICKSTER In world myth, a paradoxical figure, usually considered to be superhuman although not always a legitimate God, who mischievously assists and hampers human activity, like Coyote in Native American folklore, or Hermes in Greek myth. Also appears as a hare, raven, or spider. Pictured in human guise as the Juggler or FOOL in the Tarot.

TRIPITAKA (Tree-pee-TAHK-ah) Sanskrit, "three baskets." In Buddhism, a slang term for the three bodies of literature consisting of discipline, sermons, and metaphysics.

TROPICAL ASTROLOGY In astrology, the particular school that uses the uniform divisions of the twelve SIGNS and does not recognize the actual constellations. Constrast to SIDEREAL ASTROLOGY.

TROUBADOURS (TRUE-buh-dores) From Provençal French *trobare,* "to find." Poets, minstrels, and romantic rascals who occupied France in large numbers from about 1100 to 1400. Associated primarily with southwestern

France, the region of the ALBIGENSIANS. Also active in northwestern France (Brittany), where they were called *trouvères,* "finders," for their habit of finding and preserving old stories and legends, especially relating to the exploits of King Arthur and the Knights of the Round Table. Known for their celebration of romantic love and errant passion, outside the limits of conventional morality and marriage vows. Also closely linked to Sufism through the Moorish culture of Spain, and sometimes described as the practitioners of a Western form of Tantra, or erotic mysticism (C&B3.16).

TRUMP From Old French *tromper,* "to trick." (1) The name for any card in the Tarot, but specifically "Major Trump" for the cards numbered one through twenty-two, or zero through twenty-one; and "Minor Trump" for the remaining fifty-six cards, including one through ten, and the sixteen "Court Cards" in the four suits. (2) In ordinary card games, any card that holds rank over any other card in the deck. (3) A false call to salvation, a delusionary solution of any kind.

TRUTH In the profane and practical sense, the view of reality that conforms to the given facts or testable evidence. In the sacred and subjective sense, the view of the universe and human affairs rooted in the perspective of the free subject, which is correct, effective, and viable for that subject because it originates directly in his or her innermost source of self-trust. From the Old English *treowth,* probably tracing back to the Indo-European root *drew-,* "rooted, secure"; literally, "tree." That which grows, like a tree, from the INNATE. The aim of free seeking. See also RAPHAEL-NOVALIS IMPULSE.

TULKIT (TOOL-kit) Tote bag of special gifts and occult powers carried by a tulku from one incarnation to the next. Pictured as the juggler's bag of tricks in the FOOL card of the Tarot.

TULKU (TOOL-koo) Tibetan, "altar, shrine." In Tibetan Buddhism, the person who serves as the "seat" for the embodiment of a reincarnating LAMA, who usually predicts his own return and is identified by certain signs, such as picking out personal articles he owned in his former life.

TURNINGS A term introduced by German lyric poet Rainer Maria Rilke (C&B3.3), for the key events in the SERENDIPITY of life, suddenly leading the seeker into a whole new region of the labyrinth. Also, a turning point in life where spiritual assistance may be provided. In one of the "Sonnets to Orpheus," the poet asserts that "the directing Spirit who is master of the earth entire/loves the figure of flight not so much as the point where it turns."

TWELVE-STEP PROGRAM In recovery, the model for spiritual growth and moral-emotional integration. Developed in the late 1930s by Bill Wilson, founder of Alcoholics Anonymous. Derived from the six steps of the "Oxford Group," a small reformist society dedicated to "world-changing through life-changing," founded in England in 1921 by American evangelist Frank Buchman. Stresses the admission of powerlessness over whatever is "unmanageable" in one's life, appeal to a higher power for restoration to sanity, and a moral program requiring rigorous honesty, confession of faults, forgiveness, and making amends.

TWILIGHT ZONE   Name of a famous TV series created by Rod Serling in the late 1950s, featuring episodes of supernatural events and baffling encounters with the OTHERWORLD.

TYPHONIC CURRENT   The tradition of black magic believed to have assumed its present form in Egypt around 2500 B.C., due to a schism in the priesthood responsible for guarding the secret methods of THEOGAMY. One of the main streams of Satanic ritual, revived in modern times by Aleister Crowley, who called it "the 93 current." Uses visualizations to concentrate the forces aroused by sexual intercourse (often homosexual) into the projection of "God-forms," with the aim of acquiring superhuman knowledge and occult powers. Not exactly hard-core SATANISM, but a good start.

U

U F O Unidentified Flying Object; flying saucer. Reported to have been seen in vast numbers, worldwide, especially since the end of World War II. Believed by some to be vehicles of travel used by visitors from more advanced civilizations who may be either benevolent overseers of human affairs or (less often) invaders with malevolent intentions. Also believed to be pictured in rock drawings and sacred art (at Palenque, for instance), or described in biblical visions, perhaps attesting to our planet having been visited in very early times by ANCIENT ASTRONAUTS.

U L T R A H U M A N Term coined by Teilhard de Chardin for the next stage of our species' evolution, to be attained when the human race is unified into a single, self-regulating organism by the catalytic effect of Christ as the focus of PLANETARIZATION, conceived not as a hierarchical ordering but a progression in time, "not above but ahead."

U N C E R T A I N T Y (1) In modern seeking, often the point of critical balance between posing a question and finding the answer. (2) Specifically, the Principle of Uncertainty, proposed by Werner Heisenberg in 1927, stating that it is impossible to detect at one and the same moment both the motion and position of an atomic particle. In the new physics, often taken as evidence that the act of observation alters the process being observed; thus, an important concept in defining the paradigm-shift from a mechanical/manipulative view of nature, in which the scientist is totally detached, to a holistic/cooperative view of nature, in which the mental stance and activities of the scientist are fully involved with what is being observed.

U N C O N S C I O U S Common term in modern psychology for the activity of DENIAL, usually interpreted as if the source of denial were located in a field of hidden processes—the unconscious—that exists and operates autonomously, quite independent of the conscious, self-reflecting mind. See also COLLECTIVE UNCONSCIOUS.

U N D E R W O R L D In some mythologies and religious systems, such as the Egyptian and the Mayan, the supernatural world or psychic dimension entered upon death, where the soul undergoes trial and judgment, as in the "soul-weighing" before the God Osiris in Egyptian religion. Usually equated with the AFTERWORLD, but not always. Not to be strictly equated with the OTHER-WORLD, of which it may be a subregion. Often located in the interior of the Earth (Hollow Earth).

UNEXPLAINED   Catch-all term for all kinds of odd phenomena, associated in conventional language with the realm of the psychic and occult matters: the Bermuda Triangle, Bigfoot, poltergeists, miraculous healings, channelings, house hauntings, extreme coincidences (synchronicity), telepathy, and so forth. Often of sensational interest, events like these attract popular attention to the New Age and are frequently played up by the media, with the effect of trivializing the new spirituality in disregard for its deeper aspects. Whatever lies outside one's adopted set of belief systems may be labeled as unexplained. See also APPARITION.

UNICORN   In Celtic mythology and European folklore, a fabulous beast in the form of a horse, with a single spiraling horn growing from the center of its brow. In alchemy, a symbol of the complete mastery of phallic sexuality by ritual (nonorgasmic) intercourse, and its conversion into the forces of pure VISUALIZATION.

UNIFIED FIELD   A modern term first applied to the theories of Albert Einstein, especially concerning the work Einstein left undone, namely, the creation of a comprehensive theory (with consistent mathematical formulas) able to describe and integrate all the four known fields of measurable activity in the universe, encompassing both macroscale and microscale dimensions and galactic and subatomic structures. Ideally, the model of universal unity, including the gravitational field, the metric field, the field of the "weak force," and the field of the "strong force" in a single system. An attempt to link relativity theory and quantum theory, yet to be completed but often taken in the new physics as a hypothesis pointing toward the holistic unity of the universe.

UPANISHADS   (You-PAN-ish-shahds) Sanskrit, "teachings received *(upa-)* from sitting down *(ni-shad),"* with the implication that one sits at the feet of a spiritual master. A group of teachings on the nature of the human soul and the universe, highly instrumental in the transmission of Indian spiritual wisdom to the West (C&B1.5, also E2.3).

URANTIA BOOK   An enormous volume of channeled material, published in the 1950s by the Urantia Foundation, an occult society located in Chicago. Describes a vast scenario of world evolution from the galactic scale down to the realm of worms, including an alternative version of the life and mission of Jesus Christ, who is depicted as an Avatar working in collaboration with an immense array of hierarchical powers and spiritual executives in the "Seraphic Planetary Government," a variation on the theme of PLANETARY HIERARCHY.

U T O P I A (You-TOPE-ee-uh) From the Greek *ou-,* "no, not" + *topos,* "place," hence, no-place, nowhere. (1) A paradise or ideal world, especially a social paradise of complete equality and abundance for all. Hypothetical model for many socialist communities of the nineteenth century, as well as a prevailing mytheme of the New Age (E1.1). (2) The title of a famous book by Sir Thomas More (1516).

U X M A L (OOSH-mahl) Nahuatl, "three times rebuilt." A sacred site in Yucatán, known for the Pyramid of the Magician, where legend says the POPOL VUH was revealed by divine inspiration (C&B2.12).

V

V A J R A Y A N A (Vahj-rah-YAH-nah) Sanskrit *vajra,* "thunderbolt or diamond" + *yana,* "path, way"; thus, "way or path of the thunderbolt." A name for the teachings and practices of Tibetan Buddhism, usually applied to emphasize its deeper, more esoteric aspects. The way to perfect mental clarity, which strikes like lightning to the essence of the true nature of things (VOID).

V E D A N T A (Veh-DAHN-tah) Sanskrit, "the end (or what comes at the end) of the VEDAS." A collection of commentaries on the Vedas, originally found at the end of the main text; or the philosophical system derived from them. The philosophy of ultimate meanings, defining the nature of consciousness and the relation of inner self-knowing to the all-knowing of God or Brahma. Established in its modern form by Shankara, a great Indian philosopher of the ninth century, and transmitted to the West through a lineage culminating in Swami Vivekananda.

V E D A S (VAY-duhs) Sanskrit, from the root *vid-,* "knowledge." Collective term for the four sacred books of Hinduism, or ancient Indian religion. They consist of psalms, chants, invocations of various Gods, et cetera. They are the oldest known written teachings in world religion—believed to have been committed to writing around 600 B.C., though they embody an oral tradition supposed to have been maintained for thousands of years before being written down. They are mainly of interest for their mythological and ethnological content, as they contain no philosophical or spiritual message that would be of relevance to modern seeking.

V E G A (VEE-gah) Bright star in the constellation of the Lyre in the northern hemisphere of the skies. In the early 1980s, astronomers using high-tech telescopic equipment were able to photograph Vega and confirm that it supports a planetary system—the first hard evidence that other solar systems such as our own do in fact exist. Almost immediately, the image was adopted by Pueblo Indians of the Southwest and incorporated into their tribal art (as a motif in blanket weavings, for instance)—an example of planetary folklore in the making.

VEIL/VEILING   Key paradigm of Eastern religion and metaphysics, set in strong contrast to the Western paradigm of the FALL. Expresses the belief that the true nature of reality, or God itself, is present to us directly all the time though veiled by the condition of our minds and senses. Described in Indian metaphysics as due to the activity of SHAKTI as MAYA, the Godhead veiling itself. In other myths, attributed to the action of God as TRICKSTER.

In Tantra and Hindu devotional worship centered on KRISHNA, the playful flirtation in which the divine conceals itself, so that it can be repeatedly rediscovered, to its own eternal delight; though also described in other systems of Indian metaphysics as a painful deceit, to be overcome by total denial of the sensorial world and yogic union with God, beyond the veil.

Explained in Tibetan Buddhism as the Voidness or PHENOMENALITY of all things, and in radical Buddhism, such as Zen, as the identity of Samsara and Nirvana, appearance and essence. See also PLAY and E2.4 on the issue of contrasting paradigms (Fall).

VELIKOVSKY, IMMANUEL   (Vel-ih-KOFF-skee) Austrian-born historian, psychoanalyst, and controversial mythologist (born 1895). Known for his theory that Venus was originally a comet, released from Jupiter, which passed through the orbits of Mars and Earth around 1500 B.C., wreaking havoc described in many myths, including the parting of the Red Sea by Moses. More or less forgotten today, though hotly discussed in the 1970s, twenty years after his theories first appeared in *Worlds in Collision* (1950) and *Earth in Upheaval* (1955). See also EARTH CHANGES.

VESICA   (VES-ik-ah) Latin, "bladder, vessel." Loosely, the lentil-shaped enclosure formed when two circles overlap. More precisely, the area formed in the special case of two circles drawn with the same radius and the center of one located on the circumference of the other, the so-called Vesica Pisces (VES-ik-ah PIE-sees), "the bladder of the fishes." In geomancy and its practical and artistic applications to sacred architecture, a geometric shape containing the divine proportion, or GOLDEN SECTION, used for the laying-out of temples and cathedrals or designing stained-glass windows. A symbol of MOTHER WISDOM, the creative womb or generatrix of the world; hence, a stylization of the female organs of generation.

VIGIL   From Latin *vigil,* "awake." Historically, the watch kept by a knight, often in a churchyard, all through the night or several nights, without falling asleep; for the purpose of entering the twilight state between sleeping and waking to confront the DOUBLE or do battle with astral/supernatural entities, thus proving manhood and acquiring occult powers. In the Arthurian Path, the basic ritual of spiritual empowerment, comparable to the rites of Tantra in which the yogi visits graveyards and desolate places to face and subdue hostile entities (or speaking psychologically, to visualize and incorporate psychic projections from the realm of the "deep self" and the dark side of the unconscious). In the Celtic Revival, a technique of self-initiation being redeveloped in modern variations; essential to entering upon the QUEST. Compare to the VISION QUEST of the Native Americans.

VIPASSANA (Vee-PAHSS-san-nah) In Buddhism, a form of meditation using pure self-observation to enter into the transient nature of all things and events, and observe the interplay of body and mind with total dispassion. Supposed to be especially effective in freeing the unconscious from residual responses rooted in past lifetimes.

VIRGIN In Christianity, the name of the human mother of Jesus, who is said to have conceived him by Immaculate Conception, without sexual intercourse. In worldwide mythology and especially in Gnosticism, the image of the human soul in its original state of divine perfection, before it becomes enmeshed with sensorial existence. Also, the image of human potential in its immaculate state, yet to conceive, that is, yet to be fertilized by conscious intention. The inner repository of Mother Wisdom, she who embodies the full potential of the IN-NATE. "The Virgin is the Arcanum of the Art" (Ramon Lull, mystic and alchemist). See also FALLEN SOPHIA and compare with the FOOL, who is in some respects her male counterpart.

VISION General term for the act of seeing beyond the ordinary senses or the ordinary frame of perception fixed by habitual modes of thinking and reacting. In traditional religions, the moment of illumination that gives contact with God or spiritual knowledge, such as Moses's vision of Jehovah in the burning bush on Mount Sinai, or the direct perception of the Akashic Record described by Irish poet Æ (C&B3.9).

VISION QUEST A term made popular in the current revival of shamanism, referring to a long-established practice common to the American Indians, Siberian shamans, and Australian Aborigines, in which the seeker of self-knowledge and spiritual power (often a boy at the age of puberty) enters upon a deliberate ordeal of seclusion, fasting, and prayer, with the aim of self-purification and the hope of receiving a vision that will show him his true path in life. The supreme example occurs in the memoirs of Black Elk (C&B3.5). Equivalent to the QUEST in European folklore.

VISUALIZATION A loose term for numerous practices in which mental pictures are called up and used for different purposes: to contact someone telepathically, heal from a distance, achieve a desired state (happiness, peace, courage), attain a desired goal or possession (fame, money, sexual charm). Encompasses many popular practices now in use, though the discipline itself is very ancient and seems to have been developed in almost every culture of the past. May be divided into two classes: CREATIVE VISUALIZATION for the purpose of producing external effects, and the use of visual imagery for inner exploration of the processes of the unconscious, as in the Jungian work.

VOID/VOIDNESS In Sanskrit, *shunya* or *shunyata*. Key concept in Buddhism, expressing the belief that there is no substantial basis to reality, no primordial substance out of which things are made, for all things are apparitional, as described in the twelve similes of NAROPA. In a more sophisticated version, explained as the contingent nature of all things, the complete relativity and interdependence of all phenomena, so that no single thing exists, only a vast network of intermeshing events; for instance, if you have some change in your pocket, you have not a single coin, or when you press the palms of your hands together, the surface formed between them, which can be felt as actual warmth and pressure, has no independent existence but is pure contingency. Basis of the unified-field theory of Buddhism, often cited in the new physics. Eastern variety of radical IMMANENCE, as expressed in the haiku of Issa: "Buddha Law / Shining / in leaf dew."

Expounded by Siddhartha in the *Heart Sutra* (C&B1.7) as being identical with form *(rupa)*, thus affirming the identity of Samsara and Nirvana. Elaborately analyzed and broken down into variations in Tibetan psychology, which expostulates as many names for Voidness as the Eskimos have for snow. See also SENTIENT BEINGS, NO-MIND.

VOODOO/VOUDOU   Creole variation of West African dialect, *vodu*, "fetish, demonic force." In African and Caribbean folklore, a magico-religious system for controlling supernatural powers, usually through the use of power-objects like wax dolls, which may be used for casting spells. Involves communication with the dead and marginal forms of BLACK MAGIC.

W

WAKAN (WAH-kan) Sioux, "holy, sacred, supernatural, mysterious."

WAKAN TANKA (WAH-kan TAHN-kah) Sioux, "Great Spirit," the one who works in all things, or the supreme life-force *(wakonda)* pervading all things. Comparable to CHI and MANA.

WALDORF SCHOOL An alternative form of education derived from the esoteric psychology of Rudolf Steiner, stressing protection of the imaginative powers of the child, so that writing (believed to stifle these powers) is not taught until the seventh year. Emphasizes the value of direct participation in art and drama, and a curriculum incorporating historical periods and world mythemes supposed to correspond to stages of moral and psychological development from childhood into the teens.

WALKABOUT Among the Australian Aborigines, the rite of passage undergone by young men at the age of puberty, when they are sent almost naked into the outback to survive for a time on the skills they have learned from the elders. Associated with the aboriginal idea that the landscape and its features, such as trees and stones, are permeated with ancestral memories in the form of stories that are recalled and retold in a particular sequence as one walks about the land and encounters them—example of the archaic mode of MYTHMAKING. Title of a stirring film directed by Nicolas Roeg.

WALK-IN An entity—either from another dimension, another galaxy in this dimension, or from the realm of the dead—who suddenly intervenes and takes up residence in the body of a normal human being, thereby shortcutting longer and more tedious methods of gaining access to the planet, such as that traumatic slide down the birth canal. Usually described as benefactors from other parts of the universe, who take over the body and personality of someone who no longer cares to live, in order to bring to humanity special information and teachings not available through normal people. An example of INTERVENTION.

WARLOCK Old name sometimes applied to a man who practices WICCA. From the Old English *waerloga,* "traitor, deceiver, one who practices the arts of deception." Obviously coined by those who opposed the practitioners.

400

WARRIOR (1) Traditionally, either a man or woman who possesses extraordinary vitality and prowess due to spiritual attainment—going back to times when physical and spiritual powers were believed to exist in tandem. In both the East and the West, from China to South America to Alaska to Ireland, someone of extraordinary courage who might also be a priest or shaman, looked upon as a representative of spiritual wisdom by the tribe or clan. Often connected with the martial arts and practices of self-centering, such as Zen archery and kung fu. (2) In a general and popular sense today, anyone who enters the path of self-awareness on which life itself is taken as a continuous process of risk-taking and opening-up, with the aim of developing total acceptance, courage, and impeccability (as often cited in CASTANEDA). For instance, someone who opts to meet the unknowns and the risks that life presents as opportunities for growth, thus shifting from the attitude of a victim to that of a victor. Someone who seeks not to control or prevail, or wage battle with life, but someone who attempts to face and overcome whatever prevents him or her from entering into the natural flow of things (TAO), thereby gaining advantage over those who try to resist it. The warrior prevails by restraint and nonaggression. See also ASCETIC.

WATER BIRTH The practice of giving birth to a child underwater, believed to be more gentle than the conventional way. Linked to the belief that the ocean was the womb of our species and so it ought to be the first element we contact upon birth. Sometimes attended by dolphins.

WATTS, ALAN American philosopher, teacher, writer, and self-declared "entertainer," brilliant exponent of Zen and East/West psychology (1915–1973). One of the leading pioneers of the modern spiritual movement, known for his sanity, eloquence, and humor. Internationally known author, lecturer, and proponent of the intelligent use of drugs as sacramental tools for raising consciousness.

WEIRD/WYRD From the Anglo-Saxon root *urd,* "to wind, weave." In the old Celtic tongue, the spiritual power unique to a person. The unknown, strange, erratic, ineffable, indefinable something present in every one of us due to our all being, to some degree, mysterious and unknown to each other. Exact equivalent to the NAHUAL in Toltec sorcery, as interpreted by Castaneda. In European magic and Druidic initiation, the power attributed to those who can enter and control the sinuous, ever-winding forces of nature, exemplified in Wiccan folklore by the tying of knots to affect events. Possibly linked to the bodily forces of KUNDALINI, sometimes called the coiled, or serpent, power. Perhaps, in modern translation, the attribute of magical skill acquired through access to the inner windings of the DNA coil.

WELLNESS In holistic medicine and alternative healing, the natural and harmonious state of the human body and person, taken as an object of interest and cultivation and held to be worthy of medical study and disciplinary upkeep—as opposed to sickness, which is the main interest of conventional medicine.

WESAK (WAY-sak) From Sanskrit *vaisakha*. The festival celebrating the birth, renunciation, and death of the historical Buddha, usually set at the time of the full moon in Taurus, in late autumn. Reinstated in Western form by Alice A. BAILEY, as an occasion for worldwide meditation.

WESTERN MASTERS In the tradition of Hermetics and European Rosicrucianism, an initiate distinguished by practical vision and powers of culture-initiation applicable to the social and historical problems of humanity in his or her time. The exemplary SPIRITUAL MASTER in the West, the progressive occultist who consciously undergoes periodic reincarnation in successive historical eras in order to introduce new impulses and assist humanity with the lessons essential to its moral and spiritual progress; or the initiate, inspired by love and service, who works through linear time by SERIAL REINCARNATION to provide for humanity's inner and outer needs. Those who do special and original things, by contrast to the Eastern masters or those who exemplify what we all essentially are. Usually described as remaining behind the scenes, but sometimes cited as a single, persistent ENTELECHY who appears in famous or epoch-making personalities: one example, Joseph (the father of Jesus)/Columbus/Roger Bacon/Francis Bacon/SAINT GERMAIN. (However, this famous instance is contradicted by another school of European occultism, which attributes a different sequence of previous lives to Saint Germain!) Developing and imparting OCCULTISM is the primary task of these masters, by contrast to showing the way to God, the primary task of their counterparts in the East. They are, as it were, the executives of cocreation. See also INCOMPLETION.

WESTERN MYSTERY TRADITION The body of teachings and practices indigenous to the West (that is to say, Europe and North and South America), including the lore of dozens of ancient Mystery Schools and lost traditions, such as the Hibernian, Teutonic, Celtic, Eleusinian, Pythagorean, Mithraic, Aztec, Toltec, Mayan, Incan—everything from the Druidic Schools of Ireland to the Medicine Lodges of Native America. In contrast to the massive body of Oriental religious teachings, which emphasizes Enlightenment and liberation from the demands and illusions of the sensorial, time-bound world, the Western Mystery tradition stresses bonding with the natural world and commitment to exploring the mysterious element of TIME. Initially disclosed to the public through the Hermetica (C&B2.9 and E2.2); reputed to have its most well-known modern expression in ROSICRUCIANISM. Currently (since the early 1980s) undergoing an enormous revival within the New Age movement, though still less well-known than the Eastern paths and as yet virtually obscure to the general public.

WESTERN UNION Name applied in America to the mystical-erotic practices of sexual Yoga, or Tantra.

WESTLANDS In the Celtic Revival, the westernmost regions of France (Brittany), England (Cornwall), Wales, and Ireland (County Kerry), viewed as a single magical land in medieval folklore and Arthurian Romance. Believed to be the geographic region of the UNDERWORLD, realm of deceased souls and long-departed Gods, where the warrior-initiate goes to face spiritual testing and reap supernatural wisdom, rejuvenation, and paradisiacal pleasure. Visited by Gilgamesh on his search for the mushroom of immortality (C&B2.1).

WHALES The largest mammals on Earth; almost hairless, blubber-sheathed, warm-blooded creatures of the order Cetacea (Seh-TAY-see-uh), who inhabit the ocean but must surface continually (every five to sixty minutes) to breathe. There are dozens of varieties, of which the great blue (or "sulphur-bottomed") whale is the largest known, sometimes as much as one hundred feet long. Adopted as a symbol of planetary unity in the 1960s, when the threat of extinction was opposed by the Greenpeace movement. Along with DOLPHINS, an important part of planetary folklore. Known for their capacity to communicate and navigate by sonar—often taken as an example of long-range telepathy or planet-wide communication, a goal of New Age group efforts.

WHEEL OF REBIRTH In Buddhism, a term for the endless repetitive cycle of death and rebirth, or SAMSARA—the object of spiritual practice being, in some cases, to get off the wheel; that is, to become liberated from the vicious cycle of bewilderment and free oneself from further incarnations. In Tibetan Buddhism, a didactic system of esoteric psychology illustrated in a specific MANDALA known as the world-wheel, showing the "three poisons" (anger, lust, and aggression) at the core, the scheme of the "Six Worlds" (Gods, titans, humans, animals, ghosts, demons) of physical incarnation, and the system of the "twelve karmic links" that make up the vicious cycle of birth-suffering-death-rebirth.

WHIRLING DERVISH From Persian *darvesh*, "beggar." In Arabian mysticism and Sufism, one who seeks the ecstasy of total absorption in God by spinning the body in a counterclockwise direction until overcome by the dream-like awareness of divinity that floats like a perfume through the world. Described as a beggar because he or she forgoes all other pleasures, gives up all worldly desires, in favor of this supreme spiritual enchantment. A Sufi yogic technique, often practiced in large groups to the accompaniment of drumming and chanting. Said to have originated spontaneously as a dance of ecstatic affirmation by RUMI.

WHITE BROTHERHOOD, WHITE LODGE See GREAT WHITE BROTHERHOOD.

WHITE LIGHT Street slang from the 1960s, borrowed from *The Tibetan Book of the Dead* (C&B1.8), used in referring to an effect of the psychedelic experience: a state of clarity and mental illumination in which the "tripper" enters into a vision of pure light freed of all reflective properties, experienced as something like a lightning flash that does not fade away. Depending on the extent to which the vision can be sustained, it produces a sensation of boundless joy and sensuous ecstasy similar to the SAMADHI of Indian Yoga or the after-death illumination described in the Tibetan manual for conscious dying. Closely related to AKASHA.

WHITE MAGIC The practice, by ritual and meditation, of bringing oneself and all one's efforts into conscious harmony with the progressive activity of human evolution, of serving the will of the creative flow instead of one's selfish, separatistic ends. The use of occult power and knowledge in the selfless service of humanity, rather than to control and manipulate, as is the case in black magic.

WICCA (E29) (WICK-uh) Name applied to WITCHCRAFT by its advocates and practitioners. Adj., Wiccan (WICK-un). Worship of the nature-forces, extending to reverence for nature as a divine being, especially a feminine being, that is, Mother Nature. See also WITCH.

WISDOM ME *wis,* from OE *witan,* "to know" > IE root *weid-,* "to see, know," equivalent to Sanskrit *veda,* same root as the word *wit.* Greek *Sophia.* Direct seeing and comprehending of the divine intelligence that informs the world; understanding of life at the profound level where one participates fully in what one knows. The goal of spiritual seeking in Gnosticism and other schools of cognitive discipline. Sometimes called in modern Western occultism Love-Wisdom, the operative intelligence and healing power of the Son Principle, the Solar Logos on Earth, or Christos, the synthesis of MOTHER WISDOM and FATHER WISDOM.

WITCH From the Old English *wicce/wicca,* possibly going back to the Indo-European root *weik-,* "set aside, sacred, holy." A practitioner, usually a woman, of the old religion called Wicca by those who practice it. The masculine equivalent is the WARLOCK.

WITCHCRAFT (E29) The craft or skill of Wicca. The old religion based on worshipful reverence for the Earth and the forces of nature, usually described as having two primary deities, the Great Mother and the Horned God. Described by its advocates as the religion of our Paleolithic ancestors, an inheritance as ancient as shamanism, to which it is closely related. In a loose, crude, and popular sense, the practice of casting spells and manipulating supernatural forces for fun or profit.

WIZARD From the same root as *wisdom.* One who practices what he or she knows by virtue of possessing wisdom. Old-fashioned term for an agent of creative intelligence, someone who knows how the universe works and how to work with it. Contrast to the modern term *scientist.* See also FAUST.

WORD The LOGOS or pervasive intelligence evident in any event, such as the formation of a storm or the composition of a symphony. The archetypal seed-force informing any process; for instance, that which makes a peach pit develop into a peach tree, so that every leaf on the tree is uniformly and distinctly of the peach tree, and so that it produces the fruit of its own kind and not something else.

Cosmologically, the blueprint of creation. In genetics, the consistent pattern of organic design, the operation of the DNA code "printing itself out." In ancient religion, myth, and metaphysics, the vital breath (SPIRIT) filled with inherent patterning power, by which the universe is created. In esoteric Christianity, the Solar Logos or SON PRINCIPLE: the creative word as a life-giving medium that sustains all things, but also comes to be embodied on Earth as a specific human being in Jesus Christ or in other avatars.

The single most important principle in ancient wisdom and metaphysics, presently being reinvented in such concepts as IMPLICATE ORDER, hologrammic theory (see HOLOGRAM), MORPHOGENETIC FIELDS. See also LANGUAGE.

WORKSHOP A form of group activity popular from the 1960s onward, in which a teacher/practitioner presents knowledge and exercises to a group of people, with the aim of enabling them to apply themselves directly to the information being imparted.

WORLD-TREE A mytheme found in many cultures, expressing the belief that the world grows from a tree or somehow is a tree. In the mythology of Scandinavia and the indigenous people of England (Brythons), the realm where the God-man Woden endured hanging for nine days and nights, an ordeal that imbued him with the power of the RUNES. Figured in the twelfth Tarot trump, the Hanged Man, and appropriated by Christianity, which declares the cross on Golgotha to be a redeemed version of the tree of the knowledge of good and evil in Genesis. May be interpreted as a mythic image referring to the double-spiral structure of DNA (TREE-ALPHABET), according to the theory that many kinds of initiatory vision (especially those derived from the use of psychedelics) involve penetrating consciously into the realm of genetic information and thus accessing knowledge about all aspects of world evolution. See also TRUTH.

WORSHIP The form universally assumed by traditional religions, in which the practitioners or believers perform acts of reverence and express gratitude toward their chosen deity, either individually or in groups. Today the word has something of a homely, old-fashioned air: conventional and FUNDAMENTAL-IST Christians gather to hear sermons and testify to their experiences of struggle and salvation, loosely calling this worship, although technically it is not. The word itself is a contraction of *worth-ship,* from the Old English *weorthscipe,* "worthiness." Thus, the practice performed to make oneself feel worthy, or to overcome the feeling of worthlessness.

WU (Woo) (1) Chinese for Nothing, or Enlightenment. A name for the state of perfect mental composure achieved by silencing the babble of words in the head. (2) In esoteric alphabetics, the twenty-third letter, *w,* of the English alphabet.

WU WEI (Woo WAY) Chinese, "nothing doing" or "nothing in process." The state of supreme ease and spontaneity due to being in complete attunement with the Tao; the ideal state of effortlessness and nonresistance, in which all action proceeds by harmonious accord with the flow of the moment. Dynamic SERENITY. Philosophically, the concept of radical NONATTAINMENT: "Since Enlightenment is my own nature, which becomes self-evident when free from all distraction, I will claim it by ceasing to seek for it." See E30 on this paradoxical idea basic to Zen.

X

XANADU (ZAHN-uh-doo) Artificial paradise, experienced in an opium dream by English Romantic poet Samuel Taylor Coleridge and described in his poem "Kubla Khan." Well-known example of the OTHERWORLD.

XIBALBA (She-BAHL-bah) Nahuatl name for the UNDERWORLD, or Hell, the abode of the dead, described in the POPOL VUH as a realm of supernatural events and dark, dangerous powers, where trials of initiation occur (C&B2.12).

X-RAY VISION Occult power for seeing through dense objects, possessed by the American folk hero SUPERMAN.

Y

Y A B - Y U M   Tibetan, "pa-ma" (i.e., father-mother). Sacred intercourse, especially the union of a deity with his consort, as seen in many Tibetan and Buddhist TANKAS and sculptures, where the male deity is often shown sitting cross-legged in the LOTUS POSTURE with his consort seated on his lap, joined to him in a genital embrace that is at the same time a meditative posture. In Eastern iconography, an image of the highest sacred and psychological value, representing the union of the active (feminine) and passive (masculine) principles of creation in a state of ecstatic union and serene poise. Equivalent to SHIVA/SHAKTI in Hindu Tantra. See also MAITHUNA.

Y A G E   (YAH-hay) In South American shamanism, a powerful plant used for inducing hallucinations and altered states.

Y A N G   See YIN/YANG.

Y I N / Y A N G   In Taoism and Chinese philosophy, the dual functions of the single principle at the source of all things, consisting of active/male/Yang and receptive/female/Yin. Described at length in Chinese medicine, the martial arts, and the *I Ching* (as Heaven/Yang and Earth/Yin). Contrast with INFINITY.

Y O G A   From Sanskrit *yug-*, "to join, unite." Probably the most ancient method of religious discipline in the world; the practice of using bodily postures, breathing exercises, and concentration upon sounds and images to achieve unification with the supreme state of pure being-consciousness-bliss (SAT-CHITANANDA). Arose in India in prehistorical times and imported to the West in the beginning of the twentieth century by Buddhist missionaries and practitioners of Western magic, such as Aleister Crowley, though it did not receive widespread public attention until the 1960s. Exists in many variations, of which six main types are often cited:

Bhakti, the Yoga of devotion
Hatha, the Yoga of health and physical agility
Jnana, the Yoga of spiritual wisdom

Kundalini, the Yoga of the inner fire
Mantra, the Yoga of sound meditation
Karma, the Yoga of action or duty

Defined in the BHAGAVAD GITA (C&B1.6) as the method of uniting the higher and lower selves and attaining freedom from the necessity of rebirth. Adopted in the West as a technique for stress control and CENTERING.

YOGANANDA, PARAMAHANSA (Par-amma-HAN-sah Yo-gah-NAHN-dah) One of the first and most well-known Indian gurus to bring Yoga to the West (1893–1952), known for his gentility and kindness. Founder of the Self-Realization Fellowship, best-selling author (C&B3.12). The name means "supreme swan of blissful union."

YOGI/YOGINI (YOE-gee/Yoe-GEE-nee) Masc./fem. One who practices Yoga.

YONI (YOH-nee) Sanskrit word for the female genitalia. Compare with LINGAM.

YUGA (YOO-gah) Sanskrit, from the same root as *Yoga*. In Hindu cosmology and philosophy, an age or time-cycle, such as the KALI YUGA. Of various lengths, the briefest being 432,000 years.

Z

ZARATHUSTRA (ZAHR-uh-THOOS-tra) Avestan name for ZO-ROASTER.

ZAZEN In Zen, the technique of just sitting and staring, used for clearing the mind of all distracting thoughts so that the ultimate nature of reality can spontaneously manifest itself in a moment of sudden awakening, or SATORI. An example of WU WEI.

ZEITGEIST (TZITE-guyst) German, "spirit of the times." The trend of thought and feeling that characterizes an era of time. See also ARCHANGEL.

ZEN (E30) Japanese form of the Chinese word *Ch'an,* which itself is a contraction of the Sanskrit word *Dhyana,* "momentum, flow," or the state of concentration in which one unites effortlessly with the flow of the passing moment. The practice of inner centering aimed at achieving complete, sudden, and spontaneous awareness of perfect presence, empty and without intent. Characterized by the peculiar and paradoxical doctrine of "no-mind" or NONATTAINMENT. See also VOID, SUCHNESS.

ZEND-AVESTA Persian sacred book, supposed to contain teachings and stories passed down from the time of the great Magus Zoroaster, said to have been the first human being to bargain with God.

ZENDO Meditation hall where Zen-sitting is practiced.

ZODIAC From Greek *zoion,* "animal" + *kyklos,* "circle." Usually translated as "circle of animals," though it probably meant something more like "cycle of animations." Technically, the twelve constellations on the path of the Sun, although only three of these images are actually animals (Ram, Bull, Lion). In the ancient Mysteries, the model for initiation through a sequence of spiritual tests (the Twelve Labors of Hercules). In sidereal astrology, the starry images used for locating the planets and making up symbolical interpretations of human character and behavior. In general, a sequence of psychic images or celestial ARCHETYPES, which may possibly describe ever-recurrent aspects of human experience, such as moral equilibrium between the pairs of opposites (Balance, or

Scales), commitment to one's true passions (Lion), or self-actualization through evolving the innate (Virgin). See also SIGNS versus CONSTELLATIONS.

Z O H A R   (ZOH-har) Hebrew, "splendor, radiance," from the root *zhr*, "to radiate." In the Cabala, a sourcebook of metaphysical teachings on creation and the nature of the human soul, said to have been compiled in its present form by Moses de Leon in Spain, around 1300.

Z O M B I E   Congolese *zumbi*, "fetish-doll." In West African VOODOO, a snake deity usually related to the python, or a corpse that comes to be reanimated by magic or through possession by an entity other than the one that originally inhabited it.

Z O R O A S T E R   (ZOHR-oh-ass-tur) Greek form of the Persian name Zarathustra, (master of the) "golden star." Persian master who lived historically around 600 B.C., though the name is really a title held by a line of MAGI said to go back thousands of years. Key figure in the ancient religions of the Parsis, who held themselves to be a chosen people gifted with responsibility for handling the creative fire of God on Earth. Zoroastrianism is one of the ancient world-religions, now surviving only among the small sects of Parsis in India and Iran. Originally based on a mythology describing a battle between good and evil, Ahura-Mazda and AHRIMAN, in which the human race plays a pivotal role. See also AGNI YOGA.

Z U Ñ I   (ZOO-nyee) Tribe of southwestern American Indians, of which about five thousand survive from an original race of many thousands who called themselves *A shiwi*, "the flesh" (*Zuñi* being a Spanish corruption of this word). Associated with seven primary villages, said to have been the Seven Cities of Cibola, a realm of paradisiacal abundance sought by the Conquistadores.

AFTERWORD

Fulfilling the Great Promise

*The last degree of esoteric teaching
is plain common sense.*

A. R. ORAGE,
"Aphorisms"

S ince the way the New Age is seen depends so largely upon using the full scope of the imagination, its prospects and promises tend to be somewhat exaggerated by its self-styled exemplars. To hear some talk, you would think a momentous global revolution is at hand, a historical apocalypse of epic dimensions. Part of this is just millennial fever; another part is genuine panic at the awesome dimensions of the environmental crisis, which seems to call for solutions on a scale as vast as the damage we've done to the elements that make this planet livable. The obvious urgency of our external problems in society and the environment inspires the belief that an equivalent response from within can turn the tide.

Whether it can or not depends a great deal upon the right use of the imagination by those who designate themselves the pioneers of the age. The elements of exaggeration and make-believe, which so often discredit the movement in the eyes of its critics and skeptics, can be better appreciated as aspects of its youthful nature. When children play, they engage the imagination creatively with the actual world and in doing so transfigure it. Something similar is at work in the new spirituality, where mythmaking plays an enormous role, as I have previously noted. David Spangler, certainly one of its best representatives, has described the New Age as a stage of sociocultural transformation initiated through pretending, as when a child who plays with boats in a pond goes on to become a naval architect.

This is, to my mind, a wise and compassionate observation that can prove to be extremely helpful in fostering the great promise of the age. If at least some of the developments crucial to humanity's future have to be imaginatively playacted before they can be pragmatically enacted, then it will be unwise to dismiss the childlike, narcissistic character of many New Age pursuits. As Spangler asks, Do we criticize the movement for its stage of life, or do we help it to mature? The issue is quite unavoidable, I'd say, because it contains the challenge of how to direct and discipline the powers of human imagination, the faculty viewed by the Romantics as the primary seat of divinity within us all. Free-form spirituality engages the narcissistic creative impulses of the child and, hopefully, carries them toward full and mature expression.

My own perspective on the modern spiritual movement is rooted in historical studies, going back to the Renaissance and taking account of the upheaval of Romanticism with all its long-range aftershocks. The present configuration of New Age interests and planetary thinking is a phase of a five-hundred-year-long development that has, perhaps, another two or three centuries to go before it matures. In this perspective I can see some possible long-term advances in spiritual development, if not for humanity at large, then at least for a select portion whose mission it may be to evolve into the organ of planetary conscience. Having never joined a movement nor followed a particular master or teacher, I have always kept watch for those possibilities of individual spiritual growth that can contribute in the most profound and enduring way to this mission. If there is really a great promise, a rare and special opportunity for spiritual awakening in our time, then it lies, by my sights, in that direction.

History clearly teaches that new realities emerge when paradigms shift. In this book I hope to have shown that *seeking* is truly a new paradigm. To appreciate this point, let's say that the alternative to following is not leading, but seeking. Following is the response to authority in any form; it demands obedience and conformity. As followers, we have the security of adopting that which has been passed down or delivered to us in finished form, as tradition. *Following* is the paradigm that pertained when choices were limited to the teachings and practices of spiritual development that were available in a given time and place. It characterizes the old religious culture that requires the seeker to adopt prescribed dogmas and proceed consistently along preestablished, well-worn tracks.

Currently we are experiencing a shift away from the old paradigm of following toward a risky, free-form process of experimentation and discovery. In the modern spiritual movement all previous traditions, once spread across the world and distributed through historical time, are now simultaneously available. What was formerly obligatory, because it was practically the only thing available at a given time and place, is now completely optional. Even if it is not so easy to say exactly what an alternative path actually is, as I have argued in "From Authority to Discovery" (E2.1), it still remains true that all paths may be viewed as alternatives when they are presented within a pluralistic framework.

The seeker who undertook Yogic initiation in the Himalayas a thousand years ago did not encounter the situation found by someone who takes up Yoga today. Someone who gets involved with Wicca in a contemporary manner may draw from theories of the new physics and the findings of comparative mythology to enhance their practice, but Wiccans of the past had no comparable access to such options. No astrologer of antiquity or even Elizabethan times had the *I Ching* and depth psychology for backup systems, as Dane Rudhyar did. Modern-day mystics on videotape and Gnostic networkers who converse by modem can work toward translating personal visions into planetary programs in ways the desert eremites could not.

It is the hybrid or even synthetic character of modern spirituality that makes it truly different and, as I hope to have shown, it is this difference that demands an entirely new methodology, a technique for clear and well-founded choice-making. The discipline of *pathfinding* involves responsibilities that were unknown to seekers of the past who did not face the multiple-choice situation of our times. This discipline is twofold: First, it calls for developing an overview of the paths and options available; and second, it requires an artful selection and combination of diverse options into a curriculum, a course of life-practices, that will meet the unique needs and fulfill the specific talents of the individual seeker. By mastering this twofold discipline the seeker *becomes* self-directing. In other words, self-direction is not something we have at the outset, but something we acquire and demonstrate as we go along. The discipline of pathfinding leads to a clear, well-grounded commitment to a path; then, once the path is entered, self-direction enables the seeker not merely to *follow* the path by dint of sheer conformity, but to handle the path *progressively,* to adapt it to personal needs and aims, and ultimately to direct it in a creative way, taking it beyond its pregiven status into realms of experiment and innovation. How self-directing you are becomes evident in how you lay the thread through the winding tracks of the labyrinth, linking up the different paths you take in a way that is specific and original to you and you alone. Basically it means you direct the path to serve you rather than let it run your life.

But if free exploration and the power of choice are abdicated in favor of blind adherence to any single path, there can be no self-direction toward new forms and new expressions of spiritual experience, as Eliade suggested (see the Preamble). At best, conformity to the old paradigm of following a path rather than directing it will support personal growth in some ways, but it may not engage the seeker in the kind of intense creative involvement necessary for entering the configuration of planetary conscience.

One-track seeking is still quite common—a dozen or so years spent exclusively in Zen sitting, for instance. But going on a spiritual trip is not the same as entering a spiritual path. To clarify this distinction, I propose the term *life-path* to designate what results from directing the lessons and skills gained on any spiritual path back to life itself. No single-track teaching or practice anywhere in the spectrum of options from alchemy to Zen is adequate to be considered a life-path. Why not? Well, in the first place, it is because spiritual paths tend to be self-referential, inviting the seeker to identify and lock onto a mind-set and habits that are verified within the path they define, rather than within life itself. And then again, if seeking is multioptional, it will require carving out a number of paths and then combining them into a unique life-practice, rather than merely finding one path and following it. On a spiritual trip the itinerary is already set, but a life-path is a complex braid never to be delineated by a single set of rules or practices.

Theseus in the labyrinth does not merely find a path to the Minotaur— in fact, he finds dozens of them, some leading into the interior of the maze, some leading around the sides, some coming to dead ends. What he does is unwind his thread along a number of intersecting paths within the maze, so that eventually the thread describes a unique pattern. In the same way, every seeker can forge a life-path that is entirely original and unique, combining experiences gained from a number of different teachings and practices.

So the discipline of pathfinding—the art of wending your own way through the labyrinth—is the primary point of departure toward the great

promise, the unique and unprecedented opportunity for spiritual development in our times. In no previous era of human history has the seeker
been faced with such an exciting challenge, such a huge array of options
and alternatives. We have more isms than fourth-century Alexandria
raised to the tenth power. The image of the maze, ancient though it may
be, serves to ground a pathfinding concept, fully contemporary and crucial to the future of the quest.

Since the Renaissance, the spiritual quest has been expanding toward a
global dimension, though this does not mean that progressive self-work
of the kind that can support and inspire large-scale societal changes is
being pursued worldwide by large numbers of people. Not at all, but
there is an "infraculture" emerging, which might be viewed as a meta-
morphosis of the counterculture of the sixties. Most everyone in the New
Age movement claims the ideal of global unity as their guiding vision.
"Healing ourselves and healing the planet" is the way it often is stated.
The two leading motives of healing and cocreation, undertaken within
the specific conditions of the times, contain a high call to conscience and
intimate sharing. In keeping with this global ideal, there is no place for
the age-old methods of empowerment, even the ones that worked in the
Mystery Schools. "Group action" is a major shift from the old paradigm
of the power-elite, like the Initiates and Masters who were—paradoxically—selflessly self-empowered in the cause of the racial group they served.
Today, if there is to be individual self-empowerment, it must be qualified
by deep concern for how the individual is contributing to group activities.
Cocreation is not a control system, and the basic attitudes and approaches
necessary for implementing it are still largely undefined. At present the
dynamics of cocreation are still in the incubation phase, the cellular level
of individual activity. It may take a couple more centuries before its
complex social mechanics and economic/ecologic strategies operate ef-
ficiently in some parts of the world.

    To implement this vast visionary transformation toward a new society
along the lines of the utopian dreams sketched out in E1.1, there is,
however, no infallible pregiven agenda, no "master plan" to be handed
down from an evolutionary avant-garde of superhuman guides and
stamped with the glowing seal of divine sanction. Although conspiratorial
theories are quite inescapable when one delves deeply into the history of
occult/esoteric groups and movements, I am convinced that conspiracies,
no matter how well intended, will always defeat the vision they pro-

pound. If it is only the creative collaboration of free agents that can make a real difference in the world, then the New Age agenda will have to resemble a musical jam session a lot more than the game plan of the Planetary Hierarchy described by Alice Bailey and others.

What bonds us most strongly into the great promise of healing and renovation, as I see it, is the dual dynamic of *love* and *incompletion*. *Love*, as what collaborates and colludes, is the matrix of all shared work and play, and *incompletion*, according to the view of the alchemists, is the state of creation as we have inherited it from the superhuman powers who fashioned it. In the words of the Creative Logos from the Nag Hammadi Gospels:

> Behold, you are from the Pleroma [Divine Fullness] and you dwell now in the place where incompletion is—but see how its original light comes again from me through you.

I hope that the great promise of our time also contains the possibility of rekindling the experience of *awe* through direct encounter with the Sacred, the Divine. For me this has always been a major concern, even an obsession of sorts. As we have frequently noted, the retrieval and revalorization of ancient wisdom is a dominant theme of the modern spiritual quest. And so the questions often arise: Did people in the past know more than we do about how the universe works? Did they have sounder values, reflecting a saner and more integrated relation to nature? Were they closer to God?

Of course, we can only speculate about this, but I am convinced that ancient and aboriginal peoples were better off than us in one respect at least: Their spiritual experience and the habits of life derived from it were more deeply rooted in their vitality. What we lack today—and it may truly prove to be a grave, even fatal deficiency—is the capacity or even the desire for vital contact with the Divine, the Sacred, Spirit, God, as it presents itself directly and immediately to us, from without or within.

How can we make ourselves available to *awe,* to be contacted and touched directly by the Divine, the *Sacred?* Having had a number of experiences comparable to those described by Bucke in *Cosmic Consciousness* (C&B3.1), I was always left wondering how to have them again, as often as I liked. A lot depends on how we define the Divine, how we imagine Spirit—because the *description* we devise is itself a powerful tool that can dispose us to the experience we're seeking. The best way I know is to go back to the Sanskrit verb-root *shak-*, "to be powerful," root of the words "sacred, sacrifice, sacerdotal," et cetera. Thus *Sacred* and *powerful* are practically synonymous, but this equation will be misleading unless we look carefully into what it takes to be powerful. Certainly it is not mundane power, such as may be acquired through money or political influence, that is meant here. By my faith, the Sacred is never evident in the power of one human being over another, for its essence is fundamentally more than human. But how do we arrive at a viable conception of transmundane, extrahuman power, if it is to be something better than a wispy, ethereal fiction?

My approach to this question has been to start from the idea I've just introduced: namely, that the Sacred can be experienced deep within one's own vitality. In short, I know the Sacred is powerful because my very life depends on it. I am speaking here of all the dependencies that lie outside the realm of what human beings can do for each other, or even what I can do for myself. By contrast to all that, the power of the Sacred is evident in what is done for me. When I look at my experience of nature, for instance, I see myself as a creature involved in a vast organic system of forces, a vital web that operates all around me and in many ways quite beyond me, yet also works specifically for me without my having to know very much about how it does so. It is truly amazing that I participate so slightly in the processes that sustain my life. I digest food, perform complex habitual activities like typing, and utilize my inner resources of memory and imagination without really experiencing in depth how any of it works. I don't even know how I wake up in the morning!

So I would define spiritual power as what it takes to sustain the complexities of human life, while requiring of us only a minimal participation in its actual workings. Spirit, usually placed at the apex of the triangle of body-soul-spirit, is really the power informing the other two, operating largely undetected within all the activities of body and soul that we take so much for granted. As I write these words, I relay a series of commands to my mind and body, which then respond in a highly sophisticated way, yet I know next to nothing about how the commands are formed or how they come to be executed. I imagine the Sacred, then, as a power at large in the world, far greater than myself, which lends a fraction of itself to support my life. It sustains and directs all my vital and psychological functions while requiring almost nothing of me. And so I almost never encounter it directly; I encounter it rather through its effects, through the support and assistance it lends me in a variety of complex and intimate ways.

Yet it *can* be encountered directly, as well, and for that experience the factor of awe is essential. Of course, I can—and I hope we all can— conjure up a trace of awe by contemplating how my food is digested without my having to take part in the process, or how my memory provides a full reconstruction of an incident from my past without my having to do anything but pay attention. This is a good start, but the awe of appreciating the workings of the Sacred compares to the awe of en- countering it directly as the number one compares to infinity. I doubt, however, that we can open ourselves to the greater dimensions of awe unless we return somehow to a sense of dependence upon the Sacred, viewing it as if our lives depended upon it—which they do.

And this is not all there is to it, for there is an added element of urgency in knowing that the dependence is mutual. According to some Gnostic and alchemical teachings (such as the Nag Hammadi Gospels mentioned above), creation is incomplete. The Sacred, although it is infinitely greater than ourselves and supports our life and consciousness through its workings, nevertheless needs us to complete its workings—which is perhaps exactly why we have been left so free of having to participate in them. Cocreation is definitely set up on a volunteer basis, and awe is what inspires it.

To cultivate whatever it takes to become capable of feeling *awe* is one of two primary ways to encounter and reengage the Sacred. The other is through *faith,* but this term really needs to be redefined because its conventional use constitutes a misleading description. To this end, I find it helpful to distinguish strongly between faith and belief: *Faith* is a commitment to achieve what can be imagined, while *belief* is dependence upon nonverifiable systems of description.

As I've noted regarding the issue of alternative paths, belief is a potent force that needs to be subordinated to choice. The inherited structures of religious belief, the old grandstand religions, would hardly be able to prevail in the world as they do today if their adherents asked themselves, "Is this something I choose to believe?" Here, for sure, is a valuable guideline for clear seeking, but it can perhaps be delineated even more vividly by applying what I call the "wedge." This is a tool for separating one question into two, so that each one becomes more distinct and illuminates the other. In the case of belief, you can apply the wedge like this: Whenever one encounters something that requires belief, the essen- tial question is not "Do I believe it or not?" but "Do I *need* to believe it, or don't I?"

Now, to experience vital contact with the Divine, to be swept up in *awe* through a direct encounter with the Sacred in the form of an over-whelming supernatural force can be, needless to say, a huge distraction from running errands and other quotidian activities. Having had this experience numerous times for brief moments, I have then spent years of my life in the effort to assimilate it and return to at least a semblance of normal functioning. I must leave it up to my close friends to assess how well I have managed!

In any case, I came in the course of time to realize that there were two primary ways of encountering the Sacred, one immediate and over-whelming and the other less spectacular but a lot more practical! My initial taste of Enlightenment occurred spontaneously in a Japanese boardinghouse in August 1965 as I caught sight of an old lady who was practicing what certainly must be an ancient and esoteric method of washing the pet finch: Take a huge mouthful of water from a glass and blow it at the bird. For weeks I had been hearing this noise without knowing what it was; then one afternoon I leaned out the window of my two-and-a-half tatami room and at the moment I saw what it was I also saw that I had no concept of what it was. Seeing nonconceptually for that one instant, I had the encompassing realization that my entire perception of the world was unmediated by thought, formless and void, as the Sutras say. In just the fraction of a second before I attached a "logical explana-tion" to the sound, I was able to be aware, free of language and logic, of how the Sacred reveals itself, perpetually and unconditionally, like the sky opening to the plunge of a bird.

The satori of that moment was not, however, without conceptual con-tent. As pure appearance, the Sacred reveals itself in Suchness, that lovely word; but the Sacred is present as well even in the workings of the conceptual mind. So my experience of that moment was cognitively informed in a vivid way with two features that have profoundly shaped my views of spiritual development: While the sudden awakening I experi-enced did not contain the certainty that I could maintain it, it did contain the certainty that to maintain it required no effort or technique. So, left with the resonating insight that the Sacred is never *not* present to me, and that even if I can't be sure of maintaining contact with it, that's all right, because I don't have to; I have since sought ways to make myself available to it by putting my faith in life itself.

Now the disciplines of modern seeking are one thing, and the seren-dipity of life itself is another. The point is, let's not let the two cancel each other out. After all, it is life itself that leads us to any spiritual path—leads us, I maintain, by a course of events that exhibit an innate design of beauty and necessity that has to be appreciated as much as we appreciate what we discover upon any path we enter. This is the Principle of Free Approach. It brings us back to the matter of *faith,* because it takes faith to appreciate how the Sacred is continually, ingeniously operative in the ongoing pattern of everyday events. While on the one hand the Sacred can break in and overwhelm us in a moment of cosmic consciousness or sudden awakening, it is also present in a more modest way all the time. Perhaps it's set up this way to keep us from getting totally spoiled by the unspeakable thrills of sharp-edged satori and transcendental rapture.

Another possibility, which I want to propose for its superior practical value in everyday application, is the idea that our capacity for direct contact and communication with the Divine is always operative, free and unimpeded, but we either cheat ourselves out of the experience or indulge in delusionary substitutes for it. Spiritual practice, then, may be defined as whatever we can do, day to day, to disentangle ourselves from the delusional and denial systems we use to deprive ourselves of experiencing in a vivid, tangible, and often hilarious way how the Sacred is active in the eventualities of life itself, independent of any spiritual techniques and teachings. I am unceasingly amazed at how powerfully the dynamics of *attitude* can program and direct our experience. For instance, I suspect we undertake the elaborate subterfuge of cheating ourselves out of direct contact and communication with the Sacred so that our experience will conform to the attitude that insists we don't deserve it!

It is *belief* that locks us into such preset systems of behavior, but *faith* demands the courage to imagine that things could be otherwise. Suppose, for instance, that God is not "out there" or even "within," but something that is revealed in the warp and woof of interpersonal dynamics? Imagine God is hiding among us, Vishnu playing through the dreamers. Imagine that God is a Trickster who sometimes provides miraculous assistance and at other times throws a mischievous problem in our path so that we have to own up to an attitude that is hampering us.

There is, as far as I know, no real progress in the quest without undergoing an awkward, inconvenient process of character development, and its pitfalls are legion. Arrogance, elitism, peek-a-boo games of mystic pretension, power plays and delusions of grandiosity, seductive insight, escapism and spiritual glamor, isolationary plots, denial of personal reality, warped mythmaking—I've seen 'em all, for the most part in myself. Perhaps human character is a mystery and a conundrum even to the Gods themselves. In any case, it is at least as fascinating as the most complex formulas of the Cabala or paraphysics. Today I find that the ways I can deceive and hurt myself, at any given moment, are at least as interesting as details of Pleiadean genetic experiments begun on Lemuria.

Power-seeking is the inverse of encountering the Sacred. If it is true, as I have often suspected, that people will seek power so that they can practice behaviors that allow them to pretend they don't feel lost and purposeless, then power-seeking along spiritual paths has to be viewed with a cautious and compassionate eye. And a comedic flair. Remember, if you can't play with it, it's probably a delusion. A sense of humor, it appears, is the rite of passage into significant involvement with the great riddles.

Spiritual programs may be evaluated by observing how and to what extent they return us to learning from life itself. The less self-referential they are, the more they direct the seeker back to life, and the more they prove themselves provisional and dispensable, the more valuable they are, in my estimation. Ultimately, all spiritual teachings are merely adjuncts to common sense. They are tools, not totems: If you're standing in the garden with me and I hand you a shovel, don't plant it and worship it, please.

Going on what's revealed by life itself, I must conclude there can be no final and ultimate answers, no absolutes, but at moments it is possible and necessary to see things in a lucid, comprehensive way. We are given satori to appreciate the ordinary. All the current quandaries of modern spirituality—the revival of *awe,* the way to communicate with the Sacred, the riddle of the Divine revealing itself in a *personal* mode, the nature and purpose of suffering, the significance of pain as a force that dissolves the illusion of separation, the challenge of self-initiation as an adventure of personal discovery rather than the adoption of a prescribed methodology, the problem of establishing boundaries so that cocreation can be distinguished from the arrogant presumptions of self-creation, the narcissistic character of self-actualization and how it can move toward creative offerings, the relation between the actual and the invented, the delusions and deviations of personal mythmaking, the unfoldment of "Godseed" and the problematic human/divine hybrid—all these, it looks to me, are to be approached by first passing the sphinx of human character structure.

My own task in esoterics is to explore, nurture, and support the workings of the imagination as they influence our actual lives and, in mythology, to evaluate belief systems. In the efforts at "higher education" that I've developed from my own experiments with myth, I've tried to maintain a rigorous discipline of presenting not a message but a set of optional descriptions. The conscientious seeker does not persuade or seduce, accept or reject. Rather, he or she fosters love and respect by the courageous example of "living the questions" to the amazement and amusement of all peers.

The universe would not engage us as it does if there were not something missing. We all fill it in the best way we can, depending on our abilities to love and to imagine. The wise do not play favorites, for wisdom belongs to no one in particular.

So let's be generous in passing it around.

INDEX